The last journey  e

.g

Proverse Hong Kong

2019

From 1405, in order to maintain and expand the Ming Dynasty's tributary system, Yongle Emperor Zhu Di (reigning 1402-1424) and Xuande Emperor Zhu Zhanji (reigning 1425-1435) ordered eunuch Zheng He to lead giant fleets across the seas. But soon after Zheng He's seventh and last voyage in the 1430s, the Ming emperors put an end to this activity and ordered all records of previous voyages to be destroyed. Chinese writer Luo Maodeng (罗懋登), knowing the history of some of these voyages, wished to preserve a record of them, but, conscious of the possible penalty, decided to record the facts "under a veil", in his 1597 novel, An Account of the Western World Voyage of the San Bao Eunuch (《三宝太监西洋记》). This is what Dr. Sheng-Wei Wang has concluded after reading and analysing Luo's novel. Her book, *The last journey of the San Bao Eunuch, Admiral Zheng He*, shows the methodology and evidential arguments by which she has sought to lift the veil and the conclusions she suggests, including the derivation of the complete trans-Atlantic navigational routes and timelines of that last journey and the idea that Zheng He's last expedition plausibly reached the ancient American Indian city, Cahokia, in the U.S. central Mississippi Valley in late autumn, 1433, long before Christopher Columbus set foot for the first time in the Americas. She supports the hotly debated view that Ming Chinese sailors and ships reached farther than previously accepted in modern times and calls for further research. She hopes this book will become an important step in bridging the gap in our understanding of ancient China-America history in the era before the Age of Discovery. An interesting contribution to an ongoing debate.

SHENG-WEI WANG is a Chinese American, presently based in Hong Kong. She has a B.S. from Tsing Hua University and a Ph.D. from the University of Southern California. In her early career, she was a staff scientist at the Lawrence Berkeley National Laboratory. In 2006, as an independent scholar and freelance writer, she founded the China-U.S. Friendship Exchange, Inc. A year later, she launched an English-Chinese bi-lingual website to promote U.S.-China relations, <http://www.ChinaUSFriendship.com/>, which has attracted over a million viewers to date. She has also contributed many commentaries to the English-language newspaper *China Daily (Hong Kong)*. In 2013 she started research on Zheng He with Mark Nickless and Laurie Bonner-Nickless, and has since published two related books: the Chinese book, co-authored with the Nickless couple and the present English book, by herself. She has given invited presentations on her Zheng He research at international conferences, universities, Zheng He Societies, the Executive Global Network (Hong Kong), the Clurr Club (Zürich, Switzerland), and the Straits Forum (Xiamen, China). She is a founding member of the International Zheng He Society founded in Malacca.

The last journey of the San Bao Eunuch Admiral Zheng He

Sheng-Wei Wang

Proverse Hong Kong

The last journey of the San Bao Eunuch, Admiral Zheng He
Alternate edition published in paperback in Hong Kong
by Proverse Hong Kong under sole and exclusive licence
Copyright © Sheng-Wei Wang, November 2019.
ISBN: 978-988-8491-81-0
b/w plates

1st edition published in paperback in Hong Kong
by Proverse Hong Kong under sole and exclusive licence
Copyright © Sheng-Wei Wang, 21 November 2019.
ISBN: 978-988-8491-66-7
colour plates

Enquiries to:
Proverse Hong Kong, P.O. Box 259, Tung Chung Post Office,
Lantau, NT, Hong Kong SAR, China.
Email: proverse@netvigator.com; Web:
www.proversepublishing.com

Cover image: enciktat / Shutterstock.com
Cover design by Artist Hong Kong.

British Library Cataloguing in Publication Data
A catalogue record is available for the first paperback edition
from the British Library

ACKNOWLEDGEMENTS

I express my warm gratitude to the following individuals who played very valuable and significant roles in the genesis of this book:
Mark Nickless and Laurie Bonner-Nickless invited me to work on Zheng He in early 2013 when I had already moved from California to Hong Kong. Our collaboration from 2013 to the summer of 2015 resulted in the successful joint publication of our Chinese-language book entitled Zheng He Fa Xian Mei Zhou Zhi Xin Je《郑和发现美洲之新解》or *New Evidence for Zheng He's Exploration of the Americas* on August 1, 2015. The present book has grown out of and extended that seminal work.

Ian Hudson, co-author with Gavin Menzies of *Who Discovered America? The Untold History of the Peopling of the Americas*, and the founder of the 1421 Foundation, very kindly read my initial book draft and offered generous encouragements on its content, as well as offering helpful English corrections. He suggested a Chinese version of this book: I much appreciate his vision!

T.C. Bell, a full-time surveyor, specializing in Roman and Chinese engineering, with a background in marine engineering, foundries, plant engineering and surveying, generously sent me his precious, elaborate, and (at the time of writing) not yet published survey results of many years on Cape Breton Island and in New Zealand for publication in my book. These valuable survey results have strengthened my own conclusion that Zheng He's fleet explored both North America and New Zealand long before the Europeans did.

Paul Chiasson, who discovered Chinese ruins on top of Kelly Mountain in Cape Breton Island and authored two seminal books, *The Island of Seven Cities: Where the Chinese Settled When They Discovered America* and *Written in the Ruins: Cape Breton Island's Second Pre-Columbian Chinese Settlement*, about his discoveries, kindly read an earlier version of Chapter 5 of my book draft. He explained to me the importance of the Island where the Chinese would have settled when they discovered America.

Dr. Andrew K.P. Leung, a prominent international China specialist and now Chairman of Andrew Leung International Consultants Limited, kindly gave me my first invitation to deliver a presentation on this work, to the Executives' Global Network (Hong Kong) Ltd. on Oct. 16, 2014.

Dr. John Wong, Founder and CEO of Executives' Global Network (Hong Kong) Ltd., kindly hosted my presentation on Oct. 16, 2014, on Zheng He's voyage to North America, since Dr. Andrew K.P. Leung was out of town that day.

Hwai-Pwu Chou, Professor and Senior Vice-President of National Tsing Hua University, kindly invited and hosted me to give a presentation in May 2017 on Zheng He's exploration of America. It was a great opportunity for me to revisit my alma mater long after my graduation.

Professor Zhang Ruiqin, Department of Physics, City University of Hong Kong, graciously made the arrangement to invite me to give a presentation on Zheng He's voyages at Taian University in Taian, Shandong Province, China in 2017.

Professor Jeff Lai, the then Chairman of the Chinese Zheng He Society in Taipei, kindly invited me to give a presentation to his organization in May 2017. He later came to Hong Kong to meet me for a long and fruitful discussion of Zheng He's seventh voyage. He also invited me to participate in the International Zheng He Conference held in Kuala Lumpur and Malacca, Malaysia, in November 2018, and the Straits Forum held in Xiamen, China in June 2019.

Frank Lee, an award-winning film producer from Hong Kong, an advisor for technology companies and a venture capitalist, kindly suggested that I submit my book for publication by Proverse Hong Kong. Frank also invited me to give a presentation entitled "Did Admiral Zheng He visit America?" at his New Experience Toastmasters Club in Hong Kong on November 2, 2018.

Yau-Zhih Chen, a Zheng He researcher in Taipei, discussed with me his important paper, co-authored with Professor Sheng-I Hsu of the Department of Geography of the National Taiwan Normal University, entitled "Preliminary Study of Astronomical Navigation by Zheng He", during and after we met at the International Zheng He Conference at Malacca in November 2018. These discussions were particularly useful in understanding how accurately Zheng He's fleet could determine the latitudes of their destinations.

Walter Gander, retired Informatics Professor at ETH, Switzerland, and his wife Heidi Gander-Wolf, Dr. Phil., Pfrn. Pens, and Dr. Kurt Weiss, physicist and change initiator, for inviting me to give a presentation to members of the Clurr Club (Zurich, Switzerland) in July 2019.

Pong Chi Yuen, Professor in Computer Sciences and Associate Dean at Hong Kong Baptist University for inviting me to give a seminar in August 2019 sponsored by the Institute of Creativity of Hong Kong Baptist University.

The judges of the Proverse Literary Prize thoroughly reviewed my book draft and made very insightful and constructive suggestions to strengthen some of the viewpoints.

Stephen Chen, a *South China Morning Post* reporter, kindly brought to my attention the photograph of the Malacca mural of Admiral Zheng He and the Ming Treasure Ships, used on the front cover of this book.

The Hong Kong Maritime Museum generously issued me a license to publish the photo of Junk Keying exhibited in its Museum Hall.

The present writer's husband Michel A. Van Hove, a Physics Professor at Hong Kong Baptist University, not only critically reviewed my book draft and raised many valuable questions for further research, but also produced over 60 percent of the illustrations in this book.

Finally, Dr. Gillian Bickley not only kindly and patiently guided me through the Proverse book publishing procedure, but also offered insightful suggestions to improve the writing and the content of my book. My three meetings at Hong Kong's Discovery Bay with the Proverse founders Dr. Verner Bickley and Dr. Gillian Bickley were truly delightful and I owe them a great debt of gratitude for their continuous support in completing this book.

Any remaining errors are of course mine alone.

Illustrations Acknowledgements

Illustrations acknowledgements and sources are incorporated in each of the Table of Illustrations and the Table of Plates.

Dedicated to the sailors of the Ming Treasure Ships
for their great achievements in exploring the world

Dedicated to Luo Maodeng
for his epic account of ancient U.S.-China ties

—Sheng-Wei Wang

TABLE OF CONTENTS

PART ONE
The Ming Treasure Fleet sailed to North America
Routes and timelines

PART TWO
The Ming mariners explored the central Mississippi Valley
Evidence

The Last Journey of the San Bao Eunuch

TABLE OF ILLUSTRATIONS

the World (left panels 1-3; https://en.wikipedia.org/wiki/Kunyu_Wanguo_Quantu#/media/File:Kunyu_Wanguo_Quantu_by_Matteo_Ricci_Plate_1-3.jpg; and right panels 4-6; https://en.wikipedia.org/wiki/Kunyu_Wanguo_Quantu#/media/File:Kunyu_Wanguo_Quantu_by_Matteo_Ricci_Plate_4-6.jpg)[1]

46   Detail of North and Central America on Matteo Ricci's 1602 Kunyu Wanguo Quantu (https://en.wikipedia.org/wiki/Kunyu_Wanguo_Quantu#/media/File:Kunyu_Wanguo_Quantu_by_Matteo_Ricci_Plate_4-6.jpg; Mississippi River and its tributaries, other than the Missouri River, are outlined by Michel A. Van Hove)

47   Australia as a land mass below the southern end of Africa on Matteo Ricci's 1602 Kunyu Wanguo Quantu (https://en wikipedia org/wiki/Kunyu_Wanguo_Quantu#/media/File:Kunyu_Wanguo_Quantu_by_Matteo_Ricci_Plate_1-3 jpg; Australia is framed by Michel A. Van Hove)

48   East coast of Canada on the Japanese copy of Matteo Ricci's 1602 Kunyu Wanguo Quantu (https://commons.wikimedia.org/wiki/File:Kunyu_Wanguo_Quantu_(坤輿萬國全圖).jpg; Cape Breton Island (framed by Michel A. Van Hove) is shown as two separate islands).[2]

TABLE OF PLATES
(between Part One and Part Two)

World. Cape Breton Island is shown as two separate islands on this map as framed by Michel A. Van Hove. (https://commons.wikimedia.org/wiki/File:Kunyu_Wanguo_Q uantu_(坤輿萬國全圖).jpg)

8   Wax statue of Zheng He in the Quanzhou Maritime Museum. Photo by jonjanego. Licensed under the Creative Commons Attribution 2.0 Generic license. (https://commons.wikimedia.org/w/index.php?curid=1211478 9)

9   Statue of the young Zheng He with his father. Zheng He Park, Moon Mountain (Yue Shan), Kunyang. Adapted from photo by Vmenkov. (https://commons.wikimedia.org/wiki/File:Kunyang_-_Zheng_He_Park_-_P1350545.JPG)

10   Statue of Zheng He at the Stadthuys Museum in Malacca. Adapted from photo by Michel A. Van Hove.

11   Memorial cenotaph of Zheng He in Nanjing, built to commemorate the 580th anniversary of his voyages. Adapted from photo by Peter Pang, a direct descendant of Wenming, Zheng He's elder brother. Public Domain. (https://commons.wikimedia.org/w/index.php?curid=8623267)

12   A temple in Vietnam, built to venerate Zheng He. Photo by Bùi Thụy Đào Nguyên. Licensed under the Creative Commons Attribution-Share Alike 3.0 Unported license. (https://commons.wikimedia.org/wiki/File:Miếu_Nhị_Ph ủ.jpg)

13   Sheng-Wei Wang by the Zheng He statue, inaugurated during the International Zheng He Conference held in Kuala Lumpur and Malacca, Malaysia, November 2018. Adapted from photo by Michel A. Van Hove.

EDITORIAL CONVENTIONS

1) A variety of texts is included in this book. To emphasise clearly the origin of all contents, different type-faces are used as shown below:

Category	Example
Main text of the present book	Did the treasure fleet actually navigate across the Atlantic Ocean to reach the Americas in the early fifteenth century?
Quotation from another Chinese book	其国在古里西南可二万里。古里西南申位行，善风三月至镇，⋯。
Quotation from another English book with its author's comment in round brackets	He declared that "The expeditions of San Bao (Zheng He) to the Western Ocean wasted myriads of money and grain, and moreover the people who met their deaths may be counted in the myriads."
English translation made by the present author with her comment in square brackets	The commander-in-chief said, "Musk is fine [since it was light enough to carry by hand], but how were the porcelain articles carried over?"
English translation by another scholar with his comment in round brackets and the present author's comment in square brackets	The foreign name for it is Zhi Da; (and) there is a great chief who controls it. From Zhi Da, you go west, and after travelling for one day you reach the city where the king [caliph] resides. ...

2) Book and other text titles are given as in the examples below:

Category	Example
Title for published English book	*1421: The Year China Discovered the World*
Title for published Chinese book (with Hanyu Pinyin input) and its English translation	San Bao Tai Jian Xi Yang Gi《三宝太监西洋记》or *An Account of the Western World Voyage of the San Bao Eunuch*
Title for unpublished English booklet or manuscript	'A Chinese Boachuan (Treasure Ship): Ship Yard to Wreck'
Title for published English article	"A Third Research on the Discovery of America by Zheng He's Fleet"
Title for published Chinese article	"关于美洲由郑和船队发现的见解"
Title for Chinese Inscription (with Hanyu Pinyin input) and its English translation	Tian Fei Ling Ying Zhi Ji《天妃灵应之记》 or "A Record of *Tianfei* Showing Her Presence and Power"
Title for Chinese map (with Hanyu Pinyin input) and its English translation	Kunyu Wanguo Quantu《坤舆万国全图》or Complete Geographical Map of All the Kingdoms of the World

3) Other special cases are dealt with as shown below:

Category	Example
Special names of non-English origin	*Tianfang; Kaaba; al-Masjid al-Harām*
English translated Chinese name or special Chinese term in English	Zheng He (郑和) ; 方城 *Fang Cheng*
Ship's name	*Santa María de la Inmaculada Concepción*
Arabic: مُحَمّد, pronounced [muḥammad] , the founder of Islam	Prophet Muhammad, Mohammed, Mahomet or Mahomat; "Muhammad" is a closer transliteration of formal Arabic and is used in this book.

4) Bibliographical references in the notes follow the pattern below:

Kjeilen, Tore. "Kairouan: Cemetary of Ouled Farhane." http://i-cias.com/e.o/, LookLex, 2019, http://i-cias.com/tunisia/kairouan07.htm

Jacobs, Daniel. *The Rough Guide to Tunisia*. London, U.K.: Rough Guides, 2009.

5) Other Editorial Conventions

Interventions by the present author are indicated by "—Ed."

When there is translated text, the translator is clearly indicated.

In their original form, the Chinese texts quoted are written in either traditional or simplified Chinese. In the interests of uniformity, the present work presents all in simplified Chinese.

The Last Journey of the San Bao Eunuch

PREFACE

During the early fifteenth century in China's Ming Dynasty, Chinese Treasure Fleets, led by Admiral Zheng He (郑和; 1371–?), made seven epic voyages to many countries. A memorial stele in the Nanshan Temple in Changle, Fujian, China, was erected during the eleventh month of the sixth year of the Xuande period (December 5, 1431 to January 3, 1432), almost a year after Zheng He's fleet embarked from Longwan (Dragon Bay at Nanjing) near the Longjiang Shipyard on January 19, 1431 to start out on its seventh voyage (the fleet had to wait for the monsoon winds). The inscription on the stele is entitled Tian Fei Ling Ying Zhi Ji 《天妃灵应之记》 or "A Record of *Tianfei* Showing Her Presence and Power". (*Tianfei* means, "Heavenly Princess".)

The Inscription states:

。。。皇上嘉其忠诚，命和等统率官校、旗军数万人，乘巨舶百余艘，赍币往赍之，所以宣德化而柔远人也。自永乐三年奉使西洋，迨今七次，所历番国，由占城国、爪哇国、三佛齐国、暹罗国，直逾南天竺、锡兰山国、古里国、柯枝国，抵于西域忽鲁谟斯国、阿丹国、木骨都束国，大小凡三十余国，涉沧溟十万余里。
观夫海洋，洪涛接天，巨浪如山，视诸夷域，迥隔于烟霞缥缈之间。而我之云帆高张，昼夜星驰，涉彼狂澜，若履通衢者，。。。

"...From the time when we, Zheng He and his companions at the beginning of the Yongle Period, received the imperial commission as envoys to the barbarians, up until now seven voyages have taken place and each time we have commanded several tens of thousands of government soldiers and more than a hundred ocean-going vessels. Starting from Taicang and taking the seas, we have by way of the countries of Champa, Siam, Java, Cochin and Calicut reached Hormuz and other countries of the western regions, more than thirty countries in all.

We have beheld in the ocean huge waves like mountains rising sky-high, and we have set eyes on barbarian regions far away, hidden in a blue transparency of light vapours, while our sails, loftily unfurled like clouds, day and night continued their course, rapid like that of a star, traversing those savage waves."

—English translation abstracted from J.J.L. Duyvendak, "The True Dates of the Chinese Maritime Expeditions in the Early Fifteenth Century." *T'oung Pao*, Second Series, Vol. 34, Livr. 5, 1939, pp. 341–413

In Duyvendak's 1939 work, he omitted from his translation an important sentence "涉沧溟十万余里", which states that, even before embarking on its seventh voyage, Zheng He's fleet had sailed more than 100,000 *li* over the waters of broad oceans. (Cang Ming 沧溟 means "broad ocean".)—The circumference of our Earth is 40,075 km or 80,150 *li*. Does the inscription reveal that Zheng He's fleets had already explored the whole world?

It is not surprising that the publication in 2002 of *1421: The Year China Discovered America*, written by Gavin Menzies, a retired British submarine lieutenant-commander, sparked a continuing and lively worldwide debate over the extent of Zheng He's last two voyages. Menzies claimed that the Ming Treasure Fleet had circumnavigated the globe, "discovering" most of the world.

While some believe Menzies' claim, some negate it entirely. Many are confused and caught in the middle, not knowing which side to take. However, there can be no more than one truth, even if the process of seeking the truth may be tortuous.

In this present book, a thorough analysis of most chapters in the novel entitled San Bao Tai Jian Xi Yang Gi 《三宝太监西洋记》 or *An Account of the Western World Voyage of the San Bao Eunuch*, written by Luo Maodeng (罗懋登) in 1597,[3] is made from a fresh angle, first eliminating its fanciful portions and then verifying Luo's hidden narrative about Zheng He's seventh voyage to the Western

22

Ocean against other ancient and modern Chinese and western records. I discovered that Luo's novel provides an abundant amount of information on Zheng He's voyages, and provides historical value for our understanding of Zheng He's last two voyages in particular. Specifically, my analysis has enabled me to find that during Zheng He's seventh voyage, the Chinese fleet explored 29 countries before crossing the Atlantic and landing unexpectedly at the Labrador coast. From there, the ships entered the Gulf of St. Lawrence and around the late fall of 1433 reached the "country of Fengdu", today's Cahokia Mounds State Park in Illinois, 59 years before Christopher Columbus landed on the Bahamas. Moreover, after comparing two ancient Chinese world maps, I also found circumstantial evidence that Zheng He's crews had already explored the central Mississippi Valley in 1423, during their sixth voyage, and this gives strong support for my interpretation of Luo's narrative.

Readers should be aware that Luo's novel is an allegory, a concealed description of historical facts, which have to be extracted and interpreted to reveal the actual history hidden within his narrative. This way of writing was not uncommon in imperial China. The famous novel *Dream of the Red Chamber*, one of China's Four Great Classical Novels, exposed the hypocrisy, decay and exploitation of the upper class in the feudal era. But, by portraying a fictional dynasty, hiding the truth and circumventing political issues, the author succeeded in avoiding persecution due to his writings.

Soon after the seventh voyage of the Chinese fleet, China decided to withdraw completely from the world stage. The Confucian scholars in the imperial court, who had opposed Eunuch Zheng He's costly voyages, finally won the political struggle against the powerful eunuchs who supported the voyages of Zheng He. The treasure ships were burned at anchor and the construction of new long-range ocean vessels was strictly forbidden. It then became dangerous to talk or write about Zheng He's voyages in the post-Zheng He era. Hence, in order safely to convey to readers the events of the Chinese fleet's sixth and seventh voyages, Luo chose to hide the actual location (Cahokia) reached by the sailors, under the veil of a fictitious place ("Fengdu Ghost Country").

Contrary to the generally-held viewpoint that the Ming Treasure Fleet never sailed beyond the east coast of Africa, the detailed navigational routes, timelines and multiple lines of evidence which I have extracted from Luo's novel and present in the present book, speak for themselves: the Ming sailors explored the central Mississippi Valley during both their sixth and seventh voyages, in 1423 and 1433, respectively. This was more than 60 years before Columbus set foot in the Americas, and over 100 years before Hernando de Soto led the first European expedition to cross the Mississippi River.

From this new perspective, my decoding and in-depth, multi-layered, analysis of an ancient Chinese novel written in the late Ming Dynasty has enabled me to extract the true history of the voyages made by Zheng He's fleet to North America. This has led to a much larger and different story which may become one of the first steps in bridging the gap in our understanding of ancient China-America history in the era before the Age of Discovery. The great contributions made by the Ming sailors should not be overlooked or forgotten. They deserve a proper place in history. More research and more archeological excavations around the world are called for, in order to extend this work and to answer the question: did Chinese sailors "discover" most of the world?

Sheng-Wei Wang
Hong Kong
May 12, 2019

INTRODUCTION

The extent of the epic voyages of the Ming Treasure Fleet, led by the Chinese Admiral Zheng He (郑和; 1371–?)[4] (see Fig. 1), has sparked a continuous and lively worldwide debate. It all started when Gavin Menzies published his first book, *1421: The Year China Discovered the World,*[5] in which he claimed that the Ming Treasure Fleet had circumnavigated the globe, in the process "discovering" most of the world. In particular, the debate covers unsettled issues such as: did the treasure fleet actually navigate across the Atlantic Ocean to reach the Americas in the early fifteenth century? If so, how did the fleet do it, and how many times did Zheng He and his mariners explore the Americas? Moreover, where exactly did Zheng He go during his seventh and last voyage?

Fig. 1 Admiral Zheng He

I briefly review the background of how I got interested and involved in Zheng He's voyages. In 2006, I founded China-U.S. Friendship Exchange, Inc., and in 2007 I launched an English-Chinese bilingual website, www.ChinaUSFriendship.com, aiming at improving the Sino-U.S. relations and promoting peace between the Chinese mainland and Taiwan. The website has attracted more than one million reader visits since then. In early December 2012, Mark Nickless, one of the authors (the other author is his wife Laurie Bonner-Nickless) of the book *Chasing Dragons: The True History of the Piasa* (CreateSpace Independent Publishing Platform, 2012) sent me an email, in which he wished that my organization could promote this book. I gladly agreed to publish a flyer they sent me (the flyer was published in the News/Events Section on www.ChinaUSFriendship.com on January 1, 2013; http://www.chinausfriendship.com/article1.asp?mn=337). Shortly thereafter, they further expressed their interest of seeking a translator who could translate *Chasing Dragons* into modern Chinese to explore the Chinese market; I enthusiastically agreed to do that translation myself. Later in 2013, they also sent me their unpublished book draft 'To the Gates of Feng-Tu: Discovering the Last Ming Expedition to North America, 1433' and asked me to work on it. The goal was to combine *Chasing Dragons* (a small part of the whole Zheng He history) and their unpublished book draft 'To the Gates of Feng-Tu' into a Chinese book.

However, during the process of our collaboration, I encountered great difficulties with many of Laurie's translations and interpretations. Here is just one example:

Concerning *Chasing Dragons*, I had no problem with its initial three quarters (pp. 1–74), which dealt with a very interesting depiction of a pair of Chinese dragons, the Piasa, carved on a cliff overlooking the Mississippi River, the history of which Mark Nickless and Laurie Bonner-Nickless had investigated and linked to Zheng He's seventh voyage. The remainder of *Chasing Dragons* (pp. 75–87) dealt with some passages in Chapter 98 of Luo Maodeng's novel San Bao Tai Jian Xi Yang Gi 《三宝太监西洋记》 or *An Account of the Western World Voyage of the San Bao Eunuch*, which Laurie had translated from the Chinese and interpreted: it dealt with Zheng He's mariners sailing in the Bailongjiang or White Dragon River when several river gods came to greet Zheng He. The river god from Chengdu mentioned that in the Song Dynasty, a Chinese official passed through the region and repaired a local temple. Laurie interpreted to me that this Chinese official was one of Zheng He's artists who carved the *Piasa* and the White Dragon River was the Mississippi River, the enormous old pine tree in Luo's narrative, which had its roots in a cave, and grew in a spiral around the cave, was the pine tree on top of the Piasa Cave; and that the rainbow which appeared in Luo's narrative was the Rainbow Dragon (the Piasa). On page 87, she concludes, "Here is the gnarled pine above the Piasa, as painted by Henry Lewis."

Hence, Luo's fanciful writing in Chapter 98 was transformed into historical evidence by Laurie to explain the real surroundings and history of the Piasa Cave.

Chinese being my native tongue, I could read Luo's original text myself, unlike Laurie. I found that we often disagreed about translation and interpretation. With my scientific background, I felt that we should stay very much closer to Luo's text. I therefore omitted that quarter of *Chasing Dragons* from the Chinese version and replaced it by other aspects of Zheng He's voyage, which we published together in China in 2015 as Zheng He Fa Xian Mei Zhou Zhi Xin Je《郑和发现美洲之新解》or *New Evidence for Zheng He's Exploration of the Americas*. After the publication of this Chinese book, we basically worked in separate ways and had little communication, since we repeatedly and profoundly differed in translation and interpretation. We ultimately agreed in December 2017 to publish our separate analyses independently: hence, on one hand, the December 27, 2017 book *To the Gates of Fengtu: The first full modern translation of the final fifteen chapters of Luo Mao Deng's Epic Account of Chinese Exploration of North America* by Laurie L. Bonner-Nickless and, on the other hand, the present book by me. These two newer books have very little overlap, as we treat mostly different aspects of Zheng He's voyages. I have done a critical reading and analysis of Luo Maodeng's novel from Chapter 22 to 95, presenting some of the important passages of Luo's novel and investigating aspects related to navigation, geographical, climatological and cultural information, map analysis, archeological findings, deciphering hints in Luo's novel, and translating and analysing some other historical records. Laurie translates Luo's novel from Chapter 86 to Chapter 100, and makes her own interpretations. I remain grateful for the opportunity to work on the Zheng He project and wish that more researchers will share a similar interest in this fascinating endeavour.

After this background introduction, let us get back to the Introduction of the present book.

Many people ask whether they can be fully convinced of the achievements of the Chinese mariners, unless the navigational routes and timelines of Zheng He's seventh and last voyage in the 1430s are clearly laid out and confirmed. In this book, I have derived for the first time these navigational routes and timelines extracted by means of thorough analysis of a 1597 novel written by Luo Maodeng (罗懋登) in the Chinese Ming Dynasty. I already mentioned earlier that the title of this novel may be abbreviated as San Bao Tai Jian Xi Yang Gi《三宝太监西洋记》or *An Account of the Western World Voyage of the San Bao Eunuch*. [6] Luo's novel is believed by some scholars to provide an abundant amount of information about Zheng He's overseas voyages and to have historical value. [7] For example, the editor and translator, C.C. Low & Associates in Singapore, of *Pictorial Series of Chinese Classics & History in English & Chinese: Zheng He's Voyages to Xiyang* writes that Luo Maodeng's novel "provides an abundant amount of information on Zheng He's overseas voyages, which are of high reference value" (Low 249), and American writer Louise Levathes writes that Luo's novel is "believed to have some historic reliability" (Levathes 150). Tan Ta Sen (陈达生), a renowned Zheng He scholar, entrepreneur in Singapore, and founder of Cheng Ho Cultural Museum in Malacca and International Zheng He Society in Singapore, realises that Luo Maodeng's *Account of the Western World Voyage of the San Bao Eunuch* was written "in a novel literary style and hence its credibility has often been questioned by researchers" (Tan 38), but nevertheless suggests arguments to conclude that "it is premature and simplistic to write off Luo Maodeng completely" (Tan 38).

From these and other examples, I concluded that it was certainly worthwhile to investigate Luo Maodeng's novel as thoroughly as possible to see whether I could extract valuable historical information from his huge amount of work (100 chapters and over 750,000 characters). I hoped to obtain enough information and evidence to answer the question: what was the extent of the seventh voyage made by the Ming Treasure Fleet led by Admiral Zheng He"?

Extracting reliable historical information from Luo's novel has been challenging for both Chinese and non-Chinese researchers, since Luo's narrative is written in classical Chinese, rather than modern Chinese, and the more than 750,000-character text is full of fanciful stories mingled with an overwhelmingly large number of ancient Chinese legends and historical events. Besides, very unfortunately, shortly after the seventh voyage, the Ming government issued an edict prohibiting all future voyages and ordering the destruction of the remaining oceangoing ships. It then also became risky and dangerous to talk or write about the Zheng He voyages. Even a historical novelist like Luo Maodeng had to conceal the truth behind a veil of fiction, for example by obscuring the true geographical names and introducing misleading war episodes. This gives the impression that his book does not directly describe a voyage on Earth, but rather in the sky among the stars, so it was not at all apparent from Luo's narrative that Zheng He's fleet went to America.

This way of writing was not uncommon in imperial China. For example, Hong Lou Meng 《红楼梦》 or *Dream of the Red Chamber*,[8] one of China's Four Great Classical Novels, written by Cao Xueqin (曹雪芹; 1715 – 1763)[9] is believed to be semi-autobiographical, mirroring the rise and decline of the author's own family and, by extension, of the Qing Dynasty. The novel exposed the hypocrisy, decay and exploitation of the upper class in the feudal era. However, by using a fictional dynasty, hiding the truth and not touching on political issues, the author succeeded in avoiding political persecution for his writing.

But through in-depth analysis, and close comparisons with existing records and knowledge whenever possible, valuable historical information from Luo's narrative about Zheng He's complete navigational routes and timelines during his seventh voyage are extracted for the first time in this book.

My analysis finds that, in general, Luo's sailing descriptions are brief, but give, in general, reasonably good estimates of navigational times from port to port or country to country, in comparison with other existing Chinese records. However, many fanciful and lengthy war episodes must be ignored. The reasons will be given later in Chapter 3.

The multiple lines of evidence derived from Luo's novel resolve the confusions in the existing literature and schools of thought. They lead, for the first time, to a reasonable navigational route and estimated timeline for the Ming Treasure Fleet's seventh voyage to reach the central Mississippi Valley[10] through which the Mississippi River flows.[11] Formed from thick layers of the river's silt deposits, the Mississippi embayment was one of the most fertile regions in

North America. It was the American heartland at the time, and archaeologists define the Mississippian period as beginning from 900 AD and continuing until 1450 AD.[12] My finding shows that Zheng He's seventh voyages to the "Western Ocean" was *not* limited to the Indian Ocean, but extended as far as the Atlantic Ocean.

In addition, in Luo's novel, Zheng He's crews explored a strange city Fengdu (酆都) in North America. This city had the same name as the real city—Fengdu—in China,[13] but over the past 2000 years the latter has had the reputation of being a city of ghosts in Chinese legend. Yet Luo's narrative about this strange city, Fengdu, matches well what we know about today's Cahokia Mounds State Park in Collinsville, Illinois, United States of America, as initially suggested in the Chinese book authored by Mark Nickless, Laurie Bonner-Nickless and the present author, Sheng-Wei Wang (马克·尼克莱斯, 劳丽·邦纳尼克莱斯, 王胜炜).[14] The Cahokia Mounds State Park (or the Cahokia Mounds City, or the Cahokia Mounds complex, or simply Cahokia in this book) is located in the central Mississippi Valley. It was the largest urban centre north of the great pre-Columbus cities in Mexico,[15] and now a UNESCO designated World Heritage Site in the central Mississippi Valley. Why did Luo Maodeng give such a strange name Fengdu, to an American city? And how and why did he deliberately obscure the true identity of this city? These topics are further examined in the present book.

Luo's narrative also gives indirect information about Zheng He's sixth voyage to Cahokia, supported by circumstantial evidence I discovered after comparing the 1418 Chinese World Map[16] owned by Liu Gang (刘钢; a present-day Beijing lawyer, map-collector and analyst)[17] with Matteo Ricci's 1602 map—Kunyu Wanguo Quantu 《坤舆万国全图》[18] or Complete Geographical Map of All the Kingdoms of the World. The latter uses information from Chinese maps and was drawn after Zheng He's sixth voyage but right before his seventh voyage, as pointed out by Lee Siu-Leung (李兆良).[19]

In short, the present analysis takes us vividly back in time and describes how Admiral Zheng He's distant voyages plausibly ended in the ancient American Indian city of Cahokia in 1423 and 1433, respectively, during his sixth and seventh voyages. These events occurred almost 60 and 70 years, respectively, before Christopher

Columbus (1451–1506) set foot for the first time in the Americas on October 12, 1492[20] (his landing place was an island in the Bahamas, but the exact location is uncertain), and more than 100 years before Hernando de Soto (1496/1497–1542)[21] led the first European expedition to cross the Mississippi River in 1541 (on May 8, 1541, de Soto's troops reached the Mississippi River).

All these findings can decode the enigma that has given rise to much speculation related to Zheng He's voyages, especially surrounding his sixth voyage in the early 1420s and the seventh voyage in the 1430s.

This book also proposes a navigational route taken by some of Zheng He's mariners for their visit to Florence during their return voyage to China, most likely beginning in the summer of 1434, and presents evidence to show that some of Zheng He's mariners headed for New Zealand on their way home before ending the seventh voyage. But these mariners suffered a disastrous fate, which will be discussed in detail in Chapter 8 of this book.

In short, my work has achieved at least the following goals: first, it clearly supports the "historical relevance" of Luo's novel after its veil is removed; second, it suggests for the first time the full navigational routes and estimated timelines of Zheng He's seventh voyage; third, it has clearly distinguished where *Tianfang*/Mo-jia (ancient Tunisia in North Africa) and *Tianfang*/Yun Chong (Mecca, in today's Saudi Arabia) were located, and who visited the respective *Tianfang* (天方; heavenly square) and when. In ancient China, Mecca was called *Tianfang*—the Heaven. However, according to the interpretation of some scholars, the "country of *Tianfang*" can refer to the Arab region, or a very distant country, or any country far beyond the horizon; fourth, it shows that the Ming Treasure Fleet explored the central Mississippi Valley at least twice; and fifth, it suggests insights for future Zheng He research, which could usher in a rewriting of the existing history books.

Finally, I would like to remind readers to be aware that even the most rigorous scholars in history admit that there exist some puzzling ancient Western maps in which a number of "unknown" areas are mapped out before the Age of Discovery.[22] And most of these mysteries can be resolved if we acknowledge the historical facts that Chinese sailors explored these "unknown" places long before Europeans did.

The Last Journey of the San Bao Eunuch

PART ONE

The Ming Treasure Fleet sailed to North America: Routes and timelines

The Last Journey of the San Bao Eunuch

CHAPTER ONE

Mysteries surround the seventh voyage of Zheng He

In this chapter, I research the unanswered questions surrounding Zheng He's seventh voyage from a Chinese perspective and seek answers by first determining the treasure fleet's last trackable location before Zheng He divided the fleet into separate squadrons heading for different destinations.

This chapter will first present a quick summary of the historical background of Zheng He's seven voyages and then explain the mysteries surrounding the last two, especially the seventh.

(1) Historical background of Zheng He's seventh voyage

According to official Chinese records, in 1405, i.e. in the third year of the Yongle period (永乐; 1403–1424), the Ming Yongle Emperor Zhu Di (朱棣; reigning 1402–1424) appointed Zheng He to lead the great Ming Treasure Fleet in voyages to the countries in the Western Ocean (the sea south of China was divided into Eastern Ocean and Wester Ocean; the dividing line began at Ta Tan Island near Amoy, and passed through Brunei, Belitung Island and east of Pajajaran in western Java) for diplomacy and trade. Following the bold orders of the emperor, Zheng He's fleet sailed to explore the world systematically. But the question of the farthest reach of these voyages remains a mystery in Eastern and Western academic circles and is hotly debated among the public as well.

The fleet had more than 200 main ships and a considerable number of auxiliary ships. According to Joseph Needham,[23] the purported dimensions of the largest of these ships—the treasure ships—were 137 m/449 ft by 55 m/180 ft, which would make them at least twice as long as the largest European ships at the end of the sixteenth century. Even a medium-sized auxiliary ship was 63 m/207 ft by 14 m/46 ft. Some critics, hence, have questioned such claims, arguing that even with 21st century design techniques, building a vessel of such dimensions entirely out of wood would be almost impossible.

However, since 2015, a team of scientists and archaeologists funded by the Chinese government and using advanced military-grade sensing equipment has conducted multiple surveys of the sea floor along the Sri Lankan coastline aiming at recovering a treasure ship which sank to the bottom of the Indian Ocean (a confrontation took place between Ceylon/Sri Lanka and Zheng He's military during the third voyage of the treasure fleet). Their work has delivered some preliminary "positive results" which may contribute to this debate.[24]

Edward L. Dreyer has written a book entitled *Zheng He: China and the Oceans in the Early Ming Dynasty: 1405–1433*, in which he gives a good account of the number of ships and men carried by these ships during Zheng He's seven voyages. Dreyer writes that the first voyage started with 62 treasure ships and nearly 200 auxiliary ships, making a total of 255 ships, which carried 27,800 men (sailors and soldiers) on board (51); the second voyage consisted of 249 ships (62); the third voyage consisted of 48 treasure ships, not including other ships (66); the fourth voyage consisted of 63 treasure ships and auxiliary ships crewed by a total of either 27,670 or 28,560 men on about 250 ships (126); there is no specific evidence to tell us the number of ships or men for the fifth and the sixth voyages (126); the seventh voyage had more than a hundred large ships (126).

From 1405 to 1433 (in fact, the last voyage most likely ended in 1435, as will be discussed in Chapter 8), the fleet made seven major voyages. This sailing record is based on the statistics recorded in two memorial tablets in Taicang (太仓)[25] and Changle (长乐).[26] (In fact, there were more than seven voyages, if we include the first year of the Yongle period, or 1403, when Zheng He was sent on a diplomatic mission to Siam, today's Thailand; and in the 22nd year of the Yongle period or 1424, he was sent on a diplomatic mission to Palembang.)[27]

The seven major voyages took place at the following dates:

First voyage: From the third to the fifth year of the Yongle period or 1405–1407 (see Ming Shi《明史》 or *The History of Ming* written by Zhang Tingyu et al. 張廷玉等 in the Qing Dynasty).

Second voyage: From the fifth to the seventh year of the Yongle period or 1407–1409 (see Ming Shi 《明史》 or *The History of Ming*).

Third voyage: From the seventh to the ninth of the Yongle period or 1409–1411 (see Xing Cha Sheng Lan 《星槎胜览》 or *The Overall Survey of the Star Raft* by Fei Xin 费信 in the Ming Dynasty).

Fourth voyage: From the eleventh to the thirteenth year of the Yongle period or 1413–1415 (as recorded by the inscription on the memorial stele in the Nanshan Temple in Changle, Fujian, entitled Tian Fei Ling Ying Zhi Ji 《天妃灵应之记》 or "A Record of *Tianfei* Showing Her Presence and Power"; *Tianfei* is Heavenly Princess).

Fifth voyage: From the fifteenth to the seventeenth year of the Yongle period or 1417–1419 (see record in Lou Dong Liu Jia Gang Tian Fei Gong Shi Ke Tong Fan Shi Ji Bei 《娄东刘家港天妃宫石刻通番事迹碑》 or "Inscription on the Stele in the Temple of the Heavenly Princess at Liujiagang in Eastern Lou, Recording the History of Contacts with the Barbarians"). (Eastern Lou is Taicang in Jiangsu Province, because Taicang is in the east of Lou River.)

Sixth voyage: From the nineteenth to the twentieth year of the Yongle period or 1421–1422 (see Tai Zong Shi Lu 《太宗实录》 or *Taizong's Veritable Records of Ming*). I will show that the entire sixth voyage was most likely completed after 1423.

Seventh voyage: From the fifth to the eighth year of the Xuande (宣德) period or 1430–1433 (see Ming Shi Lu 《明实录》 or *The Veritable Records of Ming*). The Xuande Emperor was the fifth emperor of the Ming Dynasty. His Chinese-era name "Xuande" means "Proclamation of Virtue."[28] I will show that the seventh voyage was most likely completed in 1435.

We can see from the above summary that each voyage lasted for two to three years or perhaps even longer since after Admiral Zheng He returned to China, there might still be ships that had not yet returned home.

Since the number of sailors and soldiers participating in each voyage was of the order of 27,800 or more, a huge amount of food and other supplies would be needed. What did they eat and why did Zheng He's fleet not suffer the severe threat of sepsis and scurvy as did the fleets led by Christopher Columbus or Ferdinand Magellan (circa 1480–1521)? [29] This is because the Ming sailors not only could store a lot more food on their much bigger ships, but they also could carry plenty of fresh water, grow fresh fruits and vegetables, and even raise livestock on board. The abundant supplies enabled them to sail for months without stopping at harbours or islands to restock. Naturally, supervising the preparation, acquisition, preservation and storage of food, and dispatching food and human resources, required huge and skilful management operations to maintain the health of tens of thousands of seafarers and overcome difficult challenges. Therefore, the achievements of the Ming Treasure Fleet are truly remarkable and deserve our comprehension and admiration.

Zheng He is remembered as someone who generally sought to attain his goals through diplomacy. But his large army also awed most would-be enemies into submission. In Southeast Asia to this day, he is celebrated and revered as a god. At the Treasure Ship Shipyard site in Nanjing, there is a replica [30] of a medium-scale treasure boat of Zheng He's fleet. It measures 63.25 m/207.51 ft long, 13.8 m/45.28 ft wide, has six sails and eight masts, and can displace about 1,300 tons. It was built in 2005 from concrete and wooden planking. But when we compare this replica with the *Santa María de la Inmaculada Concepción*, the largest of the three ships used by Columbus in his first exploratory voyage to America, the latter had a hull length of only 17.7 m/58 ft, was about 100 tons and had a single deck and three small masts. [31] As for the general structure of the Chinese wooden boat, it consisted of a main mast, a mizzen mast, a halyard, sail battens, a quarterdeck house, a rudder, a cargo hatch, a lug sail, a topsail, and a Long Gu 龙骨 or *Dragon Bone* (like a keel) to minimise the damage caused by grounding. (A keel is a long piece of wood or steel along the base of a ship, supporting the framework of the whole. [32] Many Song Chinese ships had a ballasted and bilge keel that consisted of wooden beams bound together with iron hoops.)

(2) A hotly debated topic

As mentioned in the Introduction, the extent of the epic voyages of the Ming Treasure Fleet led by Zheng He has sparked a continuous and lively worldwide debate. It all started in 2002 with the publication of Gavin Menzies' first book, *1421: The Year China Discovered the World,* in which he claimed that the Chinese Admiral Zheng He had circumnavigated the globe, in the process "discovering" most of the world. Specifically, the debate covers unsettled issues such as: did the Ming sailors explore America during their seventh voyage? Where was Zheng He during this final voyage? Adding to this confusion is the question of the year and the place of Zheng He's death.

One school of thought is represented by the renowned Zheng He scholar, Zheng Yijun (郑一钧) in China, who believes that Zheng He died of illness in 1433 at or near Gu-li (古里)/Calicut[33] on his way home during the seventh voyage.[34] Many scholars have been led by him over the past 30 years to believe that the Ming Treasure Fleet never navigated beyond the east coast of Africa and that Zheng He died in 1433 at or near Calicut.

However, Zheng Yijun's view is based mainly on a note he discovered in 1982. The note is entitled Fei Huan An Xiang Huo Sheng Xian Ji 《非幻庵香火聖像記》 or "Record of Holy Images at the Incense- and Candle-burning Feihuan Nunnery" written in 1457 by an anonymous author, more than twenty years after Zheng He's "death". The note was originally the inscription on a monument (which no longer exists) that stood in the Nanjing Bifeng Temple (碧峰寺). Subsequently Luo Maodeng copied this note at the very end of his 1597 novel. Later an engraved note was made in the Wanli era (1572–1620).[35] Today, this engraved note is in a collection in the National Library of China in Beijing.[36] In the note, the anonymous author assumes that a few last words spoken by Zheng He to a Buddhist Master in the Bifeng Temple prior to Zheng He's seventh voyage were Zheng He's will, and this author wrote that he *heard about* Zheng He's death at Gu-li/Calicut. Then the author went on to write that, later in 1435, Zheng He's old comrades and a nephew who had gone on the voyage [or "voyages"—Ed.] with him got together and decided to set up a Buddhist statue inside the Temple for people to worship, in order to fulfil Zheng He's wish as expressed in his "will".

So, this anonymous author only "heard about" Zheng He's death, and there was no mention of Zheng He's death by any eye-witnesses. For example, was there any evidence or proof showing that these old comrades and the nephew were on the same ship with Zheng He while he was dying? Can we believe this note written in 1457 by an anonymous author about a great man's "death" more than twenty years after the event? Critics not only have doubts about the note's authenticity due to the technical mistakes contained in it, but also point out its inconsistency with the facts related to the historical materials of the Ming Dynasty, [37] which will be thoroughly examined in Chapter 3 of this book.

Later during the period of Kangxi (康熙; 1654–1722)[38] in the Qing Dynasty, the Jiang Ning Xian Zhi 《江宁县志》 or *Jiangning County Records* had this entry (transl. Sheng-Wei Wang): "San Bao Eunuch Zheng He's tomb was located in the western side of the Niushou Mountain/Cattle Head Mountain (牛首山). During the Yongle period he was ordered to sail to the Western Ocean…During the early Xuande period, he was again ordered to sail to the Western Ocean. He died in Gu-li. This place was offered by the emperor as his cenotaph." ("三宝太监郑和墓，在牛首山之西麓。永乐中命下西洋…宣德初，复命入西洋，卒于古里国，此则赐葬衣冠处也。"). But why did the record appear more than 200 years after the end of Zheng He's seventh voyage? And what was the basis of this rather late record?

In fact, Zheng Yijun's view also contradicts Ming Shi 《明史》 or *The History of Ming,* in which it states that Zheng He died of old age in his home.[39] Even the Ming first-hand historical record Ming Shi Lu 《明实录》 or *The Veritable Records of Ming* does not have any record of Zheng He's death during his seventh voyage of returning home.

Another school of thought is represented by Chen Pingping (陈平平),[40] who believes that Zheng He completed his seventh voyage and led the treasure fleet back to China in 1433, and later died there in 1435. The supporters of this school of thought also think that the Ming Treasure Fleet did not navigate beyond the east coast of Africa. They believe that Zheng He continued to serve as the defender of Nanjing and in 1433 was sent by the emperor to Tibet to fetch Buddhist scriptures, dying in 1435. But regrettably, the historian who reported the above historical event in his 1936 book did not make a rubbing of the stone carving which he said he saw in the temple, which recorded this event (that Zheng He in 1433 was sent by the emperor to Tibet to fetch Buddhist scriptures). Besides, if Zheng He died in China, why is there only his cenotaph[41] (as stated in the Jiang Ning Xian Zhi 《江宁县志》or *Jiangning County Records*) and not his real tomb? Hence, even Chen Pingping, despite complaining about Zheng Yijun for misleading China's Zheng He research for over 30 years, admits that Zheng He's year and place of death remain unsolved, and all the guesses are hypotheses—we are still waiting for the discovery of Zheng He's real tomb, inscription and reliable historical records.

A third school of thought is represented by American writer Louise Levathes who, after reading Luo Maodeng's 1597 novel, suggested that, during the seventh voyage, Zheng He's fleet left Mecca on a southwesterly course and experienced a fantastic journey in the netherworld.[42] She has reported that a tradition of Zheng He's contemporary family has him dying at sea and being buried at sea according to Muslim rites (Dreyer 166). However, if Levathes had known that the netherworld to which she thought Zheng He's fleet had gone would someday be shown to be an ancient American city, she might have had second thoughts about Zheng He's death at sea.

The fourth school of thought is represented by Gavin Menzies. He writes (*1434* 43) that during the seventh voyage, after Zheng He divided the Ming fleet near Sri Lanka, he sailed with some units for Africa and North America, settling near what is now Asheville, North Carolina, where he died. Although Menzies has not yet given any evidence to support his viewpoint, it is definitely a new research direction worthy of further investigation. Luo Maodeng's 1597 novel, being the historical record which contains the most detailed narrative of Zheng He's voyages, right or wrong, seems to be a natural starting point for us to seek clues for uncovering the truth.

From the above discussions of the four schools of thought, we can see that Zheng He's navigational routes and timelines during the seventh voyage are indeed an area of intense speculation. My aim is to find sufficient clues which can explain the extent of the Ming Treasure Fleet's navigation in the early fifteenth century. If this can be done successfully, then Zheng He's whereabouts and fate may be revealed more easily.

But before beginning such a long and deep analysis, I would like first to summarise Gavin Menzies' partial analysis of Zheng He's navigational routes and timelines during the seventh voyage. Then I

41

shall show, step by step, Luo's complete account of this remarkable seventh—and last—voyage accomplished by the Chinese mariners from the day they left their Chinese harbour.

(3) Gavin Menzies' partial analysis

In, *1434: The Year a Magnificent Chinese Fleet Sailed to Italy and Ignited the Renaissance,* Menzies suggests that, during the seventh voyage, on November 18, 1432 (actually the date was November 28, 1432),[43] the treasure fleet was south of today's Sri Lanka[44] when Zheng He divided the entire fleet into his main fleet and two squadrons (43). The eunuchs Wang Jinghong (王景弘) and Hong Bao (洪保) then led their own squadrons separately from there to several other places to complete their missions. Later, their squadrons joined up again at Calicut and were led by Wang Jinghong in April 1433 to return to China. Zheng He then sailed with his main fleet for Africa and North America.

Whether this is true or not still awaits verification, since Menzies has not provided any analysis or evidence to support his view, and no one else has given a complete and convincing account of Zheng He's seventh voyage. My research—using Luo Maodeng's 1597 novel and other related Chinese records—represents an important step towards uncovering the whole truth of Zheng He's seventh voyage.

Briefly speaking, Luo recorded that after Admiral Zheng He finished his pilgrimage to the country of *Tianfang* (天方国; this place will be identified later), he led the fleet to continue sailing westward across a big ocean, until one of his reconnaissance ships collided with a cliff and the fleet came to a halt.

(4) The main protagonists of Zheng He's last voyage

In this section, I shall introduce some of the main protagonists of the Ming Treasure Fleet's last voyage in addition to Zheng He. Among them, Hong Bao and Wang Jinghong were the most important figures.

Da Ming Du Zi Jian Tai Jian Hong Gong Shou Cang Ming 《大明都知监太监洪公寿藏铭》 or "The Inscription on the Tombstone of Eunuch Hong Bao of the Great Ming Dynasty"[45] was prepared before Hong Bao's death and was dated in the ninth year of the Xuande period (year 1434). It was discovered on Zutang Hill (祖堂山) in Nanjing and shows the important role Hong Bao played during Zheng He's voyages to the Western Ocean.

It is known that during the seventh voyage, the two Principal Envoys were eunuchs Zheng He and Wang Jinghong,[46] who were sent by the Xuande Emperor to the countries of the Western Ocean. The five Assistant Envoys were Hong Bao (洪保), Zhu Liang (朱良), Zhou Man (周满), Yang Zhen (杨真), and Zhang Da (张达). Hong Bao, as well as all other Principal and Assistant Envoys, except for Zhang Da, had the eunuch rank of Grand Director (太监 Taijian). The activities of Ming voyages to the Western Ocean were recorded in Ying Ya Sheng Lan 《瀛涯胜览》 or *The Overall Survey of the Ocean's Shores* written by Ma Huan (马欢; circa 1380s–circa 1460); in Xi Yang Fan Guo Zhi《西洋番国志》or *The Annals of the Foreign Countries in the Western Ocean* written by Gong Zhen (巩珍; his birth and death years are not known); in Ming Shi 《明史》 or *The History of Ming,* and several other historical records. Ma Huan accompanied Zheng He to sail the Western Ocean during the fourth, sixth and seventh voyages and Gong Zhen accompanied Zheng He during the seventh voyage. Not all these envoys will be mentioned again in this book, but I list their names here to show respect to these great achievers who assisted Admiral Zheng He in making these epic voyages in world history.

Actually, after the seventh voyage, both Wang Jinghong and Hong Bao made one more voyage. In 1434, Halizhihan, the younger brother of the Semudera King, came to visit China, but died of illness in Beijing. The Xuande Emperor commanded a ceremony for burying Halizhihan in China, and sent Wang Jinghong alone as an envoy to Sumatra; this was the eighth voyage for Wang, during which he visited Southeast Asian countries. Later, he died of illness at sea after 1437. From July 1441 to 1442, the over 70-year old eunuch Hong Bao led the last mission to the Western Ocean. But Zheng He seems to have *vanished* from history at some point during his last voyage. What happened to him? Why so little information?

(5) China, Europe and America, soon after the seventh voyage ended

To explain why there has been so much speculation surrounding Zheng He's last voyage, we need to understand Chinese history in the post-Zheng He era.

Soon after the seventh voyage, China decided to withdraw completely from the world stage. The Confucian scholars in the imperial court, who had opposed Zheng He's costly voyages, finally won the political struggle against the powerful eunuchs who supported Zheng He's voyages. The treasure ships were burned at anchor and the construction of new long-range ocean vessels was strictly forbidden. Dreyer has summarised the adverse situation like this: "In 1436, the building of seagoing ships was banned, and the number of smaller vessels was reduced. By the early 1500s only one or two ships were left of every ten…, and the largest warships were 400 *liao*[47] vessels crewed by 100 men" (171).

Sadly, after 1436, the Chinese presence at sea suffered a precipitous decline. The deliberate action taken by Liu Daxia (刘大夏; 1436–1516), a senior official at the Ministry of War in the post-Zheng He era, is one example. Menzies recounts the reaction and critical comment of Liu Daxia as follows (84):

Liu Daxia . . . seized the records from the archives. He declared that "The expeditions of San Bao (Zheng He) to the Western Ocean wasted myriads of money and grain, and moreover the people who met their deaths may be counted in the myriads." The goods the fleet had brought home … were useless, and all the records of these expeditions—"deceitful exaggerations of bizarre things far removed from the testimony of people's eyes and ears"—should therefore be burned. Liu then blandly reported to the Minister of War that the logs and records of Zheng He's expeditions had been "lost."

The above comments explain that due to *a lack of logs and records* of Zheng He's expeditions, we know very little about the treasure fleet's seventh and last voyage. However, some Chinese historians have not definitively concluded whether Liu Daxia truly burned and destroyed *all* the navigational records. The fact that Luo Maodeng was able to make an elaborate account of Zheng He's last voyage indicates that at least during the period (1587 to 1597) when Luo

44

was writing his novel, he still had some records on hand which are no longer in existence today.

The above gives an idea of the political sentiment in the post-Zheng He era that the Chinese people had to cope with, although the Ming emperor partially lifted the *Haijin* or Sea Ban starting from 1567. A series of related isolationist Chinese policies restricting private maritime trading and coastal settlement, were imposed during most of the Ming Dynasty and part of the Qing Dynasty. The greatest episode of Chinese sailing in world history ended. But the power vacuum created by China's withdrawal from the world stage was not left vacant for long. The burgeoning sea powers of Spain and Portugal—joined later by England, France and Holland—made that emptied stage their own, carving the Americas, Africa, Asia, and Oceania into their spheres of influence. The Age of the Great Discovery or the Age of Exploration was ushered in, which in turn propelled the European Renaissance. New routes opened up by Westerners accelerated Western capitalism and opened the way for colonialism and new waves of slave-trading, expansionism, militarism, imperialism, and, eventually, resulted in World War I & World War II.

By then, Zheng He's peaceful voyages to promote trade and diplomacy to the many countries he visited had been long forgotten.

(6) Different squadrons headed for different destinations

Now, we must understand the challenge lying ahead. I know I should investigate Luo's novel in great depth. Gavin Menzies' partial analysis gives some initial hint for me to focus on Zheng He's navigational routes, but Luo's novel is daunting to comprehend. The challenging questions are: *where* to start, and *how* to connect Luo's novel with known historical records?

In order to understand thoroughly the journey of Zheng He's seventh voyage, I finally decided to choose the last identifiable location of Zheng He's entire fleet, Sri Lanka, before it was split into a main fleet and a squadron, as the starting point for further investigation. This last location is also recorded in Qian Wen Ji • Xia Xi Yang 《前闻記•下西洋》 [48] or *A Record of History Once Heard: Down to the Western Ocean* by the Ming historian Zhu

Yunming (祝允明; 1461–1527)[49] for the treasure fleet's seventh voyage.

According to Zhu, on November 2, 1432 (October 10 in the seventh year of the Xuande period), the Ming Treasure Fleet departed from Semudera or Semudera Guo (in Luo's novel, Guo can mean a country, kingdom, or city-state) in today's northern Sumatra in Indonesia. A little less than a month later the fleet arrived at Ceylon/Sri Lanka on November 28, 1432 (November 6 in the seventh year of the Xuande period). Zhu Yunming's record shows that the Ming Treasure Fleet then departed from Ceylon /Sri Lanka on December 2, 1432 (November 10 in the seventh year of the Xuande period) after a four-day stay, and arrived eight days later at Gu-li/Calicut on December 10, 1432 (November 18 in the seventh year of the Xuande period). Calicut, also known as Kozhikode, is a coastal city in the southern Indian state of Kerala. It was a significant spice trade centre that the Ming Treasure Fleet would not want to miss, and is close to Kappad Beach, where Portuguese explorer Vasco da Gama (circa 1460s–1524) landed in 1498.[50]

At Gu-li/Calicut, envoys from the country of *Tianfang*/Mo-jia or Mo-jia Guo (默伽国 or the country of Mo-jia)[51] happened to have just arrived. There, it was Hong Bao *alone*, not Zheng He or Wang Jinghong, who gave the command to send Ma Huan and several senior officers (altogether seven of them) to accompany these envoys to head for *Tianfang*/Mo-jia for a trade mission by taking the Calicut merchants' junk.[52] This means: 1) Hong Bao was the commander of the squadron which arrived at Gu-li/Calicut on December 10, 1432; and 2) when the Ming mariners departed from Ceylon/Sri Lanka, the treasure fleet was already divided into the squadron led by Hong Bao, and the main fleet led by Zheng He and Wang Jinghong, to head for different destinations (there exists no record showing that they were separated right after Sri Lanka).

This is confirmed by Míng Shi • Wai Guo Zhuan • Tian Fang 《明史•外国传•天方》[53] or the *Tianfang Section of the Chapter of Foreign Countries in The History of Ming*, in which it is recorded that Zheng He ordered *one* of his deputy commanders to lead a squadron to Calicut (Hong Bao's next call). This deputy commander must have been Hong Bao, because he was the one issuing commands at Calicut, not Wang Jinghong or any other deputy commander. Wang was the Principal Envoy of the same rank as

Zheng He, while Hong Bao was the Assistant Envoy and thus of a lower rank. If Wang Jinghong was with Hong Bao, Wang Jinghong would be the one issuing commands at Calicut, not Hong Bao. Hong Bao arrived at Calicut in eight days. In Chapter 2, I shall analyse Ma Huan's travel log to find Hong Bao's and Ma Huan's separate journeys and timelines after December 10, 1432.

Apparently, after replenishment of supplies at Ceylon/Sri Lanka, the main fleet led by Zheng He and Wang Jinghong, and the squadron led by Hong Bao left for different destinations. Ceylon/Sri Lanka is a country which can be verified in Luo Maodeng's novel. Luo's navigational account will be thoroughly examined in Chapter 3 of this book. It seems that Zhu Yunming's record has a detailed account of the navigational routes and timelines of the squadron led by Hong Bao, not Zheng He and Wang Jinghong, after his short stay at Calicut, and this record will also be discussed in Chapter 3 of this book.

Although Zhu Yunming's record has no account of where the main fleet led by Zheng He and Wang Jinghong would head, Wang Jinghong (but not Zheng He) reappeared in history when his and Hong Bao's squadrons re-joined at Gu-li/Calicut. Hence, on April 9, 1433 (March 20 in the eighth year of the Xuande period), Wang Jinghong led all the squadrons gathered at Calicut heading for China. They arrived home in July 1433. Zhu's record gives no itinerary information on the main fleet led by Zheng He and Wang Jinghong after Ceylon/Sri Lanka.

So, at least Hong Bao's navigational routes and timelines can be analysed right away and be verified first. Xi Longfei, Yang Xi and Tang Xire (席龙飞，杨熺，唐锡仁 395–396) and later Sheng-I Hsu and Yau-Zhih Chen,[54] have analysed the Zheng He Hang Hai Tu 《郑和航海图》 or *The Charts of Zheng He's Voyages*[55] for the treasure fleet's navigational routes on its way to India and Hormuz during the seventh voyage. They have re-confirmed the specific stars the Ming mariners used for specifying the coordinates (the latitudes)[56] of their destinations. These mariners also used maps for terrestrial navigation (each map contains detailed sketches of mountains, rivers, islands, buildings, and depth of water along the sea route, etc.)[57] to set the heading direction. They used a compass to guide directions, measured the distances to sail towards their targeted destinations, and verified the observed angles of the stars with the stellar maps they had on hand for the specific destinations, to confirm their arrival at such destinations. These star maps helped them to confirm the latitudes of their destinations, and this was the method of "astronomical navigation".

Menzies in *1434* and Wang Tai Peng in his paper entitled "Zheng He's delegation to the Papal Court of Florence"[58] praised the work done by the three Chinese researchers mentioned above, then went on with their own analyses in an attempt to determine Hong Bao's and later Ma Huan's itinerary. Zhu Yunming did not record Ma Huan's itinerary. Luo Maodeng did not mention the special trip made by Ma Huan, either. But Ma Huan himself *did* make a special report in his travel log on this itinerary during the seventh voyage. This has significance and will be discussed in Chapter 2.

Both Menzies (*1434* 44) and Wang Tai Peng write that soon after Hong Bao's fleet arrived at Calicut on December 10, 1432, he immediately detached two Chinese junks full of silk and porcelain and seven senior officers including Ma Huan, as a trade delegation to join the Calicut merchants heading for *Tianfang*/Mo-jia for trade.[59] However, a close examination of Ma Huan's travel log suggests that in fact Hong Bao did not detach two Chinese junks. Instead, the Ma Huan delegation took the Calicut merchants' junk.

Menzies and Wang Tai Peng write that this *Tianfang*/Mo-jia was Cairo. But it will be shown in Chapter 2 that this *Tianfang*/Mo-jia was not Cairo, but ancient Tunisia in North Africa. There are also many scholars who have mistaken this *Tianfang*/Mo-jia as Mecca (麥加) in today's Saudi Arabia, because the Chinese pronunciations of Mo-jia and Mecca are very close.

It was natural for Mecca to be regarded as *Tianfang*, since it was the most important Muslim religious centre and part of the Mamluk Sultanate (ruled by the Mamluks), a medieval realm spanning Egypt, the Levant, and Hejaz from 1250 to 1517. The Mamluks were a class of warrior slaves who won political control of several Muslim states during the Middle Ages, after successful military resistance against the Mongol advance.

However, why Cairo came to be regarded as *Tianfang* needs some explanation. Menzies mentioned that from 1260 [1250—Ed.] to 1517, Mamluk sultans ruled an empire that stretched from Egypt to Syria and also included the holy cities of Mecca and Medina.

The Last Journey of the San Bao Eunuch

Since the Mamluk sultans organised the yearly pilgrimages to Mecca, the Mamluk capital Cairo grew in prestige. By the fourteenth century, Cairo had become the preeminent religious centre of the Muslim world and was also regarded as *Tianfang*. Both Menzies and Wang Tai Peng write that the Ma Huan delegation went to Mecca first. They arrived at Port Jeddah near Mecca and then went to Mecca on pilgrimage. Afterwards, they travelled to Cairo for commercial activities. Menzies and Wang Tai Peng write further that from Cairo, some members of this trade delegation went into the Mediterranean Sea via the Red Sea Canals and were able to visit Florence in Italy in the summer of 1434 and met with Pope Eugene IV.[60] In *1434*, Menzies argues further that some senior officers from the Ma Huan delegation then passed important maps, navigation techniques, as well as Chinese scientific and technical knowledge to the Europeans, which contributed to the Renaissance in Europe and ushered in a new era of the Age of Discovery.

So, was this the itinerary of the Ma Huan delegation?

No, it could not be, because the timeline is incorrect. Actually, a year after the Ma Huan delegation left Calicut on December 10, 1432, all the delegation members re-joined at Calicut near the end of 1433, and then returned to China together. The Ma Huan delegation could not have met with Pope Eugene IV in Florence after June 1434 as Menzies and Wang Tai Peng have suggested. Moreover, by the end of 1433, Wang Jinghong and all the squadrons had already returned to China many months previously. The itinerary of the Ma Huan delegation had no overlap with Hong Bao's, and the delegation was not with the main fleet led by Zheng He and Wang Jinghong, either. Hence Ma Huan had no knowledge of Zheng He's whereabouts after their separation at Ceylon/Sri Lanka. Not surprisingly, later in Ma Huan's travel log, he did not put down any record of Florence or Zheng He's whereabouts.

In Chapter 8 of this book, I will propose a more reasonable timeline and navigational route for the Ming sailors to meet with Pope Eugene IV during their seventh voyage. Florence was the cultural, religious and commercial centre of Europe at that time. There was no reason for the Ming envoys not to visit it.

As for Hong Bao's whereabouts, Gavin Menzies and Wang Tai Peng cite again the results of the three Chinese researchers (席龙飞,

杨熺，唐锡仁 395–396). They write that the squadron led by Hong Bao made only a short stay in Calicut, then continued north to reach Dandi Bandar (near latitude 16.2°N and longitude 73.4°E), a small city in the middle of the west coast of India; later Hong Bao's squadron crossed the Arabian Sea to pass the Jabal Khamis Mountain (22.4°N and 59.5°E) in today's northeast corner of Oman. A few days later, the fleet continued heading towards the Persian Gulf in today's southern Iran, and on January 16, 1433,[61] Hong Bao's squadron arrived at Bandar Abbas, the Gulf port of Hormuz. Hong Bao and his men stayed in the neighbourhood of Hormuz for almost two months before traveling homeward on March 9, 1433. According to Gavin Menzies and Wang Tai Peng, on March 31, 1433, the squadron led by Hong Bao returned to Calicut to meet with the squadron led by Wang Jinghong. On April 9, 1433, all the squadrons were led by Wang Jinghong to return to China. They arrived at Nanjing in July of that year. Neither Hong Bao nor Wang Jinghong made any written record of Zheng He's death.

But Luo Maodeng gave a different story. According to Luo's narrative in San Bao Tai Jian Xi Yang Gi《三宝太监西洋记》or *An Account of the Western World Voyage of the San Bao Eunuch*, after leaving Ceylon/Sri Lanka, the main fleet visited many places in India, the east coast of Africa, some Arabic countries and then Hormuz, before completing a pilgrimage at the country of *Tianfang*/Yun Chong. After leaving *Tianfang*/Yun Chong, Zheng He's main fleet sailed westward across a big ocean, until his reconnaissance ship hit land and the entire fleet came to a halt. In Luo's narrative, Zheng He and Wang Jinghong led the main fleet throughout the voyage. But from Zhu Yunming's record, we know that Wang Jinghong did not sail westward across a big ocean with Zheng He. He returned to China with Hong Bao in 1433. This reveals that at some point during this last voyage, Zheng He and Wang Jinghong seem to have gone separate ways. But, where and when?

Where was this country of *Tianfang*/Yun Chong that Zheng He visited? Was it different from the *Tianfang*/Mo-jia that the Ma Huan delegation went to? Furthermore, where did Zheng He's reconnaissance ship hit land? And what happened after that?

These complicated issues will be dealt with in the following chapters by thoroughly examining Luo's narrative as well as records written by other historians. The results derived from my analyses will clear much of the confusion related to the various locations of *Tianfang*, and shed light on revealing the navigational routes and timelines of Zheng He's seventh voyage.

The Last Journey of the San Bao Eunuch

CHAPTER TWO

Ma Huan's *Tianfang*/Mo-jia was ancient Tunisia in North Africa

In this chapter, I maintain that Ma Huan's Tianfang/Mo-jia was ancient Tunisia in North Africa. My conclusion is based on a review of Lam Yee Din's paper entitled "The Country of Tian Fang is in Tunisia"[62] and analysing the following historical records: Ying Ya Sheng Lan《瀛涯胜览》or The Overall Survey of the Ocean's Shores written by Ma Huan, Xi Yang Fan Guo Zhi《西洋番国志》[63] or The Annals of the Foreign Countries in the Western Ocean written by Gong Zhen, the Xi Yang Chao Gong Dian Lu《西洋朝贡典录》[64] or Records of Tributes from the Western Ocean Countries written by Huang Shengzeng (黄省曾), and San Bao Tai Jian Xi Yang Gi《三宝太监西洋记》or An Account of the Western World Voyage of the San Bao Eunuch by Luo Maodeng.

According to the interpretation of some scholars, the "country of *Tianfang*" can refer to a very distant country or any country far beyond the horizon. But this has created great confusion in interpreting Chinese historical records. Therefore, the issue must be analysed thoroughly in order to clarify the extent of the travels of the Ming Treasure Fleet in its last voyage.

Lam Yee Din (林贻典) is a Zheng He researcher in Hong Kong. He has performed a truly valuable analysis of the location of *Tiangfang*/Mo-jia, which in his travel record Ying Ya Sheng Lan《瀛涯胜览》or *The Overall Survey of the Ocean's Shores*, Ma Huan records as the location of the "Heavenly Hall". Lam holds a different view from Menzies, Wang Tai Peng and most other scholars about the previously discussed destination which the Ma Huan delegation visited in 1433. In Lam's paper, he argues that "the country of *Tianfang*" where the Ma Huan delegation went was in fact in Tunisia. He concludes that Mo-jia was *not* Mecca in today's Saudi Arabia; and that the mosque Ma Huan recorded as the "Heavenly Hall" was the Mosque of Uqba in Kairouan, the oldest and the largest Islamic mosque in North Africa, which was regarded as the Mecca of North Africa by Muslims.

I shall now examine this issue further, starting with an introduction of Ma Huan.

The historical figure Ma Huan joined Zheng He's treasure fleet in 1412 in his 20s. He was a Muslim from Hang Zhou Bay (today's Shaoxing 绍兴), and proficient in Persian and Arabic languages. Among the members of Zheng He's crew, Ma Huan played dual roles as an interpreter for foreign affairs and as a didactic teacher, being responsible for the dissemination of Chinese culture. He participated in the fourth, sixth, and seventh voyages of the treasure fleet. Starting in the fourteenth year of Yongle (1416), Ma Huan set to work on a book entitled Ying Ya Sheng Lan 《瀛涯胜览》 or *The Overall Survey of the Ocean's Shores,* describing his personal travelling experiences and what he had learned during his voyages about the kings, politics, customs, geography, culture and economies of the different countries he visited. After 35 years of modifications, the book was completed in the second year of Jingtai (1451).[65] Today to the north of the Spratly Islands, there is still an island called Ma Huan Island (马欢岛)[66] or Nanshan Island (南尚岛) which is named after him. He knew several classical Chinese and Buddhist texts, and learned Arabic well enough to do translation.[67] He was a keen observer of social customs and well-schooled in the Confucian classics. His book is regarded as an important record of Ming navigation.

The rest of this chapter will be devoted to identifying Ma Huan's *Tianfang*/Mo-jia and its Heavenly Hall.

(1) The Ma Huan delegation did not meet Pope Eugene IV in Florence in 1434

Ying Ya Sheng Lan 《瀛涯胜览》 or *The Overall Survey of the Ocean's Shores* has the following description of Ma Huan's journey to, and return voyage from, the country of *Tianfang*/Mo-jia:

宣德五年，钦蒙圣朝差正使太监内官郑和等往各番国开读赏赐。分综到古里国时，内官太监洪 见本国差人往彼，就选差通事等七人，赍带麝香、磁器等物，附本国船只到彼。往回一年，买到各色奇货异宝，麒麟、狮子、驼鸡等物，并画天堂圆眞本回京。其默伽国王亦差使臣，将方物跟同原去通事七人献赞于朝廷。

The English translation of the above passage after my minor modifications is shown below. The original translation is taken from *Ying-yai Sheng-lan: The Overall Survey of the Ocean's Shores (1433)*, written by Ma Huan and translated by J.V.G. Mills (published by the Hakluyt Society in 1970), pp. 177–178. Mills' comments are in round brackets and my comments are in square brackets:

In the fifth year of the Xuande (period) [1430], an order was respectfully received from our imperial court that the principal envoy, the grand eunuch Zheng He and others should go to all the foreign countries to read out the imperial commands and to bestow rewards. When a division of the fleet reached Gu-li Guo [the country of Gu-li], the grand eunuch Hong [will soon be verified as Hong Bao] saw that this country [Gu-li] was sending men to travel there [Mo-jia]; whereupon he [eunuch Hong Bao] selected an interpreter and others, seven men in all, and sent them with a load of musk, porcelain articles, and other such things; (and) they joined a ship of this country [Gu-li] and went there [Mo-jia]. It took them one year to go and return. They bought all kinds of unusual commodities and rare valuables, qilins,[68] lions, "camel-fowls" [ostriches] and other such things; in addition, they painted an accurate representation of the "Heavenly Hall", (and) they returned to the capital [Beijing]. The king of the country of Mo-jia also sent envoys who brought some local articles, accompanied the seven men—the interpreter (and others)—who had originally gone there [Mo-jia], and presented the articles to the court.

"Qilins" here refer to giraffes. They were considered a precious gift to the emperor in the Ming Dynasty. The giraffe's homeland was today's Kenya in Africa. Camel-fowls or ostriches are large

55
55

flightless birds native to Africa, and lions were found in most of Africa. Bringing giraffes, lions and ostriches back home clearly indicates that the seven men had visited Africa instead of Saudi Arabia, since the Arabian Peninsula was not the homeland of these animals in those days. Also, according to Ma Huan's record, these seven men joined a ship of "this country," meaning Gu-li, and went to Mo-jia, for trade[69] and pilgrimage. My viewpoint differs from Menzies' view that Hong Bao "detached two junks" (Menzies, *1434* 44) for the delegation to join Calicut merchants heading for *Tianfang* for pilgrimage.

Zheng He's scribe, Gong Zhen,[70] who completed the book Xi Yang Fan Guo Zhi《西洋番国志》or *The Annals of the Foreign Countries in the Western Ocean* in the ninth year of the Xuande period (1434), also gave a similar description:

宣德五年，钦奉朝命开诏，徧谕西海诸番，太监洪保分舣到古里国。适默伽国有使人来，因择通事等七人同往。

My translation of the above passage is as follows and my comment is in square brackets:

In the fifth year of the Xuande period, an order was respectfully received from our imperial court to read out the imperial commands to all the foreign countries in the western sea. When a division of the fleet led by eunuch Hong Bao reached Gu-li Guo, they found that the envoys from Mo-jia had just arrived. Hence, an interpreter and others, seven men in all, were chosen to accompany the envoys and went there [Mo-jia].

Here Gong Zhen reconfirmed that it was Hong Bao who led a division of the fleet to Gu-li. Gong Zhen's record is brief and does not mention how the interpreter (Ma Huan) and others, seven men in all, went to Mo-jia.

Based on the descriptions of Ma Huan and Gong Zhen, we can confirm that: 1) during the seventh voyage, eunuch Hong Bao *did* send Ma Huan and others, seven men in all, to the country of *Tianfang*/Mo-jia for trade. This reinforces my viewpoint expressed in Section (6) of Chapter 1 that it was Hong Bao *alone*, not Zheng

He or Wang Jinghong, who gave the command to send Ma Huan and several senior officers to accompany these envoys to head for *Tianfang*/Mo-jia for a trade mission by taking a Calicut merchants' junk. Hong Bao arrived at Gu-li/Calicut on December 10, 1432. Based on Zhu Yunming's record, the trip made by the Ma Huan delegation took place soon after December 10, 1432, because Hong Bao's squadron stayed at Gu-li/Calicut only from December 10, 1432 to December 14, 1432; 2) the seven men went to Mo-jia, since, while they were at Gu-li /Calicut (transl. Sheng-Wei Wang), "the envoys from Mo-jia had just arrived" to greet them, and the seven men accompany these envoys to their country Mo-jia; 3) the Ma Huan delegation went to Mo-jia on board a Calicut merchants' junk; 4) the country of *Tianfang*/Mo-jia was most likely in Africa, because all the rare animals that the seven men brought back to China had their homeland in Africa; 5) "It took them one year to go and return" (transl. J.V.G. Mills; Hakluyt Society, 1970) indicating that by the time all seven men returned to Calicut, it was near the end of 1433; 6) neither Ma Huan nor Gong Zhen recorded that the Ma Huan delegation visited any place other than Mo-jia; and according to this timeline, these seven men could not have met with Pope Eugene IV at Florence in the summer of 1434; and 7) according to the above timelines, Ma Huan had no knowledge of Zheng He's whereabouts after Zheng He separated from Hong Bao in Sri Lanka in November 1432.

(2) The Ma Huan delegation went to *Tianfang*/Mo-jia located in ancient Tunisia, North Africa

Regarding how these seven men went to *Tianfang*/Mo-jia, how far it was from Gu-li/Calicut and what were the local customs of the country of *Tianfang*, Ma Huan records the following:

此国即默伽国也。自古里国开船，投西南申位，船行三个月方到本国马头，番名秩达。有大头目主守。自秩达往西行一日，到王居之城，名默伽国。奉回回教门，圣人始于此国阐扬教法，至今国人悉遵教规行事，纤毫不敢违犯。其国人物魁伟，体貌紫膛色。男子缠头，穿长衣，足着皮鞋。妇人俱戴盖头，莫能见其面。说阿剌毕言语。国法禁酒。民风和美，无贫难之

家。悉遵教规，犯法者少，诚为极乐之界。婚丧之礼皆依教门
体例而行。

The English translation of the above passage after my minor modifications is shown below. The original translation is taken from the book written by Ma Huan, translated by J.V.G. Mills. *op. cit.*, pp. 173–174. Mills' comment is in round brackets and my comments are in square brackets:

This country is Mo-jia. Setting sail from Gu-li, you proceed towards the southwest—the point *shen* [申位] on the compass; after that, the ship travels for three months, and then reaches the harbour of this country. The foreign name for it is Zhi Da; (and) there is a great chief who controls it. From Zhi Da, you go west, and after travelling [by land] for one day you reach the city where the king [caliph] resides [it will be shown later that this city is not the capital Tunis, but the city where the king has one of his palaces]; his country is named Mo-jia.

The people of the country profess the Muslim religion. A holy man first expounded and spread the doctrine of his teaching in this country; and right down to the present day all the people of the country observe the regulations of the doctrine in their actions, not daring to commit the slightest transgression.

The people of this country are burly and fine looking, and their limbs and faces are of a very dark purple colour [a dark-red or purple-red colour which looks almost like a purple colour; this will be explained in more detail below].

The menfolk bind up their heads; they wear long garments and leather shoes. The women all wear a hijab covering their heads, and you cannot see their faces.

They speak the Arabic language. The law of the country prohibits wine-drinking. The customs of the people are pacific and admirable. There are no poverty-stricken families. They all observe the precepts of their religion, and law breakers are few. It is in truth a most happy country.

As to marriage and funeral rites, they all conduct themselves in accordance with the regulations of their religion.

The colour "紫" is purple. In the Chinese language, "膛" means "chest". Since "膛" has the same Chinese pronunciation as "棠" and also sounds closely to "檀", it has become a habit to use 紫膛色 in writing to represent 紫棠色 or 紫檀色. "色" means colour. "棠" is the Begonia flower and "purple Begonia colour" (紫棠色) is a dark-red or purple-red colour. "檀" is sandalwood, and "purple sandalwood colour" (紫檀色) is a dark-red colour which looks almost like a purple colour.

What is very interesting in the above passage is the description of the skin colour of the people of this country—"…their limbs and faces are of a very dark purple colour." (Transl. J.V.G. Mills; Hakluyt Society, 1970.) I have noted that this "very dark purple colour" is actually a dark-red or purple-red colour, or a dark-red colour which looks almost like a purple colour. In Northern African deserts the semi-nomadic Tuaregs are said to have "blue" or "purple" faces! They have been called the "blue people" for the indigo-dye coloured clothes they traditionally wear, and which stain their skin.[71] Actually, their real facial colour is black-red.[72] The black-red colour is the original meaning of 紫膛色, 紫棠色 or 紫檀色 in the Chinese language. The Tuaregs are believed to be descendants of the Berber natives of North Africa and have been historically influential in the spread of Islam. Tuareg women wear a face veil.[73] The menfolk bind up their heads, and wear long garments. Clearly, Ma Huan's narrative gives a good indication that this country of *Tianfang*/Mo-jia may well be in North Africa. Later, I will show with multiple lines of evidence that this country was *indeed* ancient Tunisia in North Africa.

This makes good sense, since in ancient times Tunisia was primarily inhabited by the Berbers. They founded Carthage,[74] but Carthage was defeated by the Romans in 1 BC, and the Romans occupied Tunisia for most of the next 800 years until the Arabs conquered the whole of Tunisia in 697. The Arabs brought in the Muslim religion and ruled Tunisia. The Hafsids were a Sunni

Muslim Dynasty of Berber descent (Fyle 84), who ruled Ifriqiya (western Libya, Tunisia, and eastern Algeria) from 1229 to 1574.[75] (See Fig. 2.) I shall call it ancient Tunisia. The city Tunis became the capital of Ifriqiya.

When the Ma Huan delegation visited the country, the country was ruled by Abu Faris Abd al-Aziz II, a Hafsid Caliph of Ifriqiya (reigned 1394 to 1434). (A Caliphate is a state under the leadership of an Islamic steward with the title of caliph.) For simplicity, I will use "king" when I refer to the caliph of this Muslim country as Luo Maodeng did in his novel. Ma Huan saw that the people of this country spoke the Arabic language, believed in the Muslim religion and that their limbs and faces reflected the dark blue or purple colour of the long garments they wore. Tunis was then one of the richest and grandest cities in the Islamic world, with a population of about 100,000. I shall show that the Ma Huan delegation did not meet the king at the capital, Tunis, but most likely at another place.

Knowing that ancient Tunisia in North Africa might be where Ma Huan's *Tianfang*/Mo-jia was located is very interesting for me at this early stage of my analysis. But we can gather more lines of evidence by thoroughly examining the Chinese records.

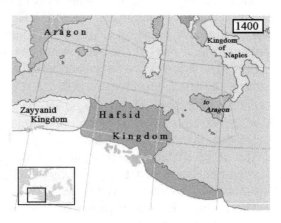

Fig. 2 Realm of the Hafsid Dynasty in 1400

In addition to Ma Huan's record, Xi Yang Chao Gong Dian Lu 《西洋朝贡典录》 or *Records of Tributes from the Western Ocean Countries*, written by Huang Shengzeng (1490–1540) in 1520 in the Ming Dynasty, also records how to get to *Tianfang*/Mo-jia, and even gives its approximate distance from Gu-li. Huang Shengzeng's book was compiled based on the materials from 1) Xing Cha Sheng Lan《星槎胜览》[76] or *The Overall Survey of the Star Raft*, written by Zheng He's scribe Fei Xin (费信; 1388–?; he joined the 1409, 1412, 1415 and 1430 voyages) in 1436; 2) Ying Ya Sheng Lan《瀛涯胜览》or *The Overall Survey of the Ocean's Shores* written by Ma Huan; and 3) other books including Jian Wei《碱位》(Zhen Wei《针位》) or *Study of Compass Measurement* (the book is no longer in existence) which was also written by Ma Huan. Huang Shengzeng's record is as follows:

其国在古里西南可二万里。古里西南申位行，善风三月至镇，番名秩潴，守以头目。秩潴西行一日至王城，本名默伽国，而又谓之天方。

My translation of the above passage is as follows and my comments are in square brackets:

The country could be 20,000 *li* southwest of Gu-li. From Gu-li, heading towards the compass direction represented by the southwest *shen* point, when encountering favourable winds, one can reach a town by sailing for three months. The foreign name for the town is Zhi Ta, and there is a chief who controls it. From Zhi Ta, travelling in a westward direction [by land] for one day, one reaches the city where the king resides [it will be shown later that this city is not the capital Tunis, but the city where the king had one of his palaces]. The real name for the country is Mo-jia, and it is also called *Tianfang*.

First of all, both Ma Huan and Huang Shengzeng recorded that where the king of Mo-jia resided was located to the west of Zhi Da/Zhi Ta; whereas Mecca is to the *southeast*, *not the west*, of Port Jeddah. This is the first sign that Mecca might not be Mo-jia.

Next, from the descriptions of Ma Huan and Huang Shengzeng, we know that to get to Zhi Da/Zhi Ta from Gu-li/Calicut by ship would require three months with favourable winds, otherwise it would take longer. This implies that the fifth year of the Xuande period was *not* the first time for ships to sail from Gu-li/Calicut to Mo-jia.

Third, the distance given by Huang Shengzeng requires examination. One *li* is 0.5 km. Here "could be" (可) shows that Huang Shengzeng did not give an exact waterway distance. But he estimated that Zhi Ta and the country of Mo-jia could be 20,000 *li* or 10,000 km/6,214 mi away from Gu-li/Calicut. I am going to examine this further. But first, I need to know the distances between some cities.

In Ma Huan's book, he states that the distance to get to Aden from Gu-li/Calicut was 6,000 *li* and the sailing time required was about one month under favourable winds:

自古里国开船，投正西兑位，好风行一月可到，其国在古里西六千里。

My translation of the above passage is as follows and my comments are in square brackets:

From Gu-li, setting sail towards the compass direction represented by due west [兑位 *dui* point], with favourable winds, the ship can reach there [the country of Aden] by sailing for one month. The country is 6,000 *li* to the west of Gu-li.

The above says that with the help of favourable winds in the navigational directions, the non-stop voyage from Calicut to Aden took about one month.[77] From Ma Huan's data, the average speed of the treasure ship can be estimated as 2.25 kn (knots).[78] Ma Huan's number of 6,000 *li* or 3,000 km/1,864 mi is reasonable since it is roughly close to the known distance of 3,349 km/2,081 mi from Port Calicut to Port Aden.[79] Next, the shortest distance (air travel distance or the distance "as the crow flies") from Aden to Jeddah (at about the midpoint of the Red Sea) is about 1,151 km/715 mi[80], and the shortest distance from Jeddah to the Holy City of Mecca is merely 64 km/40 mi.[81] This makes the shortest distance from Aden to Mecca to be around 1,215 km/755 mi after adding the above two distances together. Since the shortest distance between Jeddah and Cairo is only approximately 1,220 km/758 mi,[82] then, the shortest distance from Calicut to Cairo is approximately 3,349 + 1,151 + 1,220 = 5,720 km/3,554 mi, whereas the distance from Calicut to Mecca is approximately 3,349 + 1,215 = 4,564 km/2,836 mi. Both Cairo and Mecca are far closer than 10,000 km from Calicut. Hence, places like Cairo as suggested by Gavin Menzies and Wang Tai Peng, or Mecca in Saudi Arabia as suggested by many scholars, can all be ruled out as the country of *Tianfa*ng/Mo-jia that the Ma Huan delegation had visited.

Furthermore, the distance from Calicut to any of the harbours along the east coast of Africa or the south end of Africa is also far less than 10,000 km. For example, the shortest distance from Port Calicut to Port Mogadishu is only about 3,507 km/2,179 mi.[83] The distance from Port Calicut to Port Elizabeth in South Africa's Eastern Cape Province is 7,298 km/4,535 mi,[84] still less than 10,000 km. Hence, it is also unlikely for Mo-jia to be located at the east coast of Africa such as Port Mogadishu or the southern end of Africa.

On the other hand, if we assume that the Ma Huan delegation sailed in the southwest direction from Calicut all the way to the more distant but virtually uninhabited ice-covered landmass of Antarctica, or to more distant South America, it would not be possible for them to arrive at a Muslim country.

This leaves us only the countries in West and North Africa for consideration. This implies that "proceed towards the southwest— the point *shen* [申位] on the compass" (transl. J.V.G. Mills; Hakluyt Society, 1970) was only the initial sailing direction of the ship and, at some point, the ship must have changed its direction after crossing the Northern Indian Ocean and begun to sail along the western coast of Africa. None of the countries on the western or northern side of Africa has a harbour on its east coast and a major city to the west of this harbour, except ancient Tunisia, which is located in North Africa. The north, east and southeast of this kingdom face the Mediterranean Sea (see Fig. 2), while to the south and west are land areas. The pronunciations of Zhi Da and Zhi Ta are close to Jerba (Djerba) and Chebba (Sheba), which are the two major coast cities in eastern Tunisia.

(3) Is Jerba or Chebba in fact Zhi Da/Zhi Ta?

To resolve this issue, we need to keep in mind the important sentence written by Ma Huan (transl. J.V.G. Mills; Hakluyt Society, 1970; my comments are in square brackets): "From Zhi Da, you go west, and after travelling [by land] for one day you reach the city where the king [caliph] resides..."

A similar statement like Ma Huan's statement mentioned above was also made by Huang Shengzeng (transl. Sheng-Wei Wang, with my comment in square brackets): "From Zhi Ta, travelling in a westward direction [by land] for one day, one reaches the city where the king resides..."

Let us take a look at Jerba (Djerba) first.

Fig. 3 shows that to the due west of Jerba, there is no city which can be reached in one day. Jerba (33.81°N, 10.85°E) is an island off the coast of today's Tunisia. It is known for Mediterranean beaches and whitewashed desert towns influenced by Berber, Arab, Jewish and African cultures.[85] The nearest city to the west of Jerba is Gabes (33.89°N, 10.10°E). Since Jerba is an island, one has first to cross the water, then the combined water and land route to Gabes. The total distance travelled is about 169 km/105 mi,[86] which would take the Ma Huan delegation more than one day to reach. (If the Ma Huan delegation rode on camels with a speed of 16 km/10 mi per hour, the land route itself would take more than eight hours non-stop; the maximum speed achieved by a camel is about 25 km/16 mi per hour, but this is not sustainable.) Gabes does have a mosque, but it is of much less significance and does not need a journey of more than half a day to reach once you are in Gabes. There is the Great Mosque, the Mosque of Uqba (جـامع عقبـة بـن نـافع) in Kairouan that I am going to mention soon. However, even if the king did reside in Gabes, since the shortest distance from Gabes to Kairouan is 200 km/124 mi,[87] there is no way to reach Kairouan from Gabes in about half a day. Hence, Jerba (Djerba) can be ruled out as Zhi Da/Zi Ta, since it does not fit the descriptions written by Ma Huan and Huang Shengzeng.

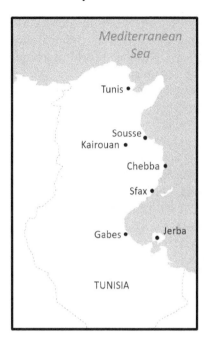

Fig. 3 Jerba, Gabes, Chebba, Sousse and Kairouan
in today's Tunisia

Next in Fig. 3, let us consider Chebba (Sheba). While there is no major city due west of Chebba, Sousse (35.82°N, 10.63°E)— Tunisia's third largest city—is located to the northwest of Chebba. It would not be unusual for the king of ancient Tunisia to have a palace in one of his major cities (most Chinese emperors had a temporary lodging built to accommodate an Imperial visit).[88] The shortest distance from Chebba to Sousse is about 78 km/48 mi.[89] If the Ma Huan delegation started from Chebba and went northwest, after travelling for one day they could be received by the king at his Sousse palace and there could be ample time for the Ma Huan delegation to take breaks during this journey.

Kairouan (35.68°N, 10.09°E) is almost due west of Sousse, and the shortest distance from Sousse to Kairouan is 55 km/34 mi.[90] The Ma Huan delegation could travel onward from Sousse, where the king resided, for a journey of more than half a day to reach the Heavenly Hall mosque in Kairouan. This justifies Ma Huan's statement mentioned earlier.

65

Kairouan, the fifth largest city in today's Tunisia, is an inland desert city and today's capital of the Kairouan Governorate in Tunisia. It is also a UNESCO World Heritage town. The name "Kairouan" means "caravan", indicating the city's origin as a settlement where desert trade caravans stopped, including the "blue" Tuaregs! We know, also, that Tunisia is a Muslim country and Tunisians speak Tunisian Arabic. Kairouan became a powerful trading hub and centre of Islamic scholarship in the ninth century, when the Arabic Aghlabid Emirs ruled Kairouan and built many of its monuments.[91] The Great Mosque or the Mosque of Uqba, on the edge of the medina (the old city), with its antique columns and imposing minaret, dates from this period and has since become a major pilgrimage site. For Muslims, seven trips made there are said to equal one hajj to Mecca.

Hence, Chebba is more likely the harbour named as Zhi Da or Zhi Ta by Ma Huan and Huang Shengzeng.

Later in Section (5), I will show that the mosque to which the Ma Huan delegation went for pilgrimage was indeed the Great Mosque or the Mosque of Uqba in Kairouan.

If Mo-jia was ancient Tunisia in North Africa, the best way to sail there would be from Gu-li/Calicut by circumnavigating southern Africa: After crossing the northern Indian Ocean the Calicut merchants' junk could sail into the fast, warm-water Agulhas Current along the east coast of Africa from north to south. The current's mean peak speed is 136 cm/sec (second) or 235 li/73 mi per day (this means 2.64 kn),[92] quite comparable to the estimated ship speed of 2.25 kn derived from Ma Huan's travel log or 3.07 kn from Ming Shi《明史》or *The History of Ming,* as I mentioned in Section (2) of this chapter. But the current can reach 245 cm/sec or 423 li/131 mi per day (i.e. 4.76 kn).[93] The ship could sail around the south end of Africa (the Cape of Good Hope is a short distance from Africa's southern tip) and continue the navigation into the slower, cold-water Benguela Current along the west coast of Africa from south to north. The mean speed of the Benguela Current is 17 cm/sec or 29 li/9 mi per day (0.33 kn); the current speed varies with seasonal winds.[94] Fig. 4 shows the courses of the warm Agulhas Current along the east coast of South Africa, and the cold Benguela Current along the west coast. Shown also in Fig. 4 is the West Wind Drift (the alternative name for the Antarctic Circumpolar Current which is an ocean current that flows clockwise from west to east around Antarctica).

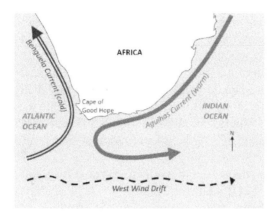

Fig. 4 The warm Agulhas Current (single line with an arrowhead) and the cold Benguela Current (double line with an arrowhead)

After leaving the Benguela Current, the ship could follow the even slower South Equatorial Current. The South Equatorial Current travels at a speed of 3–6 cm/sec or 5–10 *li*/1.5–3 mi per day.[95] Then, the ship could sail against another slow current—the Canary Current—which travels at 3–7 cm/sec or 5–12 *li*/1.5–3.7 mi per day.[96] As mentioned earlier, the Ma Huan delegation left Calicut soon after December 10, 1432. So, by the time they sailed against the direction of the Canary Current, it would have been around the late February or early March of 1433 (around late winter or early spring) when they were near the end of their journey. Lothar Stramma and Gerold Siedler's 1988 geostrophic computations indicate that the Canary Current is rather weak and variable in the winter and spring, along with the trade winds.[97] Finally, the ship could continue sailing along the north-western coast of Africa until it reached the Strait of Gibraltar and entered the Mediterranean Sea to arrive at Tunisia.

(4) How long did it take to sail from Calicut to Mo-jia? And how far apart actually were these two places?

Gavin Menzies investigated a world map showing the Indian Ocean and southern Africa (*1421* 131) drawn in 1459 by Fra Mauro, a European cartographer. Menzies estimated that a ship sailing at an average speed of 4.8 kn (a reasonably fast ship in those days) would have taken 40 days to reach the Cape Verde Islands from the Cape of Good Hope along the west coast of Africa. This would make the ship travel a distance around 8,534 km/5,303 mi (4.8 x 1.852 x 24 x 40 = 4,608 nm/5,303 mi/8,534 km) without taking into account the effect of the currents.

The actual distance and navigational time for a ship sailing at an average speed of 4.8 kn from Calicut to Chebba can be estimated by using the online sea-distance calculator[98] as follows:

1) 4,390 nm/5,052 mi/8,130 km from Calicut to Cape Town: 38 days and 2.58 hours;

2) 3,944 nm/4,539 mi/7,305 km from Cape Town to Mindelo in the Cape Verde Islands: 34 days and 4.83 hours;

3) The distance from Mindelo to Chebba cannot be calculated directly from the online sea-distance calculator, because Chebba is not stored in its database. However, we can obtain it indirectly. The online sea-distance calculator gives a distance of 2,560 nm/2,946 mi/4,741 km from Mindelo to Sfax[99] (would take 22 days and 5.33 hours). Since Chebba is only 35 nm/40 mi/64 km from Sfax[100] (see Fig. 3), and a ship would travel a shorter distance (35 nm) to reach Chebba 7.29 hours before it reached Sfax. A simple algebraic calculation would give the distance 2,525 nm/2,906 mi/4,677 km (2,560 – 35 = 2,525) from Mindelo to Chebba, and the sailing time would be shortened to 21 days and 22 hours (22 days and 5.33 hours minus 7.29 hours).

From the above information, we know that without taking into account the effect of the currents and for a ship travelling with an average speed of 4.8 kn, it would take 94 days and 5.41 hours (38 days and 2.58 hours + 34 days and 4.83 hours + 21 days and 22 hours) to complete the entire trip from Calicut to Chebba via Cape Town.

Now we can verify Menzies' estimates of navigation days and distance obtained from reading the map: how much time and what kind of distance in our calculation would it take for a ship at a speed of 4.8 kn to reach from the Cape of Good Hope to Mindelo in the Cape Verde Islands? We already know from 2) that it would take 34 days and 4.83 hours from Cape Town to Mindelo in the Cape Verde Islands. Since the distance between Cape Town and the Cape of Good Hope is 35 nm/40 mi/65 km,[101] and since Cape Town is north of the Cape of Good Hope, it would take 7.25 hours more to sail from the Cape of Good Hope to Mindelo than from Cape Town. Hence, the trip from the Cape of Good Hope to Mindelo would take about 34 days and 12 hours in comparison with Gavin Menzies' estimated 40 days.[102]

The waterway distance from the Cape of Good Hope to Mindelo is about 7,305 + 65 = 3,979 nm/4,579 mi/7,370 km, in comparison with 4,608 nm/5,303 mi/8,534 km based on Menzies' estimate by reading the map, discussed at the beginning of this section. Also, we can deduce that it would take 37 days and nineteen hours to sail from Calicut to the Cape of Good Hope (38 days and 2.58 hours minus 7.25 hours).[103]

The above estimated navigational times have not taken account of the effect of currents. For simplicity, we can neglect the effect of the slow Benguela Current, the very slow Canary and South Equatorial Currents, and concentrate on the fast-flowing Agulhas Current. As mentioned earlier, the Agulhas Current's mean peak speed is 235 li or 117.5 km/73 mi per day; but the current can reach 423 li or 211.7 km/132 mi per day.[104] With the help of the current, the ship could sail on an average of (427 + 235) li/206 mi per day[105] along the Agulhas Current, thereby saving 55 percent of the navigational time (235/427 = 0.55). So, sailing from Calicut to the Cape of Good Hope can indeed take less than 37 days and nineteen hours. The entire trip would then certainly take less than 94 days and 5.41 hours, and thus not exceed three months. This is consistent with Ma Huan's statement (transl. J.V.G. Mills; Hakluyt Society, 1970), "the ship travels for three months, and then reaches the harbour of this country."

The total distance from Calicut to Chebba is 10,859 nm (4,390 + 3,944 + 2,525) or 12,496 mi/20,111 km or a little over 20,000 km/40,000 li. Then, why did Huang Shengzeng underestimate the distance as a mere 20,000 li? Huang was a historian, not a navigator. Did he simply use the ship's speed of 2.25 kn or 200 li/62 mi per day derived from Ma Huan's travel log and multiply it by 90 days to give 18,000 li which is roughly 20,000 li?

Dreyer has given the sailing speed of the Ming Treasure Fleet on the seventh voyage as ranging from 1.4 to 3.4 kn from port to port (161). However, Ma Huan and his other delegation members sailed with the Calicut merchants in their junk which must have been a smaller and faster ship than the big treasure ships. The average speed of the ship must have been around 4.8 kn in order to explain Ma Huan's travel log related to the delegation's visit to the *Tianfang*/Mo-jia as I have just shown. In Zheng He's treasure fleet, there were also smaller and faster ships. But they had to keep pace with the big and slower treasure ships.

I have come up with a realistic waterway distance from Calicut to Chebba based on today's navigational knowledge. The effect of currents does play a role, and their inclusion shortens the navigational time from Calicut to Chebba.

Actually, failure to take into account the effect of currents in estimating the sailing distance can result in large errors. A clear example is shown in Gavin Menzies' book (*1421* 128–132), in which he notices and includes the effect of current to correct the longitudinal error, hence successfully makes the "bulge" of the west coast of Africa appear more realistically in his revised version of the 1402 Kangnido map.

Today we have the modern Global Positioning System (GPS), a space-based navigation system which provides location and time information in all weather conditions, anywhere on or near the Earth where there is an unobstructed line of sight to four or more GPS satellites, a system which was put in place in 1973. [106] Our knowledge has advanced greatly. However, we should not downplay the pioneering work the Chinese sailors accomplished over six hundred years ago when they used the best of their knowledge to diligently record the foreign lands they had explored long before other navigators did.

For the trip returning home from Mo-jia, the Ma Huan delegation would exit the Mediterranean Sea and sail along the Canary Current, the Brazil Current, the South Atlantic Current,[107] and then the South Indian Current[108] back to Calicut, before arriving at Nanjing.

(5) The "Heavenly Hall" mosque was the Mosque of Uqba in Kairouan, Tunisia

The previous analysis leads us to think that, based on the *distance* covered, Mo-jia was ancient Tunisia in North Africa. But I can provide more evidence to support this view by examining Ma Huan's description of the Heavenly Hall mosque in the country of *Tianfang*/Mo-jia.

Here is Ma Huan's description of the Heavenly Hall mosque to which he and other senior officers went on pilgrimage after they arrived at Mo-jia:

自此再行大半日之程，到天堂礼拜寺，其堂番名恺阿白。外周垣城，其城有四百六十六门，门之两傍皆用白玉石为柱，其柱共有四百六十七箇，前九十九箇，后一百一箇，左边一百三十二箇，右边一百三十五箇。其堂以五色石叠砌，四方平顶样。内用沉香大木五条为梁，以黄金为阁。满堂内墙壁皆是蔷薇露龙涎香和土为之，馨香不绝。上用皂纻丝为罩罩之。蓄二黑狮子守其门。每年至十二月十日，各番回回人，甚至一二年远路的，也到堂内礼拜，皆将所罩纻丝割取一块为记验而去。剜割既尽，其王则又预织一罩，复罩于上，仍复年年不绝。堂之左有司马仪圣人之墓，其坟垄俱是绿撒不泥宝石为之，长一丈二尺，高三尺，阔五尺，其围坟之墙，以绀黄玉叠砌，高五尺余。。。

The English translation of the above passage after my minor modifications is shown below. The original translation is taken from the book written by Ma Huan, translated by J.V.G. Mills. *op. cit.*, pp. 174–175. Mills' comment is in round brackets and my comments are in square brackets:

If you travel on from here [where the king resides] for a journey of more than half a day, you reach the Heavenly Hall mosque; the foreign name for this Hall is K'ai-a-pai (Kaaba). All around it on the outside is a wall; this wall has 466 openings; on both sides of each opening are pillars all made

71

of white jade stone; of these pillars there are altogether 467—along the front 99, along the back 101, along the left-hand side 132, and along the right-hand side 135.

The Hall is built with layers of five-coloured stones. Its shape is square and flat-topped. Inside the Hall, there are five great beams made of incense wood [that is agarwood; agarwood or aloeswood is a fragrant dark resinous wood used in incense, perfume, and small carvings],[109] and a shelf made of yellow gold. Throughout the interior of the Hall, the walls are formed of clay mixed with rosewater and ambergris, exhaling a perpetual fragrance. Inside the Hall there is a covering of black hemp silk. They keep two black lions to guard the door [it is very unlikely that two live lions were "kept" in front of the door; it rather means that they "drew the images of two lions" on the door façade to scare away evil people, since lions are not black].

Every year on the tenth day of the twelfth month, all the foreign Muslims—in extreme cases making a long journey of one or two years—come to worship inside the Hall. Everyone cuts off a piece of the hemp-silk covering [this covering is a curtain] as a memento before he goes away. When it has been completely cut away, the king replaces the old covering with another covering woven in advance; this happens again and again, year after year, without intermission.

On the left of the Hall is the burial-place of Si-ma-yi, a holy man. His tomb is entirely made with green *sa-pu-ni* gem-stones; the length is one *zhang* two *chi*, the height three *chi*, and the breadth five *chi*; the wall which surrounds the tomb is built with layers of purple topaz, and is more than five *chi* high. ...

Earlier, we learned from Ma Huan's writing that from Zhi Da, you go west (actually northwest), and after travelling for one day you reach the city where the king resided. Now we know that the trip from where the king resided to the Heavenly Hall mosque was a journey of more than half a day. In Section (3) of this chapter, I have already shown from geographical analysis that the city in which the king resided was most likely Sousse, and the Heavenly Hall mosque was located in Kairouan, which is just 52 km/32 mi away from Sousse. We also know that the Mosque of Uqba/the Great Mosque is located in Kairouan. It is one of the oldest places of worship in the Islamic world.

Does Ma Huan's description of the Heavenly Hall mosque match the Mosque of Uqba/the Great Mosque in Kairouan?

The white jade stone (白玉石) is white marble, granite or porphyry, and the five colours of the coloured stones (五色石) are blue, red, yellow, white and black. *Sa-pu-ni* (苏浡泥) or Sabuni in Persian pronunciation is a low-grade light green gem. One *zhang* is about 3.33 m; and one metre is about 3.33 *chi*.

The meaning of K'ai-a-pai in Arabic is "The Cube",[110] or "a cube-shaped building". Can we distinguish Ma Huan's K'ai-a-pai from the famous *Kaaba*, a cuboid building at the centre of Islam's holy mosque in Mecca, Saudi Arabia?

The sanctuary around the *Kaaba* in Mecca of Saudi Arabia is called *al-Masjid al-Ḥarām*, the Sacred Mosque, the Holy Shrine, the Great Mosque, or the Grand Mosque. *Kaaba*, the ancient stone building, is considered the House of God, and a place where Angels worship Allah (the Arabic name for God). Legend has it that the first man, Adam, set up the *Kaaba*. Later Abraham or Ibrahim ibn Azar, a prophet and apostle of God, reformed and built the *Kaaba*. Ishmael (司马仪 Si-ma-yi) was the son of Ibrahim, who helped his father to build this place around 2130 BC and his descendants remained the custodians of the Holy Shrine.

However, unlike the mosque described by Ma Huan, Muslims do not come to worship inside the *Kaaba* in Mecca; instead they *circle around* the *Kaaba*. But Ma Huan said that in the Heavenly Hall mosque of Mo-jia, Muslims came to worship *inside* the Hall.

Ma Huan also did not mention the famous Black Stone. If Ma Huan's K'ai-a-pai was the unique and famous *Kaaba* at the centre of the Grand Mosque in Mecca, Saudi Arabia, then the famous Black Stone[111] should be on it. The stone was venerated at the *Kaaba* in pre-Islamic pagan times. Islamic tradition holds that it fell from Heaven as a guide for Adam and Eve to build an altar, although it has also been described as a meteorite—a hypothesis.

Since then the stone has been broken into a few fragments. Now the surface of the *Kaaba*'s external wall, about 1.5 m above the eastern wall corner, is inlaid with a 30 cm long, slightly reddish-brown stone which is believed to be the famous Black Stone.

Swiss traveller Johann Ludwig Burckhardt visited Mecca in 1814. His detailed description of the Black Stone is included in the book *Zeus: A Study in Ancient Religion* (Cook 919) as follows:

It is an irregular oval, about seven inches in diameter, with an undulated surface, composed of about a dozen smaller stones of different sizes and shapes, well joined together with a small quantity of cement, and perfectly well smoothed; it looks as if the whole had been broken into as many pieces by a violent blow, and then united again. ... It appeared to me like lava, containing several small extraneous particles of a whitish and of a yellow substance. Its colour is now a deep reddish brown approaching to black. It is surrounded by a border composed of a substance which I took to be a close cement of pitch and gravel of a similar, but not quite the same, brownish colour. This border serves to support its detached pieces; it is two or three inches in breadth and rises a little above the surface of the stone. Both the border and the stone itself are encircled by a silver band, broader below than above, and on the two sides, with a considerable swelling below, as if a part of the stone were hidden under it. The lower part of the border is studded with silver nails.

This Black Stone is considered by Muslims to embody the only remaining original building relics of the *Kaaba*. If Ma Huan's country of *Tianfang*/Mo-jia was Mecca, then how could he, a devout Muslim himself, leave out this important object in his travel record, which Muslims believe to be like an icon in the Heavenly Hall mosque? This is the key point that Ma Huan's Heavenly Hall mosque *could not be* the Grand Mosque in Mecca, Saudi Arabia.

Huang Shengzeng made only a brief note about the K'ai-a-pai in Mo-jia in his book Xi Yang Chao Gong Dian Lu 《西洋朝贡典录》 or *Records of Tributes from the Western Ocean Countries* as follows:

其禮拜之寺曰天堂，其堂四方而高廣，謂之愷阿白。

My translation of the above passage is as follows:

74

Its mosque is named as the Heavenly Hall; its hall is of cubic shape, both tall and spacious. It is called the K'ai-a-pai.

Clearly, K'ai-a-pai is in general a large cuboid building for people to worship their God. Most scholars are of the opinion that Ma Huan's Heavenly Hall mosque was in Mecca. Lam Yee Din was the first to oppose that viewpoint. He, instead, proposes that Ma Huan's Heavenly Hall mosque could be the Mosque of Uqba in Kairouan, Tunisia.

There are other aspects of Ma Huan's Heavenly Hall mosque, which do not match the general description of the Sacred Mosque in Mecca. Hence, I will make a further analysis below to compare that general description with that of Ma Huan's Heavenly Hall mosque to see whether these two mosques can be considered as identical.

1. The physical characteristics of the mosque in Kairouan: The old town of Kairouan[112] is of an irregular oblong shape, surrounded by a brick wall, and pierced by five principal gates and four posterns, now closed. The Mosque of Uqba (Kairouan Sidi Oqba; Arabic: مسجد سـيدي عقبـة) or the Great Mosque of Kairouan [113] is incorporated into Kairouan's town walls. It is the oldest and most important Islamic building and the oldest Islamic mosque in North Africa, originally built by Oqba ibn Nafi, the Arab commander who founded Kairouan in 672 AD.

Fig. 5 is a view from outside the Mosque in 2010. The massive minaret is the oldest standing minaret, and its construction began during the first third of the eighth century. It was completed in 836 AD. The imposing square-plan tower consists of three sections of decreasing size reaching 31.5 m/103ft. Considered as the prototype for minarets of the western Islamic world, it served as a model for many later minarets. [114] From the outside, the Great Mosque of Kairouan is a fortress-like building. And Ma Huan was correct in his description (transl. J.V.G. Mills; Hakluyt Society in 1970) that all around the Heavenly Hall mosque "is a wall." The Mosque has several domes, the largest being over the mihrab (a niche that indicates the direction of Mecca) and the entrance to the prayer hall from the courtyard. Apart from the minaret and a few added dome structures on the roof, the mosque has a flat-topped roof as shown in Fig. 6.[115]

According to present records,[116] the Great Mosque itself has a vast irregular quadrilateral structure which consists of columns, minaret, fountain, inner court, central aisle, prayer hall, Lalla Rihana gate and entrance. (See a simplified drawing in Fig. 7.) The four unequal sides of the Mosque have the following lengths—127.60, 125.20, 72.70 and 78 m (418.64, 410.76, 235.52 and 238.52 ft), respectively—with four-metre high walls all around it on the outside. It covers a total area of 9,000 m^2/96,875 ft^2.

Fig. 8 gives detailed views of the Mosque of Uqba taken from inside the courtyard. Visible are the unusual column or pillar design of the Great Mosque later adopted by other mosques (left photo of Fig. 8) and the inner court viewed from the hallway openings (right photo of Fig. 8). Today, the prayer hall is accessed by seventeen carved wooden doors. A portico with a double row of arches leads to the spacious prayer hall which takes the shape of a rectangle of 70.6 m/231.6 ft in width and 37.5 m/123 ft in depth and can accommodate 3,000 people. Some say that along the three sides of the courtyard there are altogether 300 pillars, and inside the prayer hall there are another 300 pillars in twenty rows. Others say that in the prayer hall, there are 414 columns of marble, granite or porphyry among more than 500 columns in the whole mosque.[117]

Fig. 5 View outside the minaret (left) and entrance (right) of the Mosque of Uqba

Fig. 6 View from outside the Great Mosque of Kairouan

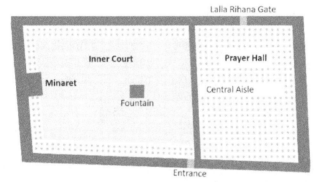

Fig. 7 Map of the Mosque of Uqba

Fig. 8 Columns in the hallway (left) and inner court viewed from the hallway openings (right)

Ma Huan gives yet another set of numbers: The wall surrounding the mosque had 466 openings and on both sides of each opening were pillars; these pillars—altogether 467—were, along the front,

77

99; along the back, 101; along the left-hand side, 132; and along the right-hand side, 135. The numbers 99:101:132:135 give ratios of 1:1.02:1.33:1.36, and these ratios do indicate that the shape of the mosque was an irregular quadrangle, in qualitative agreement with today's Mosque of Uqba (the four sides have lengths of 72.70, 78, 125.20, and 127.60 m; these give ratios of 1:1.07:1.72:1.76). Since the mosque has undergone significant changes over the past 600 years to ensure the stability of the building, the number of pillars and their positions may have changed. A legend says that people could not count these columns without going blind!

2. Special features of the Heavenly Hall mosque: I shall in this section discuss in more detail what Ma Huan described as follows: Ma Huan writes (transl. J.V.G. Mills; Hakluyt Society, 1970; my comment is in square brackets), "The Hall is built with layers of five-coloured stones. Its shape is square and flat-topped. Inside the Hall, there are five great beams made of incense wood [that is agarwood; agarwood or aloeswood is a fragrant dark resinous wood used in incense, perfume, and small carvings], and a shelf made of yellow gold. Throughout the interior of the Hall, the walls are formed of clay mixed with rosewater and ambergris, exhaling a perpetual fragrance," and "Inside the Hall there is a covering of black hemp silk. They keep two black lions to guard the door." The Hall, here, refers to the prayer hall of the mosque.

What we see today in the prayer hall of the Mosque of Uqba is that the painted ceilings are a unique ensemble of planks, beams and brackets, illustrating almost a thousand years of practice of painting on wood in Tunisia, and that the columns, floors and some other features in the prayer hall appear to have been made of colourful stones.[118] It has been said that the form of the Great Mosque is the cry of the muezzin in stone.[119] We already know from Fig. 6 that the entire mosque including the prayer hall has a flat-topped roof. However, the prayer hall is not square in shape, but is a slightly irregular quadrangle. Did Ma Huan make a mistake here? This is just one of the instances in which Ma Huan can cause some confusion.

In the interior of the prayer hall, the walls are formed of clay mixed with rosewater and ambergris, exhaling a perpetual fragrance. It is customary that Persian rosewater (scented water made by immersing rose petals in water) is used as a perfume in religious ceremonies by Muslims.[120] Since the walls enclosing the mosque are 4 m/13 ft in height, it is quite capable of holding a sub-floor made of yellow gold inside the prayer hall.

As for the hemp silk covering, in Xi Yang Chao Gong Dian Lu 《西洋朝贡典录》or *Records of Tributes from the Western Ocean Countries*, Huang Shengzeng wrote specifically that the black hemp-silk covering was some sort of curtain hanging *inside* the prayer hall.[121]

As mentioned earlier, the prayer hall in Mecca, Saudi Arabia, is quite different. It is well-known that the *Kaaba* inside the Sacred Mosque in Mecca is not very big. Most pilgrims can only circle the *Kaaba* and worship outside the *Kaaba*, and a black hemp-silk covering hangs over the entire *Kaaba*.

Next, concerning, "They keep two black lions to guard the door" (transl. J.V.G. Mills; Hakluyt Society, 1970), there is one verse of the Quran that mentions lions specifically: it describes the lion as an animal to be feared. Since lions are majestic creatures, very powerful and brave, in many Islamic countries, lions seem to be respected, and the Prophet's uncle Hamza ibn Abd Muttalib had the title of the Lion of Allah.[122] But it is most unlikely that two live lions could be "kept" in front of the door. They could attack any worshippers, not only the evil ones. Also, lions are *not* black. Hence, Ma Huan's description should be interpreted as they "drew the images" of two black lions on the door façade to scare evil people. This is another instance in which Ma Huan can cause confusion. But Louise Levathes simply writes, "...lion sculptures would have been anathema in Islam, which forbids human or animal depiction of any kind" (171).

Ma Huan's detailed description of how Muslims sincerely and devotedly came to the Heavenly Hall mosque to worship their God shows that the mosque which the Ma Huan delegation visited was a very important pilgrimage destination in the Islamic world. Indeed, the Great Mosque in Kairouan is one of the oldest and largest places of prayer and has been regarded as the Mecca of North Africa.

3. The burial sites inside the Heavenly Hall mosque: Ma Huan describes the burial site of a Muslim holy man as follows (transl. J.V.G. Mills; Hakluyt Society, 1970): "On the left of the Hall is the burial-place of Si-ma-yi, a holy man. His tomb is entirely made with green *sa-pu-ni* gem-stones; the length is one *zhang* two *chi*, the height three *chi*, and the breadth five *chi*; the wall which surrounds the tomb is built with layers of purple topaz, and is more than five *chi* high."

We know that Ishmael or Si-ma-yi, the son of Ibrahim, helped his father to build the Sacred Mosque in Mecca around 2130 BC, and his descendants remained the custodians of the Holy Shrine. Hence, most people think that the burial place of Si-ma-yi can only be inside the Sacred Mosque in Mecca, because he was the prophet of Islam. This is one of the reasons for confusing the country of *Tianfang*/Mo-jia with Mecca. But some scholars regard Si-ma-yi as Ismaili, a branch of Islam—Si-ma-yi can be interpreted as Ismaili believers (namely the Shia faction of Islam). They follow a living Imam and are known for their mystical philosophy. If you accept that Si-ma-yi are Ismaili believers, you would agree that cemeteries of this sect's Sahaabah (holy disciples) can have multiple burial sites. As Lam Yee Din has pointed out, the "burial-place of Si-ma-yi", recorded by Ma Huan, can refer to the tombs of this Islamic sect's Sahaabah, seen nowadays in Kairouan, instead of the tomb of Si-ma-yi himself.

According to Brockman (258), the Great Mosque of Kairouan may be entered through several gates, where one can find the tombs of "local saints". This is consistent with the above discussion. But the detailed dimensions or physical descriptions of these tombs are unknown, and it is impossible to compare them with Ma Huan's figures. Brockman also writes, "Nearby is a cemetery restricted to descendants of the family of the Prophet Mohammed [Muhammad—Ed.]". His sentence points to the graveyard—the cemetery of Ouled Farhane—outside the city wall to the west, about half a football pitch in size, and with whitewashed graves standing in front of the city walls and the minaret of the Great Mosque. Most of the tombs are shaped like little houses.[123] This graveyard is the cemetery of only one family and is surrounded by a low stone wall.

4. The interior of the Heavenly Hall mosque: Ma Huan gives the following description:

城内四角造四堆塔，每礼拜即登此塔喝班唱礼。左右两傍有各祖师传法之堂，亦以石头叠造，整饰极华丽。

The English translation of the above passage after my minor modifications is shown below. The original translation is taken from the book written by Ma Huan, translated by J.V.G. Mills. *op. cit.*, p. 176. Mills' comment is in round brackets and my comment is in square brackets:

Inside the wall (of the mosque), at the four corners, are built four towers; at every service of worship they ascend these towers, call to [to call] the company, and chant the ceremonial. On both sides, left and right, are the halls where all the patriarchs have preached the doctrine; these, too, are built with layers of stone, and are decorated most beautifully.

The translation of the above Chinese passage by Lam Yee Din is shown as follows:

Inside the mosque, at the four wall corners, are built four pagodas; at every service of worship they ascend these pagodas, to call the company, and chant the ceremonial. On both sides, left and right, are the halls where all the patriarchs have preached the doctrine, these, too, are built with layers of stone, and are decorated most beautifully.

Here we need to clarify where J.V.G. Mills' four "towers" or Lam Yee Din's four "pagodas" are. Only one Chinese source on the internet records that in addition to the gate being equipped with defensive facilities, there are four watchtowers at the four corners of the Mosque of Uqba in Kairouan.[124] In fact, the minaret also serves as a watchtower, in addition to calling the faithful to prayer. But until today no such watchtower can be found at the four corners of the Mosque of Uqba in Kairouan. Did the four watchtowers ever exist, especially in Ma Huan's days?

On the other hand, Lam Yee Din interprets Ma Huan's "four towers" ("四堆塔") as four pagodas; that is, the four pagodas are *multi-level towers* with each story constructed smaller than the story below it. Lam reasons, as these pagodas are for worship chanting, they should be located inside the prayer hall. He finds that, exactly on the southwest side of the Great Mosque, the prayer hall has two larger and two smaller pagodas; the total number is four as indicated by Ma Huan; the prayer hall of the Mosque of Uqba in Kairouan is divided into left and right halves; the two larger pagodas are opposite each other and are located on mid points of the longer sides of the whole prayer hall; also there is a pathway connecting the two larger pagodas; thus each left and right half prayer hall can have its own preaching doctrine hall for ancient patriarchs. Because these pagodas described by Lam Yee Din are inside the prayer hall, they cannot provide a lookout/surveillance function. Since the interior layout of the Sacred Mosque of Mecca is entirely different from Ma Huan's description, it seems not likely that the mosque described by Ma Huan was in Mecca. This will become very clear in Section (5) of Chapter 3.

5. The tombs and A-bi San-san in Mo-di-na: After the pilgrimage at the Heavenly Hall mosque, Ma Huan describes the visit to a place called Mo-di-na (蓦底纳):

又往西行一日，到一城，名蓦底纳。其马哈嘛圣人陵寝正在城内，至今墓顶豪光日夜侵云而起。墓后有一井，泉水清甜，名阿必糁糁。下番之人取其水藏于船边，海中倘遇飓风，即以此水洒之，风浪顿息。

The English translation of the above passage after my minor modifications is shown below. The original translation is taken from the book written by Ma Huan, translated by J.V.G. Mills. *op. cit.*, p. 177. Mills' comments are in round brackets and my comments are in square brackets:

If you go west again [meaning from the Heavenly Hall mosque in Kairouan] and travel for one day, you reach a city named Mo-di-na; the tomb of their holy man Ma-ha-ma is situated exactly in the city; (and) right down to the present day a bright light rises day and night from the top of the grave and penetrates into the clouds. Behind the grave is a well, a spring of pure and sweet water, named A-bi San-san; men who go to foreign parts take this water and store it at [in] the sides of their ships; if they meet with a typhoon at sea, they take this water and scatter it; (and) the wind and waves are lulled.

Many scholars think that Mo-di-na is Medina in Saudi Arabia. This cannot be correct, since the shortest distance between the two cities is 338 km/210 mi[125] and travel by land cannot take only one day. Actually, "medina" (Arabic: مدينة *madīnah*) means "city" or "town" in modern day Arabic. A medina quarter ("the old city") is a distinct city section found in many North African cities. The old town of Kairouan is called Medina, the area outlined in Fig. 9.[126] The pronunciation of Medina is close to Mo-di-na. The Great Mosque of Kairouan stands in the northeast corner of the Medina on this 1916 Map of Kairouan.

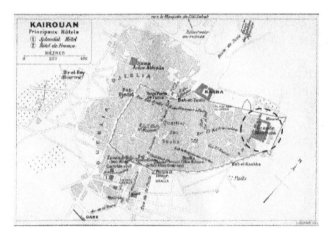

Fig. 9 Map of Kairouan (1916) showing the location of its Great Mosque in the northeast corner of the Medina (outlined)

But I disagree with Ma Huan's statement (transl. J.V.G. Mills; Hakluyt Society, 1970; my comment is in square brackets), "If you go west again [meaning from the Heavenly Hall mosque in Kairouan] and travel for one day, you reach a city named Mo-di-na." The Kairouan medina starts across the street from the mosque, a few seconds' walk from its gate. (See Fig. 9.) The medina is about 1 km/0.6 mi in length, so you can easily walk its full length in fifteen minutes: you don't need "one day" to get there. Since there is

83
83

The Last Journey of the San Bao Eunuch

no major city to the west of Kairouan, if you do travel westward for one day, you will be very disappointed if you expect to find any Medina as described by Ma Huan. (See Fig. 3.) So, Ma Huan's confusing statement must be clarified.

In Xi Yang Chao Gong Dian Lu《西洋朝贡典录》or *Records of Tributes from the Western Ocean Countries*, Huang Shengzeng gives a more precise description about the location of Mo-di-na:[127]

其国西行百里曰蓦底纳城。城之东曰谟罕蓦德神人之墓，墓顶有五色光，且夕辉煌不绝。墓后有泉，其名阿必糁糁。

My translation of the above passage is as follows:

Travelling 100 *li* to the west of this country, you can reach a city called Mo-di-na. To the east of this city is the tomb of the deity Muhammad. The top of the tomb has five-colour lights, staying ceaselessly glorious day and night. Behind it is a spring, named A-bi San-san.

Here Huang Shengzeng states (transl. Sheng-Wei Wang), "Travelling 100 *li* to the west of this country, you can reach a city called Mo-di-na." This is different from Ma Huan's statement (transl. J.V.G. Mills; Hakluyt Society, 1970; my comment is in square brackets), "If you go west again [meaning from the Heavenly Hall mosque in Kairouan] and travel for one day, you reach a city named Mo-di-na."

We must figure out the meaning of "Travelling 100 *li* to the west of this country" in Huang Shengzeng's statement. If "this country" means Kairouan, since 100 *li* = 50 km/31 mi, it is far west of Kairouan, I do not see any place called Medina or similar there. But if "this country" means Sousse, the king's residence, then 100 *li*/50 km/31 mi to its west (actually southwest) you will find Mo-di-na which was the old town centre of Kairouan. As discussed in Section (3) of this chapter, the shortest distance between Kairouan and Sousse is 52 km/32 mi, which is very close to Huang Shengzeng's 100 *li*/50 km/31 mi! This kind of distance would be a journey of about half a day, not one day. This is also in agreement with Ma Huan's earlier statement (transl. J.V.G. Mills; Hakluyt Society, 1970; my comment is in square brackets): "If you travel on from here [where the king resides] for a journey of more than half a day, you reach the Heavenly Hall mosque."

Concerning cemeteries and tombs, in the northwest corner of the city and to the west of the Great Mosque of Kairouan, the Barber Mosque (Zawiya of Sidi Sahab) keeps the relics of Abu Zama'a al-Balawi who was a companion of the Islam Prophet Muhammad[128] (pronunciation close to Ma-ha-ma in Ma Huan's narrative listed above). The legend says that the belongings include the hair of Muhammad.

In addition, there are tombs of descendants of Prophet Muhammad in Bir Barrouta[129] situated in the southwest direction, not far from the centre of Kairouan, and to the east of central Mo-di-na.[130] Huang Shengzeng's statement (transl. Sheng-Wei Wang), "To the east of this city is the tomb of the deity Muhammad" should be interpreted as a tomb for the descendant or descendants of Prophet Muhammad, because the Prophet himself, after his death, according to his will, was buried at his original residence in the Mosque of the Prophet in Medina, Saudi Arabia.

The sacred well Bir Barrouta is supposed to be able to communicate with the Zamzam well at Mecca in Saudi Arabia. The former is enclosed within a domed building and is the only one in the city. It is pumped by a blindfolded camel trudging in circles. Legend has it that its water comes directly from the well of Zamzam in Mecca. Even today, the local religious tradition says that a Muslim drinking water from Bir Barrouta a number of times is exempted from performing the pilgrimage to Mecca, a journey both long and expensive.

But neither Ma Huan's nor Huang Shengzeng's record can be considered the unique source of evidence for the existence of Mo-jia in North Africa. Luo Maodeng in Chapter 51 of his 1597 novel also has a record of this country.

Luo wrote that after the Ming sailors accepted the tributes from Semudera, more countries came to pay tributes. Among them there was a small country called Mo Jia Guo 默伽国 or Mo-jia Guo. But unlike Ma Huan or Huang Shengzeng, Luo did not call it the country of *Tianfang*. Why? Did Luo have in mind a country of *Tianfang* different from Mo-jia? I shall leave this for further discussion in Chapter 3.

The San Bao Eunuch

The Last Journey of the San Bao Eunuch

In Chapter 51 of Luo's novel, he wrote about the water of this small country, Mo-jia, as follows:

有默伽国，其先是个旷野之地，因为大食国有个祖师叫做蒲罗呼，徙居其地娶妻生一子，名字叫做司麻烟，生下地来，呱呱的哭了两三日，就把只脚照地上一顿。一顿不至紧，就涌出一股清泉来，日日长流，流成一个大井。井又有些灵验。甚么灵验，但凡飘洋的舟船遇着大风，把这个井水略洒几点，其风即止。国王闻中国宝船在苏门答剌，进上：
金刚指环一对，摩勒金环一对。

My translation of the above passage is as follows, and my comments are in square brackets:

There was a Mo-jia Guo [默伽国] which was anciently a land of wilderness. The ancestor of the Dashi [大食 Arabs] called Pu-luo-mou, moved to that land and married a woman. She later gave birth to a son, named Si-ma-yan [司麻烟]. After being born on the ground he cried for two or three days [perhaps because there was no water for her to wash the baby, she had to put the baby on the ground and went to look for water, but when she returned she was surprised at what she saw]. Then she saw her son kicking the ground with his heel. Kicking the ground was not a big deal, but a spring came forth, with the purest of water, and a stream flowed every day into a large well. The well showed some magic power. What sort of magic power? Whenever ocean going ships encountered high winds, a little sprinkle of the well water would stop the wind. The King [of Mo-jia] heard about the Chinese treasure ships at Semudera and sent in his tributes: a pair of diamond finger rings, and a pair of precious Mo-le gold bands.[131]

Da Shi Guo 大食国 or Dashi is a transliteration of "Tazi" or "Taziks" in Persian; the source was Tayyi. Dashi was the Arab Empire. Later in the Chinese Tang and Song Dynasties, the word was used by the Chinese to refer specifically to the Arabs, the Arab Empire, and the Iranian Muslim nations. Luo Maodeng wrote that

86

Mo-jia was originally a land of wilderness. This fits well with the desert environment of ancient Tunisia in North Africa. Pu-luo-mou and Si-ma-yan are Arabic names. The history of early Islamic Tunisia opened with the arrival of the Arabs who brought with them their language, the religion of Islam, and its calendar.[132] Si-ma-yan sounds close to Si-ma-yi or Ismaili and can be regarded as Si-ma-yi's followers or Ismaili believers (a branch of Islam, as we have discussed earlier).

As for the water of the well, Luo Maodeng offered another fascinating story. His description (transl. Sheng-Wei Wang), "Whenever ocean going ships encountered high winds, a little sprinkle of the well water would stop the wind," echoes well with Ma Huan's description (transl. J.V.G. Mills; Hakluyt Society, 1970; Mill's comment is in round brackets and my comment is in square brackets), "men who go to foreign parts take this water and store it at [in] the sides of their ships; if they meet with a typhoon at sea, they take this water and scatter it; (and) the wind and waves are lulled."

Since Mo-jia was a small country, the tributes sent by the king appeared to be quite moderate relative to tributes presented by other countries listed in Luo's novel. However, this kind of precious gold band was produced in India and worn around the head of the Mo-le (Mara in Sanskrit) Buddha. The fact that a Mo-le gold band showed up in Mo-jia, a Muslim country, can be explained as a trade item most likely obtained from Calicut merchants or merchants from other parts of India, who sailed to Mo-jia in those days. Ma Huan and his other delegation members who sailed with the Calicut merchants in their junk to Mo-jia, is strong evidence of the Mo-jia-India trade in the 1430s.

In summary, Luo Maodeng's Mo-jia points to the same Mo-jia recorded by Ma Huan's travel log, namely the ancient Islamic Tunisia in North Africa and the well which flowed with holy water is in Bir Barrouta. Luo's narrative on Mo-jia shows that he clearly distinguished Mo-jia from the country of *Tianfang*/Yun Chong, in his mind. This will be discussed further in the following chapter.

We begin to see that Luo's San Bao Tai Jian Xi Yang Gi 《三宝太监西洋记》 or *An Account of the Western World Voyage of the San Bao Eunuch* is giving a reliable description of this country from which Zheng He's fleet received tributes. This was also the country to which the Ma Huan delegation went for trade and pilgrimage in 1432–1433 during their seventh voyage to the Western Ocean. In later chapters, I shall show that Luo's novel also reveals amazing multiple lines of evidence linking Zheng He's sixth and seventh voyages with the far away Americas.

(5) Concluding remarks

In this chapter, I have analysed Ma Huan's description of *Tianfang*, and conclude that his country of *Tianfang*/Mo-jia was ancient Tunisia in North Africa, and the Heavenly Hall mosque the Ma Huan delegation visited was the Mosque of Uqba in Kairouan, Tunisia.

Mo-jia should not be confused with Mecca in today's Saudi Arabia. This conclusion is very important, especially for the seventh voyage. Luo Maodeng's novel is the *only* historical record which correctly distinguishes the country of *Tianfang*/Mo-jia from the country of *Tianfang*/Yun Chong which Zheng He's main fleet visited during his seventh and last voyage. But where was the country of *Tianfang*/Yun Chong? The answer will be given in Chapter 3 of this book.

It was Eunuch Hong Bao, soon after his squadron arrived at Gu-li/Calicut on December 10, 1432, who commanded the Ma Huan delegation to accompany the envoys from Mo-jia to go to their country for trade and pilgrimage by taking the Calicut merchants' ship. The outbound navigational route for the Ma Huan delegation from Calicut to Mo-jia during the seventh voyage is shown in Fig. 10 in Chapter 3. Ma Huan and Huang Shengzeng, together, have provided valuable information including the approximate distance (even if not precise), the length of travel time and the harbour, for arriving at this country.

Ma Huan's narrative relative to the Mo-jia people's black-red or purple skin colour, dress style, living conditions, customs, language spoken, religious rituals, etc., all resemble what we know of a Muslim country like ancient Tunisia in North Africa. Ma Huan also described the Heavenly Hall mosque he saw in Mo-jia, including the walls, the building shape, the building materials, the column structure, the prayer hall design, the tombs and the pagodas inside the prayer hall. His descriptions match well the existing records of the Mosque of Uqba in Kairouan.

Ma Huan and Huang Shengzeng next described nearby Mo-di-na and its surrounding tombs, well and spring water. Both their descriptions (after correcting a misleading statement made by Ma Huan) also match well existing records of the old town centre (Medina). Furthermore, having Chinese senior navigators on a Calicut merchants' junk to sail together in the years 1432–1433 from Calicut directly to the region in North Africa was a remarkable achievement at that time. The event offers *concrete evidence* that the Ming mariners and the Calicut merchants were able to sail around the Cape of Good Hope near which the Antarctic Ocean current moves with the roughest winds and giant waves, and which was a great challenge then to navigators. After overcoming this challenge, the Ma Huan delegation and the Calicut merchants could continue their sailings by following the currents along the west coast of Africa to reach North Africa, first by crossing the Strait of Gibraltar, then by entering the Mediterranean Sea. The delegation returned to Calicut one year later, near the end of 1433, with Mo-jia's envoys who brought some local articles and presented the articles to the Ming court. Such a remarkable achievement—documented in Chinese records—but not well understood previously, is now thoroughly examined and verified in this book. The event took place more than 55 years before Portugal's Bartolomeu Dias (1451–1500) sailed around the southernmost tip of Africa in 1488 to reach the Indian Ocean from the Atlantic.[133]

Equally impressive, if not more so, is that 1432–1433 might not be the first time the Ming sailors circumnavigated the southern tip of Africa. Lam Yee Din, in his Chinese article entitled "关于美洲由郑和船队发现的见解"[134] and his English article entitled "A Third Research on the Discovery of America by Zheng He's Fleet"[135] provides the following arguments: based on analysing Chinese historical records, the Ming mariners had already visited Mu-lan-pi or the country of Mu-lan-pi (木兰皮国) near today's Namibia in West Africa during their fifth voyage (1417–1419). Another Zheng He researcher, Liu Gang, has analysed the same subject and concluded that Mu-lan-pi was a border area between the Patagonia Plateau and the Pampas in South America.[136] In each case, the analysis supports the suggestion that the Ming mariners circumnavigated the southern tip of Africa even before the 1430s.

89

I conclude that the world should abandon the conventional view that the Ming Treasure Fleet sailed only as far as the east coast of Africa and the related view that the "Western Ocean" is limited to the Indian Ocean. Such a conclusion is no longer tenable after we truly understand the historical records of Ma Huan, Huang Shengzeng, Gong Zhen, Luo Maodeng, and others.

However, in terms of the timelines, Ma Huan and his fellow delegation members could not have been the envoys who met either with the famous Italian astronomer Paolo del Pozzo Toscanelli (1397–1482) or Pope Eugene IV in Florence in the summer of 1434.

CHAPTER THREE

Luo Maodeng's *Tianfang*/Yun Chong was Mecca in Saudi Arabia

In this chapter, I make a thorough analysis of the major chapters in Luo Maodeng's novel from a fresh angle, by eliminating its fanciful portion, and verifying his narrative about Zheng He's voyage to the Western Ocean against other Chinese historical records. I have extracted the navigational routes and timelines for the Ming Treasure Fleet during the seventh voyage, starting from Nanjing, to the point of arriving and then departing from Jeddah after their pilgrimage to Tianfang/Yun Chong. My results confirm that Luo Maodeng's Tianfang/Yun Chong was Mecca, Saudi Arabia.

In Chapter 2, I confirmed that the country of *Tianfang*/Mo-jia, which Ma Huan and his fellow delegation members visited in 1433, was ancient Tunisia in the Hafsid period in North Africa. This confirmation will help to clarify the confusion regarding where the main fleet led by Zheng He and Wang Jinghong sailed after they departed from Hong Bao in 1432.

In this chapter, Luo's narrative will show the different country of *Tianfang*/Yun Chong which Zheng He was going to visit. But where was this *Tianfang*? Moreover, will Luo Maodeng's 100-chapter novel give us clues about Zheng He's complete navigational routes and the timelines of his last voyage? These will be thoroughly examined to give clear answers.

(1) Countries explored and the timelines of Zheng He's fleet during the seventh voyage

In his novel, Luo Maodeng started to cover the navigational routes of Zheng He's seventh voyage to the Western Ocean in Chapter 22, in which the Ming Treasure Fleet visits the first foreign country of their journey. The list of countries that Zheng He's fleet explores is shown in this chapter. Actually a few more countries are mentioned in Luo's novel, but they are not included in the list due to their very small size, or due to other reasons including their very backward cultures. Also included in the list are the countries which the Ming

Treasure Fleet did not visit; but these countries sent their envoys with tributes to greet Zheng He when Zheng He's fleet was at Semudera in North Sumatra. In his voyages, Zheng He pursues a peaceful mission as best he can. However, during the first voyage (against pirate chief Chen Zuyi 陈祖义 at Palembang), the third voyage (against the king of Ceylon, Alagakkonara) and the fourth voyage (capturing a usurper named Sekandar against Zain al-'Abidin, the king of Semudera recognised by China), the treasure fleet was forced to defend itself militarily to put an end to war.

According to Zhu Yunming's Qian Wen Ji • Xia Xi Yang 《前闻記•下西洋》 or *A Record of History Once Heard: Down to the Western Ocean*, for the seventh voyage, the Ming Treasure Fleet led by Zheng He and Wang Jinghong embarked from Longwan (Dragon Bay 龙湾 at Nanjing, near the Longjiang Shipyard) on January 19, 1431 (Dreyer 151). While they waited for the monsoon winds, Zheng He and his crew set up two inscriptions (Dreyer 145). Both inscriptions were set up in the sixth year of the Xuande period (February 12, 1431 to February 2, 1432). One inscription, entitled Lou Dong Liu Jia Gang Tian Fei Gong Shi Ke Tong Fan Shi Ji Bei 《娄东刘家港天妃宫石刻通番事迹碑》 or "Inscription on the Stele in the Temple of the Heavenly Princess at Liujiagang in Eastern Lou, Recording the History of Contacts with the Barbarians", was at Liujiagang (刘家港) on the lower reaches of the Yangtze River. Zheng He's fleet arrived at Liujiagang on February 3, 1431, where the fleet was still present when the Liujiagang inscription was erected on March 14, 1431. The fleet arrived at Changle on April 4, 1431 and the second inscription, entitled Tian Fei Ling Ying Zhi Ji 《天妃灵应之记》 or "A Record of *Tianfei* Showing Her Presence and Power", was erected at Changle anchorage in Fujian Province (福建省) during the eleventh month of the sixth year of the Xuande period (December 5, 1431 to January 3, 1432; Dreyer 145). The fleet departed and then passed the Five Tiger Passage (五虎门) in Fujian Province before leaving the Min River (闽江) estuary on January 12, 1432 (December 9 in the sixth year of the Xuande period; Dreyer 145).

I am now going to compare the sailing routes and timelines in Luo's narrative with those in Zhu Yunming's record. The latter have been reconfirmed by the research of Xi Longfei, Yang Xi and Tang

Xire (席龙飞, 杨熺, 唐锡仁 395–396). Zhu's dates relate to the Lunar calendar and are given in parentheses.

The following list specifies the countries which Luo records in his novel, and in relation to which I have done a thorough analysis to extract the navigational routes and timelines of Zheng He's fleet during the seventh voyage, after eliminating the portions which contain Luo's fanciful descriptions:

1   Champa (金莲宝象国／占城国 or City of the Chams):[137] surrendered after failed resistance and made tributes.[138] This country was the first stop on all of Zheng He's voyages. According to Zhu Yunming, Zheng He's fleet arrived at Champa on January 27, 1432 (December 24 in the sixth year of the Xuande period; Dreyer 151) and departed on February 12, 1432 (January 12 in the seventh year of the Xuande period; Dreyer 152).

2   Bintonglong (宾童龙国):[139] surrendered without resistance and made small tributes.[140] From Luo's novel we know that travelling by boat between Bintonglong and Champa would take seven to eight days. So, Zheng He fleet's arrival and departure date at Bintonglong could be February 19 or 20, 1432 (January 19 or 20 in the seventh year of the Xuande period), since Bintonglong was a very small country the fleet would not have been interested to stay overnight. Zhu Yunming's record does not show this small country.

3   Lopburi (罗斛国):[141] surrendered after failing in an attempted resistance against the Chinese presence (Luo wrote that it took about three days to suppress the resistance) and made tributes.[142] Luo's record does not tell how long it took the fleet to sail to Lopburi from Bintonglong. Nonetheless, the fleet's departure date can be deduced as February 26, 1432 (January 26 in the seventh year of the Xuande period; see explanation in the paragraph below regarding Java). Hence, the arrival date can be deduced as February 22, 1432 (January 22 in the seventh year of the Xuande period). Zhu Yunming's record does not show this particular country.

4   Java (爪哇国):[143] According to Luo Maodeng, the country surrendered and made tributes after fierce resistance for

several years.[144] In fact, this did not happen during the seventh voyage. It was during the first voyage, when Zheng He's fleet arrived at Java's Semarang to trade and the islands of West Java and East Java were engaged in civil war. West Java destroyed East Java and killed 170 of Zheng He's soldiers. The king of West Java was afraid of the Ming military's revenge, so he sent gold to compensate for Zheng He's dead soldiers.[145] Later, the king of Java had to travel to China himself to make tribute to the Ming emperor.

We know that for the seventh voyage, Zheng He's fleet left Champa on February 12, 1432. According to Luo's narrative, it sailed for seven or eight days from Champa to Bintonglong, then spent three days calming down the attempted resistance in Lopburi, and another ten days and nights sailing from Lopburi to Java. When the fleet arrived at Java, it must have been in March of 1432. Indeed, according to Zhu Yunming, Zheng He's fleet arrived at Java on March 7, 1432 (February 6 in the seventh year of the Xuande period). From the above date, I have deduced that Zheng He's fleet left Lopburi on February 26, 1432 (a leap year) and arrived there on February 22, 1432. According to Zhu Yunming, the fleet departed from Java more than four months later, on July 13, 1432 (June 16 in the seventh year of the Xuande period).

5 Janggala (重迦罗国):[146] made small tributes.[147] According to Luo Maodeng, Zheng He's fleet only passed by this small kingdom without stopping. In Zhu Yunming's record, after the fleet left Java, the port of destination was Surabaya in eastern Java, Indonesia, near the historical heartland of the Majapahit kingdom (Dreyer 152). Zhu Yunming's record does not show the arrival and departure dates at Surabaya.

6 Palembang (浡淋邦 / 浡淋国 ; 旧港 Old Haven):[148] surrendered without resistance and made tributes.[149] According to Zhu Yunming, the arrival date at Palembang was July 24, 1432 (June 27 in the seventh year of the Xuande period). It took eleven days to arrive at Palembang from Java. The departure date from Palembang was July 27, 1432 (July 1 in the seventh year of the Xuande period).

According to Luo Maodeng, during the initial "several days" of sailing towards Palembang, Zheng He's fleet passed by five small places at which the people wanted to give their tributes. Since they were so poor, Zheng He did not accept the tributes from them. Luo also said that the fleet sailed for "a few more days" and encountered a small wealthy country that had a bad reputation for prostitution. After Zheng He gave his good advice to the chief of that kingdom, the fleet continued to sail again for "a few days" until it reached Palembang. Each time when Luo used "several days" or "a few more days" or "a few days", it is best interpreted as three or four days. This is because after summing up these sailing days, the number is eleven days (3 + 4 + 4 or 4 + 3 + 4 or 4 + 4 +3). In later cases, when Luo writes "several days", "a few more days", or "a few days", I will interpret these phrases as meaning three or four days. This interpretation gives more reliable numbers of days whenever I can cross-check against other information. So, according to Luo, it also took Zheng He's fleet eleven days to reach Palembang after leaving Java, consistent with Zhu Yunming's record.

7   The Land of Many Perfumes (女儿国):[150] surrendered after failed resistance for a few days and made tributes.[151] Luo's narrative about the sailing time to arrive at this country from Palembang and from Palembang to Malacca needs more discussion. It is shown in the next paragraph. Luo's exaggerated war narrative (resistence for a few days) seems to exist only on paper and should be ignored. Zhu Yunming's record does not mention this country.

8   Malacca (满 剌 伽 国): [152] sincerely made tributes. [153] According to Zhu Yunming, the arrival date of Zheng He's fleet in Malacca was August 3, 1432 (July 8 in the seventh year of the Xuande period). Based on Zhu's record, it took only eight days (if we also include the departure date) for Zheng He's fleet to arrive at Malacca from Palembang after the Chinese mariners left there on July 27. In comparison with Luo's narrative, it took Zheng He's fleet, first "a few days" (three or four days) to sail from Palembang to the Land of Many Perfumes, then "a few days" and "two or

95

three days" to sail from the Land of Many Perfumes to Malacca; altogether it took Zheng He's fleet from eight days to eleven days to sail from Palembang to Malacca. From this comparison, we know that Luo's sailing time from Palembang to Malacca via the Land of Many Perfumes can only be eight days, and there is no time for the fleet to stay overnight at the Land of Many Perfumes. This seems to make good sense. Would it be better not to stay at this women's country overnight when most mariners and soldiers on Zheng He's ships were male? Hence, I deduce that Zheng He's fleet arrived at and left the Land of Perfumes on July 30 or 31 (July 3 or 4 in the seventh year of the Xuande period). Zhu Yunming's record shows that the fleet's departure date from Malacca was a month later, on September 2, 1432 (August 8 in the seventh year of the Xuande period).

9 Aru (哑鲁国/亞路国):[154] received gifts from Zheng He.[155] According to Luo Maodeng, it took four days and nights to arrive at Aru from Malacca. Since Zhu Yunming's record shows that Zheng He's fleet left Malacca on September 2, 1432 (August 8 in the seventh year of the Xuande period), then the fleet would arrive at Aru on September 6, 1432 (August 12 in the seventh year of the Xuande period). Aru was a very small country and we can therefore assume that Zheng He's fleet simply passed by it without staying overnight. Zhu Yunming's record does not mention this country.

10 Alu (阿鲁国):[156] also received gifts from Zheng He.[157] According to Luo Maodeng, it took two days for Zheng He's fleet to arrive at Alu from Aru. Then the arrival date should be September 8, 1432 (August 14 in the seventh year of the Xuande period). Alu was a very small country and basically, we can assume that Zheng He's fleet just passed by it without staying overnight. Zhu Yunming's record does not mention this country.

11 Semudera (苏门答剌国):[158] surrendered after a failed uprising against the Chinese and made tributes.[159] According to Zhu Yunming, the arrival date of Zheng He's fleet at Semudera in North Sumatra was September 12,

1432 (August 18 in the seventh year of the Xuande period), and the departure date was November 2, 1432 (October 10 in the seventh year of the Xuande period). According to Luo Maodeng's narrative, Zheng He's fleet sailed for four to five days to arrive at Semudera (this is consistent with Zhu's date); and while Zheng He's fleet was still in Semudera, the following ten countries (the twelfth to the 21st in the list shown below) sent in their envoys to greet Zheng He and made tributes.[160] However, Zhu Yunming's record does not mention any of them in his record. Here are the ten countries:

12 Kulam (故临国)[161]
13 Mo-jia (默伽国)[162]
14 Battak or Nakur/Nagur (花面国/那孤儿国)[163]
15 Misr (勿斯里国)[164]
16 Mosul (勿斯离国)[165]
17 Ghazni (吉慈尼国/加兹尼国)[166]
18 Ma-li-ban (麻离板国)[167]
19 Li-fa/Li-de (黎伐国/黎代国)[168]
20 Baghdad (白达国)[169]
21 Lambri/Lamuri (南浡里国)[170]

After leaving Semudera in North Sumatra, Zheng He's fleet sailed to the 22nd country in the list shown below.

22 Sa Fa (撒发国):[171] this country no longer exists today.[172] According to Luo Maodeng, after Zheng He's fleet left Semudera in North Sumatra (according to Zhu Yunming, the departure date was November 2, 1432), the Ming sailors sailed for seven or eight days to arrive at Sa Fa. Zheng He's fleet was on its way to Ceylon. But there exist only two island groups, the Andaman and Nicobar Islands, between North Sumatra and Ceylon. Fei Xin, in his book Xing Cha Sheng Lan 《星槎胜览》 or *The Overall Survey of the Star Raft*, recorded that on November 14, 1432 (October 22 in the seventh year of the Xuande period), "because the wind and waves were not cooperating, [the fleet] arrived at Cuilanxu and was tied up at anchor for three days and

97

nights (Dreyer 154). Cuilanxu was probably the Great Nicobar Islands (Dreyer 154). Luo Maodeng could have taken the Great Nicobar Islands to be the country named Sa Fa, and it took the fleet seven to eight days' sailing to arrive at this island country. Then, the arrival date can be estimated as November 9 or 10, 1432 (October 17 or 18 in the seventh year of the Xuande period). According to Luo, Zheng He's soldiers spent two years subduing Sa Fa's resistance. This is obviously wrong and should be ignored. In fact, the fleet had only zero to four days to stay at Sa Fa before departing. My estimate is consistent with Fei Xin's record that in Sa Fa, the fleet was tied up at anchor for three days and nights. This is explained further in the following discussion of Ceylon. Zhu Yunming's record does not mention Sa Fa.

23 Ceylon/Sri Lanka (锡兰国):[173] According to Luo, Zheng He's military arrested the king of Ceylon.[174] In fact, the confrontation took place during the third voyage,[175] not the seventh voyage. According to Zhu Yunming, Zheng He's fleet departed from Semudera in North Sumatra on November 2, 1432 (October 10 in the seventh year of the Xuande period) and arrived at Beruwala on the west coast of Ceylon/Sri Lanka on November 28, 1432 (November 6 in the seventh year of the Xuande period). Ming Shi 《明史》 or *The History of Ming* said that non-stop sailing from Semudera in North Sumatra directly to Ceylon could take only twelve days and nights under favourable wind conditions. However, for the seventh voyage, it took 26 days (November 2 to 28). The Ming Treasure Fleet obviously did not encounter the most favourable wind conditions, and this resulted in a longer navigation as Fei Xin's record has shown; also stopping by Sa Fa might have taken extra days. We can estimate how many extra days it took as follows:

According to Luo Maodeng, it took seven or eight days to sail from Semudera in North Sumatra to Sa Fa, then "a few days" (meaning three or four days), followed by a series of sailings for three days, seven or eight days, and two or three days from Sa Fa, to arrive at Ceylon/Sri Lanka.

Adding up all the sailing days gives a total of from 22 days (7 + 3 + 3 + 7 +2) to 26 days (8 + 4 + 3 + 8 + 3) for the length of time to sail first from Semudera in North Sumatra to Sa Fa, and then from Sa Fa to Ceylon/Sri Lanka (here I do not include the seven days given by Luo for Zheng He's Buddhist Master to chant the scripture to pray for good luck, since this narrative may exist only on paper). Since Zhu Yunming's record shows that the trip from Semudera in North Sumatra to the west coast of Ceylon/Sri Lanka took 26 days, this leaves the treasure fleet with only zero to four days (26—26 = 0 or 26—22 = 4 days) to stay at Sa Fa, not two years as claimed by Luo Maodeng. So, the fleet would leave Sa Fa on November 13 or 14 (October 21 or 22 in the seventh year of the Xuande Period), since the fleet arrived there around November 9 or 10. Again, the war episode Luo describes between the military forces of Zheng He and the tiny Sa Fa should be discarded. But why did he repeatedly exaggerate the war episodes? The reason will be explained in Chapter 8 of this book.

According to Zhu Yunming's record, the treasure fleet departed from Beruwala on the west coast of Ceylon/Sri Lanka on December 2, 1432 (November 10 in the seventh year of the Xuande period) after a four-day stay and arrived at Gu-li/Calicut on December 10, 1432 (November 18 in the seventh year of the Xuande period). As explained in Chapter 2, at Calicut, it was Hong Bao, not Zheng He or Wang Jinghong, who commanded seven senior officers including Ma Huan to take the Calicut merchants' ship to *Tianfang*/Mo-jia in ancient Tunisia in North Africa for a trade mission. This indicates that *before leaving Ceylon/Sri Lanka, Zheng He had divided the fleet into a main fleet and a squadron*; each would head for a different destination to perform different tasks as confirmed in the *Tianfang Section of the Chapter of Foreign Countries in The History of Ming* (see discussion in Chapter 1, Section (6), of this book). Menzies argued that Wang Jinghong would lead his squadron to the Persian Gulf directly (*1434* 43). Since there is no historical record showing that Wang Jinghong led his own squadron alone to Hormuz or the Persian Gulf at this early stage of the seventh voyage, I am inclined to favour

99

the viewpoint that Zheng He and Wang Jinghong led the main fleet, and the two principal envoys explored more places together. This main fleet would have exhibited great strength of numbers to *overawe* one of their later destinations, Bengal, while Hong Bao would lead his own squadron to Calicut, his next call. But later, after reaching Aden, Zheng He's main fleet would decide to sail to yet other locations, and the two principal envoys would take separate itineraries (this will be discussed further in Section (3) of this chapter).

I will now focus on the navigational routes and timelines of Hong Bao's squadron in more detail. This is because, while most scholars consider that Zhu Yunming's record gives the extent of travel of *Zheng He's* main fleet during the seventh voyage, Luo's narrative leads me to think that Zhu's record actually reflects mainly *Hong Bao's* navigational routes and timelines after he and Zheng He (and Wang Jinghong) separated at Sri Lanka. It therefore seems suitable to discuss these first.

The navigational routes and timelines of
Hong Bao's squadron

Gavin Menzies cites (*1434* 42) the findings of Xi Longfei, Yang Xi and Tang Xire (席龙飞, 杨熺, 唐锡仁 395–396) that, given the date of departure—October 10, 1432—Zheng He's fleet was sailing in the direction of the prevailing monsoon across the Indian Ocean from Pulau Rondo (Banda Atjeh or Banda Aceh) on the north tip of Sumatra (6°04'N, 95°07'E) to Ceylon/Sri Lanka. *The Charts of Zheng He's Voyages* indicates that by measuring the angles of the given stars above the horizon, the treasure fleet finally reached Ceylon/Sri Lanka. Menzies writes that on November 18, 1432 (again, he did not indicate whether this date was in the Lunar calendar or in the Gregorian calendar), when the fleet was south of Sri Lanka (Galle, in the southern end of Sri Lanka, was its largest port), Zheng He ordered Hong Bao to lead his squadron to Calicut, their next port of call (*1434* 43). But according to Zhu Yunming's record, the treasure fleet departed from Beruwala at the west coast of Ceylon/Sri Lanka (Dreyer 153), instead of Galle in the southern end of Sri Lanka. However, Menzies' date of November 18, 1432[176] seems to be a typographical error for November 28, 1432. If Menzies' date is corrected to November 28, 1432, its corresponding Lunar calendar date would be November 6 in the seventh year of the Xuande period, in agreement with Zhu Yunming's record.

Hong Bao's fleet stayed at Calicut for only four days and departed from Calicut on December 14, 1432 (November 22 in the seventh year of the Xuande period). This means that the Ma Huan delegation left Gu-li/Calicut around December 10 to December 14, 1432. Hong Bao's squadron arrived at Hormuz on January 17, 1433 (December 26 in the seventh year of the Xuande period).

Menzies cites again (*1434* 43) the findings of Xi Longfei, Yang Xi and Tang Xire (席龙飞, 杨熺, 唐锡仁 395–396), which give more detailed itineraries: after Hong Bao left Calicut, his squadron first arrived at Dandi Bandar, farther north along the west coast of India, then crossed the Arabian Sea on a course of approximately 330 degrees to make landfall at Jabal Khamish/Khamis Jabal Mountain in Oman. After a few days, Hong Bao's squadron pushed on to Bandar Abbas, a port city and capital of Hormozgan Province on the southern coast of Iran, on the Persian Gulf, arriving on January 17, 1433, in agreement with Zhu Yunming's record. Hong Bao's squadron stayed in the neighbourhood of Hormuz for over two months, departing from Hormuz on March 9, 1433 (February 18 in the eighth year of the Xuande period), and returning to Calicut on March 31, 1433 (March 11 in the eighth year of the Xuande period), where his squadron later regrouped with Wang Jinghong's squadron.

Hong Bao and Wang Jinghong left Calicut on April 9, 1433. According to Zhu Yunming's record, their fleet reached Semudera on April 25 1433 (April 6 in the eighth year of the Xuande period), left from there six days later on May 1 (April 12 in the eighth year of the Xuande period), reached Malacca eight days later on May 9 (April 20 in the eighth year of the Xuande period), left from there nineteen days later on May 28 (May 9 in the eighth year of the Xuande period), reached Zhan City on June 12 (May 26 in the eighth year of the Xuande period), left from there three days later on June 17 (June 1 in the eighth year of the Xuande period); anchored at Liujiagang (刘家港 or Taicang) on July 7 (June 21 in the eighth year of the Xuande period); and arrived in Nanjing, on July 22, 1433 (July 6 in the eighth year of the Xuande period). In short, it took the treasure fleet about three and a half months to return to Nanjing from Calicut.

Fig. 10 shows the outbound navigational routes for Hong Bao's squadron and the Ma Huan delegation during the seventh voyage, and Fig. 11 shows the inbound navigational routes for Hong Bao's and Wang Jinghong's squadrons on their return voyage. Wang Jinghong's inbound navigational route will be explained later in this chapter.

In terms of the extent of travel, Zhu's record does not indicate that Hong Bao's squadron went to the east coast of Africa, or the southern end of the Arabian Peninsula, or the southern coast of the Arabian Peninsula. But according to Ming Shi《明史》or *The History of Ming*, the ambassadors of eleven countries including Aden (on the southern end of the Arabian Peninsula), Brava (on the east coast of Africa), Lasa (on the southern coast of the Arabian Peninsula) and Mecca (in today's Saudi Arabia) were escorted to China at the end of the seventh voyage. Since Hong Bao's squadron did not visit the above-mentioned four places, and there is no record stating that he sent squadrons to these places, I am inclined to think that Zheng He's main fleet must have visited them. Then, we must consider whether Luo Maodeng's records support this line of thinking.

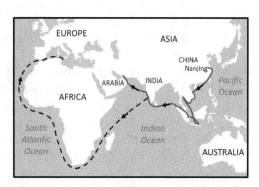

Fig. 10 Outbound navigational routes for Hong Bao's squadron (solid line) and the Ma Huan delegation (broken line) during the seventh voyage

102

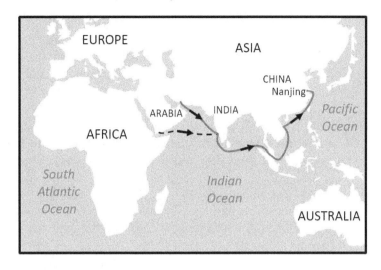

Fig. 11 Inbound navigational routes for Hong Bao's (solid line) and
Wang Jinghong's (broken line) squadrons
on their return voyage

The main fleet led by Zheng He and Wang Jinghong continued to explore more countries

In Luo's narrative, after Ceylon/Sri Lanka, the main fleet led by
Zheng He and Wang Jinghong continued its navigation to seventeen
more countries. Starting here, for the sake of convenience, the
Gregorian calendar, only, will be used for the dates mentioned:

24 Liushan/Maldives （溜山国／马尔代夫）:[177] surrendered
without resistance and made tributes.[178] From the previous
discussions we know that the main fleet led by Zheng He
and Wang Jinghong, and the squadron led by Hong Bao, left
Beruwala at the west coast of Ceylon/Sri Lanka on
December 2, 1432, separately. According to Luo Maodeng,
Zheng He's main fleet sailed for seven or eight days from
Ceylon/Sri Lanka to arrive at Liushan/Maldives. This is
consistent with the record of Ming Shi 《明史》 or The
History of Ming, that sailing south from Bieluoli in Ceylon,
it takes seven days and nights under favourable winds to
reach Liushan/Maldives. Beruwala (Bieluoli) and Galle are

103   103

close enough (the shortest distance between Galle and Beruwala is only 55 km/34 mi).[179] The fleet's arrival date can be deduced as December 9 or 10, 1432. Since the king of this small island country surrendered voluntarily and sent in tributes, Zheng He's fleet could depart on the same day as it arrived, December 9 or 10, 1432.

25 Greater Quilon/Da Gelan (大葛兰国):[180] surrendered without resistance and made tributes.[181] According to Luo, it took two or three days to sail from Liushan /Maldives to the Greater Quilon. The estimated arrival date should be around December 11 to 13, 1432. Since the king surrendered voluntarily without resistance and sent in tributes, Zheng He's fleet could depart on the same day as it arrived, December 11 to 13, 1432.

26 Lesser Quilon/Xiao Gelan (小葛兰国):[182] surrendered without resistance and made tributes.[183] According to Luo, it took three to five days to sail from the Greater Quilon/Da Gelan to the Lesser Quilon/Xiao Gelan.[184] Then, the estimated arrival date was December 14 to 18, 1432. Similarly, since the king surrendered voluntarily and sent in tributes, Zheng He's fleet could depart on the same day as it arrived, around December 14 to 18, 1432.

27 Cochin (柯枝国):[185] surrendered without resistance and made tributes.[186] According to Luo, it took two days for Zheng He's fleet to sail from the Lesser Quilon to Cochin.[187] The estimated arrival date should be around December 16 to 20, 1432. Similarly, since the king surrendered voluntarily and sent in tributes, Zheng He's fleet could depart on the same day as it arrived around December 16 to 20, 1432.

28 Gu-li/Calicut (古俚国/古里国):[188] surrendered without resistance and made tributes[189]. According to Luo, it took "a few days" (meaning three or four days) to sail from Cochin to Gu-li/Calicut.[190] This means Zheng He's fleet arrived at Gu-li/Calicut around December 19 to 24, 1432. According to my earlier discussion about Zhu Yunming's record, Hong Bao's squadron arrived at Calicut on December 10, 1432, and left from there on December 14, 1432. Zheng He's main fleet and Hong Bao's squadron did not meet at Calicut.

At Gu-li/Calicut, Zheng He held a banquet for the king and the fleet departed on the same day as it arrived, around December 19 to 24, 1432 (since Hong Bao had visited the place just a few days earlier).

29 The "Country with people with yellowish-coloured or golden-coloured eyes" (金眼国):[191] surrendered after failed resistance and finally made tributes.[192] According to Luo, it took some ten days (eleven to nineteen days; around December 30, 1432 to January 12, 1433) and then again "a few more days" (meaning three or four days; around January 2 to 16, 1433) to sail from Gu-li/Calicut to this nation of islands.[193] Luo wrote that the island nation spread for thousands of *li* around, and the climate was often hot ("周围有数千里之远。气候常热").[194] This island nation could have been the Andaman Islands in the Bengal Bay, north of the Great Nicobar Islands. The Andaman Islands in the Bay of Bengal were said to be inhabited by wolf-headed people. A mature wolf's eyes are often amber/brown or gold.[195] Luo used many chapters to describe the confrontation between this small island country's navy and Zheng He's soldiers. But it is very unlikely that this fierce combat took place or even lasted for more than two months, given the huge military disparity between the adversaries. It would require little effort to subdue the resistance of this small country, if there was any. Then peace could be restored as soon as Zheng He's fleet arrived there around January 2 to 16, 1433, and the fleet could depart from the country on the same day as its arrival around January 2 to 16, 1433.

30 Xi-ge-la/Bengal (吸葛刺国 / 榜葛刺):[196] surrendered without resistance and made tributes.[197] Zheng He's main fleet sailed for "a few days" (three or four days; around January 5 to 20, 1433) from the "Country with people with yellowish-coloured or golden-coloured eyes" to arrive at Hong Luo Mountain (红罗山) near the border of Xi-ge-la/Bengal. After briefly defeating residual resistance (Luo's war narrative should be ignored), which supported the "Country with people with yellowish-coloured or golden-coloured eyes", Zheng He's fleet arrived at Xi-ge-la/Bengal

within half a day's sailing (still around January 5 to 20, 1433). After two days (around January 7 to 22, 1433), the king surrendered and set up a banquet lasting for three days (around January 10 to 25, 1433) to welcome the Ming mariners.[198] Zheng He also held a banquet lasting for three days (around January 13 to 28, 1433) to thank the king.[199] After all the events were over, Zheng He's fleet sailed for East Africa, around January 13 to 28, 1433.

31   Mogadishu（木骨都束国）:[200] surrendered after failed resistance and made tributes.[201] Accorrding to Luo, from Xi-ge-la/Bengal, sailing for some ten days (eleven to nineteen days; around January 24 to February 16, 1433), Zheng He's fleet arrived at Mogadishu in today's Somalia. It should not have taken any time to subdue the local resistance given the huge military disparity between the adversaries, if there was any resistance at all. When peace was restored, the date would be around January 24 to February 16, 1433.

A local legend in Mogadishu says that the Ming Buddhist Master left a copper pillar near the seaport after Emperor Zhu of the Ming Dynasty sent envoys to come to the country to show friendship and to collect tributes. The pillar is carved with "namo amitfabha" on all sides to praise the Buddha. Quite amazingly, this copper pillar was mentioned in Luo's 1597 novel in Chapter 77. How did Luo know about it? How could he imagine such an event with such amazingly detailed accuracy?

He must have had some records which we do not have today.

Moreover, today in Africa, there is a strange village, Siyu, of more than 1,000 residents on a small island, Pate Island, which is only 8 km/5 mi away from the continent to the east of Kenya which borders Somalia. The villagers claim that they are the offspring of Zheng He's sailors. Some of them even went specifically to China to seek their Chinese ancestors.[202] Their skin colour is a shade between black and yellow, different from the ordinary African people. They build their tombs in a semi-circular shape and erect a monument in front of it like the Chinese do. In

Africa, they are the only ones who do it this way. They make pottery and simple porcelain artefacts using methods like those used by the ancient Chinese people. There has been a legend circulating on the island that 600 years ago, a Chinese ship hit the rocks, and dozens of sailors desperately swam upstream to reach the Pate Island. These mariners lived with the black-skinned women on the island and had children; and they were the ancestors of today's people of Pate Island.

Then, it should not be a surprise that in 2017, during the first international forum entitled "Links between China and East Africa: from antiquity to the present day" on the island of Manda (the Lamu archipelago, Kenya), a group of Chinese, Kenyan and American archaeologists reported the discovery of bone remains of three people genetically related to the Chinese and living, it is supposed, in the era of the sea voyages of Zheng He.[203]

32 Zhubu/Juba (竹步国):[204] surrendered and made tributes together with Mogadishu.[205] The date would be around January 24 to February 16, 1433, since the country was very close to Mogadishu.

33 Brava/Barawa (卜剌哇国):[206] surrendered and made tributes together with Mogadishu.[207] The date should be around January 24 to February 16, 1433, since the country was also very close to Mogadishu.

34 Lasa (剌撒国):[208] surrendered and made tributes on the day after Zheng He fleet's arrival.[209] But Luo Maodeng did not tell how many days it took the fleet to get from Brava/Barawa to Lasa. Here I try to make an estimate as follows: using an online tool for calculating distances between sea ports,[210] the distance between Port Calicut and Port Aden is approximately 1,820 nm/2,095 mi/3,371 km. According to Ming Shi 《明史》 or The History of Ming, Aden could be reached from Calicut in as few as 22 days and nights.[211] This means the ship was sailing 82.7 nm per day or about 3.4 nm per hour (3.4 kn). Since the distance between Port Mogadishu and Port Mukalla (close to Lasa)[212] is approximately 941 nm/1,083 mi/1,743 km,[213] it would take the same ship about eleven days and nine hours

to get from Port Mogadishu to Port Mukalla. So, Zheng He's fleet could have arrived at Lasa around February 4 to 27, 1433. The next day would be around February 5 to 28, 1433, when the fleet received the tributes and departed from Lasa. Luo writes that Zheng He used powerful gunpowder weapons, namely *Xiangyang Dapao* (襄阳大炮), to warn the walled city state of Lasa (Dreyer 84). I shall discuss this powerful weapon again in Chapter 8 of this book.

35 Juffair/Dhufar (祖 法 儿 国): [214] surrendered without resistance and made tributes. [215] It took eight to ten days (five or six days plus three to four days, according to Luo's narrative; around February 13 to March 10, 1433) for Zheng He's fleet to arrive at Juffair/Dhufar from Lasa. The king held a banquet lasting three days for the Chinese sailors and saw them off afterwards. The date was around February 16 to March 13, 1433.

36 Hulumumosi/Hormuz (忽鲁谟斯国): [216] surrendered without resistance and made tributes. [217] According to Luo, it took no more than "a few days" (three or four days) for Zheng He's main fleet to reach Hulumumosi/Hormuz from Juffair/Dhufar. [218] The date should be around February 19 to March 17, 1433. Since the country voluntarily surrendered and sent in tributes, Zheng He's fleet could leave the country on the same day as their arrival, around February 19 to March 17, 1433. Zheng He and Wang Jinghong could have met with Hong Bao briefly during this very brief period, since Hong Bao's squadron was in the Hormuz region from January 16, 1433 to March 9, 1433.

37 The "Country with people with silver-coloured eyes" (银眼国): [219] Luo wrote that Zheng He's fleet sailed for "a few days" (meaning three or four days; around February 22 to March 21, 1433) to arrive at this small country. It would not be a problem for Zheng He's military force to quickly subdue the resistance of the "Country with people with silver-coloured eyes," [220] if there were any. Zheng He ordered the people of this small country to assimilate with people in the neighbouring countries, and from then on, the eyes of the people of this small country gradually turned black, due to interracial mixing, and the country no longer

exists. When Zheng He's fleet left this country, the date could still be around February 22 to March 21, 1433.

38 Aden (阿丹国):[221] surrendered after failed resistance and made tributes.[222] It took some twenty days (21 to 29 days; around March 15 to April 19, 1433) for Zheng He's fleet to sail from the "Country with people with silver-coloured eyes" to arrive at Aden.[223] The country is a necessary stopping place along the sea route to Mecca in today's Saudi Arabia. Port Aden is at the southwest tip of Yemen and faces the Gulf of Aden. It is close to the opening of the Red Sea. The distance from Port Aden to Port Jeddah is about 1,151 km/715 mi, and the shortest distance from Jeddah to the Holy City of Mecca is merely 64 km/40 mi. Mecca has a Sacred Mosque containing the most famous "Blackstone" and "*Kaaba*". From the above estimated timeline, Zheng He's fleet could have arrived at Aden around March 15 to April 19, 1433. Aden was not a big country. Zheng He's fleet could have subdued any resistance there quickly. Hence it could be possible that Zheng He's mariners departed from Aden around March 17 to April 22, 1433 after Zheng He gave the king of Aden two or three days to prepare tributes. The increasing uncertainty of the estimated arrival and departure dates arises from Luo's imprecise expressions of the navigational days accumulated along the voyage.

According to Ming Shi 《明史》 or *The History of Ming,* the ambassadors of eleven countries, including Aden, Brava, Lasa and Mecca, were escorted to China at the end of the seventh voyage, whereas Zhu Yunming's record does not document the treasure fleet's journey to any of the above-mentioned four countries.

So, who escorted them to China?

It could not be Hong Bao, since he did not visit these four countries and there is no evidence or record showing that he sent squadrons to these countries. And even if Zheng He's main fleet might have met Hong Bao's squadron briefly in the neighbourhood of Hulumumosi/Hormuz and could have the ambassadors of Brava, Lasa and others transferred to Hong Bao's ship, the date was before Zheng He's main fleet visited Aden and Mecca. Hence, the ambassadors of Aden and Mecca were not yet with Zheng He in Hulumumosi/Hormuz to be transferred to Hong Bao's ship.

Could it be Wang Jinghong who escorted the ambassadors to China?

He could have stayed with Zheng He's main fleet all the time until the moment he separated from Zheng He's main fleet to escort the ambassadors of Aden, Brava, Lasa, Mecca and others to Calicut to re-join Hong Bao's squadron. This could have happened as early as the arrival of Zheng He and Wang Jinghong at Aden around March 15 to April 19, 1433, when the envoys from Mecca had arrived at Aden to greet them. Wang Jinghong had just about enough time (22 days were needed to reach Calicut from Aden according to Ming Shi《明史》or *The History of Ming*) to reach Calicut in early April[224] to re-join Hong Bao's squadron.[225] Both squadrons left Calicut on April 9, 1433. This leads me to think that Zheng He and Wang Jinghong very likely separated at Aden. According to Luo Maodeng's narrative, after leaving Aden, Zheng He's main fleet continued to navigate to the 39th country *Tianfang*/Yun Chong and the 40th country, Fengdu. Here I briefly summarise these last two visits:

39 *Tianfang* (天方国)/Yun Chong:[226] sent in tributes.[227] According to Luo's Chapter 86 (transl. Sheng-Wei Wang), "The country of *Tianfang* was a blissful paradise; the mosque in *Tianfang* was full of places of historic interest" ("天方国极乐天堂 礼拜寺偏多古迹"). But where was this *Tianfang* /Yun Chong mentioned in Luo's novel? And when did Zheng He's crew arrive and leave there? These questions will be discussed in the following sections.

40 Fengdu (酆都国):[228] sent in tributes.[229] Similar questions can be asked about Luo Maodeng's Fengdu or Fengdu Guo, as detailed in Chapters 6, 7 and 8 of this book.

(2) Wang Dayuan's "Yun Chong" was Mecca in today's Saudi Arabia

Before I thoroughly examine Luo's chapters to answer the above questions, let me first take a moment to review the translated names of the English *Mecca* (Arabic: مكة *Makkah*) in Chinese records. For centuries, many scholars have regarded Mecca in Saudi Arabia as the country of *Tianfang*. But Mecca could be confused with Mo-jia which was also called the country of *Tianfang* by Ma Huan and other historians due to their similar pronunciations. Therefore, a thorough analysis is needed to clarify this confusion.

"Mecca" was called "Ma-jia" ("麻嘉国") for the first time in Ling Wai Dai Da 《岭外代答》or *Answers to the Questions Concerning Foreign Countries*. It is not only a book about Guangdong and Guangxi local histories in the Song Dynasty (960–1279), but also a book about the history of transportation between Song Dynasty China and foreign countries.[230] It was written by Zhou Qufei (周去非; 1134–1189) in the fifth year of the Chunxi period (淳熙五年; 1178) of the Emperor Xiaozong (孝宗) of the Southern Song Dynasty. "Mo-jia" ("摩迦") also appeared in the record entitled Song Hui Yao 《宋会要》or *Decrees and Laws Collected in the Song Dynasty*. ("Hui" means meeting or imperial court appearance; "Yao" means imperial edicts and memorials. "Song Hui Yao" thus indicates the records collected in the Song Dynasty by the official historians in the imperial court after they arranged the original imperial edicts and memorials to the throne into different classifications.)[231] Moreover, "Ma-jia" (" 麻嘉 ") appeared in Zhu Fan Zhi 《诸蕃志》or *Records of Many Foreign Countries*. It is a masterpiece which recorded maritime trade and transportation between China and foreign countries from Japan in northeastern Asia to Europe, and to Morocco in North Africa; it was written by Zhao Rugua (赵汝适; 1170–1231) in 1225 of the Southern Song Dynasty.[232]

It is clear that the above-mentioned Ma-jia 麻嘉国, Mo-jia 摩迦 and Ma-jia 麻嘉 in different Chinese records could easily be confused with Ma Huan's Mo-jia 默伽. But the most important record was written by Wang Dayuan (汪大渊; 1311–1350; a traveller from Quanzhou, China, during the Mongol Yuan Dynasty

111

in the fourteenth century). He was a prominent navigator and author of a significant 1349 book Dao Yi Zhi Lue 《岛夷志略》 or *Descriptions of Barbarians and the Islands*. Between 1328 and 1333, he sailed along the South China Sea and visited many places in Southeast Asia, reaching as far as South Asia, landing in Bengal, Sri Lanka and India. In 1334–1339 he visited North Africa and East Africa.[233] Wang Dayuan recorded the local geographies, customs and products of more than 200 countries that he personally had visited during two voyages in 1330 and 1337. His book had a great influence on the geography books of the Ming Dynasty. In particular, he travelled abroad to a "paradise". There have been debates about where this paradise might be. Below is Wang Dayuan's description of this paradise which has been quoted by many historians:

地多旷漠，即古筠冲之地，名为西域。风景融和，四时之春也。田沃稻饶，居民安业，风俗好善，有酋长，无事科扰于民，刑法之治，自然淳化。不生盗贼，上下和美。古置禮拜寺，見月初生，其酋長及民下悉皆拜天，以為一國之化，餘無所施。其寺分為四方，每方九十間，共三百六十間。皆白玉為柱，黃甘玉為地，中有黑石一片，方丈餘，曰漢初天降也。其寺層次高上，如塔之狀。男子穿白長衫。地產金箔、寶石、珍珠、獅子、駱駝、祖剌法、豹、麂。馬八尺之高也，即為天馬也。貨用金銀、段疋、色絹、青白花器、鐵鼎、鐵銚之屬。乃日中不市，至日落之後以為夜市，蓋其日色熱之故也。诗曰：罕见天方国。。。

My translation of the above passage is as follows, and my comment is in square brackets:

The place has many vast deserts. This is the land of Yun Chong in ancient times, also known as the Western Regions. In the spring of the four seasons, the landscapes and climate are pleasant. The soil is fertile and produces plenty of rice. Residents live and work in peace, and social customs are kind and benevolent. There is a tribal chief, but he, also, is benevolent. Punishment is according to law and regulations to bring society naturally into harmony. The place does not

112

nurture thieves and robbers. High and low classes of people live together peacefully. There has been a mosque since ancient times. When the new moon is observed, the tribal chief and his people all worship Heaven. It is regarded as the one and only culture of this country. The mosque is four-sided. Each side has 90 sectors, making a total of 360 sectors, all of which have pillars made of white jade stones. The floors are made of yellow jade stones. In the centre there is a piece of black stone which is one *zhang* or more in breadth. It is said that it came from Heaven in the early Han Dynasty. The mosque has multi-levels and is tall, shaped like a tower. Men wear white-coloured long robes. The place produces gold leaves, gems, pearls, lions, camels, zu-la-fa [giraffes], leopards and muntjacs. Horses measuring eight *chi* in height are Heavenly horses. For trade they use gold and silver, satin, coloured silk fabric, cyan- and white-coloured flowerpots, iron tripods, and items such as iron pots. There is no market activity during the day. The night market starts after the sun sets, because it is hot during daytime. The poem says that this is the rarely seen country of *Tianfang*...

"Yun Chong" ("筠冲") is generally known as the name of a place in the Arab region and may be one of the birthplaces of Islam.[234] Note that Wang Dayuan specifically mentioned the "black stone" inside the mosque in the above passage, which *only* exists in the Sacred Mosque of Mecca in Saudi Arabia. He quoted a poem (transl. Sheng-Wei Wang) to praise this "paradise"—Yun Chong—as "the rarely seen country of *Tianfang*." Clearly, he has confirmed, in his mind, that Yun Chong was Mecca (in today's Saudi Arabia), and Mecca was *Tianfang*.

I am going to show that Wang Dayuan was correct. My analysis of Wang Dayuan's passage will firmly support the claim that Yun Chong was *indeed* Mecca, Islam's holiest city, the birthplace of the Prophet Muhammad and the faith itself.

In Wang Dayuan's passage, the term, the Western Regions (西域) refers mostly to the many countries and regions west of the Yumen Guan (玉门关 or Jade Gate Pass), or another gate Yang Guan (阳关 or Southern Pass), of the southern base of Tian Shan (天山 or Tiam Mountain)[235] in China's Han Dynasty (202 BC–220

113
113

AD). During the Sui (581–618 or 619) and Tang (618–907) Dynasties, the Western Regions expanded to Purum[236] in the north, Persia in the middle, and India in the south. In the Yuan Dynasty (1271–1368), the Western Regions expanded to include parts of Europe and Africa.[237]

Wang Dayuan's passage deserves further study.

1) Climate: He writes (transl. Sheng-Wei Wang), "The place has many vast deserts." This is consistent with the fact that Saudi Arabia is widely thought of as a desert and Mecca features a desert climate.

He also writes near the end of his passage (transl. Sheng-Wei Wang), "There is no market activity during the day. The night market starts after the sun sets, because it is hot during daytime." Mecca retains its warm temperature even in winter, which can range from 18 °C/64 °F at night to 30 °C/86 °F in the day. Summer temperatures are extremely hot, often being over 40 °C/104 °F during the day, dropping to 30 °C/86 °F at night. For the whole year, the temperature is between 30 °C/86 °F and 40 °C/104 °F on average during the months of April, May, June, July, August, September and October; and between 20 °C/68 °F and 30 °C/86 °F on average during November, December, January, February and March.[238]

The Sacred Mosque in Mecca, also called the Great Mosque of Mecca, the Grand Mosque, or the Holy Mosque (al-Masjid al-Harām) which houses the Kaaba, is geographically located in a valley. Although it rains in Mecca just like anywhere else in the desert, to produce plenty of rice, as Wang Dayuan described, the soil around the area requires heavy irrigation.

2) Commerce: According to Wang Dayuan's description, Yun Chong was an affluent society. Similarly, as early as the sixth century, Mecca was an important emporium in the Arabic world. Merchandise from the "Spice Road" of India and the "Silk Road" of China carried by cargo ships was unloaded at the ports of Yemen. The merchandise and the produce of Southern Arabia from the "Incense Road" were then carried by camel caravans to Mecca, and from there to Syria and the Mediterranean region. The caravans coming from the north also halted in Mecca before they marched on to the ports in the south of the peninsula, on the Arabian Sea.[239] Therefore, Mecca was at the crossroads for international commerce and trade, and developed into an affluent society.

3) Social order: In Yun Chong, according to Wang Dayuan (transl. Sheng-Wei Wang), "There is a tribal chief, but he, also, is benevolent. Punishment is according to law and regulations to bring society naturally into harmony. The place does not nurture thieves and robbers. High and low classes of people live together peacefully."

Similarly, Mecca was ruled by the Quraysh tribe[240] with a tribal chief, and the Islamic religion kept the society in good order. The Quraysh were a powerful merchant tribe that controlled Western Arabia including Mecca and its *Kaaba*. According to pre-Islamic and Islamic tradition, they were descended from Ishmael. Since ancient times, the pilgrim traffic has been a very lucrative source of revenue for the citizens of Mecca.

4) Religion: Wang Dayuan continues (transl. Sheng-Wei Wang), "There has been a mosque since ancient times. When the new moon is observed, the tribal chief and his people all worship Heaven. It is regarded as the one and only culture of this country."

Similarly, the Islamic name for God, Allah, derives from a pagan moon god in local Arabic mythology. The moon-god Allah in the archaeology of the Middle East including Mecca is a widely cited source of the idea that Allah is a moon-god.[241] The use of a Lunar calendar and the prevalence of crescent moon imagery in Islam is said to be the result of this origination. The Hijri year or era beginning its count from 622 AD, the year of the journey of Muhammad, is a Lunar calendar consisting of twelve months in a year of 354 days. It is used to date events in many Muslim countries and used by Muslims everywhere to determine the proper days on which to observe the annual Ramadan fasting, to attend *Hajj*, and to celebrate other Islamic holidays and festivals.

5) Mosque: Concerning the mosque at Yun Chong, Wang Dayuan writes (transl. Sheng-Wei Wang), "The mosque is four-sided. Each side has 90 sectors, making a total of 360 sectors, all of which have pillars made of white jade stones. The floors are made of yellow jade stones. In the centre there is a piece of black stone which is one *zhang* or more in breadth. It is said that it came from Heaven in the early Han Dynasty. The mosque has multi-levels and is tall, shaped like a tower."

Does the mosque in Mecca fit this description?

Fig. 12 shows Mecca in 1850. The mosque had a *Kaaba* in the centre, being four-sided and the mosque was tall and had a few

115 115

levels, shaped like a tower, consistent with Wang Dayuan's description of the mosque he saw in Yun Chong. Mecca in 1718 also shows a *Kaaba* in the centre of a four-sided mosque.[242] There is no known image of the mosque in fourteenth century's Mecca when Wang Dayuan visited there. But it must have kept the basic four-sided mosque architecture with a separate *Kaaba* in the centre. It is not clear whether each side of today's Sacred Mosque in Mecca still has 90 sectors, making a total of 360 sectors, since many renovations have been made over the years. Nonetheless, all these sectors do have pillars made of white jade stones and the floors are made of yellow jade stones. However, the piece of "black stone" in today's Mecca is no longer one *zhang* or more in breadth. In Section (5) of Chapter 2 of this book, it is written, "The stone was venerated at the *Kaaba* in pre-Islamic pagan times... Since then the stone has been broken into a few fragments. Now the surface of the *Kaaba*'s external wall, about 1.5 m above the eastern wall corner, is inlaid with a 30 cm long, slightly reddish-brown stone which is believed to be the famous Black Stone."

Fig. 12 Mecca in 1850

In Mecca, only Muslims are allowed in the city, with millions arriving nowadays for the annual Hajj (pilgrimage). Dating from the seventh century, the central Sacred Mosque surrounds the *Kaaba*.

The black cloth-covered cubic structure is Islam's most sacred shrine.

6) Clothing: In Mecca, when Muslims enter the Sacred Mosque, they wear identical white robes,[243] an act which symbolically means that they are viewed as equals in the eyes of God. Moreover, Arab men in the Arabian Peninsula, Iraq and neighbouring Arab countries also wear a long white-coloured robe (a thawb[244] or thobe; thawb is the standard Arabic word for "a garment"), because white reflects heat. All these fit Wang Dayuan's description of the men in Yun Chong.

7) Local products, animals and trading customs: Wang Dayuan writes (transl. Sheng-Wei Wang, and her comment is in square brackets), "The place produces gold leaves, gems, pearls, lions, camels, zu-la-fa [giraffes], leopards and muntjacs. Horses measuring eight *chi* in height are Heavenly horses. For trade they use gold and silver, satin, coloured silk fabric, cyan- and white-coloured flowerpots, iron tripods, and items such as iron pots." The description fits well with what Mecca produced and the local trading customs. In particular, the Arabian Peninsula produced the famous Arabian horse with a distinctively-shaped head and high tail carriage. These horses, when standing, can be as tall as eight *chi* (over 2 m/6.6 ft), similar to the horses in Yun Chong.

In conclusion, we can confidently conclude that Wang Dayuan's "Yun Chong" was "Mecca" in today's Saudi Arabia. This is important, because According to Luo Maodeng's Chapter 86, Zheng He's fleet, during their seventh voyage and after they left Aden, went to a kingdom which had the name of Yun Chong.

(3) Zheng He heard about a country which was a blissful paradise

After confirming Wang Dayun's Yun Chong as Mecca in Saudi Arabia, I now return to Luo Maodeng's narrative in Chapter 86. The king of Aden surrendered after failed (attempted) resistance (if it really did take place), and made tributes to Zheng He. Zheng He's fleet was about to depart from Aden around March 17 to April 22, 1433, according to the detailed analysis of the fleet's whereabouts in section (1) of this chapter. The date was several months after Zheng He and Wang Jinghong separated from Hong Bao at sea on December 2, 1432.

117

The king of Aden told Zheng He that his people were Muslims. Admiral Zheng He was a devout Muslim. Many of his sailors were Muslims as well. Then, the Admiral and the foreign king had the following conversation:

元帅道："贤王俱奉回回教门，回回可有个祖国么？"番王道："极西上有一个祖国，叫做天堂极乐之国。"元帅道："去此多远？"番王道："三个多月日才可到得。"元帅道："我们可得到么？"番王道："二位元帅来此有几十万里之外，岂有这两三个月日的路程就到不得的？"元帅道："中途可还有哪个国么？"番王道："小国这一带都是极西之地，天尽于此，苦没有甚么国。就是天堂国，卑末们都不曾过往。"

My translation of the above passage is as follows:

The commander-in-chief asked, "Sage kings all believe in Muhammad. May Muslims have a homeland?" The foreign king replied, "There is a homeland in the far, far away west, called the 'country of paradise.'" The commander-in-chief asked, "How far is it from here?" The foreign king replied, "It takes more than three months to get there." The commander-in-chief asked, "Can we get there?" The foreign king replied, "The two commanders-in-chief like you have come here from hundreds of thousands *li* away, how can you not be able to make a two- or three-months' journey?" The commander-in-chief then asked, "Is there any country along the way?" The foreign king replied, "The region of my small country is the westernmost land where the sky ends; there is no other country, except this 'country of paradise.' But none of us, the humble people, have ever gone there."

"番王" denotes in general a foreign king; here it is the king of Aden, who was a Muslim. The commander-in-chief who asked the questions was Zheng He. The "two commanders-in-chief" referred to are Zheng He and Wang Jinghong (in Luo's novel Wang Jinghong was the deputy commander-in-chief, but in reality, for the seventh voyage, both Zheng He and Wang Jinghong were the Principal Envoys or the commanders-in-chief). Luo Maodeng, in his narrative, keeps Wang Jinghong and Zheng He together on the same ship throughout the entire seventh voyage and they also returned to China together. This would mean that Wang Jinghong had also gone to *Tianfang*/Yun Chong/Mecca and the country of Fengdu/Cahokia (the 39th and the 40th countries on the list in Section (1) of this chapter) before returning to China. But this cannot be true, because if Wang Jinghong also went to *Tianfang*/Yun Chong/Mecca and Fengdu/Cahokia, he could not have returned to China on July 22, 1433. The additional journey would have taken about two more years to complete. This will be discussed in detail in Chapter 8 of this book.

However as mentioned earlier, ambassadors from eleven countries, including Aden, Brava, Lasa and Mecca, were escorted to China at the end of the seventh voyage. My analysis in Section (1) of this chapter has led me to believe that it was in Aden that Zheng He's main fleet separated from Wang Jinghong's squadron. It was also at Aden, that the envoys from Mecca (the "country of paradise"; to be explained in the next section) arrived to greet Zheng He, and some of them could have decided to visit China. While Zheng He would lead his fleet to Mecca for pilgrimage after his conversation with the king of Aden, Wang Jinghong would accompany the ambassadors of Aden, Brava, Lasa, Mecca and others to China. Wang Jinghong had just enough time to reach Calicut in early April to regroup with Hong Bao's squadron. The above analysis explains Wang Jinghong's inbound navigational route to Nanjing as shown in Fig. 11. But Luo's narrative does not give these important details.

Regarding Luo's description of distance in his paragraph, the shortest distance between Nanjing in China to Aden is a little more than 8,000 km/4,971 mi; the waterway has many twists and turns, hence could be over ten thousand kilometres, but not hundreds of thousands of kilometres. Luo's number is a grossly exaggerated distance.

After this, let us now refocus on Zheng He's next destination, the country of paradise, by returning to Luo's passage again.

(4) Zheng He's fleet arrived at the "country of paradise"

While Zheng He was enquiring about the country of paradise from the king of Aden, seven visitors arrived unexpectedly at Aden:

。。。把门的番官禀说道："朝门外有三个通事，四个回回，自称奉天堂国国王差遣，赍着麝香、瓷器等项物件为礼，远来迎接大明国征西元帅老爷。"。。。

My translation of the above passage is as follows:

…The foreign king's officer who guards the palace gate comes in and reports to his superior, saying, "Three interpreters and four Muslims carrying a load of musk, porcelain articles, and other such things as gifts are outside the entrance portal to the palace. They claim that they are from far away and were sent by the king of the country of paradise to greet the respected Admiral Zheng He who leads the expeditionary voyage to the Western Ocean."…

The above paragraph describes how the envoys of the country of paradise came to Aden to greet Zheng He. The following is the conversation among Zheng He, the king of Aden and one of the interpreters:

。。。元帅道："你们是旱路而来？你们是水路而来？"通事道："小的是从旱路而来。"元帅道："来了多少日子？"通事道："也不晓得多少日子，只是月生了七遭。"元帅道："月生七遭，却不是七个月？"阿丹王道："旱路迂曲，水路则折半足矣！"元帅道："你们手里拿的是甚么东西？"通事道："拿的是些麝香、瓷器之类，少充贺敬，聊表国王之诚。"元帅道："麝香也罢，瓷器怎么得来？"通事道："有个千里骆驼驮将来。"

My translation of the above passage is as follows and my comment is in square brackets:

. . . The commander-in-chief asked, "Did you come by land? Or did you come by water?" The interpreter replied, "We, the humble people, came by land." The commander-in-chief asked, "How many days did it take you to come here?" The interpreter replied, "We do not know how many days, but we noticed that the new moon appeared seven times." The commander-in-chief asked, "If the new moon has appeared seven times, isn't it seven months?" The king of Aden explained, "The land route is tortuous; if you go by sea it takes only half that time." The commander-in-chief asked, "What are you holding in your hands?" The interpreter replied, "A load of musk, porcelain articles and other such things, as a token to show the sincerity of our king's good will and high respect." The commander-in-chief said, "Musk is fine [since it was light enough to carry by hand], but how were the porcelain articles carried over?" The interpreter replied, "There was a camel which could carry our packs and walk thousands of *li*."

This passage describes the envoys from the country of paradise spending more than seven months' time to take the land route to arrive at Aden to greet the Ming envoys and show their respect. They said that carrying out the trip by boat would cut the travelling time from more than seven months to half that time. The length of travelling time seems to contain a serious error. How could a king of the country of paradise have known "seven months" in advance that Zheng He would be in Aden in those days? As soon as we know where this "country of paradise" was located, I shall explain later that this unrealistic timing was in fact due to Luo Maodeng's erroneous estimation of the travelling time from the country of paradise to Aden. But for the time being let us continue Luo's narrative further until we get to the point where things become clearer.

The following several paragraphs show that after this conversation, Zheng He decided to visit the mosque [245] of this blissful "country of paradise".

。。。元帅辞谢阿丹王，收拾开船。 七个来人仍旧要从旱路而去。元帅道："水行逸而速，陆行劳而迟。你们从船便。"道犹未了，宝船已自一齐开岸，趁着顺风，照西上直跑。来人虽欲陆行，不可得已。一程顺风，更不曾停阻。

My translation of the above passage is as follows and my comment is in square brackets:

121

. . . The commander-in-chief thanked and bid farewell to the king of Aden, then sent out an order to pack things up and to start sailing. The seven envoys still wanted to go back by taking the same land route. The commander-in-chief said, "The sea route is easier and quicker while the land route is tiresome and causes delay. You can all board the ship for more convenience." After he finished speaking, the treasure ships started to leave the shore together. Taking advantage of the favourable winds, the ships sailed in the westward direction on a straight run. Despite the envoys' wish to take the land route, it was already not possible for them [to get off the ship]. The whole journey had favourable winds, and the ships sailed smoothly without making any stop.

This passage describes the envoys boarding the treasure ships and sailing with the Chinese mariners towards the country of paradise.[246] If they were heading for Jeddah from Port Aden, the fleet must first sail in the westward direction. Once they reached the entrance of the Red Sea, the fleet had to sail in the northwest direction to get to Jeddah. However, if they intended to sail from Port Aden to Port Chebba in Tunisia (Ma Huan's country of *Tianfang*/Mo-Jia was ancient Tunisia during the Hafsid period), the treasure ships had first to sail in an eastward direction to get out of the Gulf of Aden, then sail in a southwestern direction along the coast of eastern and southern Africa until they could sail around the Cape of Good Hope, as the Ma Huan delegation and the Calicut merchants did around December 1432 to March 1433. So, in terms of the sailing direction, Zheng He's fleet was taking a different route from the Ma Huan delegation. It is unlikely that Zheng He's fleet was heading for the country of *Tianfang*/Mo-Jia in North Africa.

行了三个多月，忽一日天堂国通事到中军帐下磕头，禀说道："七日之内可到天堂本国。"元帅道："七日以后的事，怎么七日以前就知道？"通事道："本国依城四角造塔四座，各高三十六丈，其影倒垂天海，七日路外一览可见。小的适来看见影，故此晓得七日之内可到本国。"。。。再行几程，搭至七日上面，蓝旗官报道："前面却是一个国。"道犹未了，通事来禀说道："到了敝国，请元帅传令收船。"

My translation of the above passage is as follows and my comments are in square brackets:

After sailing for more than three months [it will be shown soon that this navigation time was incorrect], suddenly one day the interpreter from the country of paradise came to the commander-in-chief's tent and respectfully kowtowed. In presenting the petition he said, "The country of paradise can be reached within seven days." The commander-in-chief asked, "How do you know beforehand that we are going to arrive within seven days?" The interpreter replied, "This country has built four towers at the four corners of the city. Each is 36 *zhang* [about 108 m/354 ft] in height and its shadow overhangs from sky to sea, which can be seen within seven day's sailing distance. I, the humble person, happened to see their reflections in the water shadow and knew that within seven days we could reach my country."... After sailing further, until the seventh day, the officer holding the blue-coloured flag on the ship [for sending out signals] reported, "A country is within sight." Before he finished reporting, the interpreter came to present his request and said, "My country is reached. Please, commander-in-chief, give the order for the ships to stop sailing."

"Zhong Jun" means Army of the Centre (中军; 中 "Zhong" means centre, 军 "Jun" means army), and is usually headed by the senior military commander. Here Zhong Jun's tent was Commander-in-chief Zheng He's tent.[247]

Here Luo's narrative about the country of paradise shows a distinct difference from Ma Huan's description of *Tianfang*/Mo-jia.

Luo writes (transl. Sheng-Wei Wang), "This country has built four towers at the four corners of the city." These four towers were very tall, and visible from the sea, since each is 36 *zhang* high and their shadows overhang from sky to sea, which can be seen within seven day's sailing distance (but, this must be an exaggeration). Recall that one *zhang* is approximately 3 m/9.8 ft, 36 *zhang* is about 108 m/354 ft. While Kairouan is near the sea (the shortest distance between Kairouan and Port Sousse is 52 km/32 mi), but the four pagodas inside the prayer hall of the Mosque of Uqba in Kairouan

The Last Journey of the San Bao Eunuch

could not serve as watchtowers and could not be seen from the sea. Besides, even the single minaret in the Mosque of Uqba, which can serve in the function of a watchtower, is only 31.5 m/103 ft in height.

Mecca is also not far from the sea. The shortest distance from Port Jeddah to the Holy City of Mecca is merely 64 km/40 mi. The Sacred/Great Mosque in Mecca has very tall minarets. These minarets are slender towers and are part of the mosque, with a balcony from which a muezzin calls Muslims to prayer. These minarets are also used as watchtowers. Each minaret is up to about 90 m/295 ft in height, which would match Luo's description much more closely in height and in its function as a watchtower. The Sacred/Great Mosque was built in the seventh century and it has been modified, rebuilt, and expanded on a regular basis ever since.[248] The number of minarets also keeps increasing. Currently two 420 m/1,378 ft tall minarets are under construction, which will raise the number of minarets to fifteen after the completion of the expansion project.[249]

The first major renovation to the Sacred/Great Mosque took place in 692. Before this renovation, which included the mosque's outer walls being raised and decoration added to the ceiling, the mosque was a small open area with the *Kaaba* at the centre. By the end of the eighth century, the first minaret was added. The spread of Islam in the Middle East and the influx of pilgrims required an almost complete rebuilding of the site, which included adding more marble and three more minarets.[250] So, there was a period when the mosque had four minarets and Zheng He's visit to the mosque in 1433 happened to fall within this period. In 1629, during the reign of Sultan Murad IV, the mosque went through another renovation. In this renovation, three more minarets were added, bringing the total to seven.[251] After 1629, the number of minarets was unaltered for nearly three centuries until another major renovation under the Saudi kings was carried out between 1955 and 1973. Fig. 12 shows that in 1850 during the Ottoman period,[252] the Sacred/Great Mosque had seven minarets representing seven days of the week. We can see that all the slender and tall minarets were attached to the mosque as part of it, and the mosque had four sides.

Thus far, we have found that the country of paradise Zheng He's crew were about to visit could not be the country of *Tianfang*/Mo-

124

jia or ancient Tunis in North Africa, but could be Mecca in today's Saudi Arabia.

Luo continued his narrative in Chapter 86:

三日后。。。国王迎接进城，盛设筵宴，大飨诸将。只是不设酒，回回教门禁酒故也。元帅道："大国名天堂么？"国王道："敝国即古笃冲之地，名为天堂国，又名西域。回回祖师始于敝国阐扬教法，至今国人悉遵教门，不养猪、不造酒，田颇肥，稻颇饶，居民安业，风俗好善。卑末为民上者，不敢苛敛于民。下民也无贫难之苦，无乞丐，无盗贼，不设刑罚，自然淳化，上下安和，自古到今。实不相瞒列位所说，是个极乐之国。"。。。元帅道："大国有礼拜寺，在那一厢？"国王道："在城西，离城有半日程途。"。。。

My translation of the above passage is as follows and my comment is in square brackets:

Three days later. . . The king went to receive them [from the port] and bring them to the city, gave a big banquet to all the generals, but served no wine, because Islam prohibits the drinking of alcohol. The commander-in-chief asked, "Is your great country known as paradise?" The king replied, "My country is the land of Yun Chong known in ancient times as the country of paradise, also known as the Western Regions. The founder of Islam first expounded and spread the doctrine of his teaching in this country and until today our people all follow the doctrine taught by him, do not raise pigs, do not make wine, but the soil is fertile and produces plenty of rice. Residents live and work in peace, and social customs are kind and benevolent. I, the humble person, am above them but do not dare to levy heavy taxes upon people. The people below me do not suffer from poverty or hardship. There are no beggars, no thieves and no need for setting penalties for crime. Everything is natural and simple. From top to bottom, the society is content and in harmony. This has been the way from ancient days until today. I do not want to conceal my feelings by telling you all that this is a blissful country."... The commander-in-chief asked, "Your great country has a mosque, where is it?" The king replied, "It is to the west of the city and half a day's journey from the city.".…

Notice that the first part of Luo's long paragraph is almost a copy of Wang Dayuan's description of Yun Chong/Mecca in Dao Yi Zhi Lue《岛夷志略》 or *Descriptions of Barbarians and the Islands*, since the king told Zheng He explicitly (transl. Sheng-Wei Wang), "My country is the land of Yun Chong known in ancient times as the country of paradise, also known as the Western Regions." Moreover, the king explicitly said that his country, Yun Chong, was the birthplace of Islam. We know that Mecca was the birthplace of the Prophet Muhammad and the Islamic faith itself. Was the king implying that Yun Chong was Mecca?

Concerning the location of the mosque, Luo Maodeng quotes the king's reply (transl. Sheng-Wei Wang), "It is to the west of the city and half a day's journey from the city." A map of the modern city of Mecca (with highways)[253] shows that the Sacred Mosque (Arabic: المسجد الحرام, translit. *al-Masjid al-Ḥarām*) is shown as the small four-sided green area (with a *Kaaba*, coloured grey, in the centre) in the centre of the map. It is to the east (right), not to the west (left) of the "old" city centre (the old city centre is to the left of the four-sided green area labelled *Al-Masjid Al-Ḥarām* on the map). So, either Luo Maodeng made an error here, or the city centre has moved over time. Since the Sacred Mosque was only a few kilometres away, it would not be half a day's journey from the old city.

(5) The "country of paradise" had the Sacred Mosque of Mecca

Here is Luo's description of the mosque in the country of paradise:

到了礼拜寺，只见寺分为四方，每方有九十间，每间白玉为柱，黄玉为地。中间才是正堂，正堂都是五色花石垒砌起来。外面四方，上面平顶，一层又一层，如塔之状，大约有九层。堂面前一块拜石，方广一丈一尺，是汉初年间从天上掉下来的。堂门上两个黑狮子把门，若行香进谒的，素行不善，或是贼盗之类，黑狮子一口一个，故此国中再无贼盗。堂里面沉香木为梁栋、栌科之类，镀金椽子，一年一镀，黄金为阁阑，四面八方都是蔷薇露和龙涎香为壁。中间坐着是回回祖师，用皂苎丝罩定，不见其形。面前悬一面金字匾，说道："天堂礼拜寺。"每年十二月初十日，各番回回都来进香，赞念经文，虽万里之外都来。来者把皂苎丝罩上，剜割一方去，名曰香记。其罩出于国王，一年一换，备剜割故也。。。。

My translation of the above passage is as follows and my comments are in square brackets:

Upon arriving at the mosque, you can see the mosque is four-sided, each side has 90 sectors, all of which have pillars made of white jade stones and the floors are made of yellow jade stones. The chamber in the centre is the Main Hall built with layers of five-coloured stones. The exterior of the Main Hall [Prayer Hall] has four sides and is flat-topped; the coloured stones stack up layer by layer into an elevated structure like a tower, and there are approximately nine layers. In the front wall surface of the Main Hall, there is a stone altar, which is one *zhang* and one *chi* in breadth. It is said that it came from Heaven in the early Han Dynasty. There are two black lions drawn on the door surface to guard the entrance of the Hall. If the pilgrims are ill-intentioned or if they are thieves and robbers or the like, the [image of the] black lions would scare them as if they tried to swallow them [i.e. those pilgrims who are ill-intentioned, thieves, robbers or the like] one by one. So, the country no longer has thieves and robbers. Inside the Hall, there are beams made of agarwood [agarwood or aloeswood is a fragrant dark resinous wood used in incense, perfume, and small carvings], yearly gilded rafters, and a shelf made of yellow gold. Throughout the interior of the Hall, the walls are formed [of clay mixed] with rosewater and ambergris, exhaling a perpetual fragrance. In the middle is the Muslim holy man sitting behind a covering of black hemp silk, hidden from the view of the pilgrims. A plaque with gold characters hanging in front of him says: "Heavenly Hall mosque." Every year on the tenth day of the twelfth month, all the foreign Muslims—in extreme cases making a long journey of tens of thousands of *li*—come to worship and chant the scripture readings. Everyone cuts off a piece of the hemp-silk covering as a fragrant memento before he goes away. The covering comes from the king and is replaced once a year...

Again, the first sentence of Luo Maodeng's description is essentially identical to Wang Dayuan's description of the mosque at Yun Chong. The drawing of the Sacred Mosque of Mecca shown in Fig. 12 is still four-sided in 1850. But over the years, the mosque has undergone many renovations and now has more than four sides. According to the historical record,[254] the mosques had pillars made of white jade stones and the floors inside the *Kaaba* were made of marble and limestone (it is ordinarily white, but may be coloured by impurities, iron oxide making it brown, yellow or red and carbon making it blue, black, or grey). Luo's description is consistent with the existing historical records about the Sacred Mosque in Mecca, Saudi Arabia, and very similar to Wan Dayuan's description of the mosque in Yun Chong.

Luo continued to describe the Main Hall/Prayer Hall inside the mosque in the country of paradise. In the Sacred Mosque of Mecca, the *Kaaba* is the Main Hall/Prayer Hall. It is a cuboid building at the centre of Islam's most sacred mosque. It is the House of God or the House of Allah.

Today, the *Kaaba* is approximately 13.1 m/43 ft tall (some claim 12.03 m/39.5 ft), with sides measuring 11.03 m/36.2 ft by 12.86 m/42.2 ft.[255] It is tall, four-sided with a flat top, consistent with Luo Maodeng's description (transl. Sheng-Wei Wang): "The exterior of the Main Hall [Prayer Hall] has four sides and is flat-topped; the coloured stones stack up layer by layer into an elevated structure like a tower, and there are approximately nine layers." Fig. 13 shows the interior view of the *Kaaba*. It is a cuboid-shape structure made of granite, a very hard, granular, crystalline, igneous rock consisting mainly of quartz, mica, and feldspar and often used as a building stone. The wall of the *Kaaba* is formed by stacking these rocks layer by layer of "approximately nine layers" in Luo's words (transl. Sheng-Wei Wang), showing that the *Kaaba* is a tall and strong structure. Inside the *Kaaba*, there are *three great pillars* made of agarwood as support. This is structurally different from the *five beams* described by Ma Huan inside the prayer hall of the Mosque of Uqba in Kairouan, Tunisia.

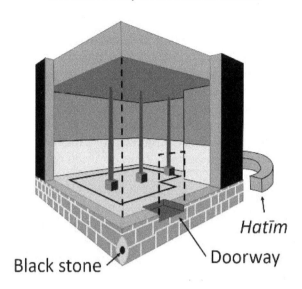

Hatīm

Doorway

Black stone

Fig. 13 Interior view of the *Kaaba*

The northeastern wall has the only door of the building, about seven feet above the ground level. Inside is an empty room with a marble floor and the three wooden pillars mentioned above to support the roof. The entire *Kaaba* structure is draped all the time with a black silk covering, upon which passages from the Koran are embroidered in gold. This is very different from the prayer hall in the Mosque of Uqba in Kairouan, Tunisia, in which there is a hemp-silk covering or a curtain inside the Prayer Hall, as I have discussed in Chapter 2 of this book.

This black silk (and gold) curtain is cut up and distributed to the worshippers, and replaced annually during the Hajj pilgrimage. Since the *Kaaba* is too small to accommodate the huge number of worshippers, unlike the prayer hall in the Mosque of Uqba in Tunisia, the Hajj requires pilgrims to walk seven times around the *Kaaba* in a counter-clockwise direction to show respect. The circling is believed to demonstrate the unity of the believers in the worship of the One God, as they move in harmony together around the *Kaaba*, while praying to God.

Luo's description is entirely consistent with what we know about the *Kaaba* in the Sacred Mosque of Mecca.

Also, Luo writes about an altar in this way (transl. Sheng-Wei Wang): "In the front wall surface of the Main Hall, there is a stone altar, which is one *zhang* and one *chi* in breadth. It is said that it came from Heaven in the early Han Dynasty." Only the main prayer hall, *Kaaba*, in the Sacred Mosque, has such a stone, the Black Stone. Islamic tradition holds that it fell from Heaven for Adam and Eve to use to build an altar. Islamic scholars have generally assumed that the *Kaaba* was constructed by Abraham around 2130 BC. But the size Luo attributes to the stone is too big and the date in the early Han Dynasty (202 BC–220 AD) is too late in comparison with the date from the Islamic legend. However, we know that the stone was broken into a few fragments over the years. Today, the surface of the *Kaaba*'s external wall, about one and a half metres high above the eastern corner, is inlaid with a 30 cm or one-foot long, slightly reddish-brown stone, which is believed to be the famous Black Stone.

At one time, there were numerous such "*Kaaba*" sanctuaries in Arabia, but only the one in the Sacred Mosque of Mecca was built of stone.[256] Both Luo Maodeng and Wang Dayuan are correct in describing the prayer hall as made of *stone*. The others also allegedly had counterparts of the Black Stone.[257] The *Kaaba* was thought to be at the centre of the world, with the Gate of Heaven directly above it. The *Kaaba* marked the location where the sacred world intersected with the profane; and the embedded Black Stone was a further symbol of this as a meteorite that had fallen from the sky and linked Heaven and Earth. Muslim pilgrims revere the stone as a powerful symbol of faith. Luo is *indeed* correct to call it an altar.

Luo also writes more realistically (transl. Sheng-Wei Wang), "There are two black lions drawn on the door surface to guard the entrance of the Hall," as opposed to Ma Huan's incomprehensible description (transl. J.V.G. Mills; Hakluyt Society in 1970)—"They keep two black lions to guard the door"—in relation to the Mosque of Uqba in Kairouan, Tunisia.

Overall, Luo Maodeng has given more detailed and accurate information on the Heavenly Hall mosque in Yun Chong than Wang Dayuan has done, especially when Luo starts to describe the tombs inside the mosque:

。。。堂之左是司马仪祖师之墓，墓高五尺，黄玉叠砌起来
的。墓外有围垣，圆广三丈二尺，高二尺，俱绿撒不泥，空石
砌起来的。堂左右稍后有各祖师传法之堂，俱花石叠砌而成，
中间俱各壮丽。寺后一里之外，地名蓦氏纳，有麻祖师之墓。
堂上毫光日夜侵云而起，如中国之虹霓。墓后有一井，名为阿
净糁，泉甚清冽，味甘。下番之人取其泉藏在船上，若遇飓风
起时，以此水洒之，风浪顿息，与圣水同。

My translation of the above passage is as follows:

… On the left of the Hall is the burial-place of Si-ma-yi, a holy man. The tomb is five *chi* in height and is built with layers of yellow gem-stones. The tomb is surrounded by a wall. The semi-circular wall has a length of three *zhang* and two *chi*, and a height of two *chi*. All of this is made with green *sa-pu-ni* gem-stones stacked up one on top of the other. On both sides, left and right, a little behind the Hall, are the halls wherein masters of the teaching of the patriarch of this faith have preached the doctrine; these, too, are built with layers of coloured stones, and are decorated most beautifully. Behind the mosque, and a *li* away, is the place named Mo-shi-na where the tomb of their holy man Ma-ha-ma is situated; and a bright light rises day and night from the top of the grave and penetrates into the clouds as the rainbow of China. Behind the grave is a well, a spring of pure and sweet water, named A-jing-san; men who go to foreign parts take this water and store it in the sides of their ships; if they encounter a typhoon at sea, they take this water and scatter it; then the wind and waves are lulled, as with holy water.

According to Luo (transl. Sheng-Wei Wang), "On the left of the Hall is the burial-place of Si-ma-yi, a holy man." Luo also gives detailed dimensions of the tomb and the dimensions, shape and the material of the low wall around the tomb. In today's Sacred Mosque in Mecca, there is a semi-circular low wall called *Hatīm*. At one time the space between the *Hatīm* and the *Kaaba* belonged to the *Kaaba* itself, and western scholars thought it was where Ishmael and his mother Hagar were buried. Today, this low wall is opposite, but not connected to, the north-west wall of the *Kaaba*. The semi-circular wall is 90 cm/2.95 ft in height, 1.5 m/4.9 ft in width and 17.75 m/58.2 ft in length. It is composed of white marble instead of green sa-pu-ni gem-stones. According to Luo Maodeng, this semi-circular low wall was two *chi* or about 67 cm/2.2 ft in height, and three *zhang*[258] and two *chi*[259] or about 10.67 m/35 ft in length. Luo did not give the width of the wall. Luo's figures are qualitatively consistent with today's known figures: 90 cm/2.95 ft in height, 1.5 m/4.92 ft in width and 17.75 m/58.23 ft in length.[260] Fig. 14 shows the *Kaaba* and *Hatīm* today.[261] Luo is the only writer who has pointed out the most salient feature, namely the *semi-circular* shape of the low wall.

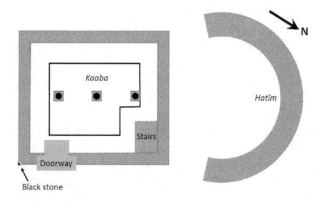

Fig. 14 *Kaaba* and *Hatīm*

Ishmael and his father Abraham reformed and built the *Kaaba* around 2130 BC; and their descendants remained the custodians of the Holy Shrine. It was natural for them to be buried near the *Kaaba* instead of in the Mosque of Uqba in Kairouan, Tunisia. Moreover, the Uqba Mosque was built at a much later date (670 AD). It would not be plausible for Ishmael and Hagar to be re-buried in the distant Kairouan in North Africa, from the Holy City Mecca in Saudi Arabia. This lends further support to my previous conclusion (as first suggested by Lam Yee Din) in Chapter 2 that the tombs mentioned in Ma Huan's Ying Ya Sheng Lan 《瀛涯胜览》 or *The Overall Survey of the Ocean's Shores* were tombs of holy Islamic disciples, instead of the tomb of Ismael himself. From the above analysis, we can see that the details reflected in Luo Maodeng's description of the burial site for Ishmael and his mother Hagar, and the peripheral wall, resemble closely the scene near the *Kaaba* in the Sacred Mosque of Mecca.

However, Luo's statement (transl. Sheng-Wei Wang), "Behind the mosque, and a *li* away, is the place named Mo-shi-na where the tomb of their holy man Ma-ha-ma is situated", needs further investigation. Ma-ha-ma is the Islamic prophet Muhammad. After his death, according to his will, he was buried inside the Prophet's Mosque, his original residence in Medina, north of Mecca. The shortest distance between Mecca and Medina is 338 km/210 mi. [262]

However, it is difficult to find a grave inside the Sacred Mosque in Mecca which is connected to Muhammad in any way. But 4.9 km/3 mi or about ten *li* southeast of the Sacred Mosque there were the famous graves of Jannatul Mualla (or Jannatul Moala, Jannatul Mualla, Jannatul Ma'la, Mualla, Moala, Mualla, Ma'laare, pronunciations all somewhat close to Mo-shi-na), [263] where Muhammad's wife, grandfather and other ancestors were all buried. In 1925, King Ibn Saud of Saudi Arabia removed these graves. The Mo-shi-na is neither the Medina in Saudi Arabia nor the Medina in Kairouan, Tunisia (see Section (5) of Chapter 2 of this book). The only explanation I can come up with is that Luo Maodeng might have mistaken "ten *li*" to "a *li*" in his narrative: it should be (transl. Sheng-Wei Wang), "Behind the mosque and ten *li* away is the place named Mo-shi-na."

Also, Luo's statement (transl. Sheng-Wei Wang), "Behind the grave is a well, a spring of pure and sweet water, named A-jing-san," cannot point to the Zamzam well inside the Sacred Mosque. The Zamzam well is located 20 m/66 ft east of the *Kaaba* inside the Sacred Mosque, whereas A-jing-san was in Mo-shi-na next to some graves. But because the Jannatul Mualla graves were removed in 1925, there is no information on the nearby A-jing-san well.

(6) Luo Maodeng's *Tianfang*/Yun Chong was Mecca in Saudi Arabia

Summing up the detailed analysis in Chapter 2 and Chapter 3, I conclude that the country of *Tianfang*/Mo-jia where the Ma Huan delegation went in 1432–1433 was ancient Tunisia in North Africa during the Hafsid period, whereas the country of *Tianfang*/Yun Chong where Zheng He's crew went for pilgrimage in 1433 was the Holy City Mecca in today's Saudi Arabia. In Luo Maodeng's novel, he has clearly distinguished Yun Chong/Mecca from Mo-jia/Tunisia. He describes Yun Chong as the country of *Tianfang* or the "country of paradise", whereas Mo-jia was "first a land of wilderness" (in Chapter 51 of his novel; transl. Sheng-Wei Wang).

Even if we accept all these findings, a serious question remains. Why would the direct waterway journey between Port Aden and Port Jeddah, plus a short land route from Jeddah to Mecca take more than three months as given by Luo Maodeng? This is a serious mistake made by Luo and must be corrected. Most Zheng He researchers have hence mistaken Ma Huan's Mo-jia as Mecca.

Recall that in Chapter 2, the distance from Aden to Jeddah (at about the midpoint of the Red Sea) is about 1,151 km/715 mi, and the shortest distance from Jeddah to the Holy City Mecca is merely 64 km/40 mi. There are two ways to figure out the navigational time from Port Aden to Port Jeddah:

1) Using Ma Huan's data (it took 30 days from Calicut to Aden for a distance of 6,000 *li* or 3,000 km), then it would take 30 x 1,151/3,000 = about 11 days from Port Aden to Port Jeddah.

2) Using the data from Ming Shi 《明史》 or *The History of Ming* (it would take only 22 days from Calicut to Aden), then it would take 22 x 1,151/3,000 = about 8 days from Port Aden to Port Jeddah.

But Ma Huan's data was from the earlier voyage, since he did not go to Aden during the seventh voyage (he went to Mo-jia by boarding a Calicut merchants' junk). I shall use the result of eight days from Aden to Jeddah, obtained by using the data from Ming Shi 《明史》 or *The History of Ming*.

Based on this revised length of travel time, and since the departure date from Aden was around March 17, 1433 to April 22, 1433, Zheng He's main fleet would have arrived at Jeddah around March 25, 1433 to April 30, 1433. After adding three days for waiting at the harbour for the king to receive them and another day for a round trip to visit the Sacred Mosque at Mecca and back to

Jeddah, we can deduce that when Zheng He's fleet departed from Jeddah, the date was around March 29 to May 4, 1433. Fig. 15 shows the navigational routes for Zheng He's main fleet, on the way out during the seventh voyage. In Chapter 4, I shall present an analysis showing how Zheng He's main fleet accidentally landed near the Labrador coast in the North Atlantic Ocean.

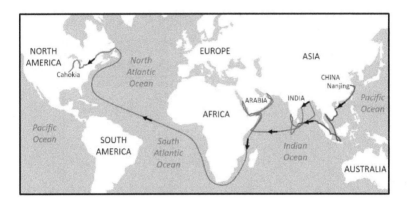

Fig. 15 Outbound navigational routes for Zheng He's main fleet during the seventh voyage

(7) Summary

Table 1 (below) gives an overall list of navigational routes (countries explored) and timelines of Zheng He's fleet, before and after he divided the fleet into squadrons at Ceylon/Sri Lanka. Each squadron headed for its destination during the seventh voyage. For the outbound voyage from China, before the separation, all the squadrons visited all the first to the thirteenth countries listed in Table 1. After the separation, the fleet which was led by Zheng He and Wang Jinghong together visited all the 14th to the 28th countries. The 29th and the 30th countries were visited only by Zheng He's main fleet (Wang Jinghong's squadron separated from Zheng He's main fleet at Aden and returned to China in July 1433). The last country which Zheng He's main fleet explored was Fengdu/Cahokia in North America, which will be discussed in detail in Chapters 6, 7 and 8 of this book. The separate navigational routes and timelines for Hong Bao's squadron beyond Ceylon/Sri Lanka, and Wang Jinghong's squadrons beyond Aden are not shown here.

Country name	Arrival date	In Lunar Calendar	Dep. date	In Lunar Calendar	In Zhu's Record? Yes/No
1. Champa 金莲宝象国 /占城国	Jan. 27, 1432	Dec. 24, the 6th year of the Xuande period	Feb. 12, 1432	Jan. 12, the 7th year of the Xuande period	Yes
2. Bintonglong 宾童龙国	Feb. 19 or 20, 1432	Jan. 19 or 20, the 7th year of the Xuande period	Feb. 19 or 20, 1432	Jan. 19 or 20, the 7th year of the Xuande period	No
3. Lopburi 罗斛国/暹罗	Feb. 22, 1432	Jan. 22, the 7th year of the Xuande period	Feb. 26, 1432	Jan. 26, the 7th year of the Xuande period	No
4. Java 爪哇国	Mar. 7, 1432	Feb. 6, the 7th year of the Xuande period	July 13, 1432	June 16, the 7th year of the Xuande period	Yes
5. Janggala 重迦罗国	N/A	N/A	N/A	N/A	No
6. Palembang 浡淋邦/ 浡淋国	July 24, 1432	June 27, the seventh year of the Xuande period	July 27, 1432	July 1, the seventh year of the Xuande period	Yes
7. Land of Many Perfumes 女儿国	July 30 or 31, 1432	July 4 or 5, the seventh year of the Xuande period	July 30 or 31, 1432	July 4 or 5, the seventh year of the Xuande period	No
8. Malacca 满刺伽国	Aug. 3, 1432	July 8, the 7th ycar of the Xuande pcriod	Sep. 2, 1432	Aug. 8, the 7th ycar of the Xuande pcriod	Yes
9. Aru 哑鲁国/ 亞路国	Sept. 6, 1432	Aug. 12, the 7th year of the Xuande period	Sept. 6, 1432	Aug. 12, the 7th year of the Xuande period	No
10. Alu 阿鲁国	Sept. 8, 1432	Aug. 14, the 7th year of the Xuande period	Sept. 8, 1432	Aug. 14, the 7th year of the Xuande period	No
11. Semudera 苏门答刺国	Sept. 12, 1432	Aug. 18, the 7th year of the Xuande period	Nov. 2, 1432	Oct. 10, the 7th year of the Xuande period	Yes

12. Sa Fa 撒发国	Nov. 9 or 10, 1432	Oct. 17 or 18, the 7th year of the Xuande period	Nov. 13 or 14, 1432	Oct. 21 or 22, the 7th year of the Xuande period	No
13. Ceylon/Sri Lanka 锡兰国	Nov. 28, 1432	Nov. 6, the 7th year of the Xuande period	Dec. 2, 1432	Nov.10, the 7th year of the Xuande period	Yes
14. Liushan/ Maldives 溜山国/ 马尔代夫	Dec. 9 or 10, 1432	N/A	Dec. 9 or 10, 1432	N/A	No
15. Greater Quilon 大葛兰国	Dec. 11 to 13, 1432	N/A	Dec. 11 to 13, 1432	N/A	No
16. Lesser Quilon 小葛兰国	Dec. 14 to 18, 1432	N/A	Dec. 14 to 18, 1432	N/A	No
17. Cochin 柯枝国	Dec. 16 to 20, 1432	N/A	Dec. 16 to 20, 1432	N/A	No
18. Gu-li/ Calicut 古俚国/ 古里國	Dec. 19 to 24, 1432	N/A	Dec. 19 to 24, 1432	N/A	No
19. The "Country with people with yellowish-coloured or golden-coloured eyes" 金眼国	Jan. 2 to 16, 1433	N/A	Jan. 2 to 16, 1433	N/A	No
20. Xi-ge-la /Bengal 吸葛剌国/ 榜葛剌	Jan. 5 to 20, 1433	N/A	Jan. 13 to 28, 1433	N/A	No
21. Mogadishu 木骨都束国	Jan. 24 to Feb. 16, 1433	N/A	Jan. 24 to Feb. 16, 1433	N/A	No
22. Zhubu /Juba 竹步国	Jan. 24 to Feb. 16, 1433	N/A	Jan. 24 to Feb. 16, 1433	N/A	No

137

The Last Journey of the San Bao Eunuch

23. Brava/ Barawa 卜剌哇国	Jan. 24 to Feb. 16, 1433	N/A	Jan. 24 to Feb. 16, 1433	N/A	No
24. Lasa 剌撒国	Feb. 4 to 27, 1433	N/A	Feb. 5 to 28, 1433	N/A	No
25. Juffair/ Dhufar 祖法儿国	Feb. 13 to Mar. 10, 1433	N/A	Feb. 16 to Mar. 13, 1433	N/A	No
26. Hulumumosi/ Hormuz 忽鲁谟斯国	Feb. 19 to Mar. 17, 1433	N/A	Feb. 19 to Mar. 17, 1433	N/A	No
27. The "Country with people with silver-coloured eyes" 银眼国	Feb. 22 to Mar. 21, 1433	N/A	Feb. 22 to Mar. 21, 1433	N/A	No
28. Aden 阿丹国	Mar. 15 to Apr. 19, 1433	N/A	Mar. 17 to Apr. 22, 1433	N/A	No
29. *Tianfang/* Yun Chong (Mecca) 天方国/ 麥加	Mar. 25 to Apr. 30, 1433 arriving at Port Jeddah	N/A	Mar. 29 to May 4, 1433 leaving Port Jeddah	N/A	No
30. Fengdu /Cahokia 酆都国/ 卡霍基亞	Late autumn of 1433*	N/A	Around Apr. to Aug. 1434, leaving the North Atlantic coast **	N/A	No

Table 1 During the seventh voyage on the way from China, Zheng He's main fleet explored thirty countries.

* *To be discussed in Section (3) of Chapter 5*
** *To be discussed in Section (3) of Chapter 8*

CHAPTER FOUR

Sailing across the Atlantic Ocean, the fleet landed unexpectedly

I continue to extract navigational routes and timelines of Zheng He's main fleet from Mecca to the North American coast, based on analysing Luo Maodeng's narrative and also referring to modern knowledge of ocean currents. The Keying Junk's global navigation over seven months demonstrates the excellence of the construction technology and performance of ancient Chinese wooden boats, and hence provides strong support of the view that Zheng He's main fleet navigated across the Atlantic.

As I have mentioned in Chapter 1, Mecca was part of the Mamluk kingdom of Egypt from 1250 to 1517. The Mamluk sultans ruled an empire that stretched from Egypt to Syria and included the holy cities of Mecca and Medina. Chapter 86 of Luo Maodeng's novel notes, that Zheng He visited *Tianfang*/Yun Chong (Mecca). The king (Mamluk sultan) sent in tributes, and Zheng He returned a salutation to the king. The king politely thanked Zheng He and left. From the analysis in Chapter 3 of this book we know that when this happened, the date was around March 29, 1433 to May 4, 1433. Soon after the king left, Zheng He's crew went back to their ships. They were about to depart from Jeddah and embark for the next destination. But after the king left, he returned and asked to see Zheng He again.

。。。元帅道："贤王有何见谕？"国王道："特来请二位元帅，宝船还向哪一边行？"元帅道："还往西行。"国王道："敝国就是西海尽头的路。 卑末并不曾听见西边还有甚么去路，就是满国中长老，并不曾传闻西边还有甚么国土。元帅还往西行，也须要一番斟酌。"元帅道："地有三千六百轴，怎么就尽于此？"国王道："区区管见，固尽于此，但凭元帅尊裁。"元帅道："多谢指教。只是我们之行，还不可止。"国王又辞谢而去。

My translation of the above passage is as follows:

. . . The commander-in-chief asked, "Sage king, what advice are you coming to offer me?" The king replied, "I especially come to ask your two commanders which direction your treasure ships plan to sail in." The commander-in-chief replied, "Further west." The king said, "My humble country is at the end of the path of the Western Sea. We humble people have not heard of any other existing path to the west. Even all the country's elders have not heard rumours about any country to the west. Even though the commander-in-chief still wants to sail in the western direction, please consider it carefully." The commander-in-chief replied, "Our Earth has 3,600 axes; how can it end here?" The king said, "This is merely an opinion, it does end here. It will depend entirely on the commander-in-chief's honourable judgement." The commander-in-chief replied, "Thank you for your advice, but our journey still cannot stop." The king politely thanked him again and left.

The concept that "Our Earth has 3,600 axes" came from ancient Chinese imagination mentioned in the book entitled Bo Wu Zhi 《博物志》 or *Natural History* (Latin: *Naturalis Historia*) [264] written by Zhang Hua (张华; 232–300 AD) in the Western Jin Dynasty (西晋时期; 266–316 AD). Today we know that the Earth has only one self-rotating axis which is perpendicular to the plane of the equator, and it is the straight line through the Earth's centre; the Earth's north and south poles are in the Arctic and Antarctic, respectively. But some ancient Chinese imagined that inside the Earth, there were four underground pillars; these pillars were 100,000 *li* apart,[265] and the Earth had 3,600 interlocking axes. This particular concept does not necessarily imply that the Earth is a sphere (but Zhang Heng, 张衡; 78–139 AD, the chief astronomer of the Eastern Han Dynasty had already written about the round Earth in one of his books entitled Ling Xian 《灵宪》 [266] or *The Spiritual Constitution of the Universe* around 120 AD). However, it does imply that the Earth is three-dimensional, though very extended, but has a finite size. Hence, if a traveller starts from a location on Earth and continues to travel in any direction, he will not reach an end point. This explains why Zheng He replied (transl. Sheng-Wei wang), "How can it end here?" and he believed that there must be unexplored territories ahead. Thus, Zheng He remained unmoved and was determined to continue to sail boldly westward even though the king earnestly tried to persuade him not to do so.

In Chapter 1 of this book, I mentioned that Louise Levathes recounts that Zheng He's fleet left Mecca on a southwesterly course shortly thereafter, and experienced a fantastic journey in the underworld, despite lengthy protests about the futility of any such venture on the part of the ruling Mamluk sultan, Al Ashraf Sayf-ad-Din Barsbay (ruled from 1422 to 1438). This ruling Mamluk sultan was the same king mentioned in the above passage from Luo's novel.

Luo's Chapter 86 will soon tell us how Zheng He's main fleet progressed in the westward direction.

(1) The Treasure Fleet sailed for almost 100 days without seeing land

We start from the time around March 29, 1433 to May 4, 1433 when Zheng He's main fleet started to sail again from Jeddah after they finished their pilgrimage at the Sacred Mosque in Mecca.

宝船开洋，无晓无夜，往西而行。只见天连水，水连天，渺渺茫茫，悠悠荡荡。一日又一日，不觉得百日将近。一月又一月，不觉得三月以来。二位元帅心上都有些费周折。。。

My translation of the above passage is as follows:

The treasure fleet set sail into the ocean moving in the westward direction, day and night without stopping. All they could see was that the sky and the water seem to merge together. What was lying beyond the horizon was unclear and the boats floated unsteadily. Day after day, nearly 100 days had passed. Month after month, imperceptibly, three months had gone. The two commanders-in-chief began to feel somewhat worried...

Now, almost 100 days later means that the date must be around early July to mid August in 1433. Although the treasure ships encountered no difficulty during these days, with no land in sight the two commanders-in-chief [267] began to wonder and became anxious. They did not know whether they should abandon the westbound adventure or continue.

. According to Luo, the treasure ships were far away from Mecca and entered a vast expanse of water. Even after sailing for more than three months there was still no sight of land. This was apparently a very wide ocean. With our knowledge of geography today we should immediately realise that this ocean must be the Atlantic Ocean, since there is no other neighbouring ocean lying far west of Mecca. But we still want to reconfirm this more closely.

Besides, how did the treasure ships manage to sail into this ocean to the west of Africa after leaving the country of *Tianfang*/Yun Chong/Mecca? And what was their most likely navigational route?

We know that to the west of the Red Sea is land. The "westward direction" (transl. Sheng-Wei Wang) in Luo's passage could not be "due west". It should be understood as a "generally western direction". And it could mean one of the following two things:

Route 1 or R1: Zheng He's fleet continued to sail in the north-westerly direction along the Red Sea from Jeddah. This would include sailing through the Great Bitter Lake and the Small Bitter Lake (now they are connected through the Suez Canal) [268] in northeastern Egypt. If in 1433 the waterways connecting the Red Sea with the Great Bitter Lake, the Small Bitter Lake, the ancient Red-Sea-Nile-Canals (man-made east-west waterways linking the Red Sea to the Nile) and the Mediterranean Sea were navigable, vessels could use this water route to enter from the Red Sea into the Mediterranean Sea as shown in Fig. 16, then pass the Strait of Gibraltar (between Morocco and Spain) into the North Atlantic Ocean. Fig. 17 [269] shows that after passing through the Strait of Gibraltar, following the ocean currents—first the Canary Current, next the North Equatorial Current and finally the Gulf Stream [270]— Zheng He's fleet would be able to cross the Atlantic and reach Central America and North America. Another possible route entails following the Canary Current, then the North Equatorial Current, the Equatorial Counter Current, the South Equatorial Current and finally the Brazil Current—this way, Zheng He's fleet would be able to cross the Atlantic and reach South America.

However, the Red-Sea-Nile-Canals were seasonal waterways. John P. Cooper has done a thorough analysis on the navigability of the ancient Red-Sea-Nile-Canals. In his research report, "Egypt's Nile-Red Sea canals: chronology, location, seasonality and function,"[271] he points out that much beyond December to January, the Nile river had typically fallen below its start-of-August level. This seasonality is also confirmed by Raoul McLaughlin in his book, *Rome and the Distant East: Trade Routes to the ancient lands of Arabia, India and China*, in which he writes that September to January was the best time to use the canals due to the swollen River Nile (86). In addition, between March and June, the waters, presumably, had been entirely drained from its bed for canal maintenance. But when Zheng He's fleet left Jeddah, it was around March 29, 1433 to May 4, 1433. If the fleet took route R1, then it would have reached the entrance to the old Red-Sea-Nile-Canals around mid April to mid-late May, and the canal would be closed.

Fig. 16 The ancient Red Sea Canals region

Based on the above analysis, the likelihood of Zheng He's fleet navigating through the old Red-Sea-Nile-Canals around mid April to mid-late May of 1433, and then entering the Mediterranean Sea and the Atlantic Ocean, appears to be negligible. Luo's paragraph states (transl. Sheng-Wei Wang) that Zheng He's crew saw no land while sailing for nearly 100 days. But the neighbourhood of the Red

Sea, the Red-Sea-Nile-Canals and the region surrounding the Mediterranean Sea is land rich. Based on these circumstances, Zheng He or Zheng He's messengers would not have taken the opportunity to visit Italy via this route to meet with Pope Eugene IV at Florence in 1433 as Menzies has suggested (*1434* 70). This will be further discussed in Chapter 8.

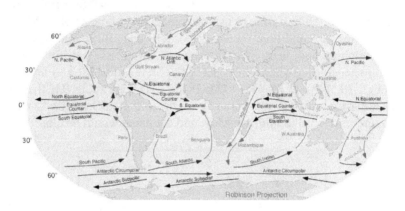

Fig. 17 World ocean current map; arrow (current direction)

Route 2 or R2: Zheng He's fleet could have left Jeddah, returned to Aden and the Gulf of Aden, and then re-entered the Indian Ocean. In this case, Fig. 17 shows that by following the Agulhas Current southward along the east coast of Africa, the fleet could round the southern tip of Africa; next, follow the Benguela Current northward along the west coast of Africa, and then the South Equatorial Current. At this point, there were three possibilities:

R2 (1): The fleet could first follow the South Equatorial Current, then the North Equatorial Current and the Gulf Stream to sail northward to the southeastern or northeastern coast of North America. If the fleet navigated northeastward, the ships could even follow the North Atlantic Drift (it is a slow-moving body of water located between about 50°–64°N and 10°–30°W),[272] leading north to the British Isles. The Gulf Stream along the northeastern coast of North America will encounter the Labrador Current[273] which moves along the northeast coast of the Labrador Peninsula. By sailing against the direction of the Labrador Current, this route could reach the northeastern coast of the North American continent.

144

R2 (2): The fleet could follow the South Equatorial Current, and then the Brazil Current to sail southward to reach the east coast of the South American continent.

R2 (3): The fleet could follow the South Equatorial Current and navigate northwestward, to reach today's Florida in the southeast corner of North America, Mexico, the Caribbean Sea and other Central American countries.

From the above analysis we can see that it is very likely that R2 was the voyage that Zheng He's fleet navigated for nearly 100 days without seeing land. The three possibilities offered by R2 could take the fleet to North, Central or South America, and the fleet could sail in the North Atlantic or the South Atlantic waters. But which route did Zheng He's fleet actually navigate during the last leg of the seventh voyage? This will become clear in the next section.

(2) The fleet sailed for two more months in mostly dark cloud and wild dense fog

Before we know where Zheng He's fleet finally arrived, let us first find out what the leaders on Zheng He's ship were discussing after they became anxious about whether they wanted to continue any further. Zheng He was already 62 years old and people respectfully called him the venerable San Bao Master. The San Bao Master started to have a conversation.

。。。"非我不肯回去，怎奈传玺不曾得来。原日白象驮玺隐入西番，正是这个西洋地面。"

My translation of the above passage is as follows:

. . . "The reason is not because I refuse to go back, but because we have not yet been able to find our country's lost Heirloom Seal of the Realm. A legend says that one day, long ago, a white elephant carrying this seal on its back disappeared into the western foreign country. That place is near this western land."

I need to make some explanations. The Heirloom Seal of the Realm, also known in English as the Imperial Seal of China,[274] is a Chinese

145

jade seal carved out of the He Shi Bi (和氏璧), a historically famous piece of jade. [275] But what was the story behind Zheng He's comment? What gave Zheng He the strong motivation to continue to navigate in the westward direction until the Imperial Seal was recovered? Was the search of the Imperial Seal the only reason?

We also need to understand the history of the Imperial Seal of China, because the seal used by the Chinese emperors has been regarded as a symbol of destiny.

In 221 BC, Qin Shi Huang (秦始皇) or the First Emperor of Qin, unified China after defeating six other countries and obtained the He Shi Bi. He ordered it made into his Imperial Seal and let the words "Having received the Mandate from Heaven, may [the emperor— Ed.] lead a long and prosperous life" (transl. Sheng-Wei Wang) be carved into the seal. After the second Qin emperor's death, the third and last Qin Emperor Ziying (秦王子婴 ; 242–206 BC) [276] surrendered to the invading military and offered the Imperial Seal of China to the first Han Emperor Liu Bang (汉高祖刘邦; 256–195 BC). However, Wang Mang (王莽; 45 BC–23 AD) usurped the Han, but was killed later, and the Imperial Seal of China went into the hands of Liu Xiu (刘秀), the Han Emperor Guangwu (汉光武帝; 5 BC–57 AD). After the Han Dynasty, the Imperial Seal of China passed to emperors of the Western Jin, Former Zhao, Later Zhao, Ran Wei, Eastern Jin, Song, Southern Qi, Liang, Northern Qi, Zhou, Sui[277] and Tang Dynasties.[278] It disappeared during the periods of the Five Dynasties[279] and the Ten States.[280] But a legend says that one day in the Yuan Dynasty (1271–1368), a copper bridge rose across the sea, and Emperor Shun (顺帝; 1333–1368) of the Yuan Dynasty drove a white elephant carrying the Imperial Seal over the bridge and disappeared. Consequently, the Ming (1368–1644) and the Qing (1644–1912) Dynasties did not have the Imperial Seal of China.

When Hongwu (洪武皇帝; 明太祖朱元璋; 1328–1398), the founding emperor of the Ming Dynasty, died, he did not pass the throne to his son but to his grandson Zhu Yunwen (朱允炆), who became Emperor Jianwen (建文帝; 1377–?). Zhu Di, the Prince of Yan (燕王), the fourth son of Emperor Hongwu, was not satisfied. He successfully invaded the capital Nanjing in 1402 and changed the era name to Yongle in 1403. After that, Emperor Jianwen disappeared. Legend had it that he became a monk or that he fled to western territories. Hence Emperor Yongle ordered Zheng He to sail to the Western Ocean not only to encourage foreigners to expand the tributary system, but also to find the Imperial Seal of China to justify the legitimacy of his imperial power, and to search for Zhu Yunwen, to eliminate any potential threat to Emperor Yongle's reign. Until the Xuande period of the Ming Emperor Xuanzhong (明宣宗; 1398 or 1399–1435), the motivation for searching for Zhu Yunwen might have subsided, but the Imperial Seal of China still had not been found. Therefore, according to Luo Maodeng, enlightening foreigners and searching for the national treasure were the missions of the voyage.

The San Bao Master's comment given above is taken from Chapter 9 of Luo's novel, in which he writes (transl. Sheng-Wei Wang), "Yuan Emperor Shun who drove a white elephant carrying the Imperial Seal, crossed a bridge over the Western Ocean and disappeared into the western countries... Therefore, this Imperial Seal that passed from dynasty to dynasty fell into the hands of the western foreigners" ("元顺帝赶着白象，驮着传国玺，打从桥上竟往西番。。。故此这个历代传国玺，陷在西番去了"). But why did Emperor Shun run away? We need to know Yuan history.

When the Ming Dynasty's first emperor Hongwu was attacking the Yuan capital Khanbaliq or Dadu, now Beijing, the last Emperor Shun of the Yuan Dynasty did not resist. He fled with only part of his family to Shangdu, also known as Xanadu, the capital of Kublai Khan's Yuan Dynasty in today's Inner Mongolia (this was before he decided to move his throne to Khanbaliq). Emperor Shun later fled to Yingchang, situated on Lake Taal in modern Inner Mongolia. This gave Zheng He strong motivation to continue to navigate in the westward direction to unknown territories until the Imperial Seal was recovered.

While the San Bao Master was speaking, other leaders of the fleet, who were present, were evaluating the progress of the navigation and the options. Although Zheng He felt that the fleet should not go back before completing the task ordered by the emperor, he still expressed his concern and said,

。。。"非咱不肯前进。只是天师牒上凶多吉少，因此上就没有了主张。" 国师道："若有甚么凶吉事，这个一则天师，一则贫僧，还须一定要逢凶化吉，转祸成祥。"二位元帅大喜，说道："若能够逢凶化吉，转祸成祥，凭他甚么阴司鬼国，也走他一遭。"

My translation of the above passage is as follows:

. . . "The reason is not because I do not want to move forward. It is only because the Daoist Master's magic figures indicate that the odds are more ominous than propitious, therefore I do not know how to make a decision." Then the Buddhist Master said, "If there is any good or bad luck, it must require either the Daoist Master or me, the monk, to turn bad luck into good luck, and disaster into good fortune." The two commanders-in-chief were overjoyed and said, "If it is possible to turn bad luck into good luck, and disaster into good fortune, there will be no problem with us visiting even the netherworld or the ghost country. We must go there."

Here we use "Daoist Master" as the title of the head of the Daoists (or Taoists) on the ship. He could practice exorcism to drive out evil spirits or ask God to bring good luck. The Buddhist Master on the ship was the eminent monk, Jin Bifeng (金碧峰). He could resolve doubts to dispel suspicion or practice virtue to pray for blessings. Then, a Buddhist disciple named Yun Gu (云谷) interrupted while standing at the side among the other members of the fleet.

。。。"前唐状元倒不是走到鬼国里面去了？前面是个鬼国也未可知"。后来果真的走到阴司鬼国，这几句话岂不是人心之灵，偶合如此！

My translation of the above passage is as follows:

. . . "Previously didn't Tang Zhuangyuan walk into a ghost country? Who knows what lies ahead? Maybe a ghost country or may be not!" Later, Tang Zhuangyuan did enter a ghost country in the netherworld. Don't these words show that people's psyche often reveals what is going to happen!

148

Tang Zhuangyuan (唐状元) or Marshall Tang, was Tang Ying (唐英), one of the military chiefs under Zheng He's command during the western expeditions. Yun Gu's comment points to Chapter 85 of Luo Maodeng's novel, in which Tang's wife, Huang Fengxian (黄凤仙), employed magic arts, using a Daoist trick to bring Tang Zhuangyuan into and out of the legendary Fengdu ghost country. The above passage implicitly reveals that Zheng He's people had some knowledge about the destination in the very distant west. "Later, he really walked into a ghost country in the netherworld" (transl. Sheng-Wei Wang) is Luo's hint to be taken up later in Chapters 5 and 6. There will be other evidence to show that this was not the first time that the Ming Treasure Fleet sailed towards a seemingly strange coast, and the land of the Fengdu ghost country.

Yun Gu's comment seems to have strengthened the Buddhist Master's stance of turning bad luck into good luck, and disaster into good fortune.

二位元帅得了天师之数，本是一忧；得了国师之言，又成一喜，放心大胆，一任前去。

My translation of the above passage is as follows:

The two commanders-in-chief were originally worried after receiving the Daoist Master's magic message but became joyful after hearing the Buddhist Master's comment. The two commanders-in-chief set their minds at ease and boldly let the ships sail ahead.

Luo's narrative continues:

又去了两个多月，先前朝头有日色，晚头有星辰，虽没有了红纱灯，也还有些方向可考。到了这两个月之后，阴云惨惨，野雾漫漫，就像中朝冬月间的雾露天气，只听见个声气。这个时候，不由你不行。掌定了舵，前面还是直西，若左了些，便不知道是哪里；右了些，也不知道是哪里。再加个转过身，越发不知去向，哪敢转过身来？

My translation of the above passage is as follows:

More than two months went by again. Previously, there was sunlight during the day and stars during the night. Even if no red gauze lanterns were used, still some directions could be taken as references. During these two months, the sky was covered with dark clouds, and wild dense fog was always present. It was just like the winter weather in China when the air is filled with mist and dew. Communications could be made only through sound. At this kind of time, you could not help but keep vigilant. If you fixed the rudder, the straight-ahead direction remained the straight west direction. But if you turned left a little, you lost track of where you were; if you turned right a little, you also lost track of where you were. If you turned around, you could lose track of your direction completely. How could you dare to turn around?

Knowing how the treasure ships communicated with one another can help us better to understand the above paragraph. When treasure ships sailed in the ocean, the sound of drums or gongs would send commands, which was loud enough to be heard between neighbouring ships. At night or in bad weather, lanterns were used as guides and as signals for exchanging information. For large distances, pigeons were sent to deliver messages.

In the Chinese Mazu (媽祖) culture, the red lantern is the symbol of booming life and prosperous business. Mazu is a Sea God belonging to the faith of people living on the coast of the mainland of China, including Okinawa, Japan, Korea, Southeast Asia and other maritime areas in East Asia. Mazu is also known as Our Lady of the Sky, the Holy Virgin of the Sky, Queen of Heaven, Goddess of the Sea, Celestial Queen, *Niang Ma* in Meizhou, etc.[281]

During the first 100 days of this crossing, there was no need to use the red gauze lanterns, since the weather conditions were good. There was sunlight during the day and stars during the night for the sailors on one ship to see the other ships by, and to identify their direction. During the first 100 days, since the fleet departed from Jeddah around March 29 to May 4, it was just before the start of the monsoon season in the Indian Ocean around May. By the time of crossing the Atlantic Ocean, the fleet would be helped by currents and favourable winds in the summer months.[282] But during the fourth and the fifth months of the sailing, the sky was so dark and the fog was so thick that even light from the red gauze lanterns on other ships could hardly be seen by the sailors. Evidently, the fleet had entered an area with very unfavourable weather conditions for navigation.

So, after adding these two extra months to the previous travelling time, it must now be around early-mid September to mid-late October in 1433. But according to Luo, the weather was just like the winter months in China.

We know that neither South America (which could be reached by taking the **R2 (2)** navigational route) nor Central America (reachable by taking the **R2 (3)** route) has the kind of coastal weather conditions around early-mid September to mid-late October, which would fit Luo's description. So, Zheng He's fleet could not be in the vicinity of Central or South America; the fleet was most likely in the North Atlantic Ocean (reachable by taking the **R2 (1)** route). We shall soon see that *only* the **R2 (1)** navigational route could lead Zheng He's fleet to an area with the weather conditions in Luo's description.

To support this finding, we must know the following weather condition, that as the Gulf Stream[283] reaches Cape Hatteras in North Carolina, the cold Labrador Current that flows from the north separates it from the coast; at this confluence, the warm Gulf Stream waters combine with the cold winds accompanying the Labrador Current, forming one of the densest concentrations of fog in the world, and the foggiest place on Earth is the "Grand Banks" off the island of Newfoundland. The Grand Banks is a vast and shallow continental shelf to the east of Newfoundland. (See Fig. 18.) It is different from the general continental shelf. It is formed by deposits carried from dissolved sea ice or ice from melted icebergs and is one of the world's prolific fishing grounds due to its shallow water.

Comparing Luo's narrative with the above facts gives a reasonable inference that during the fourth and the fifth months, Zheng He's fleet was sailing in this foggy coastal area near North America until the fleet was in the foggiest Grand Banks where the air was always filled with mist and dew, and visibility was limited to within an arm's length.

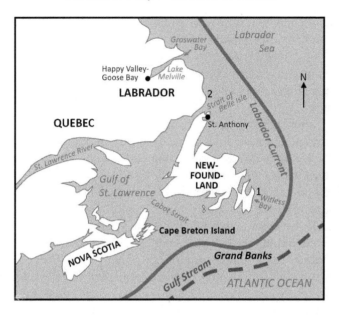

Fig. 18 The "Grand Banks" are located where the southbound cold
Labrador Current (solid line) mingles with the eastbound
warm Gulf Stream (broken line)

(3) Sailing another month before a reconnaissance boat bumped against a steep cliff

Luo continued,

兢兢业业，又走了一个多月。只见前哨船撞着在个黄草陡崖下。蓝旗官报到中军帐，元帅道："既有陡崖，一定是个国土。且住下船，再作区处。"即时传令，大小宝船一齐收住。这时候，正是：云暗不知天早晚，雪深难辨路高低。一会儿乌云陡暗，对面不见人，伸手不见掌，想是夜得来了。

My translation of the above passage is as follows:

Cautiously, the fleet sailed on again for more than a month when, suddenly, a reconnaissance boat bumped into a steep cliff covered with yellow grass. The officer who held the blue-coloured flag came to the commander-in-chief's tent to report.

152

The commander-in-chief said, "Since there is a steep cliff, there must be land. Just stop the boat, get off and then deal with it." The order was instantly sent out and the large and small ships all stopped at once. At this time, dark clouds made day and night indistinguishable, and deep snow made it difficult to tell the height of the ground. In a little while, the clouds suddenly became so dark that you could not see the person right in front of you. If you stretched out your hand, you could not see it before you. Night must have arrived.

At the end of this cautious month, the date was around early-mid October to mid November. Where was Zheng He's fleet? It must have been near the Labrador coastal region. This will be discussed in detail in Chapter 5.

(4) Comparing Junk Keying's global navigation with Zheng He fleet's voyage

The previous section describes the treasure fleet as it cautiously sailed on for more than a month, until a reconnaissance boat bumped against a steep cliff covered with yellow grass and Zheng He decided to stop the entire fleet. The colour of the grass indicates that this incident took place in the *autumn* season. *My estimate from analysing Luo's narrative also gives a timeline of the autumn season around early-mid October to mid November in 1433.* The fleet had already left Jeddah and sailed for more than six months. Was this time long enough to cross the Atlantic Ocean and reach the North American coast? Was this long navigation possible? Can this kind of navigation by a Chinese wooden boat be repeated?

Authors Wang Enshuang and Ren Jianmin (王恩双 任建民), in a Chinese article entitled "中国第一艘远洋木帆船—'耆英号'"[284] or "The first Chinese ocean-going wooden ship—Junk Keying"[285] (transl. Sheng-Wei Wang) point out that in the 26th year of the Daoguang Emperor (道光二十六年; 1846) of the Qing Dynasty, a Foochow (福州) Chinese trading junk's global sailing set the distance record for Chinese sailboats. Fig. 19 shows a model of Junk Keying displayed at the Hong Kong Maritime Museum.

Fig. 19 Junk Keying (© Hong Kong Maritime Museum)

Junk Keying, a 50 m/164 ft long, 10 m/33 ft wide, 5 m/16 ft deep, three-masted wooden boat, having a displacement tonnage of 750 tons (slightly smaller than the medium-sized ships in Zheng He's fleet) was piloted by a British captain, Henry Kellett, with 30 Chinese and eleven British sailors. The ship left Hong Kong on December 6, 1846. While rounding the Cape of Good Hope on March 14, 1847, it met and survived a violent hurricane. Almost four and a half months later, on April 17, 1847, Junk Keying reached St. Helena Island in the South Atlantic Ocean.[286] After leaving the Island, while the ship's original destination was London, it deviated from the route and headed for the Americas because of the more favourable *winds and currents* (the same currents shown in Fig. 17 and discussed in Section (1) of this chapter; the trade winds and currents also helped Zheng He's fleet to cross the Atlantic). When the crew experienced shortages of food and drinking water, they almost rioted. (Zheng He's fleet had far better supplies as we have mentioned in Chapter 1 of this book; and as a fleet with many ships navigating together, they could work as a team to minimise problems and risks.) Captain Kellett changed his mind and decided to head for New York (a similar route was taken by Zheng He's fleet in the early fifteenth century). The boat sailed

 154

into New York Harbour in early July 1847, about four months after the boat rounded the Cape of Good Hope. The crew visited Boston in November 1847. After leaving Boston on February 17, 1848, it took only *21 days* to cross the Atlantic Ocean by following the North Atlantic Drift to reach Port St. Aubin at Jersey in the Channel Islands on March 15, 1848.[287] Keying's global navigation of over seven months proves the excellence of construction technology and performance of ancient Chinese wooden boats.

While Junk Keying was able to sail from Hong Kong to New York in about seven months, Luo's narrative indicates that it took Zheng He's fleet more than six months (obtained by adding 100 days to more than two months and adding again to more than one month) to sail from Jeddah until a reconnaissance boat hit land off the coast of the North Atlantic. In Chapter 5, I will show that this location was most likely near the Labrador and Newfoundland coastal area off the Gulf of St. Lawrence.

To verify whether Luo's more than six-months' time for Zheng He's fleet to make this trans-Atlantic voyage is realistic or not, some simple calculations can be made as follows:

The waterway distance from Hong Kong to New York is not much longer than that from Jeddah to the Labrador and Newfoundland coastal area. Using the online tool for calculating distances between sea ports,[288] the former can be approximated as 6,917 nm from Hong Kong to Cape Town plus 6,789 nm from Cape Town to New York. The total is 13,706 nm, and the voyage took over seven months. The latter can be approximated as 4,653 nm from Jeddah to Cape Town, plus 6,672 nm from Cape Town to Newfoundland's St. John's. The total is 11,325 nm, and the voyage took over six months. The ratio of these two distances, 13,706/11,325, is 1.21. When we divide seven months by six months, the result is 1.17. The two ratios are very close. Hence, *the navigational time given by Luo Maodeng for Zheng He's fleet to complete the said trans-Atlantic navigation appears to be very realistic and cannot be explained simply as another "coincidence"!*

The Last Journey of the San Bao Eunuch

CHAPTER FIVE

Travelling from the Gulf of St. Lawrence to the country of Fengdu

In this chapter, I consider the initial landing site in North America of Zheng He's main fleet, the possible temporary shelter of the fleet near that landing site, and the timelines for the crew to proceed until Zheng He's scout Wang Ming encountered the country of Fengdu. I also describe the transportation methods used by these Chinese sailors from the initial landing site of their fleet to the neighbourhood near Fengdu.

When a reconnaissance boat of Zheng He's fleet hit a steep cliff covered with yellow grass, the entire fleet's forward progression ended. Luo's description of the scene of the incident is like this (transl. Sheng-Wei Wang): "At this time, dark clouds made day and night indistinguishable, and deep snow made it difficult to tell the height of the ground." It is apparent that the sky was not visible because of the overwhelming layers of clouds, and that snow had accumulated everywhere. The above sentence seems to indicate that the Chinese sailors could not decide whether it was day or night when the incident occurred due to dark cloud covering the sky.

Then follow the next three sentences (transl. Sheng-Wei Wang): "In a little while, the clouds suddenly became so dark that you could not see the person right in front of you. If you stretched out your hand, you could not see it before you. Night must have arrived." The statement indicates firmly that the fleet reached the coast in the evening, after sunset, and it would have been night.

Luo's narrative indicates that during the last month Zheng He's fleet had passed the foggy area of the Grand Banks and sailed further north to the colder coastal area. There, the Chinese sailors saw scenes of deep snow in the autumn season (the unexpected collision occurred around early-mid October to mid November of 1433). This area was most likely near the present-day Newfoundland and Labrador Province of Canada. However, to determine where approximately the incident took place, we need to understand the October and November weather conditions of a few representative locations along the North Atlantic coast in North America to validate the above prediction.

(1) Locating the initial landing site of the treasure fleet

First, I examine the climate of the Grand Banks. The following are temperatures in a town of "Grand Bank, Newfoundland" in southern Newfoundland. It is near the Grand Banks, and I use the data for this town as an example. Its mean maximum and minimum temperatures (in degrees Celsius) in October are, respectively, 11.7 and 4.1 °C, while in November they are 6.7 and 0.3 °C.[289] It seems that the Grand Banks region should have a similar climate as the town of Grand Bank in Newfoundland, and the region is not likely cold enough to see scenes where "deep snow made it difficult to tell the height of the ground" from early-mid October to mid November.

Next, I examine the climate of Witless Bay in Newfoundland. (See Fig. 18, position 1.) Newfoundland is a large Canadian island off the east coast of the North American mainland. Witless Bay (47°17'11"N, 52°49'28"W) is a town on the Avalon Peninsula in the province of Newfoundland and Labrador, 35 km/21 mi south of the provincial capital, St. John's, and air distance 221.56 km/137.67 mi from the town of Grand Bank. The latitude of Witless Bay is slightly to the north of the latitude of Grand Bank (47°06'0"N, 55°47'0"W), and both are ice-free harbours. I expect that the mean maximum and minimum temperatures in October and November in Witless Bay are perhaps slightly cooler than, but not much different from the Grand Bank region. It is also usually not cold enough to see scenes where "deep snow made it difficult to tell the height of the ground" around early-mid October to mid November.

Finally, I examine more closely the Newfoundland and Labrador Province. The province includes, to the south, the island of Newfoundland and its nearby islands, as well as, to the north, the Labrador Peninsula and its nearby islands, with the Strait of Belle Isle separating the province into two geographical divisions. The province includes over 7,000 small islands. Both the southeast corner of Labrador and the western region of Newfoundland face the Gulf of St. Lawrence, while other coastal areas of these two regions all face the North Atlantic Ocean. Most of Newfoundland and Labrador are *uninhabited*, and harbours are *frozen* in winter. Northern Labrador is classified as having a polar tundra climate (it

158 158

has cool summers and very cold winters; a polar climate results in treeless tundra, glaciers, or a permanent or semi-permanent layer of ice),[290] whereas southern Labrador is considered to have a subarctic climate (a climate characterised by long, usually very cold winters, and short, cool to mild summers).[291] Most of Newfoundland would be considered to have a cool summer subtype of a humid continental climate, because the sea breeze plays a role in regulating the temperature. The winter in Newfoundland is not too cold, and summer not too hot. Hence, it is also not very likely to have deep snow around early-mid October to mid November. However, the coast of Newfoundland does have many cliffs which would be covered with yellow-coloured grass around early-mid October to mid November.[292]

For navigation, along the Newfoundland coastline from St. Anthony to the north of Nain in Labrador, there is a sea route of approximately 2,000 km/1,250 mi, which could have been taken by Zheng He's fleet during the last stretch of their voyage. But notice Luo's description (transl. Sheng-Wei Wang): "Cautiously, the fleet sailed on again for more than a month." Why did they have to sail "cautiously?"

The Labrador coast borders the Labrador Sea which is part of the North Atlantic Ocean. During the first half of the year, the Newfoundland and Labrador waters could be covered with sea ice or "floating ice" which differs from icebergs. (An iceberg[293] is a large piece of freshwater ice that has broken off a glacier or an ice shelf, and is floating freely in open water.) Since icebergs are bulky and have a hard texture, they often cause shipwrecks due to collisions with ships. A famous example is that of the *Titanic*, which took place in 1912 in that area. While sea ice or floating ice in the Newfoundland and Labrador waters consists of smaller pieces of sea ice that float on the sea surface, it can also make navigation difficult. Hence seafarers must stay vigilant. As winter advances, sea ice formation and movement off the coasts of Labrador and northern parts of Newfoundland also lower temperatures. But around the Avalon Peninsula[294] and off much of the south coast, the ice concentration is usually lighter or non-existent, allowing temperatures to be moderated by the open water.[295] From the beginning of January each year, the sea ice of the Labrador Current begins to move southward; until about April the ice melts faster than the speed of the current so that the ice cover begins to retreat

 159

northward. However, Zheng He's fleet should have been able to sail in the above-mentioned sea route of the North Atlantic Ocean from St. Anthony to the north of Nain without encountering sea ice during the month from early-mid October to mid November of 1433 before winter set in. The southeast coast of Labrador is also not short of cliffs covered with yellow grass in autumn. However, to sail from the Grand Banks to the Labrador coastal region, the treasure fleet had to make an extra effort to sail against the direction of the Labrador Current and required these Chinese mariners to make more effort.

While the mean maximum and minimum temperatures in Newfoundland's coastal town of St. Anthony are, in October, 6.5 and 0.4 °C, and, in November, 1.0 and -4.8 °C, [296] the mean maximum and minimum temperatures of Labrador's Goose Bay (located in the central part of Labrador on the coast of Lake Melville and the Grand River) in October, are 7.0 and -0.6 °C, and in November, -0.3 and -7.6 °C.[297] The more you go north, the colder it becomes. Also, the mean maximum and minimum temperature in the inland Labrador City are, respectively, 3.8 and -2.9 °C in October and -4.2 and -12.0 °C in November.[298] It means, the further you are away from the coast, the colder it becomes. Hence, the Chinese sailors could have seen that the Labrador inland area was covered with deep snow around early-mid October to mid November, while the Labrador and Newfoundland coastal region were unfrozen and therefore allowed ships to sail.

From the above weather comparisons, we can see that during the final month of the voyage, Zheng He's fleet might have sailed to a place close to the Labrador area, or a Newfoundland coastal area which was also close to the Labrador coast (for example, St. Anthony). The place was at higher latitude and was colder than the Grand Banks so that Zheng He's mariners would have been able to see deep snow covering the ground at night. But as Fig. 18 shows, regardless of whether the fleet was near position 1 close to the Newfoundland area, or position 2 close to the Labrador area, it was in either case near the Gulf of St. Lawrence. The Strait of Belle Isle, between Newfoundland and Labrador, connects to the north with the Labrador Sea, and to the south with the Gulf of St. Lawrence. The Strait is 145 km/90 mi long and 20 km/12 mi wide, being the narrowest passage separating Newfoundland from the mainland of Canada. Before and after the departure of the Norse people,[299]

160

Newfoundland was inhabited by aboriginal populations. In 1497, Italian navigator John Cabot[300] became the first European since the Norse settlers to set foot on Newfoundland. The island is separated from Cape Breton Island by the Cabot Strait as shown in Fig. 18, and blocks the mouth of the St. Lawrence River, creating the Gulf of St. Lawrence, the world's largest estuary.

The Chinese sailors would soon be able to enter the Gulf of St. Lawrence to find a more suitable place for them to anchor their ships while they proceeded to explore the North American mainland. Such a place was most likely to be Cape Breton Island as shown in Fig. 18, which is part of Nova Scotia, one of Canada's four Maritime Provinces (New Brunswick, Nova Scotia, Prince Edward Island, and the easternmost province of Newfoundland and Labrador). Once inside the Gulf of St. Lawrence, Zheng He's fleet would very likely find Cape Breton Island, also called the Island of Seven Cities. [301] Surrounded by oceans, the weather there is moderate and the climate is closer to a maritime than a continental climate. Hence, its climate is very suitable for human habitation.

(2) Cape Breton Island: The Chinese North Atlantic base

When Gavin Menzies published the Chinese edition of *1421: The Year China Discovered America*, he told reporters that in the Nova Scotia region, in an area of about 50 sq km/19 sq mi, there remain the ruins of a once prosperous harbour city. These ruins were discovered in 2002 by Paul Chiasson, a local Canadian architect born on Cape Breton Island (his ancestors came from France; he is the thirteenth generation). He happened to see these ruins while hiking up Kelly's Mountain—a hill he had never explored on Cape Breton Island—and found that the ruins contained a lot of oriental cultural characteristics. Because he knew about Menzies' work, he notified Menzies about the ruins. Soon Menzies went to investigate there in person with T.C. Bell, a full-time surveyor, specializing in Roman and Chinese engineering, with a background in marine engineering, foundries, plant engineering and surveying.

When Chiasson discovered the ruins, he said that the place had been "off the beaten track" for centuries. Even the nearest residents knew nothing about the existence of these ruins. In 1497, the first batch of Europeans who arrived in this area described it as a thriving beautiful harbour; the Indigenous People of the region, the Mi'kmaq, had oriental features, used strange hieroglyphs, and wore clothing with golden oriental patterns and Chinese-style earrings. The Mi'kmaq claimed that aliens rode on huge ships coming from the sea, and then these mysterious aliens returned to their homes on the far side of the North Pole. Chiasson repeatedly stressed that *no European ever saw the city, which has not appeared on any European map to this day.*

Chiasson's research result was published in May 2006 in a book entitled *The Island of Seven Cities: Where the Chinese Settled When They Discovered America.* [302] The seven cities were known to Europeans and are shown in Fig. 20. In alphabetical order, they are Cape Dauphin, Chéticamp, Ingonish, Louisbourg, St. Ann's, St. Peter's, and the area now known as Sydney.

Cape Dauphin[303] is one of the peninsulas of Cape Breton. It is 300 m/984 ft high, heavily forested, with steep cliffs on three sides. To its west is St. Ann's (Englishtown) [304] harbour [305] which is situated on the southwestern shore of St. Ann's Bay. Cape Dauphin divides St. Ann's Bay to the north from the Great Bras d'Or channel to the south. According to Paul Chiasson,[306] St. Ann's would have had a fort built by the Chinese because of its location at the opening to St. Ann's Bay and so, although small, it would have been considered a settlement by the earliest European settlers and therefore one of the seven cities. Chéticamp is a fishing village on the west coast of the Cape Breton Island; the Chéticamp River flows into the Gulf of St. Lawrence.[307] Ingonish (known as Portuguese Bay) is located along the northeast coast of Cape Breton Island and was one of the first areas settled on Cape Breton Island.[308] The harbour Louisbourg (also known as the English Harbour) is situated on the east shore of Cape Breton Island and on the Atlantic coast. It had been used by European mariners since at least the 1590s.[309] The French military founded the Fortress of Louisbourg in 1713 and its fortified seaport on the southwest part of the harbour. After the French settlers left, the English settlers built a small fishing village, across the harbour from the abandoned site of the fortress.[310] St. Peter's (also known as St. Peters) is a small village located on a narrow isthmus which separates the southern end of Bras d'Or Lake (where a modern canal connects it to the Atlantic), known as St. Peter's Inlet, to the north from St. Peter's Bay and the Atlantic Ocean to the south.[311] Sydney, the major town to the east of Bras d'Or was also known by early Europeans. It was called Spanish Bay because of its use by Spanish fishermen just as Ingonish was known as Portuguese Bay because of its use by sixteenth century Portuguese.[312]

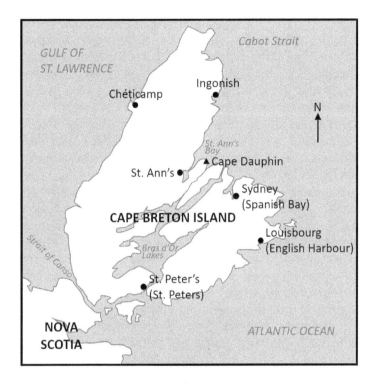

Fig. 20 Cape Breton Island

In 2005, T.C. Bell visited the Chinese Settlements on Cape Dauphin, Louisbourg and St. Peter's on Cape Breton Island, and Canso on the mainland of Nova Scotia. [313] He summarises his findings as follows:[314]

On Cape Dauphin, ruins of walls stretch out for about two miles; water storage facilities and tombs are also found, defining a city. The layout of the city appears to be Chinese and the scale of the whole endeavour is mind-blowing.

Two forms of tombs were located via magnetic anomaly surveys. These tombs were positioned horizontally and oriented in a North-South direction. Near these tombs, there was a group of inhumations with human bodies in

163

flexed position or like foetus burials in vertical position, which is a standard Chinese method. Two Viking Hogback stone grave markers were also discovered.[315] They were at the lower end of the main road to the Chinese site from the Bras d'Or, an inland sea. The presence of the two Viking Hogback grave markers which were the first located in North America, on the main road to the Chinese settlement on Cape Dauphin,[316] proves that the Chinese Road existed *prior to* the Viking arrival in North America in the tenth century.[317]

The survey work covers the three sides of Cape Dauphin's peninsula, at sea level. The remains of extremely large, well-engineered and well-defended Chinese settlements with a religious core were discovered. They were all supplied by roads and canals to access the coastal deep-sea harbours by canalized local rivers (brooks) fitted with ladder locks. The photo in Fig. 21 (taken by T.C. Bell in 2005) shows a close up of detail of terrace stonework at the Chinese religious site at Cape Dauphin. Another photo (taken also by T.C. Bell in 2005) in Fig. 22, shows a dump which includes stonework derived from the said adjacent Chinese religious site. The dumped pile held a number of carved stone faces of animals, like those on the roofs of the Chinese temple in the Forbidden City. Several sections of semi-square pillars were also noted; the centres of the pillars held iron bolts to link them together. The pillars do not have carved faces on them.

Evidence of smelter ramps, ore crushers and ore exploitation were noted. The Chinese built the island's major harbour by constructing a barrier across St Ann's Bay, leaving a 70 m/230 ft wide gap, now crossed by a chain ferry. The Chinese and later the French and English all built forts to control the gap. Shore-side harbours suitable for 47 m x 11 m (154 ft x 36 ft) vessels were noted on both the eastern and western side of Cape Dauphin. During the survey on the east coast, excavations had exposed the stone quays of an inland harbour capable of berthing four 47 m x 11 m (154 ft x 36 ft) vessels. The harbour accessed the channel to the Bras d'Or by a short length of canal and locks. This harbour connected with two canalized brooks which accessed the upper Chinese sites.

Slot harbours designed for two 47 m x 11 m (154 ft x 36 ft) vessels were also noted opposite the French Fortress of Louisbourg. Overlooking the ferry access ramp, alongside the cannon presented by Louisbourg Fort, is the clear outline of the platform of a Chinese 36 m x 4 m (118 ft x 13 ft) walled barrack block. A scan indicated the distinctive outline of the foundations of the six barrack blocks.

St. Peter's, south Cape Breton Island, lies alongside a sheltered bay. It has a superb natural harbour, fought over by both the English and the

French. Most unusually it has a 5 fathom[318] (30 ft), circa 9 m/29.5 ft deep, vertical-sided channel alongside the main land. Here the Chinese left a fort, a walled barracks capable of housing the crews of two large junks, alongside a 100 m/328 ft long paved quayside and a slot harbour designed to take a 47 m x 11 m (154 ft x 36 ft) vessel. The harbour plus a 6 m/19.7 ft flanking canal of Chinese design can access the Bras d'Or, the inland sea. The first Chinese canal—which has been rebuilt twice—is now used by fishing craft.

It is noteworthy that the standard Chinese 36 m x 4 m (118 ft x 13 ft) barracks, with one paved and eight unpaved rooms, was found at *every* site surveyed on Cape Breton and mainland Canso, and also at the more than 50 Chinese sites located in New Zealand.[319]

Cape Dauphin, Cape Breton Island, being at the gateway to the St Lawrence Bay, was well suited to explore the Canadian hinterlands including the Great Lakes. While the Chinese mariners went ashore to explore, they needed a base to dock their big ships and to serve as an operational headquarters. Cape Breton Island would appear to have been the Chinese North Atlantic base during their earlier voyages[320] as well as during Zheng He's seventh voyage when his fleet landed near the Labrador (or Newfoundland) coastal region. A similar conclusion is also suggested by the massive evidence of two waves of Chinese operations in Britain, including wrecks, located by T.C. Bell. In Britain, the Chinese settlements used 30 m x 10 m (98 ft x 33 ft) three-room houses, the centre room paved, the others unpaved. The sailors used 36 m x 4 m (118 ft x 13 ft) barracks. The size difference in houses and barracks could indicate the arrival of two Chinese settlers at two widely different dates and their different operations and practices.[321]

Bell's findings lend strong support to Luo Maodeng's narrative that Zheng He's fleet landed near the Labrador-Newfoundland coastal area near the Gulf of St. Lawrence during his seventh voyage, and also suggest that the most likely operational headquarters for Zheng He's crew to explore the North American heartland in the 1430s was Cape Dauphin, Breton Island.

Fig. 21 Close-up of detail of terrace stonework
at Chinese religious site at Cape Dauphin

Fig. 22 Dump which includes stonework from the adjacent Chinese
religious site at Cape Dauphin; the dumped pile held a number of
carved stone faces of animals, like those on the roofs of the Chinese
temple in the Forbidden City

166

(3) Zheng He's scout, Wang Ming, arrived at a densely populated city

Now let us continue to read Luo Maodeng's narrative to find out what happened in the early morning on the day after Zheng He's fleet landed on the previous night.

。。。二位元帅坐在中军帐上，传令夜不收上岸去打探。夜不收不敢去。老爷道："着王明去。"王明道："天涯海角都是人走的，怕它甚么雾露朦胧！"一手拿着隐身草，一手一口戒手刀，曳开步来就走。走到十数里路上，天又亮了些。再走，又走到十数多里路上，天又亮了些。再又走，走到十数多里路上，天愈加亮净了。虽则有些烟雨霏霏，也只当得个深秋的景象，不是头前那样黑葳葳的意思。。。
。。。却说王明行了三五里路，前面是一座城郭，郭外都是民居，又尽稠密。。。

My translation of the above text is as follows and my comment is in square brackets:

…The two commanders-in-chief sat inside the military tent. They ordered the reconnaissance officer to go ashore and probe the situation. The reconnaissance officer did not dare to go. The revered master said, "Let Wang Ming go." Wang Ming responded, "Even the end of the Earth can be walked over by people, what is there to be afraid of in this misty fog!" Carrying a straw shield in one hand and a knife in the other, he started to walk without hesitation. He walked some ten *li* [between 10 *li*/5 km and 20 *li*/10 km], and the day broke slightly. He walked another some ten *li*, and the day broke again a little more. Still he walked another some ten *li*, and the day broke even more and became brighter. Though some misty rain was falling, the scene was only like late autumn, unlike the darkness of the previous night. …
. . . Then Wang Ming walked for another three to five *li* and saw in front of him a city with an outer wall. Outside the wall were closely packed residential dwellings. …

167

The above description (transl. Sheng-Wei Wang), "Carrying a straw shield in one hand" implies that Wang Ming (王明), one of Zheng He's sergeants, could hide himself from view under the cover of this straw shield to avoid being discovered by others.

(4) Detecting clues in Luo Maodeng's novel

A closer examination of Luo Maodeng's narrative reveals a few inconsistencies that must be clarified for a better understanding of the time sequence and progress of Zheng He's crew after they landed in the coast of North America.

First, while the analysis of the sea currents tells us that the reconnaissance boat of the Ming Treasure Fleet collided with a steep cliff covered with yellow grass around early-mid October to mid November 1433, according to Luo, the climate of the inland area where Wang Ming was exploring was that of *late autumn* (November). The passage of the seasons gives us a hint, an important clue. Seasonal change represents time change. What had happened during the time interval between the fleet's landing date and Wang Ming's arriving at a densely populated city?

Second, we should also pay special attention to Luo's description of Wang Ming's walk. The fact that Wang Ming "started to walk without hesitation" (transl. Sheng-Wei Wang) implies that it was easy, and it seems to indicate that he was not near the same cliff as the night before, where deep snow buried the ground (it would be very unlikely for the deep snow to melt overnight). Then we should try to understand what these sentences mean. Wang Ming walked some ten *li* (between 10 *li*/5 km and 20 *li*/10 km) three times, and each time the day broke more and became brighter. Then Wang Ming walked for another three to five *li*, he saw in front of him a city with an outer wall. Outside the wall were closely packed residential dwellings. We may estimate how many kilometres Wang Ming walked in all, until he discovered the walled and densely populated city named Fengdu or Fengdu Guo in Luo Maodeng's novel. As one *li* is 0.5 km, the three times of walking some ten *li* (each time between 10 *li*/5 km and 20 *li*/10 km) would cover around fifteen to 30 km. Adding the last 1.5–2.5 km (three to five *li*) still gives a total that was, at most, a little over 30 km/19 mi. That is to say: starting from the steep cliff covered with yellow grass, Wang

Ming walked a total of, at most, a little over 30 km/19 mi, before he encountered a densely-populated strange city. But, near the Labrador and Newfoundland coasts or in the area of the Gulf of St. Lawrence, no densely populated and walled city existed in those days (the entire area was sparsely populated then). So how do we explain this? Where was Wang Ming actually?

It seems that Luo's narrative fails to mention some circumstances. What circumstances?

(5) Luo's omission leaves blanks to be filled

From the moment the Chinese reconnaissance boat collided with the steep cliff until Wang Ming made his walk and encountered a strange city, it is entirely possible that Zheng He's mariners travelled to a different location, Fengdu, a location that was away from their landing site and had a very different environment from the Labrador and Newfoundland coastal region. Such a scenario would give a logical and satisfactory explanation for the distance Wang Ming had to walk over land, the manner in which he walked, the late autumn landscape he saw, and the densely populated city he encountered.

What is missing in Luo's narrative is the *progress* of Zheng He's mariners from near the Labrador and Newfoundland coasts or the Gulf of St. Lawrence to the river bank near Fengdu. It is not clear to me how this omission happened. It could be that Luo Maodeng did not have the complete record so as to be able to write about the progress of Zheng He's crew, or that he did it on purpose to obscure this part of the journey. In any case, even in describing the very challenging trans-Atlantic navigation he used only a few short paragraphs. So, it is also possible that he might have decided to simply skip the details of the Chinese mariners' sailing in the inland waterways. What he might have ignored, or even intended to leave out, makes it difficult for us to work out what happened. But his omission gives us the opportunity to fill in the blanks he created.

In summary, my interpretation and findings are as follows: 1) in those days, near the Labrador and Newfoundland coasts or the Gulf of St. Lawrence, there was no walled city like Fengdu, described by Luo Maodeng as being on a significant scale, with densely populated residential dwellings; 2) when Zheng He's reconnaissance boat collided with the steep cliff, the date was

169

around early-mid October to mid November in 1433; hence, Wang Ming should not have seen the late autumn scene. Such *a change of season means advancement in time*. It means that when Wang Ming saw the city, it was already a couple of weeks or more than a month after the entire fleet was halted at the cliff side. After walking for, at most, a little over 30 km/19 mi, Wang Ming encountered the outskirts of Fengdu, implying that the Chinese sailors had advanced for a couple of weeks or more than a month to a water area, at most, a little over 30 km/19 mi away from Fengdu; 3) Luo Maodeng describes in the later chapters of his novel how several of Zheng He's armed generals also rode on horseback and walked, at most, a little over 30 km/19 mi from their boats, to arrive at Fengdu; this further implies that Wang Ming and Zheng He's generals were all coming ashore from the same body of water not far from Fengdu.

Where was this body of water, which was, at most, a little over 30 km/19 mi from Fengdu? And where was Fengdu?

In the following chapters I shall list the multiple lines of evidence which show that the country of Fengdu that Wang Ming encountered was Cahokia—today's *C*ahokia Mounds State Historic Site—in the central Mississippi Valley, one of the ten amazing cities from the ancient world.

(6) The Chinese sailors arrive in the central Mississippi Valley

The missing details in Luo's narrative and the actual route for the Chinese sailors to arrive at Cahokia, the heart of the Mississippi River Valley, can be understood as follows:

Today it is obvious from any map that the part of North America's eastern coast that includes the Gulf of St. Lawrence is the one and only water route from the Atlantic Ocean to the Great Lakes, and then to the heartland of North America by taking the Mississippi River and its major tributaries. But is it obvious to us that in the early fifteenth century, the Chinese mariners also had this knowledge? The 1418 Chinese World Map owned since 2001 by Liu Gang (a present-day Beijing lawyer, map-collector and analyst) was unveiled in 2006.[322] It shows the entire North America eastern coast, but does not show the Great Lakes and the rivers connecting with these lakes. Even the prominent 1602 map—Kunyu Wanguo Quantu 《坤輿万国全图》 [323] or Complete Geographical Map of All the Kingdoms of the World does not show the Great Lakes, although it does show the Mississippi River and its major tributaries (in Chapter 9 of this book, I shall list evidence to show that this map incorporated information from Chinese maps made around 1428 to January 19, 1431). It then became clear to me how courageously Zheng He's mariners had tried to explore this new waterway route to reach inland North America during their seventh voyage after they accidentally landed on the North Atlantic coast. It is known today, that, until the nineteenth century, water transportation was often used to travel through North America. Zheng He's main fleet must have found this route by being in touch with the natives to reach the American heartland, but they had to pass two short land portages connecting different sections of the water route.

Fig. 18 and Fig. 23 show, that from the Labrador and Newfoundland coasts, Zheng He's boats could enter the Gulf of St. Lawrence through the Strait of Belle Isle, then the St. Lawrence River. Fig. 23 shows that the St. Lawrence River (upper right corner) is connected to Lake Ontario which is the first of the Great Lakes.

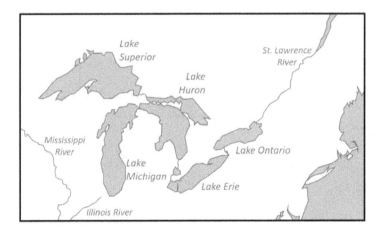

Fig. 23 The St. Lawrence River (upper right corner) connects the Gulf of St. Lawrence to the Great Lakes

Between Lake Ontario and Lake Erie are the Niagara Falls which are about 51 m/167 ft high. Before the Welland Canal was constructed in 1824, transportation between Lake Ontario and Lake Erie must have relied on a land path between today's Chippewa and

171 171

Queenston (马克·尼克莱斯等 114–115). Fig. 24 shows the connection of Lake Ontario, Lake Erie and the Niagara Falls. Chippewa lies by the Niagara River in Canada, about 2 km/1.2 mi upstream from the Niagara Falls; Queenston lies also by the Niagara River in Canada, about 5 km/3.1 mi downstream from the Niagara Falls. After this short land journey, the Chinese sailors could use the boats they transported over land or make new boats to enter Lake Erie, then Lake Huron, and finally Lake Michigan. They did not need to use the fifth Great Lake of North America, Lake Superior, during this voyage.

Fig. 24 Lake Ontario, Lake Erie and Niagara Falls. On the left is the current Welland Canal with a total of eight locks, on the right is the Niagara Falls region

After reaching Lake Michigan, there is a swampland between Lake Michigan and the Illinois River. Fig. 25 shows the connection between Lake Michigan, the north section of the Chicago River, the south section of the Chicago River, the Des Plaines River and the Illinois River. The Chicago Portage in the middle was the marshes. In the dry autumn, Zheng He's boats, horses and troops could be transported over land to cross this swampland (马克·尼克莱斯等 115–116). Hence, land connections linking seas, lakes and rivers had special significance and importance. Following these land routes which connected the seas, lakes or rivers, involved carrying boats and equipment. The entire land and water transportation route was identified by the local Indians and the early European explorers as the main route leading inland into North America from the North Atlantic coast (马克·尼克莱斯等 117).

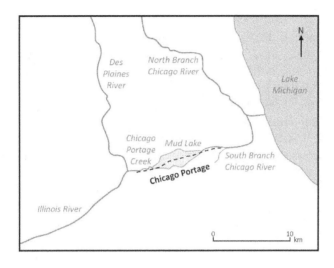

Fig. 25 Topography surrounding the Chicago Portage

The formation of the Chicago Portage [324] was related to the sedimentary clay of the glacial lakes. After the last glacier of the Lake Michigan basin retreated, a big lake formed between the retreating ice and the depositional ridges. The depositional ridges marked the furthest reaches of the glacier. The lake eventually shrank to the current size. However, the Lake Michigan area was filled with sedimentary clay from the much bigger glacial lake, Lake Chicago.[325] The clay prevented water from penetrating deep into the ground, thus forming a landscape of swamps. There are many residual lakes and sloughs in the Chicago area. One of them is known as Mud Lake. (See Fig. 25.) The wetland in its centre was located approximately in the lowest area of the drainages. The drainages included the Chicago River which flowed to the east into Lake Michigan, and the Des Plaines River which flowed southwest into the Illinois River, and then into the Mississippi River. Seasonally, this was a shallow waterway or a muddy slough of 13

173

km/8 mi across,[326] forming the critical link between the Chicago River and the Des Plaines River to the west. In very wet weather the river water rose and the Des Plaines River and the Chicago River were connected, so there was no need to use land transportation. However, most of the time, porting was necessary for travellers in the early days. Early visitors pulled their canoes and carried them through the boundary marshes between the two rivers until they arrived at the deep-water area where they could embark in their boats again. In 1803, the U.S. federal government built Fort Dearborn beside the Chicago River to guard this portage. Today the words "Chicago Portage National Historic Site" are marked on a sign at the western end of the old portage to commemorate the unique importance of this ancient passageway.[327]

Here I would like to summarise how land transportation took place across the Niagara Falls and the Chicago Portage. In the dry season, Indian canoes and small boats could be carried on the shoulders or pulled by manpower through the two land routes mentioned. For centuries, they provided for the Native Americans and the later Europeans a unique way to travel inland from the North Atlantic coast.

The Chinese expedition could also build punts for transporting horses, food, or instruments. These punts could be larger than Indian canoes, but still small enough to be moved or pulled by human power or horsepower (马克·尼克莱斯等 117). Alternatively, the Chinese could use wooden rollers to transport or drag medium-sized boats on the two land routes to traverse the Niagara Falls and the Chicago swampland. Later, the Europeans could even move boats weighing several tons through these difficult passages (马克·尼克莱斯等 117). Probably new larger boats were needed after crossing the Niagara Falls to sail the length of three of the Great Lakes to Chicago. Would they build them (if there was enough time to build them) or buy them from the natives? I have no doubt that the Chinese expedition teams would have made their best decision. Today, canals bypass the Niagara Falls and the Chicago swampland.

The Illinois River flows into the Mississippi River near today's Grafton[328] (approximately 25 mi/40 km northwest of downtown St. Louis and about 20 mi/33 km upstream from the confluence of the the Mississippi and Missouri Rivers). Near this junction lie the rolling hills of the Pere Marquette State Park. Steep cliffs start here and continue until south of today's Alton before turning into gentle terrain. The river junction is about 50 km/31 mi from Cahokia as the crow flies. If Zheng He's boats docked near the junction of these two rivers (the Illinois River and the Mississippi River), due to the cliffs, Wang Ming and later Zheng He's five generals would not be able to come ashore easily. They would have to walk or ride horses along the Mississippi River bank for more than 50 km/31 mi to reach the Cahokia Mounds complex (the Mississippi River makes a bend after passing Alton). This longer distance does not match the afore-mentioned 30 km/19 mi distance, as given approximately by Luo Maodeng.

However, if Zheng He's river boats docked near the confluence of the Missouri River and the Mississippi River (the river rounds the northern side of St. Louis to join the Mississippi River on the border between Missouri and Illinois), then the shortest distance from this confluence to the Cahokia Mounds complex is no more than 30 km/19 mi. If Wang Ming and Zheng He's five generals went ashore from here by foot and on horse, then in no more than 30 km/19 mi they could see the densely populated city of Cahokia. In addition, we must understand that when Zheng He's boats sailed the Mississippi River downstream (from north to south) after passing by Grafton, on the left bank of the river, near today's Elsah and Alton, there are continuous cliffs stretching all the way to the south of Alton. Only near the confluence of the Missouri River and the Mississippi River is the terrain flatter. There is *no* cliff at the junction of the two rivers. This explains why Wang Ming could come ashore and simply start to walk without hesitation. This leads me to think that Zheng He's riverboats most likely docked near the confluence of the Missouri River and the Mississippi River, in particular near the bank of the calmer Mississippi River. Fig. 26 shows the general areas surrounding the two river junctions mentioned above.

The water and land journey from the Labrador and Newfoundland coasts or the Gulf of St. Lawrence to the Mississippi Valley takes time. This explains the reported seasonal transition from around early October to mid October into late autumn (late November) when Wang Ming arrived at Fengdu. If we imagine that Fengdu was the Cahokia Mounds complex, then it is quite reasonable for Wang Ming to walk from the docked boat in the neighbourhood of the confluence of the Mississippi River and the

175
175

Missouri River to Cahokia in no more than a little over 30 km/19 mi as shown in Fig. 26 (the distance is actually about 18 km/11 mi). This finding is fully in line with the actual geographical environment near the Cahokia Mounds complex. Later in Chapters 6 and 7, I shall go through multiple lines of evidence to show that the Cahokia Mounds complex was *indeed* Luo Maodeng's Fengdu in North America.

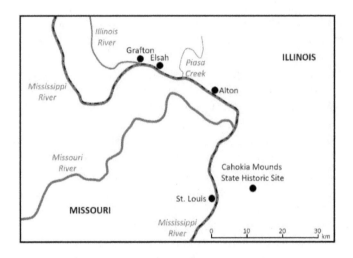

Fig. 26 Area surrounding today's St. Louis

The Chinese sailing experts would have been able to draw on thousands of years of celestial navigation to find their way in an open, stormy ocean. The treasure fleet's unexpected collision with a steep cliff certainly would not have deterred these brave, skilful and determined mariners, let alone prevent them from sailing in rivers and lakes! Indeed, the Ming Treasure Fleet had arrived at the Mississippi River bank in late November 1433, nearly sixty years before Christopher Columbus reached America in 1492 and over a hundred years before Hernando de Soto led the first European expedition to cross the Mississippi River in 1541.

**1. The Yongle Emperor (reigned 1402-1424) who sent Admiral Zheng
He on the first six of his seven voyages.**

Plate 1　　　177

2. Da Ming Hung Yi Tu (Amalgamated Map of the Great Ming Empire) painted AD 1389.

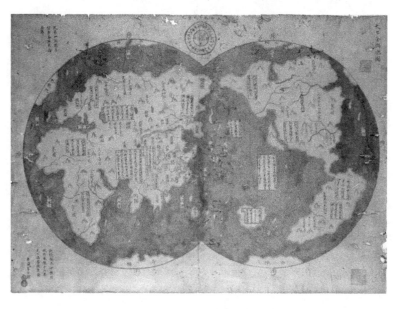

3. The 1418 Chinese World Map.

Plate 2   178

4. Seventeenth Century Japanese copy of Matteo Ricci's 1602 Kunyu Wanguo Quantu or Complete Geographical Map of All the Kingdoms of the World.

Plate 3

**5. Giraffe, variously said to have been brought to China
by Zheng He's treasure fleet or as tribute by Bengali envoys.**

Plate 4   180

**6. Detail of North and Central America
on Matteo Ricci's 1602 map.
The Mississippi River and its tributaries,
other than the Missouri River, are outlined.**

**7. East coast of Canada on the Japanese copy of Ricci's 1602 map.
Cape Breton Island (framed) is shown as two separate islands.**

Plate 5   181

8. Wax statue of Zheng He in the Quanzhou Maritime Museum.

Plate 6

9. Statue of the young Zheng He with his father. Zheng He Park, Moon Mountain (Yue Shan), Kunyang. By Vmenkov.

10. Statue of Zheng He at the Stadthuys Museum in Malacca. By Michel A. Van Hove.

11. Memorial cenotaph of Zheng He in Nanjing, built to commemorate the 580th anniversary of his voyages. By Peter Pang.

Plate 7   183

12. A temple in Vietnam, built to venerate Zheng He.

13. Sheng-Wei Wang by the Zheng He statue inaugurated during the International Zheng He Conference held in Kuala Lumpur and Malacca, Malaysia in November 2018.

Plate 8

PART TWO

The Ming mariners explored the central Mississippi Valley: Evidence

185

The Last Journey of the San Bao Eunuch

CHAPTER SIX

Wang Ming encounters his ex-wife in Fengdu and explores the city

Luo Maodeng describes how Wang Ming encountered his ex-wife (or wife presumed dead ten years earlier) Liu Shi. Their unexpected reunion in Fengdu, North America, gave Wang Ming the opportunity to explore the city which is named the country of Fengdu in Luo's novel. By analysing Luo's narrative, multiple lines of evidence are discovered, which expose Fengdu's true identity— Cahokia—today's Cahokia Mounds State Historic Site in the central Mississippi Valley. The emotional conversation between Wang Ming and Liu Shi further reveals that the Chinese mariners had explored the same neighbourhood in 1423 during their sixth voyage to the Western Ocean.

Earlier in Chapter 3, I successfully extracted the navigational routes and timelines of Zheng He's main fleet from Nanjing to Mecca, based on analysing Luo Maodeng's narrative and ancient Chinese records. Then in Chapter 4, I successfully teased out the navigational routes and timelines of Zheng He's main fleet from Mecca to the North American coast based again on analysing Luo Maodeng's narrative and modern knowledge of ocean currents and weather conditions. Later, in Chapter 5, I addressed the initial landing site of Zheng He's fleet in the North Atlantic coastal region. These three chapters are extremely important in setting the stage for properly interpreting Luo's narrative on Wang Ming's adventures in the country of Fengdu to be discussed in this chapter. Had Louise Levathes had this knowledge when she investigated Zheng He's navigational routes and timelines, she would have logically realised that Zheng He's fleet had landed in North America during the seventh voyage. Then, it would have been very unlikely for her to propose that after leaving Mecca and heading on a southwesterly course, Zheng He's fleet experienced a journey in the "netherworld". Levathes' viewpoint exposed a contradiction, namely, that there was a "netherworld", Fengdu, in the "real world", North America.

In Chapter 5, I also pointed out that the part of North America's eastern coast that includes the Gulf of St. Lawrence is the only water route from the Atlantic Ocean to the Great Lakes. Until the nineteenth century, water transportation was often the fastest way to travel through North America. Thus, it is very likely that Zheng He's main fleet could have explored this route to reach the American heartland with the help of Native Americans, but the Chinese mariners had to pass two short land portages connecting different sections of the water route. In the same chapter, I also gave the timelines for Zheng He's crew to proceed on their journey, up to the time when Zheng He's scout, Wang Ming, arrived at the country of Fengdu in late autumn of 1433.

In this chapter, I shall list and translate some of Luo Maodeng's narrative in his Chapter 87 to share with both English and Chinese readers. I shall revise and enhance some of the viewpoints expressed in the earlier Chinese book Zheng He Fa Xian Mei Zhou Zhi Xin Je 《郑和发现美洲之新解》 or *New Evidence for Zheng He's Exploration of the Americas*, jointly published by Mark Nickless, Laurie Bonner-Nickless and the present author Sheng-Wei Wang (马克·尼克莱斯, 劳丽·邦纳尼克莱斯, 王胜炜) in 2015. This Chinese book represents a preliminary study of Zheng He's seventh and last voyage to North America and has received positive responses from readers. [329] But further insightful studies are definitely needed in order not only to work out the complete navigational routes and timelines of the different squadrons during Zheng He's seventh voyage, but also to offer a fresh look at the multiple lines of evidence I gathered, to present a comprehensive understanding of China's pre-Columbus exploration of America. With this in mind, I am including the many new insights and discoveries I have accumulated over the past several years into this new English book.

In particular, in this chapter, my aim is to reconfirm that Luo Maodeng's country of Fengdu in North America was *indeed* Cahokia—today's Cahokia Mounds State Historic Site—in the central Mississippi Valley, as initially suggested in the above-mentioned Chinese book. [330]

Luo's Chapter 87 is entitled (transl. Sheng-Wei Wang), "The treasure fleet arrived at the shores of Fengdu; Wang Ming encountered his ex- or presumed-dead wife" ("宝船撞进酆都国 王明遇着前生妻"). This chapter describes the emotional scene of how Wang Ming encountered his ex-wife (or presumed-dead wife) and how Wang Ming was overwhelmed with what he saw, because she had been missing for about ten years in the strange foreign land of Fengdu.

I shall start by discussing Luo Maodeng's general writing background for Chapter 87.

(1) Luo Maodeng borrowed the writing style from *Journey to the West*

Luo Maodeng introduced the country of Fengdu to his Chinese readers in his 1597 novel. Actually, there is a city called Fengdu, in China. To avoid confusion, we must have some understanding of this Chinese city and distinguish it clearly from the country of Fengdu in North America, which is mentioned in Luo's novel.

As already said, the Fengdu in China[331] is a real city and it is not the city state Fengdu presented in Luo Maodeng's novel. This will become clear later in this chapter. The Fengdu in China is located on the Ming Mountain or Fengdu Ming Mountain in Fengdu County of the present Chongqing Municipality in mid-west China. The city was established in the Eastern Han Dynasty (25–220 AD) and has almost 2000 years of history. It consists of a large complex of shrines, temples and monasteries built with concepts related to Chinese mythology and Buddhism that signify the netherworld or hell. Over a long period of time, a Chinese legend has developed around this historical, cultural and touristic place, in which it is projected to be a ghost town ruled by Yama, King of Hell, and the destination of the dead. Luo Maodeng in his novel has skilfully used the name and the image in Chinese legend imposed on the real Fengdu City in China to obscure the true identity of the Fengdu which Wang Ming encountered after Zheng He's main fleet landed near the North Atlantic coastal region. However, a careful reading shows that Luo's novel also explicitly reveals through Wang Ming's conversation with his ex-wife (or wife presumed-dead ten years earlier) Liu Shi (刘氏),[332] when they were unexpectedly reunited at Fengdu, that the Fengdu Wang Ming encountered was a different city from the Chinese Fengdu in Chongqing. This will soon become very clear in this chapter.

Notice that my analysis in the previous chapters has already led me to conclude that in November 1433 Zheng He's scout Wang

Ming encountered a densely populated city, Fengdu, located in North America. Then, no matter what name Luo gave to this city, what image he was trying to project, and for whatever purpose he tried to conceal the truth behind a veil of fiction, there is no doubt that Fengdu City or the country of Fengdu in North America was a "real" city in the "real" world, not a ghost town in Chinese legend. Hence, my task is to show what this Fengdu in North America did represent. If the true identity of Fengdu in Luo's novel can be determined, it would be much easier to find out what might have happened to Zheng He's crew after they arrived in North America.

I can see that on the one hand, Luo has deliberately obscured the true identity of Fengdu in North America, but on the other hand, he has also consistently and strategically presented his narrative about Fengdu as real-life scenes, but taking place as if they were events in the netherworld, including the names for some protagonists in Chapter 87 and in his later chapters. For example, one of the three protagonists, Cui Jue (崔珏), is a character in the famous Chinese classical mythical novel Xi You Ji《西游记》or *Journey to the West*,[333] written by Wu Chengen (吴承恩; 1506–1582) in the mid-sixteenth century of the Ming Dynasty. In the novel Cui Jue was a judge whose official rank was lower only than that of Yama (shown in Fig. 27), King of Hell, in the court of Yama. Cui Jue was responsible for handling trials for the ghosts who came to register themselves in the netherworld. The other two protagonists are Wang Ming and his ex-wife Liu Shi. Cui Jue, an aboriginal American, was Liu Shi's new husband in Fengdu.

Lu Xun (鲁迅; 1881–1936),[334] a leading figure of modern Chinese literature, once commented on Luo Maodeng's San Bao Tai Jian Xi Yang Gi《三宝太监西洋记》or *An Account of the Western World Voyage of the San Bao Eunuch*. Lu said that Luo's novel imitated some of the writing style from *Journey to the West*. Clearly, the use of the name Cui Jue and his title as a court judge in the netherworld are all borrowed from Xi You Ji《西游记》or *Journey to the West*.

So, how and why did Luo Maodeng want to hide under the veil of a Chinese ghost city the true identity of the city Wang Ming arrived at? How can it be explained? After reading through my analysis in Chapters 6 and 7, readers will hopefully come to a better understanding of Luo's motives. Now, in order to proceed with my analysis, my focus on Luo's narrative will shift from the treasure fleet's wide range of activities to Wang Ming's personal experiences in this strange Fengdu.

Fig. 27 Yama, King of Hell

(2) Wang Ming arrived at the strange Fengdu

At the very beginning of Chapter 87, Luo wrote:

。。。却说王明行了三五里路，前面是一座城郭，郭外都是民居，又尽稠密。。。

My translation of the above passage is as follows:

…Wang Ming then walked for another three to five *li*, and saw ahead a city with an outer wall. Outside the wall were closely packed residential dwellings. …

To make a direct connection between Luo's narrative about Fengdu and the previously mentioned Cahokia Mounds complex, we must first review a computer-generated sketch of the Cahokia Mounds complex in Fig. 28, which is based on one of the paintings produced by William R. Iseminger[335] after some simplifications. The painting

183　　　　　　191

is what an artist decided that Cahokia might have looked like during the time of the city's apex.[336]

I reiterate that in this book, when I use "Cahokia", "Cahokia Mounds complex", or "Cahokia Mounds City", they all refer to today's "Cahokia Mounds State Historic Site".

The main part of the Cahokia Mounds complex is the wall-enclosed "downtown" Cahokia, as referred to by archaeologists doing work there.

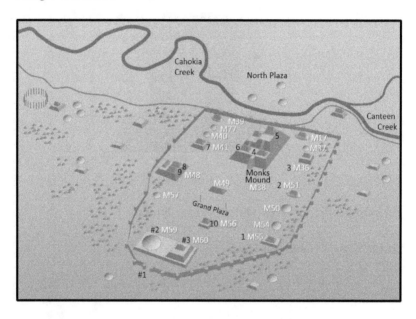

Fig. 28 Site map of the Cahokia Mounds complex. All the mounds in "downtown" Cahokia are labelled. The numbers 1–10 and #1–#3 are explained in Section (6) of this chapter

Over the years, archaeologists have identified more than 100 mounds in the Cahokia Mounds City, and many names and numbering systems have been applied to the Cahokia mounds. In this book, the numbering system is based on the work developed by John J. R. Patrick, who produced the first accurate and detailed map of Cahokia in 1876 (Fowler 11). Many of the mounds are outside downtown Cahokia. The eighteen mounds in downtown Cahokia are:

▪️und 38 (Monks Mound). It received its name from the group ￮st[337] monks who lived on nearby Mound 48; it is the

184   192

largest mound and a tiered platform mound (a platform mound is a four-sided truncated pyramid), which has multiple terraces. It is also the only mound with more than two terraces at the Cahokia site and indeed throughout much of eastern North America; Mound 38 is indicated by positions 4, 5 and 6; 2) Mound 56 (Jesse Ramey Mound) at position 10, a tiered platform mound; 3) Mound 55 (Murdock Mound) at position 1, also a tiered platform mound;[338] 4) Mound 54, a small conical mound (cone or oval-shaped mound) adjacent to Mound 55; 5) Mound 50, a small conical mound adjacent to Mound 51; 6) Mound 51 (Persimmon Mound) at position 2, an oval-shaped platform mound; 7) Mound 36 at position 3, a platform mound; 8) Mound 37, a small conical mound connected to the northwest corner of Mound 36; 9) Mound 17, near the northeast corner of Monks Mound; an oval-shaped platform mound with its major axis east-west (Fowler 72); 10) Mound 39 (Sawmill Mound), a small, rounded mound; originally it was probably a rectangular platform mound; 11) Mound 77, a small conical mound; 12) Mound 40, a small conical mound; 13) Mound 41 at position 7, directly west of the south half of the Monks Mound, a platform mound; 14) Mound 48 (the second largest mound) at positions 8 and 9, almost a square platform mound (112 m/367 ft north-south by 111 m/364 ft east-west); 15) Mound 57, at about 100 m/328 ft south of Mound 48, a relatively round or conical mound; 16) Mound 49 (Red Mound), very near the geometric centre of the plaza, might be a marker mound used for the layout of the community, a ridgetop mound; 17) Mound 59 (Round Top Mound), a classical conical mound at position #2; and 18) Mound 60 (Fox Mound), a classical platform mound at position #3. Mound 59 and Mound 60 are the two largest mounds in terms of height, about 12 m/40 ft, after Monks Mound. The Grand Plaza[339] (a ceremonial plaza that served as the central focus of the community) is in the centre area of downtown Cahokia. According to the archaeological findings presented by Melvin L. Fowler, among the above eighteen mounds, ten of them are regular platform or oval-shaped platform mounds; the ten mounds are 55, 51, 36, 17, 38, 39, 41, 48, 56 and 60 (counterclockwise starting from Mound 55).

Also, in Fig. 28, on top of each platform mound there is at least one palace-temple. For example, Mound 38 has four, of which three are large and one is small; Mound 48 has three; the other platform mounds all have one palace-temple each. These palace-temples are shown symbolically as small and brown-coloured house-like structures on top of the platform mounds.[340] Based on Fig. 28, there are altogether twelve palace-temples (1 + 1 + 1 + 4 + 1 + 3 + 1) at positions 1 to 10, on top of the seven *major* platform mounds inside downtown Cahokia. I shall mention these palace-temples again in Section (6) of this chapter.

Cahokia was a city of massive earthen structures. These mounds were built in a wide range of sizes and shapes, and served different functions.[341] The Cahokia Mounds State Historic Site is directly across the Mississippi River from modern St. Louis, Missouri. It is the largest pre-Columbian settlement north of Mexico. Besides the mounds, the snaking line at the top of Fig. 28 is the Cahokia Creek, which is inside the city, but outside downtown Cahokia. The downtown area was surrounded by a low wall (palisade) made of wood and then plastered over with clay, and there were several gates in this wall to facilitate entry for the populace.[342] According to Luo, Wang Ming saw a city with an outer wall. But the wall in Fig. 28 is a wall inside the city. It is not the outer wall of the city Wang Ming saw initially.

Did Fengdu in Luo's novel also have a river inside the city? Did Fengdu also have the same kind of low wall like the one enclosing downtown Cahokia? These questions will soon be answered.

However, we can at least be sure that *both Fengdu and Cahokia were densely populated cities* at that time. According to records, Cahokia was a city that, at its peak, from 1050 to 1200, was larger than many European cities, including London. The city was spread out over 6 sq mi /16 sq km and had a population of 6,000 to 40,000 people at its peak.[343] So, Luo's description of *Fengdu's dense population is consistent with the situation of Cahokia in those days.*

Then, after entering into the city of Fengdu, Wang Ming saw people who all looked somewhat strange and this made him fearful. These people were aboriginal Americans. They wore horned headdresses like the heads of oxen or horses. They had hairstyles that stood erect like horses' manes. They carried live snakes in their mouths. They had prominent noses like a hawk's beak and coloured their faces. They had fangs or prominent teeth (马克·尼克 莱斯等 122–124). Here, Luo's description of *Fengdu's people begins to show Cahokia's Native American flavour.*

The Last Journey of the San Bao Eunuch

(3) By chance, Wang Ming met his ex-wife in Fengdu

After seeing these strange people in the city, what happened next is the most emotional scene in Luo's novel:

。。。王明看见这些古怪形状，心下就有些害怕哩。大凡人的手脚，都管于一心，心上有些害惶，手就有些酸，脚就有些软。王明心上害怕，不知不觉，就像脚底下绊着甚么，跌一毂碌，连忙的爬将起来，把一身的衣服都跌污了。王明跌污了这一身衣服，生怕起人之疑，找到城河里面去洗这污衣服。就是天缘凑巧，惹出许多的事来。怎么天缘凑巧，却又惹许多的事来？王明在这边河里洗衣服，可可的对面河边，也有一个妇人在那里洗衣服。。。

My translation of the above passage is as follows:

. . . Upon seeing these odd people, Wang Ming's heart felt a bit afraid. Since people's hands and legs are generally controlled by their hearts, when the heart feels afraid and becomes anxious, the arms would then feel sore, and the legs weak. Wang Ming was afraid. Unaware of what was going on, and as if his feet stumbled over something, he suddenly fell down to the floor. After he hurriedly scrambled back onto his feet, his clothing was all covered with dirt from the fall. Wang Ming's fall had soiled all his clothing. For fear of other people's suspicions, he found the city river and went there to wash his dirty clothes. It was this lucky coincidence that stirred up a lot of events—"how", you ask? Wang Ming was washing his clothes on this side of the river, while there was also a woman washing clothes on the opposite side of the river. ...

The above passage clearly indicates that Wang Ming entered into the city (Fengdu was actually a city state in Luo's novel), and that the *Fengdu in North America was like Cahokia, also having a river inside the city.*

187

。。。王明看着那个妇人，那个妇人也看着王明。王明心里有些认得那个妇人，那个妇人心里也有些认得王明。你看我一会，我看你一会。王明心里想道："这妇人好像我亡故的妻室。"那妇人心里想道："这汉子好像我生前的丈夫。"。。。

My translation of the above passage is as follows:

. . . Wang Ming looked at that woman, that woman also looked at Wang Ming. In Wang Ming's heart he could somehow tell that he recognised that woman, and in that woman's heart somehow, she could also tell that she recognised Wang Ming. They kept looking at each other on and off for a while. In Wang Ming's heart, he thought, "This woman looks like my deceased wife." In that woman's heart she thought, "This man looks like my ex-husband before I was almost sentenced to death." . . .

After looking at each other for a moment, it was Wang Ming who spoke first.

。。。王明道："我是大明国征西大元帅麾下一个下海的军士，姓王，名字叫做王明。为因机密军情，才然到此。"那妇人道："你原来就王克新么？"。。。王明道："。。。家中父亲早年亡故，母亲在堂，还有兄弟王德侍奉。有妻刘氏，十年前因病身亡。为因官身下海，并不曾继娶，并不曾生下子嗣。"。。。那妇人却晓得是他的丈夫，心如刀割，两泪双流，带着眼泪说道："你从上面浮桥上过来，我有话和你讲哩！"王明走过去，那妇人一把扯着王明，大哭一场，说道："冤家！我就是你十年前因病身亡的刘氏妻室。"王明听见说道是他的刘氏妻室，越发荡了主意，好说不是，眼看见是，口说又是；好说是，十年前身死之人，怎么又在？半惊半爱，说道："你既是我妻刘氏，你已经死了十数年，怎么还在？怎么又在这里相逢我哩？你一向还在何处躲着么？"刘氏说道："街市上说话不便，不如到我家里去，我细细的告诉你一番。"

My translation of the above passage is as follows:

. . . Wang Ming said, "I am a sergeant going to sea for expeditionary voyages under the command of the Great Admiral Zheng He of the Ming Dynasty. My surname is Wang, and my full name is Wang Ming. I came here to gather information." The woman asked, "Was your original name Wang Kexin?" . . . Wang Ming answered, ". . . My father passed away in early years, my mother stayed at home, and my brother Wang De took care of her. I had a wife who died of illness a decade earlier. Due to my official duties at sea, I have not remarried and do not have any child." . . . But this woman already knew that he was her husband and felt as if a knife was piercing her heart. She was in tears and said, "You come over the pontoon bridge and I have something to tell you!" Wang Ming walked over. The woman pulled Wang Ming to her, broke into tears again and said, "Dear! I am your wife Liu Shi whom you thought died of illness ten years ago." The more Wang Ming heard that she was his wife Liu Shi, the more he lost his mind. If she was not his wife, he had her right in front of his eyes. If she was his wife, how could a person who died ten years ago reappear again? With half shock and half love, he asked, "You are certainly my wife Liu Shi, but since you died over ten years ago, how could you have returned again? How could you still meet me here? Where have you been hiding all this time?" Liu Shi replied, "It is not suitable to talk in the street. It is better to go to my house. I will tell you all the details."

The above passage describes how Wang Ming encountered his ex-wife (or presumed-dead wife) Liu Shi and found that she was still alive. They recognised each other and had an unexpected reunion in Fengdu. Both of them were very excited and deeply emotional. Originally Wang Ming thought that Liu Shi was missing and had died ten years earlier due to illness. Since Wang Ming arrived at Fengdu in the late fall of 1433 (in November of 1433 in the Gregorian calendar), we can deduce that Liu Shi was assumed to have died *in November 1423*, approximately ten years earlier.

转一弯，抹一角，进了一个八字门楼三间横敞，青砖白缝，雅淡清幽。进了第二层，却是三间敞厅，。。。

My translation of the above passage is as follows:

After making a turn and walking around a corner, they entered into a house with a roof over its entrance gate. This was a storied house with a sharply peaked roof. On the ground floor there were three spacious rooms separated by walls. The walls were built of bricks with white seams, while the rooms looked simple, tasteful and quietly elegant. Upon entering the second floor, there were three spacious halls with wide-open entrances...

Liu Shi led Wang Ming back to her house after making a turn and walking around a corner. "八字门楼" is a gate tower (门楼), with a roof shaped like the Chinese character, " 八 ". The unearthed Mississippian houses (including those in Cahokia) also had sharply-pointed thatched roofs and made of straw. A painting by Michael Hampshire shows Cahokia as it may have appeared around 1150 AD.[344] The walls of these houses were usually plastered with white mud and straw daub (马克·尼克莱斯等 126). But with time, the colour could gradually become darker. Then the appearance of these walls viewed from a distance could look like "bricks" with white seams (there were wall areas which did not become darker and still showed the original white colour) as Luo's narrative describes them. Luo's description tells us that *the houses in Fengdu in North America and Cahokia had a similar style in its appearance of roof and walls.*

(4) The Ming sailors also explored Fengdu in 1423 during their sixth voyage

Luo's previous passages have already provided strong multiple lines of evidence to show that the Fengdu in North America had a different identity from the legendary ghost town Fengdu in China. In this section, I show that Wang Ming sadly discovered that Liu Shi was forced to marry Judge Cui Jue in Fengdu, the second man after Yama, in order to escape death.

190

。。。王明道："你这是哪里？"刘氏道："你不要忙，我从头告诉你。我自从那年十月十三日得病身故，勾死鬼把我解到阴曹，共有四十二名。灵曜殿上阎罗王不曾坐殿，先到判官面前，把簿书来登名对姓。"王明吃慌说道："你说甚么阎罗王？说甚么判官？终不然你这里是阴么？"刘氏道："你不要慌，我再告诉你。那判官就叫做崔珏，他登了名，对了姓，解上阎罗王面前。一个个的唱名而过，止唱了四十一名。阎罗王道：'原批上是四十二名，怎么今日过堂只是四十一名？'崔判官说道：'内中有一个是错勾来的，小臣要带他出去，放他还魂。'阎罗王说道：'此举甚善，免使冤魂又来缠扰，你快去放他还魂。'崔判官诺诺连声，带我下来。来到家里，我说道：'你放我还魂去吧。'判官道：'你本是四十二个一批上的人。我见你天姿国色，美丽非凡，我正少一个洞房妻室。我和你结个鸾凤之交罢了。'我说道：'你方才在阎罗王面前说道放我还魂，怎么这如今强为秦晋？这是何道理？'崔判官说道：'方才还魂的话，是在众人面前和你遮羞，你岂可就认做真话！'我又说道：'你做官的人，这等言而无信。'崔判官说道：'甚么有信无信，一朝权在手，便把令来行。你若违拗之时，我又送你上去就是。'我再三推却，没奈何，只得和他做了夫妇。"

My translation of the above passage is as follows and my comments are in square brackets:

. . . Wang Ming asked, "Where are we now?" Liu Shi replied, "Do not rush, I will tell you everything from the beginning. I was taken away while I was ill on October thirteenth that year and I was at death's door. I was then sent by a Gou Si Gui [devil ghost; a local guard] to a court in the netherworld [the palace court of Cahokia]. A total of 42 prisoners on death row were waiting there. Yama, the King of Hell, was not at his seat yet in the Ling Yao Palace [Ling Yao means 'the sun']. I had first to appear in front of the judge to register my first and last name in the book." Wang Ming was shocked to hear this and frantically asked, "Whom did you mention, Yama? What judge? Is your place here in the realm of the dead?" Liu Shi replied, "Do not panic, I will tell you more. The judge's name is Cui Jue. He recorded my first name, verified my last name, and then took me before Yama. Cui Jue chanted our names one by one stopping after finishing the 41st name. Yama then said, 'The original batch had 42 names, how come today only 41 are arraigned?' Judge Cui replied, 'One of them was taken by mistake. I will take her out and let her be freed.' Yama said, 'This act is good. It can avoid the ghost of the wronged coming back to appeal again. You can quickly take her out and free her.' Judge Cui obediently and repeatedly said 'yes', and took me out. Upon arriving at his home, I told him, 'Please, let me be freed.' Judge Cui said, 'You were originally one among the 42 [to be sacrificed]. I saw you heavenly beautiful, so unusual, and I am just short of a wife. You and I should be united as man and wife.' I argued back, 'You just said in front of Yama that you will let me be freed; how is it that now you are forcing me into marriage with you? What reason do you have?' Judge Cui responded, 'What was said then to the public was to give an excuse in front of people to save your life, how can you take it as the truth?' I asked again, 'As an official, how can you fail to be faithful?' Judge Cui said, 'What is faithful or faithless? Once having power, I give the orders. If you disobey me, I will take you back there.' I declined over and over. I had no alternative but to be married with him as man and wife."

In Chinese legend, Gou Si Gui (勾死鬼) is the ghost whose task is to take away the human soul and take it to the netherworld. The Chinese term 鸾凤 (鸾 luan is a mythical male bird related to the phoenix; 凤 feng is the female phoenix) means "male and female phoenix"; and 鸾凤之交 describes "a happy married relationship between husband and wife, or a good relationship between the two families as relatives". In the above passage, it means to "get married as husband and wife".

Luo's long paragraph reveals at least the following important information:

First, Wang Ming confirmed that his presumed-dead spouse Liu Shi was in fact still alive. Liu Shi confirmed that Wang Ming was her husband before she was taken captive due to illness in a raid.

Second, in traditional Chinese culture, Yama dominated Fengdu, the netherworld. Where he lived was called the Ling Yao Palace

192

(these points will be discussed in detail later). Ling Yao is the "sun". Similarly, Cahokia was a civilisation with a defined social structure which was ruled by a chief; he lived at the Monks Mound (today's name)[345] inside the walled downtown Cahokia. This head of the Cahokians, the so-called Great Sun Chief, was the one who ruled the earth and spoke to the sky, and his counsellors were members of the élite class composed of priests and chieftains.[346] So, Luo's description confirms that the *Fengdu in North America was like Cahokia, in having a supreme leader; Fengdu's king of hell, Yama, lived at a palace named the Ling Yao Palace, the Great Sun Chief of Cahokia lived at the Monks Mound.*

Third, Liu Shi was forced to marry Judge Cui Jue in order to escape death. Cui Jue in *Journey to the West* and in Luo Maodeng's novel was a court judge ranking after Yama. He had the authority of determining the life or death of people who were sent to the court. Similarly, in Cahokia, the ancient natives in North America, who were not the Maya or Aztecs of Central America, but had a culture that arose in the Mississippi Valley in what is now Illinois, also practiced human sacrifice[347] (often using prisoners to feed gods).

Fourth, the details of Liu Shi's disappearance reveal a very important historical event, namely: Chinese mariners also reached the Fengdu area on *October 13 in the 21st year of the Yongle period (in November 1423),* during the treasure fleet's sixth voyage to the Western Ocean, and they faced local resistance. This date was approximately ten years before the reunion of Wang Ming and Liu Shi in late November 1433. Hence, the earliest time for the Chinese mariners to return to China after they completed the sixth voyage would most likely be in 1424. This finding not only lends support to Gavin Menzies' previous claim that the Ming Treasure Fleet visited the Americas in the 1420s, but also explains why Yun Gu thought that Tang Zhuangyuan was not unfamiliar with Fengdu and actually went into a ghost country, as described in Section (2), Chapter 4, of this book. Later, my analysis in Chapter 9, based on ancient maps, will reveal circumstantial evidence in support of Luo's revelation.

(5) Luo's Fengdu Ghost Country was not the legendary ghost city Fengdu in China

The conversation between Wang Ming and Liu Shi continued:

193

王明道："你这里却不是个阴司？"刘氏道："不是阴司，终不然
还是阳世？"王明道："既是阴司，可有个名字？"刘氏道："我
这里叫做酆都鬼国。王明道："可就是酆都山么？"刘氏道："这
叫做酆都鬼国。酆都山还在正西上，有千里之遥，人到了酆都
山去，永世不得翻身。那是个极苦的世界，我这里还好些。"王
明道："你这里可有个甚么衙门么？"刘氏道："。。。鬼国
就是十帝阎君是王，其余的都是分司。"。。。

My translation of the above passage is as follows:

Wang Ming asked, "Isn't your place *yin si*, the netherworld?"
Liu Shi replied, "If this place is not the netherworld, isn't it the
world of the living?" Wang Ming asked, "Since it is the
netherworld, does it have a name?" Liu Shi replied, "My place
here is called the Fengdu Ghost Country." Wang Ming asked,
"But is it the Fengdu Mountain?" Liu Shi replied, "Here is the
Fengdu Ghost Country. The Fengdu Mountain is due west, a
thousand *li* away. People who go to the Fengdu Mountain
have no chance to be revived again. It is a very bitter world
there. My place here is all right." Wang Ming asked, "Do you
have a government office here?" Liu Shi replied, "...In this
ghost country, there are ten kings in charge of the
netherworld. Yama is the Emperor, others are subordinate to
him." ...

When Wang Ming heard Liu Shi mentioning "Yama" and the
"judge", he was struck with panic and immediately asked (transl.
Sheng-Wei Wang), "Isn't your place *yin si*, the netherworld?" In
Section (1) of this chapter, I point out that Luo has imitated the
writing style of *Journey to the West*. On the one hand, he has
deliberately obscured the true identity of Fengdu in North America;
but on the other hand, he has also consistently and strategically
presented his narrative set in Fengdu as real-life scenes that took
place as if they were events in the netherworld, including but not
limited to the names he borrowed from *Journey to the West*. These
can cause confusion. Hence, we should not be surprised at Luo's use
of "*yin si*", the netherworld, or the Fengdu Ghost Country, in the
above paragraphs.

But do we know where the Fengdu Mountain was located?

In the Chinese legend, the Fengdu [Ming,—Ed.] Mountain was located in the Fengdu County of the present Chongqing Municipality in mid-west China. It was the mountain where the ghosts and the Fengdu Emperor (Yama) resided (transl. Sheng-Wei Wang; 酆都大帝居住在酆都山),[348] hence it was a bitter world. Naturally, the ghosts who lived at the Fengdu Mountain had no chance to be revived again (to live again); whereas Liu Shi lived a normal life, in the world of the living, with her new husband. Not surprisingly, she said (transl. Sheng-Wei Wang), "My place here is all right." Besides, the Fengdu Mountain was approximately due west to the Cahokia Mounds complex; it was tens of thousands *li* away, as can be seen from today's map.

Here, Luo Maodeng's narrative *explicitly* reveals that *the legendary ghost city Fengdu in China was a very distant and different place from the Fengdu Ghost Country in his novel.* But in reality, the two places are approximately 12,168 km/24,336 *li*/7,561 mi[349] apart, not only a thousand *li* away! Luo underestimated the distance.

Next, concerning the city state of Fengdu in North America, Liu Shi's reply revealed that in the ghost country where she lived, there were ten kings in charge of the government; Yama was the Emperor, and others were subordinate to him. In the Chinese legend, the historical Fengdu's supreme ruler was Yama, and he was in charge of the administration of the ten palace-temples in the netherworld, each had its own lord. Similarly, Cahokia also had a supreme ruler called the Great Sun Chief, or the Birdman[350] of Mississippi society, who ruled the earth and spoke to the sky. The Great Sun Chief was responsible for the administration of the ten major ceremonial palaces (mounds) in downtown Cahokia. *Fengdu in North America and Cahokia each had a ruler with supreme power under an organised ruling system.*

As soon as Wang Ming and Liu Shi finished talking, and while Wang Ming was planning to leave and to report to his commander-in-chief, Judge Cui arrived back home. Liu Shi introduced Wang Ming as her brother and explained to her present husband that Wang Ming had been accompanying Admiral Zheng He on the Western voyage. He was sent by the commander-in-chief to explore the country, but strayed into this city. Judge Cui politely greeted Wang Ming and they started a conversation.

195

。。。判官道："。。。请问大舅，你是大明国人，随着甚么征西大元帅来下西洋？"王明道："有两个元帅，一个是三宝太监，叫做郑某；一个兵部尚书，叫做王某。"判官道："还有哪个？"王明道："还有一个江西龙虎山引化真人，号为天师；一个金碧峰长老，号为国师。"判官点一点头，说道："金碧峰就在这里。这等还好。"王明道："大人曾相认金碧峰来？"判官道："虽不相认，我晓得他。共有多少船来？"王明道："宝船千号，战将千员，雄兵百万。"判官道："甚么贵干？"王明道："下西洋抚夷取宝。"判官道："可曾取得有宝么？"王明道："取的宝不是以下之宝，是我中朝历代帝王传国玉玺，并不曾取得。"判官道："怎么走到我这里来了？"王明道："只因不曾取得有宝，务死的向前。故此就来到这里。"

My translation of the above passage is as follows:

. . . The judge asked, ". . . Great brother-in-law, you are from the Great Ming. Are you accompanying some commander-in-chief on an expedition to the Western Ocean?" Wang Ming replied, "There are two commanders-in-chief: one is Eunuch San Bao, his last name is Zheng, the other one is the Minister of the Board of War, his last name is Wang." The judge asked, "Who else?" Wang Ming replied, "There is also a Daoist called Yĭnhua Zhenren from the Dragon Tiger Mountain of the Jiangxi Province, revered as the Celestial Master, and a Buddhist elder Jin Bifeng with the title of Buddhist Master conferred by the emperor." The judge nodded and said, "Jin Bifeng does come here. That is good." Wang Ming asked, "Respected judge, are you acquainted with Jin Bifeng?" The judge replied, "Though not acquainted with him, I have heard about him. How many ships have come?" Wang Ming replied, "There are 1,000 treasure ships, 1,000 military commanders, and 1,000,000 brave soldiers." The judge asked, "What are they coming here for?" Wang Ming replied, "The purpose of the voyage to the Western Ocean is to enlighten the foreigners and recover our missing national treasure." The judge asked, "Have you recovered the treasure?" Wang Ming replied, "The treasure to be recovered is not ordinary. It is the Imperial Seal kept by the ancient Chinese emperors from

196

dynasty to dynasty. It has not been recovered." The judge asked, "How did you manage to come to my place here?" Wang Ming replied, "Because the national treasure has not been recovered, we sailed ahead relentlessly. That is how we arrived here."

At this point, readers may wonder how Judge Cui and Wang Ming could engage in conversation. There is no need to worry about how the two exchanged their ideas, since during the conversation Liu Shi was with them. She could serve as the interpreter.

The judge's question (transl. Sheng-Wei Wang), "Are you accompanying some commander-in-chief on an expedition to the Western Ocean," and the reply (transl. Sheng-Wei Wang), "Though not acquainted with him, I have heard about him," indicate that earlier the judge had either heard about the Ming Treasure Fleet and Jin Bifeng perhaps from his Chinese wife Liu Shi, or the treasure fleet and Jin Bifeng had been in Fengdu during the fleet's previous voyage. All these observations, including Liu Shi being taken away ten years previously by natives, corroborate the finding that the Ming sailors were in Fengdu before their seventh voyage. But Luo's description (transl. Sheng-Wei Wang), "There are 1,000 treasure ships, 1,000 military commanders, and 1,000,000 brave soldiers," is clearly an exaggeration of the size and strength of the Ming Treasure Fleet.

Wang Ming and Judge Cui continued their conversation as follows:

判官道："。。。你前日可曾到天堂极乐国么？"王明道："已经到来。"判官道："天堂国是西海尽头处。我这里叫酆都鬼国，是西天尽头处。。。。"

My translation of the above passage is as follows:

The judge asked, "…Earlier, did you go to the country of paradise?" Wang Ming replied, "I have been there." The judge then said, "The country of paradise is situated at the end of the Western Ocean. My place here is called the Fengdu Ghost Country. It is at the end of the western sky. … "

197

I have shown in Chapter 3 that the country of paradise in Luo's novel was Mecca, which is situated near the end of the Indian Ocean. But Judge Cui lived inland in North America. How did he know of the existence of the far away country of paradise? How did he also know that the country of paradise was at the end of the "Western Ocean"? [He meant the Indian Ocean, since Mecca is situated near the end of the Indian Ocean.—Ed.] There is no better way to explain how Judge Cui could have received such accurate geographical knowledge than from his wife Liu Shi who had been a member of the Ming Treasure Fleet during its sixth voyage which must have navigated from the Indian Ocean to Fengdu in North America. However, when Judge Cui said that Fengdu was at the end of the western sky, we should have no reason to doubt him as to this particular point of geographical knowledge. He lived in Fengdu in North America and all the land directly across the Atlantic Ocean was at the end of Fengdu's eastern sky. Hence, Fengdu was at the end of their (people who lived across the Atlantic Ocean) western sky. Clearly, Luo's narrative reconfirmed that *Luo's Fengdu was like Cahokia, that is land at the end of the western sky, and this land in a broader sense was North America.*

On the next day, Judge Cui led Wang Ming around the city while Liu Shi stayed at home. Some of the details of Luo's account continue to emphasize that Fengdu's civilisation appeared to be identical to that of Cahokia in the early 1400s, including the strange facial appearances of the two guards at the city gate. One of the guards had fangs and his face was coloured green. The face of the other was coloured in stripes of five different colours like colourfully glazed ceramics (马克·尼克莱斯等 135–136).

After walking for a little while, Wang Ming and Judge Cui saw two tall platforms in front of them:

王明跟定了崔判官，走了一会，只见左壁厢有一座高台，四周围都是石头叠起的，约有十丈之高。左右两边两路脚擦步儿，左边的是上路，右边的是下路。台下有无数的人，上去的上，下来的下。上去的也都有些忧心忡忡，下来的着实是两泪汪汪。王明低低的问说道："姐夫，那座台是个甚么台？为甚么有许多的人在那里啼哭？"判官道："大舅，你有所不知，大凡人死之时，头一日，都在当方土地庙里类齐。第二日，解到东岳

庙里，见了天齐仁大帝，挂了号。第三日，才到我这酆都鬼
国。到了这里之时，他心还不死。阎君原有个号令，都许他上
到这个台上，遥望家乡。各人大哭一场，却才死心塌地。以此
这个台，叫做望乡台。"

右壁厢也有一座高台，也是石头叠起的，也有十丈之高，却只
是左一边有一路脚擦步儿，却不见个人在上面走。判官道：
"。。。这个台叫做上天台。。。可上而不可下，故此只一条
路。。。为人在世，能有几个上天的？"。。。

My translation of the above text is as follows and my comments are
in square brackets:

Wang Ming followed Judge Cui firmly. After walking for a little
while, they saw on the left a tall platform with a solid walled
base which had the appearance of a stone façade and the
platform was about ten *zhang* in height. On the left and right
side of the platform, there were narrow footpaths. The left
path was used for going up and the right path for going down.
At the foot of the platform, there were many people. Some
were walking up, others were walking down. Those who
walked up looked somewhat worried and those who walked
down were really brimming with tears. Speaking very softly,
Wang Ming asked, "Brother-in-law, about that tall platform,
what sort of platform is it? Why are so many people weeping
so bitterly there?" The judge replied, "My revered brother-in-
law, here is something you may not know about. Generally,
on the first day after an ordinary person dies, the dead
person's body is kept in the local Land Deity Temple,[351] which
is the temple for the 'lord of the soil and the earth.' On the
second day, the dead person's soul is sent with an escort to
the temple of the god of Mount Tai,[352] to see the supreme lord
for registration. Only on the third day, does the dead person's
soul come to my Fengdu Ghost Country [for the funeral
ceremony], which is the centre of the netherworld. Before the
dead person's soul arrives here, if the soul is still unwilling to
fully pass into the world of the dead, Yama will issue a final
decree to allow the soul to come forward to ascend at that
time onto this tall platform so that the deceased can look at
his distant home village. Then, all the souls weep mightily

while they gather there. For this reason, the platform is called 'the terrace of the last look homeward.'"
On the right there was also a tall platform with a solid, walled, base which had the appearance of a stone façade and the platform was also about ten *zhang* in height. But on the left side there was a narrow foot path, no one was walking on top of it. ... The judge said, "This is the terrace from which the soul can ascend to Paradise. ... They can only go up, not down, therefore there is only one path. ... Living in this world, how many can conduct themselves properly [for their souls] to ascend to Paradise?" ...

Here Luo used the above two passages to explain the funeral culture of Fengdu. Wang Ming and Judge Cui were actually witnessing a funeral ceremony taking place. But before going any further, let us first have some basic understanding of the descriptions in the above passages.

In Section (2) of this chapter, I have explained that downtown Cahokia was surrounded by a low wall. The wall was approximately three metres tall, and was made of wood and then plastered over with clay. The Cahokia Mounds complex when surrounded by these palisades would have given the walls the appearance of stone when viewed from a distance, and matched the walls of the platforms' bases in Fengdu as observed by Wang Ming and Judge Cui.

One *zhang* is about three and one-third metres, so ten *zhang* is more than 30 metres. Luo said that these remarkable platforms were more than 30 m/100 ft high, as high as today's ten-story buildings. The unearthed Cahokia Mounds complex is also very spectacular. The largest mound, the Monks Mound,[353] where the Great Sun Chief of Cahokia lived is, in fact, taller than 30 m/100 ft. It is 291 m/955 ft long, including the access ramp at the southern end, 236 m/775 ft wide,[354] and could support a wooden structure on the summit. It is the largest pre-Columbian earthwork in the Americas and the largest pyramid north of Mexico.[355] The Cahokia mounds were constructed almost entirely of layers of basket-transported soil and clay. In summary, the *Fengdu in North America had platforms which match the height of those in Cahokia and with bases similarly appearing to be made of stone.*

In Fengdu, on the first day after an ordinary person dies, the dead person's body is kept in the local Land Deity Temple which was the temple for the "lord of the soil and the earth." The ancient Chinese used the five elements, metal, wood, water, fire and earth, to compose the physical universe and later used traditional Chinese medicine to explain various physiological and pathological phenomena. Similarly in astronomy, the ancient Chinese combined their visual observation of planet Saturn's colour, a beautiful pale yellow with hints of orange, like the colour of soil or earth, with their theory of the five elements and gave Saturn the Chinese name "土星",[356] meaning the star (星) of soil or earth (土). Bear in mind that the solar system is heliocentric, in which the Earth and planets revolve around the sun.

Then, according to Luo (transl. Sheng-Wei Wang), on the second day, the dead person's soul was sent with an escort to the temple of the god of Mount Tai, which was the temple of the supreme lord in charge of birth, death, illness and old age in the netherworld, before the soul was sent to see the supreme lord, Yama, for registration. Mount Tai is in the east of China; therefore this supreme god is the Master of the East, or the Eastern Great Emperor (东皇太; 东 means "east", 皇太 means "supreme god"), or Tianqi Emperor (天齐帝). All these are the Chinese names for Jupiter (木星), the largest among the planets in the solar system.[357]

Since Wang Ming and Judge Cui were watching a funeral ritual, there is no surprise that, according to Luo (transl. Sheng-Wei Wang), "At the foot of the platform, there were many people. Some were walking up, others were walking down. Those who walked up looked somewhat worried and those who walked down were really brimming with tears", because there must have been many sad or worried family members, relatives, friends of the deceased, as well as on-lookers at the funeral ceremony.

The unearthed Cahokia relics also had several pairs of large mounds, for example: Mound 67[358] is a conical mound (Fowler 137), and Mound 68[359] is a flat-topped platform mound (Fowler 137). Fowler (188) writes as follows in *The Cahokia Atlas, Revised: A Historical Atlas of Cahokia Archaeology, No. 2 (Studies in Archaeology)*, "The association of conical and platform mounds indirectly strengthens the hypothesis that conical mounds are burial mounds," and "In the early historic period of the Southeast, there are eyewitness accounts of the practice of storing human remains in charnel houses.[360] These mortuary warehouses were emptied and the remains of the individuals were burned in mounds at intervals." His hypothesis is that the platform mounds represent the location of charnel structures and the associated conical mounds were the burial mounds. In *Envisioning Cahokia: A Landscape Perspective*, Rinita A. Dalan, *et al.* also write that at Cahokia, conical mounds were paired with platform mounds, reinforcing the traditional notion of conjoined function: the platform mound housed the temple/charnel house of the gods, and the conical mound housed the dead (151). But Fowler also points out that there are small conical mounds which might have served functions other than for burial (188). Later in Chapter 7, Luo's narrative shows that a large conical mound, Mound 59, served functions other than for burial.

Under Fowler's hypothesis, Mound 68 had the character of a funeral home doing preparatory work for the dead (mortuary services), which was related to the planet Saturn just mentioned, and Mound 67 was meant for the burial of the dead (137), which was related to the planet Jupiter. From Judge Cui's explanation of Fengdu's funeral ritual we can understand *the close correlation of Fengdu's funeral ritual with Cahokia's; and Luo's descriptions of Fengdu's funeral ritual are also consistent with the archaeological findings of the Cahokia Mounds City.*

Wang Ming and Judge Cui continued to explore the city and soon came across a pair of large, tall mounds:

走了一会，只望见左右两座高山，一边山上烟飞火爆，烈焰腾空。王明问道："姐夫，那座山怎么这等火发？"判官道："叫做火焰山。为人在世，肚肠冷不念人苦，手冷不还人钱，冷痒风发，不带长性；这一等人见了阎君之后，发到这个火焰山上来烧，烧得他筋酥骨碎，拨尽寒炉一夜灰。"那一边山上刀枪剑戟，布列森森。王明问道："那座山怎么有许多凶器？"判官道："那叫做枪刀山。为人在世，两面三刀，背前面后，暗箭伤人，暗刀杀人，口蜜腹剑，这一等人见了阎君之后，发到这个枪刀山上来，乱刀乱枪，乱砍做一团肉泥。。。。"

My translation of the above text is as follows and my comments are in square brackets:

After walking for a while, they saw on both sides a pair of large, tall mountains [mounds]. From the very top of one of them smoke and flames rose roiling into the air. Wang Ming asked, "My revered brother-in-law, why is this mountain [mound] generating fire?" The judge replied, "It is known as the mountain [mound] of raging fires. Living in this world, we should conduct ourselves properly. Those who are cold and indifferent to the suffering of others, or stingy and unwilling to pay back the money they owe, or are easily agitated and without stable character, are sent to see Yama first. After that, they are taken to this mountain [mound] of roiling fire, where their bodies are exposed to great heat when they are placed there to bake and to burn until their sinews are crisp and bones break, and this is continued until night when the fires of the ovens are allowed to burn to cold ashes." The mountain [mound] on the other side was a ghastly place with knives, lances, swords and halberds. Wang Ming asked, "Why does this other mountain [mound] have so many weapons?" The judge replied, "It is known as the mountain [mound] of lances and knives. Living in this world, those who are two-faced, who hurt or kill people either directly or with 'secret arrows,' or who hide malicious intent under the guise of kindness, are sent here after seeing Yama. And after that they are taken to this mountain [mound], where they are sliced and stabbed into pieces with lances and knives. ..."

The above two passages note that Wang Ming and Judge Cui visited the two mounds in Fengdu, where evil people were punished. On one of the mounds, those who had been cold and indifferent to the suffering of others in life were burned until the fires of the ovens were allowed to burn to cold ashes. On the second mound, those who had been two-faced and had hurt people with "secret arrows" were sliced to pieces with lances and knives (this was the kind of mound, a platform mound, in which preparatory work for the dead was made). Luo's pair of large, tall "mountains" (山) should be interpreted as two "mounds", because mountains are usually a minimum of several hundred metres high, while mounds are only a few tens of metres high. It is also more realistic to burn dead bodies on a mound than on a mountain (unless the mountain has a cave).

203

But the Fengdu in North America did not have a mountain, and as explained by Liu Shi to Wang Ming at the beginning of this section, the Fengdu Mountain was in China, tens of thousands of *li* away. The "mound" description also fits well with Cahokia's environment as a city of mounds, not mountains.

As mentioned earlier, the unearthed Cahokia relics have several pairs of large mounds consisting of a conical mound (for the burial of the dead) in association with a platform mound (for mortuary services). The historical records document that survivor cultures of the Mississippians smoked their dead in a kind of mummification process, involving heat on the top of the mounds (马克·尼克莱斯等 137).

The dialogue between Judge Cui and Wang Ming highlights that *the Fengdu in North America was like Cahokia, being the world of the living: both had similar funeral customs.*

(6) Luo's narrative reveals more of Fengdu's true identity

After Wang Ming and Judge Cui witnessed the funeral practices in Fengdu, they continued to explore the city. Finally, they stood atop a long strip of high ground to watch people coming from and going to the city. This long strip of high ground or mound was approximately three to five *li* (1.5–2.5 km/0.9–1.6 mi) in length. They saw drunkards, the poor, the sick and more. They continued their conversation until they passed the end of the strip. Luo's narrative tells readers that the Fengdu in North America was as real as cities in any other countries where all kinds of people lived. *The Fengdu in North America, like Cahokia, was a "living" city, not a netherworld.*

Then, Wang Ming and the judge were in front of a second gate:

王明抬头一看，前面又是一个总门，门楼上匾额题着"灵曜之府"四个大字。。。。

My translation of the above passage is as follows:

Wang Ming looked up and ahead was another main gate. On the plaque of the gatehouse were written the four characters, "Ling Yao Government Offices." ...

I have explained in Section (4) of this chapter that Ling Yao is the "sun" which is full of light and energy. The Ling Yao Government Offices featured a set of palace-temples. The Ling Yao Palace was Yama's palace where he resided and had his court. The entire complex of the Ling Yao Government Offices had a main gate in the front, which is where Wang Ming and Judge Cui stood. Similarly, in Fig. 28, the walled downtown Cahokia also has a gate at position #1.

As mentioned previously, Yama, known as the King of Hell or King Yan (阎王) or King Yanluo (阎罗王),[361] is a wrathful god, said to judge the dead and preside over the "Hells" and the cycle of death and rebirth to which life in the material world is bound. Yama divides hell into ten courts or ten palace-temples, each with the name of their Lord or King, and each court has a different kind of hell. The phrase "ten Courts of Hell"[362] started from the Tang Dynasty (618–907) when Buddhism blossomed in China. The tenth court is the palace-temple of the King of Wheel Turning, who is in charge of receiving all the ghosts or souls sent from other courts, and gives monthly notification to the King of Qínguang of the first court for registration. There, after separating the good from the evil and categorizing the souls, the ghosts are destined for reincarnation. This is the folk belief in karma, and eliminating vice and exalting virtue was reflected in the "Yama" concept.

Then, Wang Ming and Judge Cui entered through the main gate:

。。。进了总门，却是一带的殿宇峥嵘，朱门高敞，俨然是个王者所居气象。走近前去，一连十层宫殿，一字儿摆着。一层宫殿上一面匾额，一面匾额上一行大字。从右数过左去：第一，秦广王之殿；第二，楚江王之殿；第三，宋帝王之殿；第四，五官王之殿；第五，阎罗王之殿；第六，变成王之殿；第七，泰山王之殿；第八，平等王之殿；第九，都市王之殿；第十，转轮王之殿。王明道："这些殿宇，都是些怎么府里？"判官道："轻些讲来。这正是我们十帝阎君之殿。"王明道："两廊下都是些甚么衙门？"判官道："左一边是赏善行台，右边是罚恶行台。"

My translation of the passage quoted is as follows and my comments are in square brackets:

205

... After entering through the main gate, they saw a tall and steep palace-temple with a wide-open red door resembling a king's residence. When approaching closer, they saw a series of ten palace-temples in a scattered arrangement. Each palace-temple had a plaque on it, inscribed with a line of large characters. Counting from right to left in a counter-clockwise direction, the first was the palace-temple of the King of Qínguang; the second was the palace-temple of the King of Chujiang [River Chu]; the third was the palace-temple of the King of Song [宋]; the fourth was the palace-temple of the King of Five Officials; the fifth was the palace-temple of King Yama; the sixth was the palace-temple of the King of Bian City; the seventh was the palace-temple of the King of Mount Tai; the eighth was the palace-temple of the King of Equality; the ninth was the palace-temple of the King of Urban Areas; and the tenth was the palace-temple of the King of Wheel Turning. Wang Ming asked, "What kind of palace-temples are they?" The judge replied, "This is easy to explain to you. These are the 'ten Courts of Hell' of Yama." Wang Ming asked, "What kind of offices are those on each side of the entrance porch near the gate?" The judge replied, "On the left side is the structure consisting of mansions for rewarding good conduct, and on the right side is the structure consisting of places for penalizing evil conduct."

The above passage indicates that the "Ling Yao Government Offices" had a main gate; upon entering through this main gate from outside, on its left side was a structure consisting of mansions (I shall explain this soon) for rewarding people with good conduct, and on the right side was another structure consisting of places (I shall explain this soon, too) for penalizing people with evil conduct. The "ten Courts of Hell" were palace-temples in scattered distribution inside the main gate behind the two structures I just mentioned. They were not a ten-story palace-temple building at one location.

From the very beginning, Luo artificially gave the North American Fengdu an identity as the netherworld. Hence, he also consistently tried to connect the many palace-temples which Wang Ming saw with the "ten Courts of Hell" of His Highness Yama. He started from right to left in a counter-clockwise direction to identify their positions within the Ling Yao Government Offices. The fifth palace-temple was where Yama had his court and residence. Apart from the palace-temples of Yama and the King of Wheel Turning, Luo provided no further information on the functions of the remaining eight palace-temples. Luo mentioned the individual names and locations of the "ten Courts of Hell" in North American Fengdu only once in his novel. Luo's silence perhaps hints that these palace-temples were not the different kinds of hell described in Buddhism.

As shown earlier in Fig. 28, inside the walled downtown of Cahokia, there are twelve palace-temples on top of the seven major platform mounds (55, 51, 36, 38, 41, 48 and 56, in a counter-clockwise direction), which served as the government offices for the Great Sun Chief. Since the phrase, "ten Courts of Hell", was known during the Tang Dynasty (618–907), long before the existence of the Cahokia Mounds complex (1050–1450), I do not expect that the North American Fengdu described in Luo's novel on the one hand and the downtown Cahokia on the other hand had an exact match in the numbers of their respective palace-temples. Who knows the exact number of mounds and palace-temples in the days of the Chinese visits? These structures might have changed continuously in the long history of a city. But the Great Sun Chief residence and office on top of the Monks Mound (Mound 38), like Yama's, can still be numbered as the fifth in downtown Cahokia. Hence, we know that the "ten Courts of Hell" can closely match the number of palace-temples in Cahokia. And, if we exclude the small palace-temple on the Monks Mound, while including only the two front palace-temples on top of Mound 48, we also have ten palace-temples or offices at positions 1 to 10, to match the "ten Courts of Hell" of His Highness Yama. (See Fig. 28.) Each palace-temple or office was occupied by a Lord of the city to conduct certain functions for the government. More important is that the Great Sun Chief's residence and office was central among all the other offices in Luo's statement and in Cahokia's actual landscape. Melvin L. Fowler first proposed both a north-south and an east-west axis for the Cahokia site, and placed Monks Mound at the crossing point of these two axes. Monks Mound was the biggest mound in downtown Cahokia, showing its prominent position.

Cahokia people called their highest ruler the "big sun". The Great Sun Chief represented the ruler of the Cahokian people, and he was the Birdman. The palace where he worked and lived was on top of the "Monks Mound", as it is known today. Inside the walled downtown Cahokia, there were at least ten major government offices conducting the daily functions of the city of Cahokia. Luo's narrative leads us to conclude that the *North American Fengdu was just like Cahokia. It had a chief, Yama, and this chief had a government and an administrative ruling system, while the chief in Cahokia was the Great Sun Chief or Birdman in charge of the ten major government offices.*

In conclusion, this chapter has listed twelve prominent similarities between the North American Fengdu (the Fengdu in Luo Maodeng's novel) and the Cahokia Mounds complex:

1) Luo's description of Fengdu's dense population is consistent with the situation of Cahokia in those days.
2) Luo's description of Fengdu's people shows Cahokia's Native American flavour.
3) Fengdu was like Cahokia, having a river inside the city.
4) Fengdu and Cahokia had similar styles of houses.
5) Both Fengdu and Cahokia had a supreme leader. The former had a palace named the "Ling Yao Palace"; "Ling Yao" is the "sun". The latter represented Cahokia's Great Sun Chief or the Birdman who had his palace on top of the Monks Mound as it is known today. Fengdu was like Cahokia, with a government and an administrative ruling system.
6) The physical descriptions of Fengdu's "mountains" matched Cahokia's "mounds". Fengdu had tall platforms which matched the height of the mounds in Cahokia and with a similar solid walled base which had the appearance of a stone façade just like Cahokia's.
7) Fengdu was like Cahokia, both being land at the end of the western sky, and this land in the broader sense is the North American continent.
8) Fengdu's funeral ritual matched Cahokia's funeral practices; and Luo's description matches the unearthed relics of the Cahokia Mounds City.
9) Yama's "ten Courts of Hell" matched the Great Sun Chief's ten major government offices.

10) Fengdu, like Cahokia, was a "living" city, not a netherworld.

11) Fengdu's Ling Yao Government Offices were enclosed by low walls just as downtown Cahokia was by palisades.

12) Only Cahokia can match Fengdu geographically, in such a way that Wang Ming and later Zheng He's five generals could reach it without much difficulty by walking or by riding horses (or both) from where their boats were docked. Other than the Cahokia Mounds City, which other city could match Luo's geographical description of Fengdu so closely?

Now Wang Ming and Judge Cui were standing at the gate in front of the Ling Yao Government Offices. On their left side was the structure consisting of mansions for rewarding people with good conduct and on their right side was the structure consisting of places for penalizing people guilty of evil conduct. Behind these two structures were the "ten Courts of Hell." Similarly, as shown in Fig. 28, in front of the walled downtown Cahokia, there is a gate at position #1, and two mounds at positions #2 (Mound 59/Round Top Mound)[363] and position #3 (Mound 60/Fox Mound),[364] respectively. These two mounds are right behind the gate of the walled downtown Cahokia which housed the ten major government offices of the Great Sun Chief. These ten major government offices correspond to the "ten Courts of Hell" of Yama in North American Fengdu. But in Luo's novel, the two mounds are not the burial mound and charnel structure proposed by Melvin L. Fowler. Fowler proposes that these two mounds represent the mortuary precinct for the leaders of Cahokia who lived on the other platform mounds within the palisaded area (195). There has been no professional digging in Mound 59 and Mound 60 (Fowler 122–126). It would be worthwhile to conduct archaeological studies relating to these two mounds, since the mounds have also not been cultivated, and they retain much of their original sizes and forms. In Luo's novel, Mound 59 and Mound 60 serve two very different functions. It is possible that Luo Maodeng set things up in order to achieve certain goals. I shall discuss Luo's narrative in great detail in Chapter 7 of this book and leave it to archaeologists to do future work in examining these two mounds to reveal more information.

Finally, Luo's narrative vividly tells us through the emotional conversation between Wang Ming and Liu Shi that the Chinese sailors not only reached Fengdu/Cahokia in North America during

209   217

their seventh and last voyage to the Western Ocean, but also reached the same area around November 1423 (on October 13 in the 21st year of the Yongle period during their sixth voyage). Hence the "Western Ocean" the Chinese sailors reached included not only the Indian Ocean, but also the Atlantic Ocean.

CHAPTER SEVEN

Fengdu's mansions of the immortals and places of punishment

Fengdu in Luo Maodeng's novel was in North America. It shared with the Cahokia Mounds City the same moral standards and rewarded people who showed good conduct and punished or reformed people who behaved badly. These new lines of evidence further support the conclusion that the North American Fengdu was indeed the great pre-Columbian Native American city now known as Cahokia Mounds State Historic Site—a UNESCO World Heritage Centre, some 18 km/11 mi from the confluence of the Mississippi and Missouri Rivers. It was the largest pre-Columbian settlement north of Mexico.

After introducing the names and the layout of the palace-temples inside the main gate of the Ling Yao Government Offices, Luo Maodeng began to describe the moral standards of Fengdu in North America. Judge Cui introduced Fengdu's noble lords to come out to greet Wang Ming. Fengdu's ethical standards overlapped in many ways with those of the Cahokia Mounds City.

(1) Mansions for rewarding people with good conduct

Luo's narrative (we are still in Luo's Chapter 87) starts as follows: Wang Ming and the judge were in front of the two structures near the main gate of the Ling Yao Government Offices.

。。。王明道："两廊下都是些甚么衙门？"判官道："左一边是赏善行台，右边是罚恶行台。"
王明道："可看得看儿？"判官道："我和你同去看看。"判官前走，王明随后。先到左一边赏善行台。进了行台的总门里面，只见琼楼玉殿，碧瓦参差。牵手一路，又是八所宫殿，每所宫殿门首，都是朱牌金字。第一所宫殿，朱牌上写着："笃孝之府"四个大字。判官领着王明走将进去，左右两边彩幢绛节，羽葆花旌，天花飞舞，瑞气缤纷，异香馥郁，仙乐铿锵，那里说个甚么神仙洞府也？

211

The judge then showed Wang Ming the way inside. The left

My translation of the above passage is as follows:

… Wang Ming asked, "What kind of offices are on each side of the entrance?" The judge replied, "On the left side is the structure consisting of mansions for rewarding good conduct and on the right side is another structure consisting of places for punishing evil conduct."
Wang Ming asked, "Can we take a look?" The judge replied, "I will go with you to take a look." The judge walked ahead and Wang Ming followed him. They went first to the structure on the left, where people who had conducted themselves well were rewarded. After entering through the main gate, they saw a richly decorated jade palace-temple with a roof made of tiles glowing with greenish colour. As the judge held Wang's hand and walked along, they saw that a set of eight more palace-temples were inside. In front of the gate of each palace-temple, there was a red placard inscribed with characters in gold colour. On the red placard of the first palace-temple was written in large characters: "Mansion for the enjoyment of those who have shown earnest filial piety." The judge then showed Wang Ming the way inside. The left and right sides of the mansion were decorated with colourful flags and bright-red banners. Flags and banners were bedecked with feathers of every possible colour and design, and an auspicious sentiment was also present everywhere. Variegated feathers floated and danced in the sky reflecting celestial phenomena portending peace and prosperity. The air was filled with exotic fragrance, and the reverberation of bells, musical instruments and clapping stones seemed to have come from Heaven. Was this the abode of fairies and immortals?

We may hypothesise that position #2 on the site map of Cahokia shown in Fig. 28, supported the set of eight palace-temples for rewarding people with good conduct. I have mentioned in Chapter 6 that in Luo's narrative, Mound 59 does not fit Melvin L. Fowler's hypothesis that the conical mounds are all burial mounds.

The judge explained to Wang Ming that these palace-temples were the mansions for the enjoyment of those who 1) showed earnest filial piety; 2) did their duty as a younger brother; 3) had the moral integrity of loyalty; 4) had the virtue of faith and honesty; 5) were respectful to others and observant of propriety; 6) valued righteousness; 7) were honest and upright; and 8) had a sense of shame. For brevity, I shall present my detailed analysis only on the first palace-temple which was named the "mansion for the enjoyment of those who have shown earnest filial piety."

From the above passages we know that, if the North American Fengdu was Cahokia, then the golden characters on the placard of each of the palace-temples could not be Chinese characters. In fact, the inhabitants of Cahokia did not use a writing system, and researchers today rely heavily on archaeology to interpret what they discovered. So, what Wang Ming saw could be some sort of hieroglyphics that were unreadable to him. Wang Ming would need Judge Cui to explain the meaning of these hieroglyphics. Red placards inscribed with characters in gold colour are often seen in front of the entrance of ancient Chinese houses, palaces, temples and buildings. Colour has significant meanings in Chinese culture: Red corresponds to fire, symbolizes good fortune and joy; gold symbolises wealth and riches. In fact, no matter where you are in the world, gold represents wealth.

Did the Cahokia people also like the colour red? Maybe the answer can be obtained indirectly from an understanding of the Mayan civilisation. The ancient Maya believed that certain colours were sacred and carried significant spiritual meaning. The colour red represented the East and the gods named Ix Noh Uc, Ox Tocoymoo, Ox Pauah Ek and Ah Miz (Appleton 162). East was the most important and sacred direction since it is where the Sun was born. In the Maya concept of direction, East rather than North would always be at the top of maps.[365] The fact that the supreme leader in Cahokia is known as the Great Sun Chief shows that the Cahokia people also respected the Sun (which of course rises in the East), and hence the colour of the sun—red—when it rises.[366] This is an indication that Cahokia shared this cultural characteristic with the Mayan civilisation.

As for gold, since it represents wealth, then it was natural for the Cahokia people to write hieroglyphics in gold colour on the placard.

Notice that Luo used flowery Chinese language to describe the mansion for the enjoyment of Fengdu's immortals. For example (transl. Sheng-Wei Wang), "...they saw a richly decorated jade palace-temple with a roof made of tiles glowing with a greenish colour." In the Chinese imagination, majestic and tall palaces are built with beautiful jade; they are the fairyland existing only in the mythological world. But Cahokia's mounds were made of soil and clay (the aboriginal Americans did not know how to make tiles then). Hence, Luo's description should be understood to mean that Cahokia mounds' magnificent and tall appearance was as majestic and impressive as Fengdu's mansions for the enjoyment of the immortals.

Cai Chuang Jiang Jie 彩幢绛节[367] means colourful flags and bright-red banners in the Chinese description. Yu Bao Hua Jing 羽葆花旌[368] can be translated as flags and banners bedecked with feathers of every possible colour and design. Luo's description (transl. Sheng-Wei Wang)—"The left and right sides of the mansion were decorated with colourful flags and bright-red banners.… flags and banners were bedecked with feathers of every possible colour and design"—matches the poles found at Cahokia which were used to fly such flags and banners. See, for example, Swanton's description (184–185) of the poles and flags used during the funeral of the Choctaws:

When the husband dies the friends assemble, prepare the grave, and place the corpse in it, but do not fill it up. …Poles are planted at the head and the foot, upon which the flags are placed; …

…While the supper is being served, two of the oldest men of the company quietly withdraw and go to the grave and fill it up, taking down the flags. …

As for Fengdu's "reverberation of bells, musical instruments and clapping stones," which "seemed to have come from Heaven," (transl. Sheng-Wei Wang) the description is in line with the Aztec nobility being fond of wearing bells, an implication that Cahokia's civilisation shared this cultural characteristic with the Aztec civilisation (马克·尼克莱斯等 151).

Luo's narrative continues:

。。。判官到了府堂上，请出几位来相见。出来的都是通天冠、云锦衣、珍珠履，左有仙童，右有玉女。分宾主坐下。。。

My translation of the above passage is as follows:

… The judge arrived at the hall, and politely asked a few noble lords to come out to greet the guests. Those who came out all wore tall headdresses. Their garments were made of delicate and flossy silk, and their shoes were inlaid with rare pearls. Each of them was accompanied on his left side by a young man and on his right side by a young lady. All of them sat down accordingly as hosts and guests.…

The description of "tall headdresses" could match the type of Native Americans' feather headdress now referred to as a "cockroach" or "cigarette butt" (马克·尼克莱斯等 152).

Yun Jin 云锦[369] is a kind of traditional Chinese jacquard silk brocade.[370] It is soft and lovely as the clouds and valuable as gold. 衣 yi, means clothes, garment. 云锦衣 is a garment made of jacquard silk brocade.

The production of silk originated in China around the fourth millennium BC (spanning the years 4000 through 3001 BC), and the technique spread to other parts of the world after the Silk Road opened during the latter half of the first millennium BC.[371] The Crusades[372] in the medieval period brought silk production to Western Europe, in particular to many Italian states, which saw an economic boom exporting silk to the rest of Europe.[373] Here according to Luo, these noble lords in Fengdu, North America, wore garments made of delicate and flossy silk. Was Luo implying that the Native Americans already knew how to extract raw silk by cultivating the silkworms on mulberry leaves in the early fifteenth century?

Very interestingly, a photo of silkworm cocoons is displayed in the Madison County Historical Museum, Edwardsville, Illinois, and the cocoons are kept inside the museum's Sutter Collection Box. They were donated by Mr. Thomas T. Ramey's estate after his death. Mr. Ramey lived on Cahokia's Monks Mound and collected artefacts from the Mound (马克·尼克莱斯等 187–188). More research is needed to determine the age of the cocoons. But what we can already be sure of is that Luo's narrative is making us think that the Cahokia people also liked to dress gorgeously at official functions.

215

Concerning Fengdu's noble lords wearing "shoes inlaid with rare pearls" (transl. Sheng-Wei Wang), we all know that pearls have been a much-loved symbol of beauty and purity for centuries in China as well as elsewhere in the world. In Cahokia, archaeologists have found over 20,000 marine shell beads in Mound 72, a small ridge-topped mound with a height of 3.05 m/10 ft, located less than 0.8 km/0.5 mi south of the Monks Mound (Fowler 141), and large quantities of shell beads at other mounds—these were beads from the Gulf Coast on the western side of Florida (Baires 1–47). Hence, Fengdu's noble lords, like the Cahokia people, were fascinated by pearls.

In Chapter 6 and in this Chapter, I have shown that Cahokia shared some cultural characteristics with the Mayan and the Aztec civilisations. But beyond trade, did the Cahokia people also have other contacts with Mexico, the Aztec Empire or the Mayan civilisation?

David Carballo has written a short summary of pre-Columbian trade in the Americas,[374] which seems to indicate that Cahokian trade was focused on the North American landmass and did not extend to Mexico in a significant way. However, Cahokia was strategically located near the confluence of the Missouri, the Illinois and the Mississippi Rivers. The Mississippi River either borders or passes through today's states of Minnesota, Wisconsin, Iowa, Illinois, Missouri, Kentucky, Tennessee, Arkansas, Mississippi, and Louisiana. The Illinois River is a tributary of the Arkansas River in the U.S. states of Arkansas and Oklahoma, and it flows through Illinois, Wisconsin, Indiana, and southwestern Michigan. The Missouri River flows through Montana, North Dakota, South Dakota, Nebraska, Iowa, Kansas, and Missouri. Hence, the Cahokian people could trade regularly with these regions, including those from today's Minnesota in the north to the Gulf of Mexico in the south. And through the Gulf of Mexico, Cahokia would have direct water links with modern Mexico City, the Aztec Empire or the Mayan civilisation. This trade must have been accompanied by other exchanges, since corn or maize, which was first cultivated in southern Mexico about 9,000 years ago, spread throughout the North and South Americas by trade.[375]

From Luo's novel, we can understand that certain common cultural characteristics existed between the Cahokian and the Mayan and the Aztec civilisations, which might also be due to trade-initiated exchanges over a long period of time. Soon I shall show that there was more overlap of these civilisations. And this requires me to return to Luo's narrative again where we left off earlier....

The judge introduced his wife's "brother", Wang Ming, to everyone and said that Wang Ming came with the Ming Treasure Fleet sent by the great Ming emperor to explore the Western Ocean under the command of Admiral Zheng He. As a scout for the treasure fleet, he lost his way and arrived at Fengdu. He was impressed with what he saw and wished to take the opportunity to explore the city.

。。。那几位说道: "我们同是大明国, 但有幽冥之隔耳。"王明道: "在下肉眼不识列位老先生。"判官道: "列位都是事父母能竭其力, 笃孝君子。我略说几位你听着: 这一位姓刘, 尊讳殷 , 孝养祖母, 天雨粟五十钟, 官至太保; 这一位姓严, 尊讳震 , 割股疗父, 天赐舜孝草, 涂所割处, 即时血止痛除; 。。。"

My translation of the above passage is as follows and my comments are in square brackets:

… Several of those noble lords responded by saying, "We are all from the same country, now called Ming China, but the difference is that we are in the netherworld." Wang Ming said, "But by my humble naked eyes, I do not recognise any of the old gentlemen sitting here." The judge said, "All those sitting here are gentlemen who have exerted their utmost strength to serve their parents in fulfilling filial piety. I can give you a brief account of some of them and you can listen. This gentleman's surname is Liu; his revered first name is Yin. Since he took such good care of his grandmother, Heaven even rained 50 zhong[376] [钟 was an ancient unit of capacity] of millet onto Earth to help him. Later he became the Grand Protector, a very-high-ranking official close to the throne. This other gentleman's last name is Yan; his revered first name is Zhen. He cut his thigh and used his flesh to make soup to treat his sick father. Heaven praised his filial piety, recognised him for being as devoted as the ancient great Emperor Shun [舜][377]

and blessed him with a special herb to spread over his cut wound, which instantly stopped his bleeding and pain. ..."

I have pointed out in Chapter 6 that Luo Maodeng borrowed the style of *Journey to the West* and deliberately obscured the real identity of the North American Fengdu by consistently and strategically presenting his narrative about Fengdu as if all the real-life events took place in the netherworld, including the names he used for some protagonists. Here he continues this practice.

Liu Yin (刘殷; ?–312)[378] was a high-ranking official in the imperial court in the Jin Dynasty (晋朝; 265–420), and a dutiful son. He lost his father at the age of seven. At the burial ceremony, he commemorated his father in deep grief and continued to mourn his father for three years. Yan Zhen (严震; 724–799)[379] was a famous minister, and dutiful son in the Tang Dynasty (唐朝; 618–907). He made the sacrifice of cutting his thigh and taking his flesh to make soup to treat his sick father. They were historical figures who lived in earlier Chinese dynasties than Wang Ming's.

Because of Luo Maodeng's artificial setting, the noble lords in North American Fengdu had Chinese names and they had to say (transl. Sheng-Wei Wang), "We are all from the same country, now called Ming China, but the difference is that we are in the netherworld." However, did they really mean that they lived in the netherworld? No, that could not be, because they all sat animatedly in front of Wang Ming. They were Native Americans who lived in North America. From the beginning Luo wanted to give readers a false impression by artificially setting up Fengdu as a netherworld. So, he had to consistently give these noble lords revered names of deceased Chinese historical figures. Wang Ming's response was normal and truthful. On the one hand, he was a military officer living in the early fifteenth century; hence, it was not surprising for him not to know people living in the previous Chinese dynasties. On the other hand, since these noble lords were Native Americans living in North America, there was also no reason for Wang Ming to recognise any of them at this first meeting. Luo quoted the dutiful sons in Chinese history, who practiced filial piety, to show the similar kind of self-sacrifices these native noble lords had made for their family members. Mayan and Aztec civilisations also advocated

218

self-sacrifice to heal the wounds of mankind (马克·尼克莱斯等 153-154) for their people to be granted revered positions.

In Chapter 6, I have listed twelve prominent similarities between the North American Fengdu and Cahokia. Luo's narrative above may be suggesting that *Cahokia like the North American Fengdu, also shared cultural characteristics with Chinese civilisation.*

After Wang Ming and the judge finished their visit to the first mansion for rewarding people who had performed earnest filial piety, Luo also gave full descriptions of how they toured the remaining seven mansions in his Chapter 88. At each mansion, a similar scene was repeated. Hence, I shall not repeat my analysis again here.

Luo's narrative details the Chinese ancient culture on ethics, including filial piety, loyalty and family values, and the Cahokian people also promoted these cultural values. In fact, these ethics are also highly appraised values throughout today's world.

But did Judge Cui really know all the names and detailed Chinese stories of these dutiful sons in Chinese ancient history as Luo presented them? This is unlikely. These noble lords were Native Americans and must have had their local names and their own stories. Then, did Luo first write a true historical novel and then conceal it by moving its locale to an imaginary world? Quite possibly! But, why would he have done so?

Luo arranged for Wang Ming and Fengdu's judge to meet with Fengdu's administrative officials to show the substantial overlap of the great Chinese traditional cultural enlightenment with the moral education of Cahokia. At the same time, through the mouth of the judge, Luo tried to indoctrinate Chinese readers to motivate them to save the decaying Ming Empire from the brink. But unfortunately, it was to no avail. Luo's novel was completed in 1597. In less than 50 years, on April 24, 1644, the Ming capital, Beijing, fell to a rebel army[380] led by Li Zicheng (李自成), a former minor Ming official who became the leader of the peasant revolt. On April 25, 1644, the last Ming Emperor Chongzhen (崇祯) either hanged himself or strangled himself with a sash.[381] Li then briefly ruled over China as the emperor of the short-lived Shun Dynasty (大顺; 1644-1645) before his death a year later.

In Chapter 88, Luo tells us that after visiting the eight mansions for the immortals, the judge wanted to lead Wang Ming to the places for punishing people who had been evil. Wang Ming felt that since they were evil people, there was no need to see them. Instead, he asked a different question and discovered that Fengdu's legal system for reward and punishment was that men and women were treated independently at different places. This was similar to Cahokia's court systems (马克·尼克莱斯等 156). But Judge Cui discouraged Wang Ming from seeing the two places for dealing with women. Instead, he led Wang Ming to see "hell". Luo's "hell" here refers to the prison with a total of eighteen cells for punishing or reforming civilian prisoners in North American Fengdu.

(2) Wang Ming was startled by the eight cells of punishment

Luo's narrative continues as follows:

。。。判官领头，王明随后。行了有三五里之远，只见另是一般光景，日光惨淡，冷风飕飕，周围一带都是石头墙，约有数仞之高。前面一所门，门都是生铁汁灌着的。门上一面黑匾，匾上一行大白字，写着"普掠之门"四个大字。。。

My translation of the above passage is as follows:

…The judge took the lead and Wang Ming followed him. After they walked as far as three to five *li*, the scene was already quite different. The sunlight was pitifully weak and the wind was chilly. The surrounding area had many walls of several *ren* in height and with façades that looked like stone. In the front a gate was firmly in place as if it was cast from molten iron. And above that gate was a black placard upon which was written a line of large characters in white colour, which reads: "Gate of the Pu Lue Hell." [382] …The judge walked into the gate and Wang Ming also followed him in.

The words (transl. Sheng-Wei Wang), "After they walked as far as three to five *li*, the scene was already quite different," suggest that Wang Ming and the judge must have walked away from the splendid and walled Ling Yao Government Offices and reached a different location where stood the hell or prison for locking up convicted prisoners. The site map of Cahokia in Fig. 28 shows that the distance from the Monks Mound to the main gate at position #1 is about 0.5 km/0.3 mi or one *li*. Thus, three to five *li* is somewhat distant from the eight mansions for the immortals (position #2 in Fig. 28) and is also outside the walled downtown Cahokia.

The area of "hell" was surrounded by many walls about several *ren* tall. Since Luo's "several" has been interpreted as "three or four" in Chapter 3 of this book, "several" *ren* means "three or four" *ren*. One *ren* is about seven to eight ft.[383] Hence, several *ren* means a height of 21 to 32 ft or about six to ten metres.

Luo's six to ten metres is two or three times the known height (about three metres) of the palisades (Krus 227–244) surrounding downtown Cahokia.[384] It is necessary to build higher walls to keep prisoners away from the common people and to prevent the prisoners from escaping the prison by climbing or jumping over these walls, but Luo's figure seems too high to build.

Interestingly, despite the fact that the Native Americans in Fengdu did not know how to work iron in those days, Luo writes (transl. Sheng-Wei Wang), "…a gate was firmly in place as if it was cast from molten iron.," which provides a good connection between Fengdu's prison walls and Cahokia's palisades. The palisade was a wooden stockade with a series of watchtowers or bastions at regular intervals and was about 3.2 km/2 mi long, enclosing the whole downtown Cahokia including the Monks Mound. These palisades often included baffle gates (gates that permit passage in one direction only) with great posts and many long rails for controlled entry (Midlarsky 66). They matched the strength of the fixed gates in Luo's description. Thus, it is understandable that for the walls surrounding Fengdu's prison, having palisades with baffle gates for controlled entry like the ones discovered in Cahokia, must also have been a necessity.

Luo's narrative describes the guards at the prison gate in this way:

。。。两边走出两个小鬼来，都是牛头夜叉，形容古怪，眼鼻峻嶒，。。。判官一竟走进去，王明也跟定着他走进去。

My translation of the above passage is as follows and my comment is in square brackets:

221   229

... A ghost [guard] emerged from each side of the gate. Each ghost's head resembled that of a bull. The pair looked strange with deep-set eyes and prominent noses. ... The judge went through the gate and Wang Ming also went with him.

In Chinese Buddhism, when the two characters—夜 (ye, meaning "night") and 叉 (cha, meaning "cross" or "intersect")—are combined, they become the name of a ghost.[385] This ghost's body sometimes turns into a beast with a horse's head, or a bull's head (牛 niu, meaning "bull"; 头 tou, meaning "head"). In short, this ghost looks terrifying. Niu Tou Ye Cha 牛头夜叉 means a ghost whose head resembled the head of a bull. Earlier in Section (2) of Chapter 6, I have already mentioned that the aboriginal Americans wore horned headdresses like the heads of oxen or horses, which would fit well with Luo's description of the two guards coming out of the gate.

The characters 眼 (yan, meaning "eye") 鼻 (bi, meaning "nose") 崚 (ling, meaning "erect" or "lofty") 嶒 (ceng, meaning "lofty") imply that each guard had deep-set eyes and a prominent nose. Such a description certainly does not fit a Chinese look. But Cahokia's Birdman[386] had a hooked nose and deep almond-shaped eyes. (See Fig. 29.) Interestingly, an incised sandstone tablet with a birdman has been excavated from the east side of Monks Mound in 1971.

Fig. 29 Cahokia's Birdman

The judge went through the gate and Wang Ming followed him closely. Inside the gate there were eighteen hells of punishment, each with its particular design of torture. Convicted prisoners were first sent to the office waiting to hear the judgement for their evil conduct, then, according to the categories of their crimes, they were sent to the different cells for the actual punishments.

The first cell of punishment was right near the entryway and was called the "Wind and Thunder Hell" (Feng Yu Zhi Yu "风雨之狱"), where those who had committed crimes were tied up and bound to an upright copper column to be tortured. Luo wrote that a beaten copper ring[387] was set up to encircle the standing copper column. Attached to the copper ring were short and sharp knives. When the torturer whipped the copper ring, the ring would turn and produce a whirling rush of wind and loud sound. The faster it turned, the stronger the wind and the louder the sound, until it was as loud as thunder. The knives would cut through the flesh of the prisoner standing in the centre of the ring while fixed against the column, causing his blood to flow all over the ground. But the torturer made sure that the prisoner would not be killed. Finally, the torturer would hit the ring again to stop its turning, and then the wind and the thunderous sound dissipated.

The above "punishment" in Fengdu can be related to the Sun Dance, [388] a ceremony practiced by some Native Americans. Individuals made personal sacrifices on behalf of the community to pray for healing. However, the sun dance was actually a physical and spiritual test that the dancers offered in sacrifice for their people. Young men danced around a pole to which they were fastened by "rawhide thongs pegged through the skin of their chests."[389] Wang Ming and Judge Cui apparently were seeing this kind of "dance" as a punishment to the prisoners for their evil conduct in the first Fengdu cell.

Next, the judge and Wang Ming arrived at the second cell of punishment, called the "Jin Gang Hell" (Jin Gang Zhi Yu "金刚之狱"). The four "Jin Gang"[390] are its four Heavenly guardians—Dhṛtaraṣṭra, Viruḍhaka, Virupakṣa and Vaisravaṇa—at the entrance to a Buddhist temple; each is called a Jin Gang and they are tough and strong as a diamond. All Wang Ming could see was that, on the ground, there was a crude grinding stone with a large surface area. The four sides of the stone tray were of equal length and the surface could fit a circle with a radius of approximately 8 *chi*/2.7 m measured from the centre of the stone's surface. Eight well-muscled men sat at eight equidistant positions around this massive stone, each held in both hands a pounding hammer made of iron (Cahokians did not know how to make iron, so the pounding hammer could be made of stone or wood). Four more strong men standing on the four sides were very skilful. One at a time, each would grab a prisoner and use one leg to kick him onto the grinding stone for the eight sitting men to strike the prisoner at the same time with their hammers, as if they were making a persimmon dumpling. When the punishment was about over, two more men came in. They said that they were just trying to shape him into a better person like shaping a persimmon dumpling. After smoking the prisoner over tobacco embers (Luo used Yan Tou 烟头, meaning "cigarette butts", but in those days the Native Americans might not have cigarettes, so 烟头, would mean tobacco embers) for a little while, they took him out of the grinding stone tray for a rest. The prisoner would recover and be returned as a normal person. The stone tray Wang Ming and Judge Cui saw was similar to metates used by ancient Native Americans, except here it was much bigger in size (like a grinding slab) in order to kick and pound the prisoner on top of the tray. (Metate[391] is a flat or slightly hollowed oblong stone on which materials such as lime-treated maize are ground using a smaller stone. Maize is an indigenous word from the prehistoric Taino people for the maize plant[392] and other organic materials during food preparation in traditional Mexicon culture.) Similarly, scientists think that the Cahokia Mounds State Historic Site rose to prominence after 900 AD owing to successful maize farming.[393] Hence, metates must have been used for grinding maize. Winter (196–197) has reported that both tobacco seed and grinding stones were found at Cahokia.

They next visited the third cell of punishment, called the "Fire Wheels Hell" (Huo Chez Zhi Yu "火车之狱"), where evil persons were placed on top of a wheeled cart with fire spurting out from underneath. The faster the wheels turned, the hotter the fire burned. The torturers could sprinkle water from time to time over the wheels to control the level of the flames and to prevent the prisoner from being killed by overheating. But I have not been able to find examples of a wheeled cart with fire spurting out from underneath at Cahokia. The Cahokians used baskets to carry soil to build their mounds. Was it possible that they invented some sort of wheel or

224

roller (possibly made of wood) and used the baskets pulled by men as carts? Then, it would not be a surprise to find that they could invent their primitive carts with fire spurting out from underneath to punish their prisoners. This awaits closer investigation.

Then they reached the fourth cell of punishment, called the "Damp and Cold Hell" (Ming Leng Zhi Yu "溟冷之狱"), where evil persons were thrown into a round pool of clear water and swallowed one by one by a big catfish with an exceedingly wide mouth until the pool was full of catfish. These catfish would then turn into a kind of carp (smaller than catfish) which shimmered like metal[394] and had spikes. After the punishment, the evil prisoners would be spat out by the carp and would reappear. At the Cahokia Wedge site, which is one of the two previously recorded French colonial sites,[395] large blue catfish were present (Morgan 61). Carp were also collected at a sampling station located at the Sand Prairie Lane Bridge, 0.8 km/0.5 mi north of Cahokia Mounds State Historic Site (Federal Highway Administration 82). Did Cahokians actually feed evil prisoners into the wide mouths of these fish? Or did Luo Maodeng merely want to tell us that there existed big catfish and carp in Fengdu? This remains an open question for us to think about.

They then saw the fifth cell of punishment, called the "Oiled Dragon Hell" (You Long Zhi Yu "油龙之狱"), where there were a large number of posts to which each evil person was tied down naked and covered with "hot oil" coming down from the mouth of a dragon which dangled upside down from the top of the post. Then the torturer would pour boiling water on the skin and muscles of the evil person to end the punishment. Here the "hot oil" could mean the poisonous venom from the dragon's mouth injected into the evil person; and the "boiling water" could mean the detoxification liquid used to save the evil person's life, or simply hot water to dilute and wash away the poisonous venom from the naked prisoner's skin. When this punishment was practiced at Cahokia, a "snake" dangling upside down from the top of the post would replace the "dragon" in Luo's narrative.

Then they arrived at the sixth cell of punishment, called the "Scorpion Pit Hell" (Chai Pen Zhi Yu "虿盆之狱"). A man grabbed a prisoner and threw him into a deep pit in the ground, where poisonous snakes and evil scorpions buzzed like flies, and swarms of bees would jump on him, inject poisonous venom into his skin and sting his flesh. Even if he could still survive, his flesh would be torn to shreds and his body would be ravaged all over. The man then grabbed another prisoner and repeated the punishment. He would continue the procedure until finally another man came to stop the punishment, and blew a flute to order these prisoners to climb up from the pit. As they walked up, they appeared to have no part of their bodies unhurt. Cahokia and the nearby Mississippi River Valley are not short of venomous creatures.[396] Mound 66 (a long, ridge-topped mound)[397] is one of the largest mounds at the Cahokia site and is referred to by the U.S. Geological Survey as the Rattlesnake Mound. What was locally referred to as Rattlesnake Mound (Mound 64) was partially destroyed by the construction of the railroad tracks. Nests of rattlesnakes were found at these mounds. Therefore, the Cahokians could easily use the "Scorpion Pit Hell" to punish their evil prisoners.

They then arrived at the seventh cell of punishment, called the "Mortar and Pestle[398] Hell" (Chu Ju Zhi Yu "杵臼之狱"). Here, evil persons were pounded by pestles in a huge mortar of a few *zhang* in width by four torturers standing at the mortar's four sides. The punishment would continue until the evil-doers were pounded like garlic, but not to the extent to cause death. Luo's "a few" *zhang* means three or four *zhang*. Since one *zhang* is about 3.3 m, three or four *zhang* is about 10–13 m/32.8–42.7 ft. In ancient America, mortars and pestles had many sizes. But I am sceptical about Luo's size of the mortar, 10–13 m/32.8–42.7 ft, which was extreme.

As for garlic at Cahokia, E. Barrie Kavasch has published a book entitled *The Mound Builders of Ancient North America: 4000 Years of American Indian Art, Science, Engineering, & Spirituality Reflected in Majestic Earthworks & Artifacts*. In his book, he has this record (95), and my comments are in square brackets:

Agricultural fields lay outside the city, where Cahokians grew corn, squash, and beans, along with sun flowers, pigweed [can mean any of a number of weedy plants which may be used as pig fodder], Jerusalem Artichokes, and lambsquarters [various edible species of goosefoot, or pigweed; Chenopodium album, includes spinach and beets] as the principle crops. They also managed great stands of wild rice, marshelder [an herbaceous annual plant native to much of North America], maygrass [a spring-maturing grass], tobacco, wild onions, and garlic ...

We see both tobacco and garlic mentioned. Thus, the Cahokians could easily use the "Mortar and Pestle Hell" to pound their prisoners like they pounded garlic.

Then they continued to the eighth cell of punishment, called the "Cutting Blade Hell" (Dao Ju Zhi Yu "刀锯之狱"). Evil men and women were punished here by clubs with cutting blades fixed along the edges, while they were sandwiched between two thin wooden boards. Every single one of them would have multiple scars, and blood would flow from their wounds. Similar punishing methods were practiced at Cahokia (马克·尼克莱斯等 159).

So far, Wang Ming and Judge Cui had already explored eight well-guarded punishment sites in Fengdu. Without any doubt, the world of the judge was both splendid and brutally savage. In Luo's novel, he wrote that there were ten more hells/cells for punishment waiting to be explored. In Buddhism, there are eighteen different kinds of hell in the netherworld, depending on the length, and degree of suffering. This by no means implies that Cahokia actually had eighteen hells. Luo Maodeng had projected the image of North American Fengdu as a netherworld all along, so he had to be consistent in using the Buddhist analogy to describe the hells in North American Fengdu.

But at this stage the judge was suddenly notified by three of Yama's messengers to rush back to Yama's court to attend to matters involving his official duty. Thus, he could no longer accompany Wang Ming to see the rest of the hells. Then they re-entered the gate of the Ling Yao Government Offices, where the judge told Wang Ming to return home to wait for his return after he took care of his official duty. Wang Ming took the opportunity to say goodbye to the judge and then left the Ling Yao Government Offices. He found his way back to the judge's home and saw Liu Shi again. Meanwhile, the judge went inside the palace-temple where Yama worked and resided. Yama was already there waiting for him.

From Luo's amazingly detailed narrative, we learned that North American Fengdu and Cahokia shared the same moral standards and rewarded people who showed good conduct and punished or reformed people who behaved badly.

(3) Fengdu was the great pre-Columbian Native American city now known as Cahokia Mounds State Historic Site

As I have written at the beginning of Chapter 6, Luo Maodeng borrowed his writing style from *Journey to the West*. He not only deliberately obscured the real identity of Fengdu in North America, but also consistently and strategically presented his narrative about Fengdu as if all the real-life events took place in the netherworld. But the thorough analysis presented in Chapters 1 to 5 in extracting the navigational routes and timelines of the Ming Treasure Fleet during their seventh voyage, leaves no room to doubt that around early-mid October to mid November 1433, Zheng He's fleet accidentally landed near the Labrador or Newfoundland coastal region in the North Atlantic Ocean. Then the fleet members took the only water route from the Atlantic Ocean, through the Great Lakes, to the central Mississippi Valley, after they passed two short land portages connecting different sections of the water route. Wang Ming, Zheng He's courageous scout, was sent ashore to explore this foreign land where he not only met his long-missing wife, but also explored the great city of Fengdu.

By now, readers can well comprehend that Fengdu in Luo's novel was in North America and it was actually the great pre-Columbian Native American city now known as Cahokia Mounds State Historic Site—a UNESCO World Heritage Centre, some 18 km/11 mi from the confluence of the Mississippi and Missouri Rivers, and near Collinsville, Illinois. It was the largest pre-Columbian settlement north of Mexico. This conclusion is based on the step-by-step detailed analysis of Luo Maodeng's narrative in Chapters 5 to 7 of this book, and I have listed twelve multiple lines of evidence at the end of Chapter 6 as support. Now in Chapter 7, I have shown the additional evidence that both Fengdu and Cahokia shared the same moral standards and rewarded people who showed good conduct and punished or reformed people who behaved badly.

Luo Maodeng has hidden Fengdu's true identity under the veil of fiction with much effort and for so long (more than four hundred years). But now we can see clearly that there is no other place in the world that could match Fengdu so well in so many ways and to such detailed extent as Cahokia. The truth is finally unveiled.

The Last Journey of the San Bao Eunuch

CHAPTER EIGHT

Zheng He's generals force their way through the Fengdu gate, but later decide to return home

Yama expressed misgivings about Zheng He's military activities and the loss of life during the expedition, and Zheng He agreed to end the seventh voyage in Fengdu/Cahokia. Three routes and timelines are proposed for the Ming Treasure Fleet's return voyage back home. One route, based on Luo's narrative, would lead the Chinese sailors almost straight back home around June to October 1435. The second route would support Gavin Menzies' position that some of the Ming sailors visited Florence after June 1434, transferring the latest Chinese knowledge, navigational maps and technology to Europeans, thereby significantly enhancing the Renaissance and ushering in the era of the Age of Discovery; in this case, the Chinese sailors would have returned home around early summer or even into the autumn of 1435. Those treasure ships which took the third route to New Zealand around mid-January to mid-May 1435 would regrettably be wiped out. But did Zheng He return to China with his mariners? Perhaps Cahokia's mysterious disappearance could be related to Zheng He's unknown whereabouts after his seventh and last voyage.

According to Luo, the civilian prison had eighteen hells/cells of punishment. The judge and Wang Ming visited only eight of them. There was not enough time for them to see the rest of these chambers, because Yama sent three messengers to order the judge to return to the Ling Yao palace-temple to process court cases dealing with grievance complaints. So, Wang Ming had to return to Judge Cui's home and his role from this point on was minimal.

Luo's narrative of the last ten paragraphs in Chapter 88, the entire Chapter 89 and the first half of Chapter 90, deal with the 32 cases of complaints from countries which had resisted Zheng He's demands for surrender and tributes according to Luo's novel.

Of these 32 cases, six were from Champa, one from Lopburi, seven from Java, one from Palembang, two from the Land of Many Perfumes, four from Sa Fa, three from Ceylon, four from the

231

"Country with people with yellowish-coloured or golden-coloured eyes", one from the Hong Luo Mountain and three from the "Country with people with silver-coloured eyes". According to Luo, these cases involved the killings of foreign kings, generals, soldiers, women, horses, livestock, and so on, ordered by Zheng He himself or his generals when they travelled through the above-mentioned countries where they had met with local resistance. But as I mentioned earlier in Chapter 3 of this book, much of the military confrontations were non-existent and they were Luo's fanciful writing. Luo did it for a purpose which will become clear in this chapter.

(1) Yama's misgivings about Zheng He's military activities and the loss of life on the expeditions

In the court of Yama, the judge very quickly went through the great record book and made the verdict for each case. Those with evil records in life were sent either to the King of Wheel Turning to be reincarnated in a new human body, to the Livestock Bureau to be reborn as livestock, to the Ghost Bureau to be placed instantly at the foot of the ghost mountain,[399] or to the Criminal Bureau to be locked up in hell to prevent them from being reborn, and so on; others who had conducted themselves well were sent to the mansions where good conduct was rewarded with enjoyment (discussed in Chapter 7). After the trial was completed, all the complainants were taken away, but five of them refused to accept the verdicts and ran amok. They took away the judge's pen and criminal records and wrestled with him. The judge lost the fight. Luo described their fight vividly in Chapter 90 of his novel. In short,

。。。把头上的晋巾儿也打掉了，把身上的皂罗袍也扯碎了，把腰里的牛角带也蹬断了，把脚下的皂朝靴也脱将去了。。。

My translation of the above passage is as follows:

… They pulled his scarf off his head, tore his black silk robe into pieces, trod on his waist belt decorated with buffalo horn, and broke it. Then they pulled his imperial black boots from his feet. …

The word 皂 (zao) is the colour black, 罗 (luo) is a thin silk fabric, and 袍 (pao) is a robe. 皂罗袍 is thus a robe made of a thin black silk fabric. In ancient China, robes made of blue-black fabric indicated that the wearer was a court official. 牛(niu) means ox or buffalo, 角 (jiao) means horn, and 带 (dai) means belt. Thus, Niu Jiao Dai 牛角带 is a belt decorated with horns (or jade).[400] 朝 (chao) means imperial court, 靴 (xue) means boots, and Zao Chao Xue 皂朝靴 is black-coloured long boots with thick white soles worn by ancient Chinese officials when they appeared in the imperial court to report to the emperor. Luo's description of Judge Cui's outfit was typical of that worn by officials in imperial China, because Luo treated him as if he were a Chinese and had given him a Chinese name, "Cui Jue", borrowed from *Journey to the West*. But we already know that Fengdu was Cahokia and Cui Jue was a high-ranking native working for the Great Sun Chief. Then, was Luo's description of Cui Jue's dress also consistent with him being a Native American?

In Chapter 7, we learned that Cahokia's Mississippian civilisation shared some common cultural characteristics with the Aztec and Mayan civilisations. The resemblances are also evidenced here in Cui Jue's dress. In Mayan civilisation, for public events, the Mayans' outfits would usually include large feathered headdresses.[401] Luo tells us that in Yama's courtroom Judge Cui wore a kind of "scarf" over his head as a "headdress". For sports, the Mayan wore a horseshoe-shaped yoke around the waist[402] to reduce injuries, and the tonsured Maya maize deity wore a thick belt around his waist[403] just like Judge Cui did. Moreover, in Chapter 6 we also learned that Cahokia's Great Sun Chief was the one who ruled the earth and spoke to the sky, and his counsellors were members of the élite class composed of priests and chieftains.[404] Cui Jue wore a black silk robe just like those priests wearing black-coloured robes (the Aztec priests wore dark green or black robes[405] hanging over their faces reeking of blood from past sacrifices). From the above comparison, Luo's description of Cui Jue's dress is consistent with him being a Native American.

But, did the fight actually take place? Was it realistic that 5,000 foreign soldiers, hundreds and thousands of wild buffalos, hundreds and thousands of rhinoceros, over 500 women, 300 to 500 men whose terrible appearance resembled a log of firewood burning from within, another 500 foreign soldiers, 3,000 infantrymen, thirteen foreign generals, another group of several women, 50 security guards, ten headless victims, a senior commander of the troops, a group of white elephants, 500 headless and brainless victims and so on, all crowded together inside one courtroom in Fengdu? Since Fengdu was Cahokia, could this scene be played out inside the Monks Mound, the office and residence of the Great Sun Chief high up in the sky? Besides, was it possible for so many victims to come to Fengdu/Cahokia from their far, far away home countries in those days?

It seems quite plausible that Luo invented the story of 32 cases of grievance, and that the above fight inside the court house did not take place in real life. Perhaps Luo invented this story to express his personal criticism against the negative impact caused by Zheng He's military actions during all his past voyages. Luo lumped together all the military activities and the loss of life from the previous expeditions into the seventh and last voyage, while the seventh voyage itself was basically a journey of peace and diplomacy. From the beginning of his novel, he has exaggerated all the previous military actions including their length and scale. Hence, his narrative of the 32 cases of grievance raised by these victims is likely imaginary and these victims who came to Fengdu/Cahokia existed only on paper.

Originally many scholars and researchers thought that restoring China's naval supremacy might have been behind Luo's popular Ming novel written in 1597 on Zheng He. This was because the aging Ming Dynasty had become weak due to internal problems and external threats. However, after reading Luo's novel and especially the narrative in Chapter 91, Goodrich (88–96) has expressed a somewhat different viewpoint in her book, *Chinese Hells*, as follows, and her comment is in round brackets:

Similar motives (to restore China's naval supremacy) may have been behind Luo's popular Ming novel about Zheng He, written in 1597... And for the first time we have the hint, albeit clothed in fiction, that the Chinese may have had some misgivings about Zheng He's military activities and the loss of life on the expeditions.

In this chapter, we also see Luo expressing his misgivings about Zheng He's military activities and the loss of life during the expeditions. To avoid persecution for his writings in the post-Zheng He era, Luo must have decided to obscure the matter from the outset by calling Fengdu a netherworld, using covert techniques to reveal Chinese mariners' visits to North America during their sixth and seventh voyages, assigning wrong years and a wrong duration of the seventh voyage (mistakenly from the seventh year to the fourteenth year of the Yongle period), creating 32 cases of complaints from countries which had resisted Zheng He's demands for surrender and tributes, and so on.

(2) Yama sent a gift to Zheng He's five military commanders and a letter to the Buddhist Master

While Luo was describing how the five accusers were engaged in fierce fighting with the judge at Yama's court, Zheng He's mariners were on the ships docked near the Mississippi River bank waiting anxiously for Wang Ming's return:

。。。王明去了有一七多些，还不见个回报。这一七中间，天色渐明，虽有些烟雨霏霏，却不过像中朝深秋的景致。 。。

My translation of the above passage is as follows:

… Wang Ming had been gone for more than seven days, but had not yet returned to make his report. During these seven days, the weather gradually cleared a little. Although some misty rain was falling, it still looked like the late autumn landscape in China. …

The sentence reveals that the Chinese sailors had arrived at the Mississippi River bank more than a week previously and the weather condition implies that it was still in the month of November 1433.

The supreme commander San Bao Master onboard the ship began to feel worried. As a result, five of his military commanders, including Marshall Tang, volunteered to go onshore. They went on horseback, carrying weapons to check things out:

四员将军前跑，一个唐状元后随。跑了有十数多里

235

头。。。。却又是走了十数多里路头。。。。五个大将军打伙儿又跑，再又跑了十数多里路头，只见远远的望见有一条矮矮的墙头儿，中间有一个小小的门儿，五员将，五骑马，五般兵器，一抢而入。。。

My translation of the above passage is as follows:

Four military commanders rode on horseback in front of Tang Zhuangyuan. They ran some ten *li*. … Then again, walked some ten *li*… The five generals rode horses together again for some ten *li*. All they could see in the distance was an extensive low wall with a small gate in the middle. The five military commanders on horseback, carrying five different weapons, surged forward and forced their way through the gate. …

Tang Zhuangyuan, or Marshall Tang, was one of the military commanders under Zheng He's command during the western expeditions (he has already been introduced earlier in Section (1) of Chapter 4).

Later Luo wrote (transl. Sheng-Wei Wang) that the "small gate" which the five military commanders saw was the "gate of hell" (Gui Men Guan "鬼门关"). It is unclear whether this "gate of hell" actually existed in Cahokia Mounds City. When Wang Ming was sent to do his reconnaissance work, he did not have first to enter through this "gate of hell" before he encountered the outer gate of Fengdu/Cahokia.

From the place where the five military commanders left their boats, they rode on horses or walked for some ten *li,* altogether three times. Summing up, the distance was more than 30 *li*/15 km/9.3 mi but less than 60 *li*/30 km/18.6 mi, basically the same distance Wang Ming had walked, from where he got off the boat, to where he arrived at the outer gate of Fengdu/Cahokia.

Luo repeatedly revealed that the Chinese sailors' boats most likely anchored near the confluence of the Mississippi and Missouri Rivers, where the land was flat and the distance was approximately 18 km/11 mi; *indeed*, this distance was more than 30 *li*/15 km/9.3 mi but less than 60 *li*/30 km/18.6 mi from the confluence of the two rivers to today's Cahokia Mounds State Historic Site! Other than

244

Cahokia Mounds City, which other city could match Luo's geographical description of Fengdu so closely?

五骑马，一会儿就跑到城门之下。只见城上有一面牌，牌上写着"古酆都国"四个大字。。。

My translation of the above passage is as follows:

The five military commanders on horseback soon reached the front of the city gate. They saw a sign affixed on the city wall with four big characters written on it, "Ancient City-State of Fengdu." ...

This was the same city gate which Wang Ming encountered before he entered Fengdu/Cahokia. The five military commanders advanced through the gate after quickly defeating the guards.

。。。一会儿又跑到一座城门之下。这一座城较矮小些，这一座城门较窄狭些，阴风飒飒，冷雾漫漫。众将抬头一看，只见城上也有一面牌，牌上写着"禁城"两个字。。。

My translation of the above passage is as follows:

... In a little while they arrived at the front of another gate. This city looked a little smaller than the outer city, and this gate was also a little narrower. A chilly wind was blowing hard and dense fog was boundless. When they looked up, all they could see was another sign affixed on the city wall with the two characters "Forbidden City" written on it...

Luo used the two words "Forbidden City" (transl. Sheng-Wei Wang) to describe the "downtown Cahokia" mentioned in Chapter 6, and named by Fowler (193). The unearthed Cahokia Mounds complex shows a gate located in the proximity of the palace-temple known now as Mound 51 (known locally as the Persimmon Mound),[406] indicated by position 2 in Fig. 28. This corresponds to the location of the second palace-temple of King Chujiang in the Ling Yao Government Offices of North American Fengdu as discussed in Section (6) of Chapter 6. Apparently the five military commanders did not run to the same gate as Wang Ming did (position #1 in Fig. 28), because they saw a different sign "Forbidden City" on the plaque of the gatehouse from the sign "Ling Yao Government Offices" seen by Wang Ming. Similarly, Luo did not mention that the five military commanders saw on their left side the mansions for rewarding good conduct (the big Mound 59/Round Top Mound[407] at position #2 in Fig. 28) and on their right side the places for punishing wicked conduct (the big Mound 60/Fox Mound[408] at position #3 in Fig. 28).

In Section (2) of Chapter 6, I mentioned that there were several gates on each side of the palisade wall surrounding downtown Cahokia to facilitate entry for the populace. Luo's narrative mentioned two of them. Since North American Fengdu was Cahokia, from Luo's passage above, we know that the walled "Forbidden City" in Fengdu was downtown Cahokia, the same place where Yama's "ten Courts of Hell" or Ling Yao Government Offices was located. It was also the same place where Cahokia's Sun Chief or Birdman had his temple-palace where he lived and worked. This will become even clearer in Luo's passage shown below.

Once again, the five military commanders defeated the guards, and then entered the Forbidden City.

。。。一会儿却进到一个处所。这却不是城墙，这却不是城门，只见无限的朱门高敞，殿宇峥嵘，俨然是王者所居的气象，宫门上也有一面牌，牌上写着 "灵曜之府" 四个大字。。。

My translation of the above passage is as follows:

… Quickly they advanced to a certain place. This place was not a city wall, nor a city gate. In front of them was a tall and wide-open red door leading into the towering palace-temple and the seemingly endless sky. The scene created the atmosphere of a king's residence. On the plaque of the gatehouse was a sign with four large characters, "Ling Yao Government Offices," written on it . . .

I have mentioned in Section (1) of Chapter 7 the significance that Chinese culture attaches to colours; red, corresponding to fire, symbolises good fortune and joy. The ancient Chinese liked to paint their house doors or palace-temple gates red. According to Luo, the door colour of the Fengdu palace-temple was red. Similarly, the Cahokia people, like the ancient Maya, believed that the colour red represented the Sun, and the East. East is the most important and sacred direction, since it is where the Sun was born, and the rising Sun's colour is red.

Just like Yama's "Ling Yao Government Offices", the stairway leading up the front of the great Monks Mound[409] in the Cahokia Mounds City is also very long, and steep, reaching the seemingly endless sky. (See Fig. 30.)

Fig. 30 Monks Mound front view

As mentioned earlier in Section (5) of Chapter 6, the Monks Mound where the Great Sun Chief of Cahokia lived is taller than 30 m/100 ft: it is 291 m/955 ft long, including the access ramp at the southern end, 236 m/775 ft wide, and could support a wooden structure on the summit. Diagrammatic sketches of the Monks Mound, as it is thought to have been originally, were drawn by Byron W. Knoblock in 1938 (Fowler 89) and by William R. Iseminger on the cover page of his book, *Cahokia Mounds: America's First City*, published in

2010. (See Figs. 31 and 32.) In both figures there is a ramp which follows the approximate course of the ancient wooden stairs and goes up to the first terrace. But in Fig. 31, Knoblock did not draw any ramp for going from the first terrace to the second, the third and the fourth terraces on the Monks Mound. Also, no building structure is drawn on Monks Mound in his sketch.

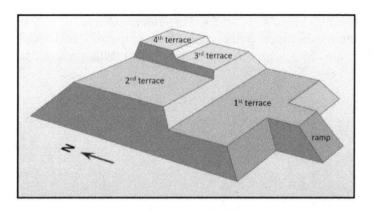

Fig. 31 Monks Mound (drawn after Byron W. Knoblock)

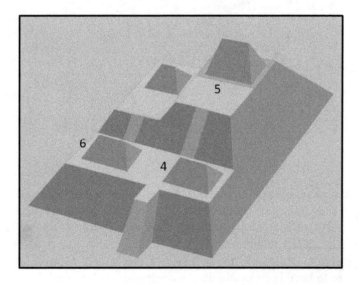

Fig. 32 Monks Mound (drawn after William R. Iseminger)

Both Figs. 31 and 32 show four terraces, but Fig. 32 differs from Fig. 31 in several aspects. Based on William R. Iseminger's model, there are three major palace-temples on the Monks Mound (the fourth one is small). In addition to a stair leading up to the first terrace, there is a palace-temple (at positions 4 and 6) on each side of the first terrace. Furthermore, there are two stairs on the first terrace: one goes up to the second terrace where a small palace-temple is located, and the other goes up to the third terrace. The third terrace has no palace-temple, while the fourth terrace is where the Great Sun Chief had a truly majestic and towering palace-temple as his residence and office (at position 5).

。。。五条猛汉，五骑马，五般兵器，一拥而入，已是进到灵霄府阎罗王殿下。

My translation of the above passage is as follows:

… Five intrepid men on five horses carrying five different weapons all rushed in. They quickly arrived at the celestial mansion of His Highness Yama.

The five military commanders forced their way into the sacred plaza area and rushed toward the great mound and the palace temple of Yama/the Great Sun Chief. While Yama was still trying to pacify the five accusers who were attacking Judge Cui in the courtroom, he heard several urgent reports that five military commanders were also rushing into the courtroom. Suddenly the five accusers quietened down and obediently accepted their fate (their role ended). Judge Cui was terrified, and Yama had no idea how to deal with these five military commanders except to send the judge to meet them to find out from where, and for what, they came here, in order to avoid a confrontation with them. Yama himself went to hide in the rear courtroom of the palace-temple. Luo's Chapter 90 ends here.

Chapter 91 entitled (transl. Sheng-Wei Wang), "Yama sent a message to the Buddhist Master … Yama gave a gift to the five commanders" ("阎罗王寄书国师 阎罗王相赠五将"), starts with Judge Cui's conversation with one of the military commanders, Tang Zhuangyuan:

241   249

判官勉强支起架子，走下殿来，说道："你们还是强神？你们还是恶鬼？我这里是个十帝阎君所居之处，。。。"唐状元见他说是阎君所在，也以礼开谈，说道："你不要吃惊，我们号为五虎将军，日战阳间夜战阴。"判官道："你这些将军，还是阳世上人？还是阴司里人？"唐状元道："你这里还是阳世？还是阴司？"判官道："将军说话也好差了。一行告诉你，这是十帝阎君所居之处，岂可又不是阴司！况兼你们一路而来，先过鬼门关，次进酆都城，又次进禁城，却才进我灵曜府。。。。"判官道："列位可是阳世上人？"唐状元道："是阳世上人。"判官道："还是哪一国？"唐状元道："是大明国朱皇帝驾下差来的。"判官道："既奉朱皇帝钦差，怎么走到我这鬼国来？"唐状元道："为因兵下西洋，抚夷取宝，故此轻造。"判官道："我这鬼国是西天尽头处，却也是难得到的。"

My translation of the above passage is as follows:

The judge reluctantly stretched his body, walked down the hall, and asked, "Are you people mighty gods or vicious devils? This is the residence of Yama of the 'ten Courts of Hell'. ..." Tang Zhuangyuan heard the judge saying that this place was Yama's court, he also reciprocated politely and said, "Please do not be surprised. We are called the five tiger-like military commanders. We can fight wars both in daytime in the world of the living and at night in the world of the dead. The judge continued, "You are military commanders. Are you people in the world of the living or in the world of the dead?" Tang Zhuangyuan did not reply to the question directly. Instead he asked, "Is your place the world of the living or the world of the dead?" The judge said, "Commander, your way of talking is not so good. I have already told you that here is the 'ten Courts of Hell' of Yama, how can it not be the world of the dead! Besides, you came all the way here by first passing through the 'gate of hell' to enter into the netherworld, then the gate to enter into Fengdu City, then the gate for entering into the Forbidden City, and now you arrive at the Ling Yao Government Offices. ..." The judge then asked, "Are you people all from the world of the living?" Tang Zhuangyuan replied, "We are people from the world of the living." The judge asked again, "From which country did you come?" Tang Zhuangyuan replied, "We were sent by Emperor Zhu of the Great Ming Dynasty." The judge continued, "Since you are imperial envoys of Emperor Zhu, how did you come to this ghost country?" Tang Zhuangyuan replied, "We imprudently came by here as a result of sailing to the Western Ocean with our soldiers to console foreign countries and find our national treasured item. The judge then said, "My ghost country is at the end of the western sky. It is very hard to reach."

While the judge said that the Ling Yao Government Offices were the "ten Courts of Hell" of Yama and the world of the dead, he also pointed out that his country had a real physical location—at the end of the western sky—which was different from the legendary ghost city of Fengdu in the Sichuan Province of China (in those days, China was not considered to be at the end of the western sky). After presenting all the evidence in previous chapters, by now, we should no longer be confused about the true identity of the North American Fengdu. Also, Judge Cui knew that Zheng He's five military commanders were ashore.

However, before Tang Zhuangyuan had the chance to speak again, the outpost Deputy Chief Commander of the Western Expedition Zhang Bo (张柏) or Zhang Langya (张狼牙)[410] became impatient and demanded the judge to send in the surrender document and pay tribute, or else face military confrontation. Apparently, Zhang Bo thought that the judge was making excuses and was reluctant to comply with the Ming demand by *faking* that the place was a world of the dead (once again, Luo revealed that Fengdu was a "living" world, not a netherworld). Other military commanders also started to chase after the judge with their weapons. Since Tang Zhuangyuan wanted to seek a peaceful resolution, he hurriedly shouted to his comrades and stopped them from using force against the judge.

Yama, standing in the rear courtroom of the palace-temple, heard the disturbance. He walked out of the room and asked:

。。。"下面甚么人？敢持刀骤马，逼勒我判官么？"判官正在没走处，一直跑上了殿。

243　　　　251

My translation of the above passage is as follows:

… "Who is in the lower court room? How dare you hold knives and ride horses at full gallop to pressure my judge?" Since the judge could not find a place to escape, he just ran all the way up to the palace hall.

Tang Zhuangyuan saw that the man who questioned them in the hall of the palace-temple wore a royal crown (headdress) and was dressed like a king, so he realised that the man must be His Highness Yama/the Great Sun Chief. Tang then reined in his horse and loudly replied that they were the envoys of the Ming emperor who sent them to the Western Ocean to enlighten the foreigners and recover a national treasure; since they had not been able to find the missing national treasure, by chance they had trespassed into the Ling Yao Government Offices. Yama said that, in this case, they should not pressure the judge but should return home. Tang replied that they needed Yama's surrender paper and tribute to take back to their superior when they returned to their docked ships. Yama then warned them as follows:

。。。阎罗王道："你们下洋之时，枉杀了千千万万的人命。他们这如今一个个的负屈含冤，要你们填还他性命。虽然是我崔判官和你们硬断，到底是怨气冲天，无门救解。大小宝船，却有沉覆之危。"。。。

My translation of the above passage is as follows:

… "When you made this expedition to the Western Ocean, you killed thousands of people. They suffered from un-righted wrongs or grievances and now want to take your lives in repayment for their lives. Although my judge, Cui Jue, has decisively settled the matter for you, the souls of the dead still show resentment. This matter has not been truly resolved. Your treasure ships may face the danger of being sunk.". . .

Although Yama gave this warning to the five military commanders, he was also impressed with their bravery and tried to find a solution to ease their demands. To show his hospitality he agreed to give the five military commanders a gift by putting it inside a red box together with a short letter which had four sentences in it for them to take back to their Buddhist Master on board the ship for his interpretation. Tang Zhuangyuan received the red box from the judge. After repeatedly thanking him, the five military commanders galloped out of the hall on horseback.

The above passage shows that Luo and Yama/the Great Sun Chief shared the same feeling about Zheng He's military activities and the loss of life during the Ming Treasure Fleet's expeditions to the Western Ocean. We begin to understand why Luo Maodeng lumped together all the military activities from the earlier expeditions into the peaceful seventh and last voyage, and exaggerated the lengths and scales of Zheng He's military actions in preparation for the present condemnation.

(3) Holding ceremonies to release souls from purgatory to avoid trouble

Back on board the ship, the five military commanders respectfully went to see their two commanders-in-chief. It turned out that Wang Ming had already returned and was also there talking about his adventures during his absence of about ten days. Both Wang Ming and Tang Zhuangyuan were able to confirm that they had been to the same place, Fengdu/Cahokia, and met with Judge Cui and His Highness Yama/the Great Sun Chief.

元帅道："里面风景何如？"唐状元道："阴风飒飒，冷雾漫漫，不尽的凄凉景色。"元帅道："居止何如？"唐状元道："照旧有街道，照旧有房舍。有个鬼门关，有座酆都城，有座禁城，却才到灵曜之府。中有阎罗王的宫殿，朱门宏敞，楼阁峻嶒，俨然王者所居气象。元帅道："阎罗王何如？"唐状元道："冕而衣裳，俨然王者气象。"元帅道："可看得真么？"唐状元道："觌面相亲，细问细对。他还有一封短札，拜上国师；还有一件礼物，赏赐末将们的。"元帅道："怪哉！怪哉！连阴司之中也征到了，连阎罗王也取出降书来，也取出宝贝来。今日之事，千载奇事。"即时请过国师、天师。唐状元递上书，国师拆封读之。。。

My translation of the above passage is as follows and my comment is in square brackets:

The commander-in-chief asked, "What was the scenery like inside that country?" Tang Zhuangyuan replied, "A chilly wind was blowing hard and dense fog was boundless. There was endless gloom and sadness." The commander-in-chief asked again, "What were the residential areas and the streets like?" Tang Zhuangyuan said, "There were normal streets and houses, a gate to enter the city of hell, the city of Fengdu, a Forbidden City, and then the Ling Yao Government Offices within which was the palace residence of His Highness Yama. There was a tall and wide-open red door, leading into the towering palace-temple and the seemingly endless sky, resembling the scenery of a king's residence." The commander-in-chief asked further, "What did His Highness Yama look like?" Tang Zhuangyuan replied, "He wore a royal crown [headdress] and was dressed just like a king." The Commander-in-chief then asked, "Did you truly see him?" Tang Zhuangyuan replied, "I was with him face to face. He asked me detailed questions and I gave detailed answers. He also gave me a short letter to be delivered respectfully to the Buddhist Master and a gift awarded to the lesser commanders like us." The Commander-in-chief said, "Strange! Strange! Our expedition has gone to the netherworld. Yama has even presented the surrender document and given us a gift. What has happened today is unheard of." He then immediately asked the Buddhist Master and the Daoist Master to be present. Tang Zhuangyuan handed over the letter and the Buddhist Master opened the envelope of the letter to read. ...

Here the "commander-in-chief" was Zheng He. The description (transl. Sheng-Wei Wang)—"A chilly wind was blowing hard and dense fog was boundless"—is very similar to the windy and foggy autumn weather of the Mississippi Valley. With the Mississippi River nearby, Cahokia's humidity is high, and in the cold late autumn and winter, when Zheng He's mariners were there, it could often have foggy days.

In Chapters 6 and 7, we learned that the Cahokia Mounds City[411] was like the Fengdu Ghost Country described in Luo Maodeng's novel, having streets, a river, houses (with sharply pointed thatched roofs), city gates, the Grand Plaza, the walled downtown area, and the Monks Mound (where the Great Sun Chief/Birdman[412] resided. (See Fig. 30.)

Once again, Luo used "netherworld" and "His Highness Yama" in place of the real-world Cahokia Mounds City and its real leader the Great Sun Chief to obscure the true story.

But the conversation between Tang Zhuangyuan and Zheng He (transl. Sheng-Wei Wang), such as "Did you truly see him?" and "I was with him face to face," send a clear message that Fengdu's Yama was a living person and Fengdu was a real world. Luo did not miss this great opportunity to tell his readers that His Highness Yama was *truly* a "living" person, not a ghost!

The remaining part of Luo's Chapter 91 and the entire Chapter 92 thoroughly explore the true meaning of the four sentences in Yama's letter and the origin of the gift. The title of Luo's Chapter 92 is (transl. Sheng-Wei Wang), "Buddhist Master thoroughly investigated the message in Yama's letter and decided to release souls from purgatory" ("国师勘透阎罗书 国师超度魍魉鬼"). The broad meaning of Chao Du 超度[413] in Buddhism is chanting to relieve ghosts from misery. The deeper meaning is to pass through life and death and to reach the other side of Nirvana.[414]

After the Buddhist Master gave detailed explanations, Zheng He and his crew on board the ship finally understood that Yama's real intention was to condemn Zheng He and his soldiers for unjustly killing thousands of people and animals during their expeditions to the Western Ocean. To vent resentment, the souls of the dead could seek revenge and the treasure ships might face the crisis of being capsized and sinking in the ocean. In the letter, Yama warned the Chinese sailors that unless these souls were released from purgatory, Zheng He and his crew might not be able to avoid trouble.

。。。元帅道："我和你今日来到酆都鬼国，已自到了天尽头处，海尽路处。。。况兼阎罗王也说道：'可以止矣。'。。。只一件来，沿路上钢刀之下，未必不斩无罪之人，'超度'两个字最说得有理，伏望国师鉴察。"国师道："这也是理之当然。"

My translation of the above passage is as follows:

… The Commander-in-chief said, "Today I come with you all to the Fengdu Ghost Country which is already the end of sky and the end of sea. … Besides, Yama also said, 'You can stop here.' … However, there is one more thing on my mind, namely that during our journey we inevitably killed innocent people with our steel knives. 'Release souls from purgatory' are the words best said. I sincerely hope that our Buddhist Master can look into this matter." The Buddhist Master responded, "This of course is the way it should be."

The respected Commander-in-chief Zheng He was aware that the voyage had reached the end of sky and sea. Although the national treasure was not recovered, the courageous sailors of the treasure ships completed the Ming emperor's order of enlightening foreigners to maintain and expand the tributary system. Besides, they had reached North America, the end of sky and the end of sea in those days! Was there still any reason for them not to go home? Eunuch San Bao agreed with Yama's suggestion (transl. Sheng-Wei Wang), "You can stop here", by not entering Fengdu/Cahokia any further. It was time to go home. Releasing souls from purgatory is the benevolent practice of Chinese Buddhism.

The Buddhist Master Jin Bifeng agreed with Zheng He's decision. Jin then set up an altar on the land and an altar on the ship to perform Buddhist rituals needed to release souls from purgatory. The rituals lasted for 49 consecutive days and nights[415] in order to suppress ghouls and bogeymen who tried to make complaints to Yama.

In addition, the Buddhist Master also received Zheng He's approval to set up another altar to worship the Sea God. Afterwards, a huge banquet was offered to officials of all ranks and descriptions, and awards given to all soldiers. Since the Buddhist Master also received Zheng He's approval to set up an altar to worship the Sea God, this indicates that by this time the Ming sailors had already left the Fengdu/Cahokia area and had taken the original route, but in the reverse direction, back to where their big sea ships were anchored near the Gulf of St. Lawrence. Because now, they were by the Atlantic Ocean and they could set up an altar to worship the Sea God before going home.

。。。日上清风送行，晚上明月送行。。。直送仙舟返帝京。。。又生受野花行者。。。直送仙舟返帝京。。。又生受芳草行者。。。直送仙舟返帝京。。。

My translation of the above passage is as follows:

... During the daytime, gentle breezes bade them farewell, and during the night the bright moon bade them farewell. ... Wished them to sail safely back towards the Ming capital. ... Messengers of wild flowers and green grass also bade them farewell. ... Wished them to sail safely back towards the Ming capital. ...

The above description no longer shows the late autumn scene they saw previously in the area of Fengdu/Cahokia Mounds City in 1433. The gentle breezes, wild flowers and green (and fragrant) grass bidding farewell tell that the season had changed into the spring or summer of 1434.

But before the Ming mariners sailed home, they erected a memorial stele on a small mountain above the cliff previously covered with yellow grass (by now, the grass must have turned green due to seasonal change). This is described in detail in Luo's Chapter 93. The idea was suggested by the Buddhist Master. He thought that the achievements of the Ming Treasure Fleet far exceeded what the great military strategist Ma Fubo (馬伏波 or 马援 Ma Yuan)[416] had accomplished in the Eastern Han Dynasty (25–220 AD). This time the Chinese sailors explored far beyond the traditionally known "Western Ocean" (Indian Ocean) to reach the land of Fengdu, now known as the Cahokia Mounds State Historic Site in the central Mississippi Valley, many tens of thousands of *li* away from the Chinese territory.

The Buddhist Master made the recommendation to follow Ma Fubo's example of placing a stone stele as a historic commemorative sign to demarcate the boundary that Ming sailors reached. His idea was supported by the fleet members. Thus, a stone column was erected on the small mountain near the cliff. The column had eight faces. One face was engraved with the official title of Zheng He, and the remaining seven faces were engraved with praises to the Buddha. Then the Daoist Master suggested erecting a

249

second stone stele with an inscription on it. The stone stele was shorter than the stone column and stood in front of the column.

After the formal ceremony of erecting the column and the stele, the officer who held the blue-coloured signalling flag instructed the ships to start sailing. The fleet then navigated towards home.

(4) When did the Chinese mariners leave North America?

So, for how long did the Chinese mariners stay in North America? According to Luo's narrative in Section (3) of this chapter, when the Chinese mariners left North America the season had changed into the spring or summer of 1434, namely, they left most likely between March 1 and August 31 of 1434. They could not have left after the end of summer (August 31) of 1434, because in the Labrador coastal area, autumn would not have gentle breezes, wild flowers and green grass.

Here I have tried to work out the timelines of the stay of Zheng He's mariners in North America as follows: 1) when Wang Ming returned to the ship after ten days' reconnaissance work, the date was near the end of November 1433; 2) it took 45 days and nights for the Buddhist Master to perform the rituals to release souls from purgatory; then the date passed to around mid-January 1434; 3) it took a few weeks or a month for the Chinese mariners to sail from Fengdu/Cahokia back to the cliff area; then the date might have passed to around mid- or late February 1434; 4) it took a number of days to perform Buddhist rituals to worship the Sea God; 5) it took a number of days to offer a huge banquet to officials of all ranks and descriptions, and awards to all soldiers; and 6) it took a number of days to erect a memorial stone stele and stone column on a small mountain above the steep cliff covered with yellow grass (which now must have turned green). Luo did not give the actual days spent for carrying out the activities listed in items 4) to 6), or mention the days spent during which the Chinese mariners surveyed the land and the coastal area they had visited before leaving. All I can be sure of is that, according to Luo Maodeng's narrative, the Chinese mariners might have left North America around spring time (March, April and May) to summer time (June, July and August) of 1434. Leaving the Labrador coastal area shortly before the end of August when the grass was turning yellow again, would pose no problem in navigation because the harbours would not be frozen. But could they leave as early as March?

Bear in mind that the Labrador coastal harbours are frozen in winter. In Section (1) of Chapter 5, I mentioned that, from the beginning of January each year, the sea ice of the Labrador Current begins to move southward until about April, when the ice melts faster than the speed of the current and the ice limit begins to retreat northward. It would be much safer for the treasure fleet to sail in the sea route of the North Atlantic Ocean without encountering sea ice. Hence, I would favour the estimate that the *earliest* time for the Chinese mariners to leave the North American coast would be in *April 1434*. Luo's description of having the gentle breeze, the wild flowers and the green grass to bid farewell to the Chinese mariners is not only consistent with the general spring or summer weather condition of the North Atlantic coastal region, but also with the favourable condition of its harbour and the sailing condition in the sea route of the North Atlantic Ocean.

In summary, we now have a good understanding of the whereabouts and the timelines of the Ming mariners from the moment of their unexpected landing at the steep cliff covered with yellow grass near the Labrador coastal region *around early-mid October 1433 to mid November 1433*, to their departure from the same cliff area around *early April to late August 1434* (after August, the grass will turn yellow again).

(5) The treasure fleet might have visited Florence on its way home in 1434

。。。时光迅速，。。。不觉的宝船回来，已经一个多月。每日顺风。。。忽一日，云生西北，雾障东南，猛然间一阵风来：。。。马船上早已掉下一个军士在海里去了。。。

My translation of the above passage is as follows:

… Time passed quickly. … It had been over one month since the treasure ships sailed towards home. Every day they encountered favourable winds. … Suddenly, one day, clouds started to form in the north-western sky and mist blocked the sight in the south-eastern direction. A gust of wind came all of

251

a sudden. … A sergeant on board the horse ship had already fallen into the sea. …

First, what does a "horse ship" mean? The treasure fleet used several types of ships: the Treasure Ship was the largest ship in Zheng He's fleet, equivalent to the flagship; the Troop Ship was a large warship; the Horse Ship was also known as the Horse Clipper, which was an early Ming large-scale high-speed ship for battles fought on the sea or on a river, as well as for transporting horses and a large number of goods; the Grain Ship was for carrying food, grain and logistics items; the War Ship was used as a special escort ship and designed to be manœuverable in battle; and the Water Ship was an auxiliary boat for storing and carrying fresh water.

When the above incident occurred, it was around May to September, over a month after the fleet left the cliff around April to August 1434. Not only did they encounter favourable winds every day in the Atlantic Ocean around this period of time, but their sailing was also a lot easier because, for this eastbound (homebound) journey, they could follow the Labrador Current, which would naturally bring them to the neighbourhood of the Grand Banks. Recall that in Chapter 5, their westbound (outbound) journey to the Labrador coastal region was against the flowing direction of the Labrador Current;[417] they had to sail cautiously. It also took over a month. But can Luo's narrative confirm the above viewpoint?

So, where was the treasure fleet when "a sergeant on board the horse ship had already fallen into the sea?" (Transl. Sheng-Wei Wang.) Does Luo give any hint?

We are at the end of Luo's Chapter 93 and the answer is in Luo's Chapter 94.

In Chapter 94, the drowning sergeant, Liu Guxian (刘谷贤), was luckily rescued and told the San Bao Master that he was saved by a big fish as he was about to drown in the sea. The revered San Bao Master then asked what kind of fish it was.

。。。谷贤道："其鱼约有十丈之长，碧澄澄的颜色，黑委委的鳍枪。是小的掉下去之时，得它乘住，虽然风大浪大，它浮沉有法，并不曾受半点儿亏"。。。谷贤道："是它口里说道：'你去罢。'不知怎么样儿，小的就在船上。。。"

My translation of the above passage is as follows:

… Guxian answered, "The fish was about ten *zhang* in length and in ghostly blue colour, with a dark-coloured fin sprouting out from its body like a spear. It was when I fell into the sea that this fish let me ride on it. Although the wind rolled turbulently and the waves were whipped up, the fish was able to swim up and down on the water skilfully and I did not suffer a bit."… Guxian added, "It was that fish which told me to 'go ahead and leave.' Not knowing how it happened, I was back on board our ship . . ."

Guxian was the first name (his last name was Liu 刘) of the sergeant who had fallen into the sea earlier. Is there any kind of "fish" that would fit Guxian's description?

It has been suggested that the "fish" was the narwhal (马克·尼克莱斯等 172–173) living in the Gulf of St. Lawrence (there is a debate whether narwhals are fish or mammals). Luo's narrative confirms that the Ming Treasure Fleet was in the Grand Banks region near the Gulf of St. Lawrence, which is rich in narwhals.

However, an adult narwhal's body length can be at most 4–5 m/13–16 ft, plus the male's tusk can be up to 3 m/9.8 ft, making the total length only a fraction of 30 m/98 ft; hence, far shorter than Luo's description of ten *zhang* (over 30 m/98 ft). Was it Luo's error, or his exaggeration? Only blue whales can have body lengths of more than 30 m/98 ft. But other than body lengths, they do not possess the "spear" described by Luo.

In short, we can conclude that the treasure fleet was in the neighbourhood of the Grand Banks in the North Atlantic Ocean, on its way home, and the date was around May to September 1434.

After the sergeant was rescued and returned to the ship, the fleet continued to sail towards home and could have taken one of the following routes:

Route 1 (sailing home, passing by the southern end of Africa):
After leaving the Grand Banks area around May to September of 1434, the Chinese sailors could have followed the North Atlantic Drift, then the Canary Current, the Brazil Current, the South Atlantic Current,[418] and the South Indian Current, to return home.

(See world ocean current map in Fig. 17.) This route could avoid sailing across the highly disputed Mediterranean Sea and traversing the dangerous Arabian Peninsula, while taking advantage of the dominant SSW winds associated with the Southwest Monsoon season from around April to October.[419] It could also avoid the threat of tropical cyclones—rapidly rotating storm systems, characterised by strong winds, and a spiral arrangement of thunderstorms which produce heavy rain.[420] The threat increases across the North Indian Ocean[421] as the Southwest Monsoon becomes established in April and May. Besides, the Ming Treasure Fleet had visited all the foreign countries commissioned for their expedition; it was time to take the most efficient route to go home as quickly as possible.

According to Luo's Chapter 95, the treasure fleet revisited only Malacca more than eight and a half months after it left the Labrador coastal area around April to August 1434. When the fleet arrived at Malacca, it was consequently around mid-January to mid-May 1435.

After leaving Malacca, the fleet passed an area near a magnetic mountain that is the highest ridge located on today's Hainan Island in the China coastal area. By then, it was more than eleven months after they had left the Labrador coastal area.

Finally, the treasure fleet returned to Nanjing more than a year after they left the Labrador coastal area. The date would be *around June to October 1435.*

In Chapter 3, I have shown that, for the seventh voyage, the Ming Treasure Fleet, led by Zheng He and Wang Jinghong, embarked from Longwan on January 19, 1431. So, by the time these Chinese mariners completed their trans-Atlantic voyage to North America and returned to China in mid-late 1435, more than four years had elapsed. Emperor Xuande (1389 or March 16, 1399 to January 31, 1435) had passed away a few months earlier. The sixth Emperor Yinzhong (英宗) or Emperor Zhengtong (正統帝; November 29, 1427 to February 23, 1464) of the Ming Dynasty, aged seven, ascended the throne on February 7, 1435.

From Chapter 3 of this book, we know that Wang Jinghong led his and Hong Bao's squadrons, returning to Nanjing on July 22, 1433 (July 6 in the eighth year of the Xuande period). Comparing this return date with the return timeline of the mariners who were led by Admiral Zheng He and made the trans-Atlantic voyage, the latter arrived at Nanjing approximately two years later. This timeline shows that Zheng He could not have been reappointed as the defender of Nanjing in 1433, if he had gone to North America.

More than 60 years later, on July 8, 1497, Portuguese explorer Vasco da Gama[422] led a fleet of four ships with a crew of 170 men from Lisbon in Portugal in search of a route to India. The motivation was also because traveling the ocean route would allow the Portuguese to avoid sailing across the highly disputed Mediterranean Sea and traversing the dangerous Arabian Peninsula. The round-trip route to India followed in Vasco da Gama's first voyage is shown in Fig. 33.

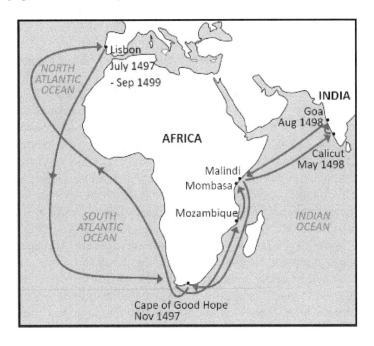

Fig. 33 The round-trip routes to India followed in
Vasco da Gama's voyage

Vasco da Gama's initial sailing after leaving Lisbon was to follow the Canary Current, and then the Brazil Current. This part of the voyage was similar to that of Route 1 taken by the Ming mariners in 1434 for returning home. On November 4, 1497, the expedition made landfall on the African coast. After that, da Gama basically followed the east coast of Africa against the Agulhas Current and stopped by Mozambique, Mombasa, and Malindi. He left Malindi for India on April 24, 1498. After crossing the Northern Indian Ocean with the help of the SSW winds, he landed in Calicut on May 20, 1498. The entire journey from Lisbon to Calicut took ten months and twelve days. The distance travelled in this journey was much shorter than the distance Zheng He's mariners had travelled from the Labrador coastal area to Malacca in just eight and a half months. To reach Malacca from Calicut, Vasco da Gama had to sail non-stop for approximately another 24 days (24 days was the length of time for the squadrons led by Wang Jinghong to make the same journey before returning to China in 1433). (See Section (1) of Chapter 3.) The Chinese mariners' Route 1 is far more efficient!

Route 2 (visiting Florence before going home): After leaving the Grand Banks area around May to September 1434, the Chinese sailors could follow the North Atlantic Drift, the Canary Current, and then enter the Strait of Gibraltar which is a narrow strait of approximately 14 km/9 mi wide at its narrowest point[423] connecting the Atlantic Ocean to the Mediterranean Sea. Recall from Section (4) of Chapter 4 that it took Junk Keying only 21 days to make the trans-Atlantic voyage from Boston to Port St. Aubin on Jersey in the British Channel Islands. It should take a comparable time for the Ming sailors to reach Port Gibraltar from the Grand Banks area. The arrival date would be around June to October 1434. Due to the importance of Florence[424] at that time as a centre of medieval European trade and finance and one of the wealthiest cities of that era, it would be really surprising and unlikely that the Ming envoys would omit to visit this important city and not meet Pope Eugene IV at Florence after June 1434 (in June 1434, the pope had to flee a revolt in Rome and began a ten-year exile in Florence).[425] Florence is considered the birthplace of the Renaissance, and has been called "the Athens of the Middle Ages".[426] Such a meeting would support Gavin Menzies' stance that the Ming envoys transferred the latest Chinese knowledge, navigational maps and technology to the Europeans in Florence, hence, significantly enhancing the progress of the Renaissance after 1434 and ushering in the New Age of Discovery.[427] But exactly how long the Ming envoys would have stayed in Florence or in the Mediterranean area is not known.

264

One possibility is that, after visiting Florence, the Chinese mariners could stay in the Mediterranean area longer. Since September to January was the best time to use the Red-Sea-Nile-Canals due to the swollen River Nile, they could navigate the ancient canals around September 1434 to January 1435 to Cairo, another important city to visit. After Cairo, they could sail from the Red Sea port into the Red Sea to reach Aden in less than a month, then to Calicut after sailing for less than another one month. By then, it would be around November 1434 to March 1435. They had to wait at Calicut until the direction of the winds became favourable[428] to sail home (as Wang Jinghong and Hong Bao did on April 9, 1433). But this could mean many months of waiting at Calicut. When they returned to Nanjing, the time would be *around July 1435*.

Alternatively, they could leave the Mediterranean area after visiting Florence by exiting the Gibraltar Strait, and then take Route 1 to return home. In this case, however, they would have arrived at Nanjing *later than around June to October 1435* (this was the arrival time without making the Florence visit).

Luo did not record the treasure fleet's Florence visit in his novel. Similarly, Luo also did not record Ma Huan's visit to *Tianfang*/Mo-jia, perhaps because the visit was under Hong Bao's command, not Zheng He's. Does this mean that the Florence visit, if it did occur, was also not under Zheng He's command, hence, escaped from Luo's record? Then, in this case, could it be that Zheng He did not return to China with his sailors? If so, where was he? Was he still in Fengdu/Cahokia? But, why? I shall come back to this point at the end of this chapter.

In summary, both Route 1 and Route 2 would bring some of the Chinese mariners who had made the trans-Atlantic voyage with Zheng He to North America, back to Nanjing in the early summer or even into the autumn of 1435. However, there is at least one other option, to be discussed next.

(5) The treasure fleet's tragic fate in New Zealand

The third route would bring some of the Chinese mariners first to New Zealand, on their way home. But sadly, their wish of returning home was not fulfilled. This section will detail what might have happened to them:

257   265

Route 3 (visiting New Zealand, but never making it home): After leaving the Grand Banks area around May to September of 1434, the Chinese sailors could follow the North Atlantic Drift, then the Canary Current and the Brazil Current as in Routes 1 and 2. Then, instead of following the South Atlantic Current to sail eastward, the treasure fleet could pass through the Strait of Magellan[429] to sail along the west coast of South America by following the South Pacific Current, then the South Equatorial Current (flowing from east to west) to reach New Zealand. (See world ocean current map in Fig. 17.) I label this route, Route 3 (1).

Another route was to follow the Brazil Current, then the Antarctic Circumpolar Current to reach New Zealand. (See Fig. 17.) (Fig. 34 shows Australia and New Zealand.) I label this route, Route 3 (2).

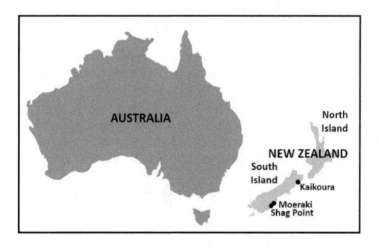

Fig. 34 Australia and New Zealand

In my earlier discussion of Route 1, I mentioned Luo's record that it took eight and a half months for the Chinese mariners to reach Malacca after they left the Labrador coastal area around April to August 1434. For Route 3, based on a crude distance estimate, it would take an approximately similar amount of time for the Chinese mariners to reach New Zealand after they left the Labrador coastal area by either Route 3 (1) or Route 3 (2). This means that when the

Chinese mariners arrived in New Zealand the date would be around mid-January to mid-May 1435.

But why would the Chinese be interested in New Zealand, instead of the much bigger Australia? New Zealand was rich in metallic ores and had very large trees suitable for ship-building and masts. Hence, it appeared to be a more valuable site for the Chinese mariners to set up an operational base. A shipyard capable of building China`s largest vessels was located in the South Island, according to T.C. Bell,[430] who did not wish to give the actual location of the evidence to protect it from being destroyed.

In New Zealand, Bell has also located Chinese rammed earth walls with stone cores; the largest Chinese city in the North Island was complete with a Weng Cheng 瓮城 or *Weng Cheng* (瓮 weng, meaning urn or earthen jar; 城 cheng, meaning city), a semi-circular enclosure built on the outside of the city gate,[431] the hallmark of a Chinese development. (See Fig. 35.)

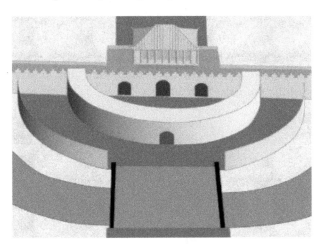

Fig. 35 *Weng Cheng* in Beijing

When the enclosure is in square shape, it is called Fang Cheng 方城 or *Fang Cheng* (方 fang, meaning square). (See Fig. 36.)

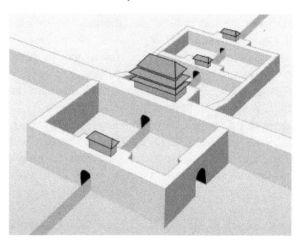

Fig. 36 *Fang Cheng* in Nanjing

Fig. 37 shows a rock which formed part of the outer gateway of the walled road to an "unknown"[432] location in the North Island of New Zealand. An "eye" carved in the rock kept watch on those entering the gate. Some writing has been carved into the rock face. Sadly, the broken area of the rock marks a recent attempt to destroy the evidence of the pre-Māori occupation.[433]

Fig. 37 A rock which formed part of the outer gateway of the walled road to an "unknown" location in New Zealand

Bell summarises his survey work as follows and his comments are inside round brackets:

Summary of New Zealand surveys. Fifty plus Chinese sites, from three cities to ore exploitation sites were located. Carbon dates are from 190 BC to iron smelting in 1066 AD. Petroglyph dates are at least circa 500 BC, or earlier (by Chinese expert in China).

About 75 wrecked sand covered Chinese vessels were located; including 24 circa 120 m x 48 m/394 ft x 157 ft vessels and 23 super-junk harbours specifically designed for these large vessels with keel slots, flushed to remove debris and hull support pads at low tide (I have ignored the number of harbours located for the other junks). The entire fleet and coastal sites were wiped out in circa 1435/1436 AD by the heat from a falling meteorite, and then the carbonized vessels were washed out of their harbours by the Tsunami created when the meteorite hit the ocean south of New Zealand. The Tsunami also covered most of the coastal settlements with debris from the sea bed. Many of these vessels might have been part of the Pacific fleet gathering cargoes from the Pacific islands and might have involved some from the Chinese seventh fleet. Sadly, they chose the wrong time to meet in the fixed harbours, hence the demise of circa 35,000 sailors. And we will never know how many residents and their Maori workers/slaves died.

Moeraki[434] was the largest Chinese harbour site we located in New Zealand. Examinations of the "famed" Moeraki balls found were made. Natural concretions were brought to Moeraki for onward shipment. They came under two prime classifications. One type are the natural concretions coated externally by the Chinese to form a sphere (to form pure balls), then used for some function on the larger vessels. In North Island we also located one large dump of uncoated concretions alongside a harbour ready for shipment; these concretions had modified ends to insert timber, so that they (these concretions) can be rolled from the locations where they were found to the harbour ready for shipment. The presence of Moeraki balls is evidence of the wrecks of large Chinese vessels.

Basically, the evidence shows that the Chinese had occupied New Zealand from at least 500 BC, until being virtually wiped out in 1435/1436 AD.

The Moeraki Treasure Ship provides us with the information that the size of the Chinese treasure ships had not been exaggerated (circa 120 m x 48 m/394 ft x 157 ft) and the hull was stiffened with concrete, bonded to the hull with rice adhesive.[435]

Fig. 38 shows Chinese stone cannon and mortar balls (ammunition)—the "famed" Moeraki balls, located in New Zealand. The two stone cannon balls, each weighing 10 kg/22 lb and measuring 200 mm/8 in (in diameter), are from a Chinese wrecked vessel located near Shag Point, South Island. A similar sized cannon ball was also recorded on the sand below the Moeraki Treasure Ship.

Fig. 38 Chinese stone cannon and mortar balls located near Shag Point, South Island in New Zealand

Fig. 39 shows stone mortar balls with a diameter of 300 mm/12 in which were found partially exposed on the sand below the Moeraki Treasure Ship and photographed when Bell was filming with Television New Zealand (NZTV). According to Bell, three similar stone mortar balls have been recorded, still visible within the hull of the treasure ship, and stone mortar balls of 430 mm/17 in (in diameter) have been recorded from a North Island treasure shipwreck and by the South Island Shag Point treasure shipwreck.[436] Fig. 40 shows stone mortar balls from the nearby Chinese wrecks on display at a memorial on the 1836 site of a whale station in Moeraki.[437] They are cannon/mortar balls from Chinese vessels, carbonised by the 1435/1436 meteorite passing over New Zealand, then either washed out of their harbour or washed ashore by the Tsunami which was created by the meteorite crashing into the sea, south of New Zealand. Later in 2017, an earthquake lifted up the

262

New Zealand seabed by around one metre and displayed several spherical stone balls and the base of the Chinese harbour in Kaikoura,[438] South Island, New Zealand. These balls are identical to those located in several parts of New Zealand adjacent to the sites of the Chinese wrecks explored by Bell. The usage of these cannon/mortar balls will be further discussed towards the end of this section.

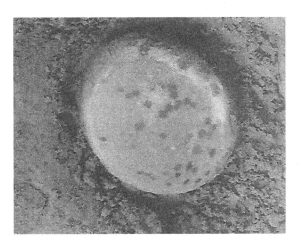

Fig. 39 This 300 mm diameter mortar ball was found partially exposed on the sand below the Moeraki Treasure Ship

Fig. 40 Mortar balls from nearby Chinese wrecks on display at a memorial on the 1836 site of a whale station in Moeraki, New Zealand

263

Bell was the first to record the existence of large concrete blocks, cannon and mortar balls which had fallen onto the beach from a Chinese vessel. Among the concrete blocks, some showing signs of timber and rice adhesive, was one with a *Chinese Government stamp imbedded in it* and another inscribed with some lovely artistic work, a goose, a porpoise jumping and some smaller animals— presumably the work of a talented sailor.[439]

Bell has also discovered in New Zealand that every Chinese vessel he has surveyed had a special kind of anchor in two sizes and they always identify a Chinese junk.[440] They consist of two blocks approximately 3 m/9.8 ft long and 0.5 m/1.6 ft wide. Bell describes them as follows and his comment is in round brackets: [441]

The blocks are shaped to form a fluke at each end. A square hole was formed at the centre of each block and the blocks are connected by an eight-metre long wooden stock. The anchor cable (rope) was attached to the centre of the stock. The design ensured that the two flukes always dug into the sea bed. This design was adopted as the modern ships' anchors and they are far superior to the Admiralty anchors [442] which engaged only one fluke at a time and are difficult to stow. The sections of worn/broken Chinese anchors were also located off the California coast. This unique design identifies wrecked junks.

Bell's survey findings reveal that New Zealand would appear to have been the Chinese Southern Pacific base during Chinese mariners' earlier voyages (we do not know when) as well as during their seventh voyage. Wear and tear of the Chinese ships required both repairs and replacement. Returning to China for repairs was out of the question due to the distance and with an unseaworthy vessel.[443] The seventh voyage took place about ten years after the sixth voyage; the Chinese mariners would most likely want to revisit their old base in New Zealand to check things out or plan for future voyages before returning home. Sadly, it would seem that they all vanished with their ships on a foreign coast.

Unlike those Ming sailors who had explored Cahokia and were able to return home safely to leave records of their adventurous voyage, Luo Maodeng had no knowledge of any Chinese mariners who vanished at New Zealand during the seventh voyage. But the Moeraki balls lying silently on the sandy beach of the South Island of New Zealand may be revealing secrets related to Zheng He's fleet using the Xiang Yang Da Pao 襄阳大炮 or *Xiangyang Dapao*[444] (大 da, meaning large and 炮 pao, meaning cannon) or *Xiangyang Cannon*[445] described in Luo's Chapter 78. Let us find out!

Xiangyang Dapao, also known as the huge stone catapult, was named after its use in the famous Battle of Xiangyang.[446] It is an important battle in the war between the Southern Song Dynasty (1127–1279) and the Mongols. The Mongols applied the counterweight technology they learned from the Persians to the huge stone catapults which they used in their siege of Xiangyang in 1268–1273 (Dreyer 86), and thereby finally succeeded in conquering the Southern Song Dynasty in 1279.[447] *Xiangyang Dapao* could throw large stones to destroy the enemy's city walls and cause severe damage. They were important weapons prior to the advent of artillery cannon. The book Ma Ke • Bo Luo You Ji《马可•波罗游记》or *The Travels of Marco Polo* (1254–1324)[448] has documented the detailed process of the Mongol siege of Xiangyang using the *Xiangyang Dapao*.

Luo's Chapter 78 also has a vivid narrative describing how Zheng He's military commanders were ordered to set up *Xiangyang Dapao* to lay siege to the city of Lasa (a city state; the 34th country on the list given earlier in Chapter 3; Lasa was near Mukalla, a seaport and today the capital city of Yemen's Hadhramaut governorate) to pressure its surrender in early 1433 during their seventh voyage.

。。。蓝旗官报："前面又到了一个国，不知是个甚么国，禀元帅老爷，即可差下夜不收前去打探明白，以便进止。"。。。即时传令四营大都督，各领本营军马，围住他四门。各营里安上云梯，架起襄阳大炮，许先放三炮，以壮军威。。。可可的这个国叠石为城，城有四门，守城番将看见军马临门，连忙闭上城门。一门上一个都督，一道云梯。一道云梯上九个襄阳大炮。各门上一个号头，连放三个大炮。这三个炮还顺了人情，不曾打他的城门，只照着城墙上放，把城墙上的石头，打得火星迸裂。。。地动山摇。。。连番王的营殿都晃了两三晃。满城中官民人等，只说是掉下了天，翻转了地，吓得魂飞魄散，胆战心惊。

My translation of the above passage is as follows and my comment is in square brackets:

... The officer who held the blue-coloured flag reported, "In front is another country. I do not know what country it is, hence, I come to make this report to my revered commander-in-chief and request you to send a reconnaissance officer to check things out in order to decide what to do next." ... Immediately an order was sent out to the military commanders of the four battalions to lead their army and horses to surround the four gates of this foreign city state. Each battalion set up a cloud ladder [scaling ladder], erected the *Xiangyang Dapao* near it, and was allowed to fire three initial shots to show military might... However, this foreign country had built strong city walls by stacking stones and the city walls had four gates. The defenders saw soldiers and horses coming to the gates, they quickly closed them. In front of each gate, there was a military commander and a cloud ladder. Near each cloud ladder were placed nine *Xiangyang Dapao*. In front of the gate there was also a trumpeter to send the necessary signal. Then, three shots were launched consecutively. These three volleys were meant to be warning shots only. They were not aimed at each city gate, but rather at the city wall. The stones on the walls sparked and cracked. ... And the earth shook. ... Even the foreign king's palace shook two or three times. The city's officials and people felt as if the sky had fallen and the ground had turned upside down. They were shattered, terror-stricken and struck dumb.

In the above passage, Luo Maodeng described how Zheng He's military commanders ordered their soldiers to erect the *Xianyang Dapao* to be in combat-ready mode and to set up the mobile "cloud ladders".[449] (See Fig. 41.) (The cloud ladder was used in ancient wars for climbing city walls and attacking cities. It was invented during China's Spring and Autumn Period[450] which corresponds roughly to the first half[451] of the Eastern Zhou Period.) During the siege, the ladder was positioned under the city wall and the movable upper ladder was added for climbing to the top of the wall.

The *Xiangyang Dapao*, which required considerable space for their launching operation, were too big to be mounted on a cloud ladder, contrary to the suggestion made earlier by Dreyer (86). The cannon could be operated independently as free-standing machines on the ground; hence, the recoil force they generated after launching artillery shells could avoid impacting the stability of the cloud ladder. With this understanding, the *Xiangyang Dapao* described in Luo Maodeng's novel could be the powerful stone-throwing machines similar to those used by the Mongols in the Xiangyang War, instead of merely "bombards" or cannons of some sort as suggested by Dreyer and J.J.L. Duyvendak without giving further details (Dreyer 86). T.C. Bell's discoveries of stone cannonballs or mortar balls weighing ten kilos and with diameters ranging from 200 mm to 430 mm, located in several parts of New Zealand adjacent to the Chinese ship-wrecks, suggest that *Xiangyang Dapao* were not born out of Luo's imagination. They had been used by Zheng He's soldiers for the siege of Lasa, and later transported to New Zealand by the treasure ships. They were true *Xiangyang Dapao* using stone/mortar balls as ammunition.

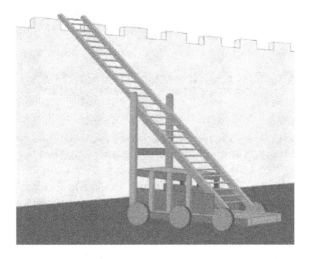

Fig. 41 Model imitating the ancient Chinese cloud ladder

To appreciate fully what Luo wrote about Zheng He's use of the *Xiangyang Dapao* for the siege of Lasa, we need a true knowledge

267

of its power. These were stone-throwing machines (重力抛石机)[452] called Counterweight Trebuchet or Trabutium, which first appeared in twelfth century Europe (after being invented by the Persians) and then entered China via the Mongols as I have said earlier. They were the largest type of trebuchet. A model is shown in Fig. 42.

Fig. 42 Model of *Xiangyang Dapao*

The simplest *Xiangyang Dapao* is a lever that holds a heavy object at one end and a cannonball at the other end, then throws the projectile at a suitable angle.[453] (See Fig. 43.) Before launching, the end on which the ammunition was placed must be pulled down with a winch, pulley or directly with human power, while the other end with the weight rises at the same time. Then, the stone cannonball is let go by releasing it or cutting off the rope so that the heavy weight at the other end falls, throwing the lighter stone cannonball into the air at high speed. The maximum range that a *Xiangyang Dapao* can reach is determined by several parameters. For example, if a heavy counterweight of one ton drops by 2 m/6.6 ft, then this *Xiangyang Dapao* can throw up to ten kilos of artillery cannonballs to a distance of approximately 400 m. The maximum range is inversely proportional to the weight of the cannonball, so that the lighter it is, the farther it will go. Typically, the ratio of the counterweight and the cannonball weight is about 100:1. Until the advent of modern artillery, the giant trebuchet dominated the battlefield because of its extensive supply of cannonball material, huge strike power and tolerance to climate.

Yuan Shi • A Li Hai Ya Chuan《元史•阿里海牙傳》or *The Biography of Ali Hai Ya in the History of the Yuan Dynasty* has this description. My translation is as follows:

When the machine launches a shell, it shakes heaven and earth. The world is completely destroyed by the attack, and the bullet penetrates seven *chi* into the ground.

For Zheng He's voyage, the *Xiangyang Dapao* were carried on ships; hence, the size of the cannon and the cannonballs had to be optimised. The Moeraki balls weigh ten kilos. According to Luo, after twelve stone cannonballs were launched (three shots near each gate) at the Lasa city walls, the natives were terrified.

Using such horror tactics was meant to scare the enemy into avoiding a real war. And unsurprisingly, Lasa surrendered and offered tribute to Zheng He on the day after the treasure fleet's arrival.

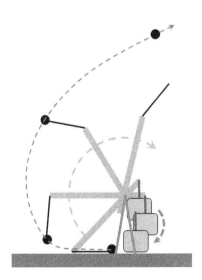

Fig. 43 Operational principle of the *Xiangyang Dapao*:
the weight swings the beam upward,
launching the projectile like a slingshot

269 277

The Last Journey of the San Bao Eunuch

Dreyer has suggested the idea that "Cannon were certainly used in the wars of the Ming founding, and Emperor Yongle's recognition of his army in Beijing included a major headquarters devoted to firearms training. It is certainly possible that Zheng He's fleet carried firearms as part of its armaments, but Luo Maodeng's novel does not add to the evidence on that point. In fact, his use of the term *Xiangyang Dapao* suggests that he wove his narrative of the fight at Lasa from the history of the historical siege of Xiangyang plus some awareness of the firearms in existence in the 1590s, which had contributed to Ming China's victory over the Japanese in Korea in that decade" (87–88). But after reading the analysis in this section and showing T.C. Bell's discoveries of the many stone cannon/mortar balls from the wrecked Chinese vessels located at various sites in the North and South Islands of New Zealand, we realise that Luo's narrative proves amazingly realistic and well connected with the known archaeological facts. Any doubt about Luo's credibility on this issue will inevitably collapse of itself!

(6) The end: Cahokia's disappearance

In Chapters 6 and 7 and this chapter, I have presented multiple lines of evidence to show, that the Fengdu Ghost Country in Luo Maodeng's novel was today's Cahokia Mounds Historic Site in the central Mississippi Valley, one of the most sophisticated pre-Columbian settlements north of Mexico; and that Zheng He's mariners visited this great city during their sixth and seventh voyages. Strangely, archaeological records show that the Cahokia Mounds complex became an empty city, mysteriously and abruptly abandoned by the original Cahokians in the fifteenth century between the years of 1400 and 1450. During the two centuries after year 1400 (Lorenz and Schleh 102),[454] Cahokia was abandoned with no sign of Native Americans living there. Until French explorers came across the ruins of Cahokia in the late 1600s, that area was rarely a place of human habitation. The Illiniwek Indians living in the area were not necessarily descendants of the original Mississippian-era people living in the area. The Osage people passed by there in the sixteenth century, but they continued their westward migration.

There have been many theories surrounding Cahokia's mysterious disappearance; including a series of major flood events

270   278

on the Mississippi River;[455] the city's growing population becoming unsustainable, leading to resource depletion and deforestation;[456] unpredictable weather conditions in the 1200s; internal turmoil such as political instability, warfare and the decline of trade; or a combination of factors. [457] However, these theories have not provided enough convincing evidence to resolve the issue.

On the other hand, the disappearance of the Cahokia Mounds City overlaps with Zheng He's seventh voyage to North America. Did the Chinese expedition have anything to do with Cahokia's disappearance between 1400 and 1450, since the Chinese sailors' visits there were during the 1420s and the 1430s?

While the Chinese explorers, like the later Europeans, had a wide spectrum of immunity to childhood illnesses such as measles, influenza, and chicken pox, the natives of Cahokia would have had no protection, due to a different blood type. Any introduction of even the milder of these contagions would have resulted in pandemics with death tolls numbering in the thousands, if not tens of thousands (马克·尼克莱斯等 183). Did Zheng He and some of his crew members have to stay at Cahokia to deal with a sudden and unfortunate event such as the pandemics mentioned here, and as a result some of them did not have the chance to return home? But why did the visit in the 1420s not cause such pandemics and wipe out Cahokia earlier than the visit in the 1430s? And why did the intimate contact of Liu Shi and Cui Jue as husband and wife not result in Cui Jue contracting illnesses such as measles and chicken-pox?

Since Luo's novel gives no indication of the occurrence of any plague in Fengdu/Cahokia introduced by the Chinese expedition, we still do not know what actually happened.

Then, early in the 21st century, a plain copper medallion of seven centimetres in diameter with the inscription "Authorised and awarded by XuanDe of Great Ming" (transl. by Lee Siu-Leung) was unearthed four inches under the surface in North Carolina. The site was several hundred miles inland from the American east coast, at the centre of the Cherokee Indians' homeland that used to be a major battleground with the first European settlers. This old copper piece is considered to be the medallion awarded to Zheng He by Ming Emperor Xuanzong before Zheng He embarked on the seventh voyage.[458] What is the connection between this Xuande

Medallion and Zheng He's final whereabouts? Who can rule out the likelihood that Zheng He stayed in North America and died there?

Only further archaeological research can provide more evidence to resolve the issue of Cahokia's disappearance and any connection it may have with Zheng He's final fate.

Over some 100 years after 1450 (when the Cahokia Mounds City turned into an empty quarter), the Ming emperor in China decided to partially lift the *Haijin*, or Sea Ban, starting from 1567. By then, China had lost the knowledge and technology of making ocean-going ships for more than a century and there were no Chinese ships making the trans-Atlantic crossing.

So, who fed Luo Maodeng all the information about Cahokia for his writing in such a detailed and realistic way?

The Cahokia Mounds City was "discovered" by French explorers in the late 1600s, after Luo had completed his novel. So, it was not the French who did it.

At the time when the French reached there, the mounds were inhabited by Illiniwek people who were different from the original Cahokians. (The mounds received their name because the Cahokia tribe was living in the area.)[459] So it was not these new Cahokia inhabitants who did it, either.

Then, who else?

Although Hernando de Soto is recognised as the explorer who led the first Spanish and European expedition deep into the territory of the modern-day United States through Florida, Georgia, Alabama, Mississippi, and most likely Arkansas,[460] and as the first European documented to have crossed the Mississippi River, he did not discover the Cahokia Mounds City. Hence, it was not Hernando de Soto who did it.

Could it be other Europeans or Asians?

At the beginning of the sixteenth century (during the middle of the Ming Dynasty), the Portuguese and Spanish colonists, while colonizing the Americas, also crossed the Indian Ocean and the Pacific Ocean, respectively, and met near southern China. The Portuguese took China's Macao and India's Goa as bases, and opened the sea route connecting Macao-Goa-Lisbon-Brazil. The Spanish took the Philippines as a base and opened the even more important sea route connecting Seville (Spain)-Acapulco (Mexico)-Manila (the Philippines)-China's Fujian and Guangdong ports. Hence, they established a link between China and the Americas so that the Chinese silk goods could be continuously shipped to the Americas and exported to Europe.[461] So the ancient Chinese "Silk Road" to the West was transferred to the Pacific Ocean, resulting in the formation of the "Pacific Silk Road". However, people travelling on this new Silk Road did not discover the Cahokia Mounds City. Hence, it was not Europeans or Asians travelling on the "Pacific Silk Road," who did it, either.

Since Luo's narrative covers materials much beyond imagination, and also beyond records written by Ma Huan, Gong Zhen, and other Ming and Qing historians, I am led to think that Luo's knowledge about the Cahokia Mounds City most likely came from Ming mariners who had actually participated in the sixth or seventh voyage (or both) to the central Mississippi Valley and later returned to China. However, a proven answer to this question is still challenging to all of us who are creative in making proposals and tirelessly seeking the truth.

The Last Journey of the San Bao Eunuch

CHAPTER NINE

Secrets revealed by ancient maps

In this chapter, I briefly review the ancient Chinese knowledge of a round Earth, and their invention and use of the compass for maritime navigation. With their advanced knowledge and long history of navigational exploration, the Chinese produced the first world map on a scroll, the 1418 Chinese World Map. Later Matteo Ricci's map—Kunyu Wanguo Quantu—was to become the earliest known Chinese world map in the style of European maps with Chinese characters. By comparing these two world maps, I have identified circumstantial evidence which shows that Ming mariners did indeed explore the central Mississippi Valley during their sixth voyage to the Western Ocean, thereby supporting Luo Maodeng's account.

In previous chapters I have shown multiple lines of evidence in support of Ming mariners' exploration of the central Mississippi Valley during their seventh voyage to the Western Ocean. Then, in Sections (3) and (4) of Chapter 6, based on the conversation between Zheng He's scout Wang Ming and his ex-wife Liu Shi, I have deduced that Chinese mariners had also explored the neighbourhood of Fengdu/Cahokia Mounds City on October 13 in the 21st year of the Yongle period (in November 1423).—This is because the date overlapped with the Ming Treasure Fleet's sixth voyage to the Western Ocean.

According to Luo Maodeng's novel, Wang Ming confirmed that his presumed-dead spouse Liu Shi was in fact still alive and well; and Liu Shi confirmed that Wang Ming had been her husband before she was taken captive due to illness, in a raid by the natives in 1423. Since extensive map analyses have been carried out by researchers working on the Zheng He project, readers may wonder whether evidence can also be found in ancient maps to verify Luo's account.

However, before connecting Luo's account with our knowledge of world maps, readers must be aware that even the most rigorous historical scholars admit that there exist some puzzling ancient Western maps in which a number of "unknown" areas had been mapped out before the Age of Discovery. Most of these mysteries can be resolved only if we acknowledge as historical fact that Chinese sailors had explored these "unknown" places long before Europeans did.

(1) Chinese knowledge of a round Earth and their ancient navigational history

Some people believe that until the Italian Jesuit priest, Matteo Ricci (利马窦; 1552–1610)[462] showed them the 1602 map of the world with Chinese characters, the Chinese people did not know that the Earth was round and did not know how to make circular maps. Therefore, it is imperative for me, first, to give a brief summary of what the ancient Chinese knew about the universe and the world, before returning to the topic of seeking evidence from maps to support the finding that Chinese mariners visited the neighbourhood of Fengdu/Cahokia Mounds City during their sixth voyage to the Western Ocean.

Concerning the Chinese knowledge of a round Earth and the stars, ancient Chinese showed that they doubted whether the Earth was square by asking the question in 221 BC: if the Earth was square and the sky was round, how could they match?[463]

In Chapter 4, I have introduced the famous astronomer Zhang Heng (78–139 AD)[464] in the Han Dynasty (202 BC–220 AD), who theorised that the universe was like an egg with the stars on the shell and the Earth as the yolk in the centre. Zhang Heng compared the celestial circle to the *diameter* of Earth and obtained a ratio of 736:232, thus obtaining $\pi = 3.1724$ (the correct value is $\pi = 3.14159...$).[465] In addition to documenting about 2,500 stars in his extensive star catalogue, Zhang also posted theories about the moon and its relationship to the sun. Specifically, he discussed the moon's sphericity, its illumination by sunlight on one side and the hidden nature of the other, and the nature of solar and lunar eclipses.[466] Modern scholars have compared his work in astronomy to that of the Greco-Roman Claudius Ptolemy (86–161).[467]

The ancient Chinese first invented the magnetic compass as a device for divination as early as in the Han Dynasty.[468] The compass was used in Song Dynasty China (960–1279) by the military for navigational orienteering by 1040–1044, and was used more generally for maritime navigation by 1111–1117. The compass reached Europe by the twelfth century, and the use of a compass was recorded in Western Europe and in Persia around the early thirteenth century.

The astronomer, mathematician and hydrologist, Guo Shoujing (郭 守 敬 ; 1231–1316) [469] of the Yuan Dynasty (1271–1368), predicted that the Earth was round by using a large amount of data.

Tian Wen Zhi《天文志》or *Astronomical Records*,[470] one of the volumes in Jin Shu《晋书》or the *Book of Jin*,[471] has an explicit account on the shape of the Earth. It reflects the concept of Hun Tian Shuo "浑天说"[472] or the "Theory of Sphere-Heavens" or the "Geocentric Theory in Ancient Chinese Astronomy", which was one of the three ancient Chinese theories of the universe. The other two theories were Ge Tian Shuo "盖天说"[473] or the "Theory of Canopy Heavens", and Xuan Ye Shuo "宣夜说"[474] or the "Theory of Unlimited Universe with Celestial Bodies Floating in the Void". Until the early fifteenth century, the "Theory of Sphere-Heavens" dominated ancient Chinese views on the universe. The central idea was like this:

。。。天地之体，状如鸟卵，天包地外，犹壳之果黄也；周旋无端，其形浑浑然，故曰浑天也。。。半覆地上，半在地下。其二端谓之南极、北极。。。两极相去一百八十二度半强。。。赤道带天之纮，去两极各九十一度少强。

My translation of the above passage is as follows:

… The shape of the celestial body is like a bird's egg. The celestial body has an outer space surrounding the Earth. It is outside the Earth like the egg shell covers the egg yolk. The celestial body rotates like a wheel and does not stop. Its extent is uncertain; hence, it is called the fuzzy celestial body. … Half of the mass is above the ground and the other half below the ground. The two poles at the two ends are called the South Pole and the North Pole. …The two Poles are a little more than 182.5° apart. The Equator is the celestial body's belt, being a little more than 91° to each Pole.

The shape of the egg yolk inside an egg shell is spherical. In an article entitled "Chinese Knowledge of the Spherical Earth Centred on the Sun,"[475] Gunnar Thompson pointed out that not only did the ancient Chinese know that the Earth was round,[476] but some of the ancient Chinese astronomers also knew that the Earth and the moon revolved around the sun. They have since successfully applied their knowledge of astronomy to navigation and made great achievements in assisting in the exploration of the world. The fact that Chinese people knew the existence of two celestial poles gave one of the most compelling reasons that the Earth was round in their minds.

At the beginning of the eighth century, the ancient Chinese already grasped the technique of measuring latitude on the Earth by observing the height of the Polaris star in the Northern Hemisphere or by observing the height of the sun. This is a very important fact for us to appreciate. These techniques required the use of angle gauges[477] and levels.[478] The length of the meridian of one degree was measured by Monk Yi Xing (僧一行; 683–727; who became a monk in his youth; Yi Xing was his Dharma name, his original name was Zhang Sui 张遂), an astronomer in the Tang Dynasty (618–907). However, historical records show that only in the mid-fifteenth century did European navigators and cartographers learn the techniques of measuring latitude in the Northern Hemisphere using these two methods. Furthermore, until the mid-sixteenth century, their measurements of the latitudes were still not very accurate. For the Southern Hemisphere, only in 1598 and 1600 were the Europeans able to determine the precise location of the Southern Cross constellation.[479] Without this knowledge, they would not have been able to find the geographical locations of Australia, New Zealand and the Antarctic region and their outer contours.

In Section (6) of Chapter 1 of this book and the references therein, I have also mentioned the four cross-ocean stellar maps contained in Zheng He Hang Hai Tu 《郑和航海图》 or *The Charts of Zheng He's Voyages*, which were used by Zheng He's fleet for determining the coordinates (latitudes) of their destinations in their astronomical navigation. These charts show that Zheng He's mariners knew how to measure latitude with good accuracy. For longitude, it could also be measured or calculated by observing certain astronomical phenomena. Some of the methods we know

278

today, which could be used on land or at sea, are proposed on Gavin Menzies' website.[480]

Specifically, the ancient Chinese sailors at sea needed some simple and practical methods to determine the longitudes of their destinations. This could be done as long as they had a clock which kept time accurately during the whole period of their journey. It would be hard to imagine that they sailed for long journeys without measuring the time during their travel. The sailors would set their clock at their starting point as the reference time and start recording the time (days and hours) and writing their navigation diaries. At the starting location and the destination, they would read the time from their clock when the sun went through transit (namely when the sun rose to its highest point above the horizon), or alternatively to show midnight when a particular star went through transit at night (reaching its highest point above the horizon). Clearly, if the clock at the destination read noon in daytime (or midnight at night), the ship was still on the same meridian as the origin. But suppose that the clock showed a sun transit time of 7:00 am, time X, at the destination, which is 5 hours before their clock's 12:00 noon at the origin: then they knew that they were on a meridian east of their starting point by 5/24 of a full revolution around the world, namely 5/24 x 360 = 75 degrees of longitude to the east of their starting point. Likewise, a sun transit time of 3 hours, a different X value at the destination, after their clock's 12:00 noon at the origin meant that they were on a meridian that is 3/24 x 360 = 45 degrees west of their starting point. This method was valid regardless of the latitudes of the origin and the destination, as long as transit times were used, and not, for example, sunrise or sunset times, which depend on latitude. I don't think currents and winds matter. The measurements I describe above depend on the sun and star transit times only, and not on the time of travel. It is true that the time of arrival does depend on currents and winds, but this did not bother them in measuring the sun and star transits; what they had to do was to wait until the next sun or star transit to work out their longitude.

Hence, the success of measuring/calculating longitude using the above methods depended on measuring the time differences as accurately as possible. The ancient Chinese had invented various methods for measuring time on land and at sea (for example, at sea, the Chinese could burn specially made large incense candles to record time).

But between the fifteenth and the eighteenth centuries, the Europeans knew only how to measure longitude by using dead reckoning[481] and magnetic declination.[482] These methods were very inaccurate. After a long voyage, cumulative errors in dead reckoning frequently led to shipwrecks and a great loss of life. Also, before the mid-seventeenth century, the Europeans had not invented a way of measuring time at sea. Only in 1756 did English carpenter and clockmaker, John Harrison (1693-1776), design a small clock which could measure time accurately during navigation. To be conservative, neither the Europeans nor the Arabs knew how to measure latitude and longitude accurately until the sixteenth century.

According to Jiu Tang Shu • Tian Wen 《旧唐书•天文》 or the *History of the Early Tang Dynasty on Astronomy* (the Tang Dynasty spanned from 618 to 907), the Chinese people had reached the coast of the Arctic Ocean before the tenth century.[483] An ancient wooden world map in a late eleventh century Chinese Daoist tomb (dated 1093; in the middle of the Song Dynasty), located to the northeast of Beijing, shows the profile of the world's five inhabited continents, including the Americas and Australia. This evidence reveals that *the Chinese had completed the feat of mapping the coastlines of these continents in 1093, 400 years before Columbus reached the New World.*[484] I shall mention this map again soon. Undeniably, the use of the magnetic compass invented by the Chinese for navigation, starting from the eleventh century, the methods for measuring time on land and at sea, and the advanced technique of astronomical navigation were the major technical contributors to their remarkable success.

Later, Ling Wai Dai Da 《岭外代答》 or *Answers to the Questions Concerning Foreign Countries* by Zhou Qufei recorded that by the twelfth century during the Song Dynasty, Chinese people could reach inland of Mu-lan-pi.

But where was Mu-lan-pi? Is it the border area between the Patagonian Plateau and the Pampas in South America, as suggested by Liu Gang, or Namibia in West Africa, as suggested by Lam Yee Dim? It is still under debate. Then, in the Yuan Dynasty, the Chinese already extended their reach to almost all inlands of the continents in the world. In 1267, a Mongolian scholar in China was able to make a wooden globe to represent the Earth, with 70 percent of its surface area in green colour as water and the remaining 30 percent in white colour as land. The ratio was almost the same as modern geographical survey results.[485]

By the fourteenth and early fifteenth centuries, even before Zheng He's fleet started its first voyage in 1405, the Chinese cartographers had a good knowledge of the shape of Africa and knew the existence of an ocean to the west and south of Africa. The 1389 map—Da Ming Hun Yi Tu 《大明混一图》[486] or Amalgamated Map of the Great Ming Empire, was made by Chinese cartographers. The 1402 map—Hun Yi Jiang Li Li Dai Guo Du Zhi Tu《混一疆理历代国都之图》[487] or The Kangnido Map or Map of Integrated Lands and Regions of Historical Countries and Capitals, was made by Koreans based on two ancient Chinese maps and supplemented with maps of Korea and Japan.[488] Both maps show the interior of Africa and the existence of an ocean—today's Atlantic Ocean—to the west and south of Africa. This knowledge was the fruit of continuous reports of the topography—coastal and internal—of Africa, by Chinese and non-Chinese merchants and mariners, who, for centuries, had frequent and extensive contacts with cities alongside the Southern coast of China.[489] In contrast, Europeans reached the south of Africa much later: Portuguese navigator and explorer Bartolomeu Dias led the first European expedition to round the Cape of Good Hope in 1488; another Portuguese explorer, Vasco da Gama, reached India from the Atlantic Ocean in 1497 to 1499.

Also, map projection, a method of converting the Earth's spherical surface onto a flat-surface drawing of a map, through complicated mathematical calculations, was not necessarily introduced by Western missionaries who came to China in the seventeenth century, as some scholars believe. Long before the Christian era, the Chinese had already begun to study map projection.[490] Zhou Bi Suan Jing《周髀算经》or *Classic of Arithmetic from the Gnomon of the Zhou Sundial* (China's first astronomical book on calendar calculations and a collection of Chinese mathematics) was completed around the first century BC.

Charles H. Hapgood (1904–1982)[491] was an American college professor and author, best known for his claim of a rapid and recent pole shift with catastrophic results, who once served as the executive secretary of Franklin Roosevelt's Crafts Commission. (In 1958, Hapgood published *The Earth's Shifting Crust: A Key To*

Some Basic Problems of Earth Science, in which he denies the existence of continental drift and included a foreword by Albert Einstein.) In another of Hapgood's famous books, *Maps of the Ancient Sea Kings: Evidence of Advanced Civilization in the Ice Age*, he analyses many Portolan charts.[492] In one case, Hapgood selected a few geographical points on the 1137 Ancient Chinese Map[493] (Hua Yi Tu 《华夷图》 or Map of China and Barbaric Countries) from the northernmost part to the southernmost part of China and determined their latitudes, and did the same thing for the longitudes (Hapgood, *Maps* 135–147). He then made the following discovery: the accuracy of the map suggested the use of spherical trigonometry, and the form of the oblong grid, very much like that of the Caverio Map,[494] suggested that the original projection might have been based on spherical trigonometry. The accuracy of the map is startling. This would further support the idea that the Chinese knew the Earth was spherical. If that was the case, then there would be no problem for the ancient Chinese to draw lines of latitude and longitude for the Earth.

It is equally startling that the 1137 Ancient Chinese Map was originally carved in stone and actually existed before 1137. The map's source was Hai Nei Hua Yi Tu 《海内华夷图》 or Map of China and Barbaric Countries within the Seas, drawn by Jia Danyu (贾耽于; 730–805) in 801 of the Tang Dynasty. All these maps predate the Portolan charts which existed in the European Middle Ages (1300–1500).—The earliest dated navigational chart extant by Pietro Vesconte (fl. 1310–1330)[495] is said to mark the beginning of western professional cartography.

The connection of the 1137 Ancient Chinese Map with the portolan charts suggests that their mapmakers mapped virtually the entire globe with a uniform general level of technology. This prompted Hapgood to conclude that his findings settle the question as to whether the ancient culture that penetrated Antarctica, and originated all the ancient western maps, was indeed *worldwide* (Hapgood, *Maps* 145).

As I have mentioned earlier, in fact, the ancient Chinese had already explored the world even before the appearance of the 1137 Ancient Chinese Map. The 1093 Chinese Wooden World Map (Zhang Kuang Zheng Shi Jie Di Tu 《张匡正世界地图》 or Zhang Kuangzheng World Map)[496] unearthed in 1971 in an ancient Daoist tomb in Beijing, drew the world inside a circle. It lends strong support to Hapgood's finding and strengthens the viewpoint that the ancient Chinese knew the Earth was spherical and had circumnavigated the entire world. Later, the 1722 map—Tian Xia Quan Tu《天下全图》[497] or 1722 Complete World Map—shows a close resemblance to the 1093 map and to better representations of Europe, Africa and the Americas, indicating that the 1722 map might be an updated version of the 1093 map.

From the discovery of the 1093 Chinese Wooden World Map and the 1137 Ancient Chinese Map, it is clear that the Chinese already knew that the Earth was spherical and had circumnavigated the entire world. Moreover, they had mastered the technique of map projection.

(2) The 1418 Chinese World Map

Knowing these facts will help us understand the importance of the 1418 Chinese World Map shown in Fig. 44, owned today by Beijing lawyer, map collector and analyst, Liu Gang. The map shows, for the first time, North America, South America and the major continents of today's world, on a scroll. The 1418 Chinese World Map—Tian Xia Quan Yu Zong Tu《天下全舆总图》[498] or Overall Map of the Geography of All Under Heaven—was a rendition made by Mo Yi-tong (莫易仝) in 1763 in the Qing Dynasty, based on the 1418 Ming map, Tian Xia Zhu Fan Shi Gong Tu《天下诸番识贡图》[499] or Map of the Barbarians from All under Heaven Who Offer Tribute to the Court. Gavin Menzies calls this map, Zheng He's Integrated Map of the World, 1418.

Fig. 44 shows the full 1418 Chinese World Map and the right-side map shows the portion containing mainly Australia, New Zealand, North and South America, the Antartic, and some small islands, etc.

During a press conference in Beijing in March 2006, some reporters and historians claimed that the "dual-hemispheric projection" for maps was invented in Renaissance Europe. Hence, Mo Yi-tong's rendition would have to be a copy of a European map made in the sixteenth century.

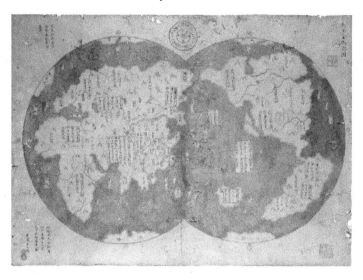

Fig. 44 1418 Chinese World Map

However, Gunnar Thompson strongly refuted the above viewpoint as follows.[500] His comments are in round brackets and my comment is in square brackets:

...To begin with, the design of the 1418 Map does not have the kind of adjacent circles that are always shown on European maps of this type; instead, it has overlapping circles or "conjoined circles." Furthermore, the 1418 Ming Map is not a "projection" of continents into spherical equivalents but is instead more a composite of land areas from otherwise flat maps that have been fitted into a circular shape. It is possible that the original artist distorted the land areas to some extent in order to mimic the effect of curvature of the earth. Even so, the Ming Map does not have the characteristic grid of longitudes and latitudes that are seen on Renaissance maps.

A book on Taoism by Stephen Little, Ed., et al., (*Taoism and the Arts of China*, Art Institute of Chicago, 2000, pp. 344–347) clearly shows that the "conjoined hemispheres" as seen in Mo Yi-tong's map relate to a Taoist artistic explanation for the phases of the moon or for patterns of daylight and night as the shadows of Yin/Yang pass across the planet. Two illustrations in Little's book show two overlapped hemispheres (called "conjoined hemispheres") representing both sides of the moon. The same kind of illustration would have served to explain the patterns of light and dark or daylight and nighttime [day and night] on the surface of the earth. The writer says that the Qing-era illustrations on a scroll were copies of the same designs that were used on a Southern Song Dynasty scroll (1127–1279). He says that the same text was used in a Ming Dynasty Taoist Canon or book of philosophy. Zhang Boduan (984–1082) is identified as the originator of the spiritual text. This concept of "conjoined hemispheres" was prevalent in Taoist art during the Song, Yuan, and Ming Dynasties. In other words, the claim on the part of Eurocentric historians that use of such a design on the 1418 Ming Map represents a copy of the Renaissance European maps is totally unfounded.

The Taoist Scroll is called Jinye huandan yinzeng tu or "Sealed Verification of the Golden Elixir of the Reverted Cinnabar." The present location of the scroll is at the White Cloud Monastery in Beijing. So, we can be certain that this kind of artwork served as an inspiration for the artist Mo Yi-tong working in Beijing. It seems quite possible that Europeans acquired this idea of dual-hemispheric map design from Ming Chinese or Arabian sources. ...

Moreover, Mo Yi-tong's rendition of the 1418 Chinese World Map placed the horizontal centre line approximately at latitude 37°, whereas the Renaissance European cartographers used the Equator as the horizontal centre line, an imaginary line on the Earth's surface, equidistant from the North Pole and South Pole, to divide the Earth into the Northern Hemisphere and Southern Hemisphere. Before the end of the Ming Dynasty, most ancient Chinese maps placed the horizontal centre line approximately at latitude 37°, since that was the main region where the ancient Chinese culture originated.[501]

To emphasise that the original 1418 Chinese World Map did exist, Gavin Menzies wrote a memo which summarises the evidence for his contention that the famous Portuguese cartographer Albertin de Virga, who made the Albertin de Virga Map,[502] obtained a copy of Zheng He's Integrated Map of the World, 1418, which he copied.

Here is Menzies' viewpoint,[503]

... He substituted his own 1409 map of the Mediterranean for those parts on the 1418 map. He also used Arab maps for depictions of North Africa and the Persian Gulf. Di Virga then published his map with the amendments in 1419.

Menzies especially noted that both de Virga's map and Zheng He's map are centred on the Salt Lake in Central Asia's Kazakhstan and depict the same eastern hemisphere of the world centred on the same place, showing rivers from the Orange River in S. Africa to the Amur in Siberia, centuries before Europeans reached there; and also showing the same Islands from the North-West Atlantic to the N. Pacific.[504] How can this be a coincidence? Moreover, some of the errors in Zheng He's 1418 Integrated Map of the World soon appeared in European maps, the most striking being the presentation of California as an island. Both maps were published before European voyages of exploration started.

Liu Gang also made similar comments, except he thinks that both maps centre on Samarkand, a major city in Uzbekistan,[505] which is not far from the Salt Lake in Kazakhstan.

Additionally, Gunnar Thompson has written an article in which he concludes that the 1418 map that the Beijing Lawyer, Liu Gang, found is quite remarkable and further states that the Chinese exploration of the world not only inspired, but also guided the voyages of the Renaissance Europeans.[506] The latter point is beyond the scope of the present book and I will not get into this area of discussion here.

(3) What the 1418 Chinese World Map reveals

The 1418 Chinese World Map was drawn in the middle of Zheng He's fifth voyage (1417–1419). Then, was the information on the map gathered entirely during the fifth voyage?

On December 28, 1416, the Yongle Emperor Zhu Di[507] ordered Zheng He to undertake the fifth voyage and to escort all the envoys of the nineteen different countries who had visited Zhi Di at the imperial court back to their homes. The fleet embarked in the autumn of 1417 (Dreyer 83) and returned to China a little over one year and seven months later, on August 8, 1419.[508] This time they escorted more envoys back with them, in time to be ready for the implementation of Zhu Di's plan to move the capital from Nanjing to Beijing.[509]

Where was Mu-lan-pi?

First, recall that the 1093 Chinese Wooden World Map already showed the profile of five continents, revealing that the Chinese had completed the feat of mapping the coastlines of these continents no later than 1093 AD. It is fair to say that after 1093, it was under the guidance of some existing Chinese maps that the Ming Treasure Fleet revisited and remapped the world along the waterways opened up by ancient Chinese mariners.

To understand the extent of the navigation of the fifth voyage, Lam Yee Din analysed ancient Chinese records and formed the view that Zheng He's fleet reached as far as the country of Mu-lan-pi in today's Namibia,[510] but did not have time to sail further, deep into the Atlantic Ocean, because Zheng He's fleet had to return home in preparation for Emperor Zhu Di's plan of moving the capital of the Ming Dynasty from Nanjing to Beijing in 1421.

If Lam is correct, then the 1418 Chinese World Map reaffirms the viewpoint that the Ming Treasure Fleet did not visit any land beyond Namibia, and the Americas shown on the map are a reflection of Ming cartographers' knowledge about that part of the world based on the work already accomplished by earlier Chinese explorers before 1418. Thus, it is not surprising to see that California was mistaken as an island by the ancient Chinese explorers, and the mistake was later corrected in Matteo Ricci's 1602 map, Kunyu Wanguo Quantu,[511] which will be discussed soon in this chapter.

However, Liu Gang has a different viewpoint. He has offered strong arguments to show that Mu-lan-pi is today's border area between the Patagonian Plateau and the Pampas in South America. The area was already known by the Chinese in the Song Dynasty.[512] The Patagonian Plateau is a sparsely populated region located at the southern end of South America, shared by today's Argentina and Chile. The region comprises the southern section of the Andes Mountains as well as the deserts, pampas[513] and grasslands east of this southern portion of the Andes.[514] Patagonia has two coasts. They are the western coast facing the Pacific Ocean and the eastern coast facing the Atlantic Ocean, whereas the Pampas, facing only the Atlantic Ocean, are fertile South American lowlands that include some of the Argentine provinces; all of Uruguay; and the southernmost Brazilian State, Rio Grande do Sul.[515]

If Liu Gang is correct, then, it is fair to say that, during the fifth voyage, Zheng He's fleet, or most likely some squadrons of the fleet, made a trans-Atlantic voyage to arrive at South America. Then, the 1418 Chinese World Map reaffirms the viewpoint that it reflects Chinese mariners' re-mapping of that part of South America. Due to their limited time, it is doubtful that they could re-map other parts of the Americas during this voyage. Then, it is also not surprising to see that California was still mistaken as an island on the map, since it was surveyed by Chinese mariners before 1418.

Having considered both viewpoints, I feel, at this point of time, that there is not enough evidence to confirm that the Ming Treasure Fleet had explored South America during the fifth voyage before the Chinese cartographers drew the 1418 Chinese World Map. It is a research area which deserves more future attention.

The 1418 Chinese World Map has changed our perceptions

The discovery of the 1418 Chinese World Map has changed our perceptions. In school, some of us were taught that the Cape of Good Hope was "discovered" by the Portuguese explorer Bartolomeu Dias in 1488; the Americas were "discovered" by Christopher Columbus in 1492; the Gulf of St. Lawrence was "discovered" by French navigator Jacques Cartier in 1534; Australia was "discovered" by the Dutch navigator Willem Janszoon in 1606; Hudson Bay was "discovered" by the British colonist and explorer Henry Hudson in 1610; New Zealand was "discovered" by Dutch navigator Abel Tasman in 1642; the Bering Strait was "discovered" by Danish-born Russian explorer Vitus Jonassen Bering in 1648; the Antarctic continent was "discovered" by Russian, American and British explorers in 1820. But *all these places are shown on the 1418 Chinese World Map*, implying that the ancient Chinese seem to have explored all these places before the Europeans did!

Mo Yi-tong's 1763 rendition of the 1418 Ming map of Tian Xia Zhu Fan Shi Gong Tu 《天下诸番识贡图》 or Map of the Barbarians from All Under Heaven Who Offer Tribute to the Court is strong evidence showing that, before 1418, Chinese sailors had completed a circumnavigation of the Earth and surveyed it. Their contribution to the exploration of the world was immense. Unfortunately, however, they later gave up their global ocean voyages and *by 1477 most of their records were destroyed* as explained in Section (5) of Chapter 1, and detailed by Dreyer (165–186). But the knowledge acquired by the Chinese people had passed through the Portuguese and through the Italian merchant and explorer Niccolò de' Conti (circa 1395–1469) who had participated in the Chinese voyages and helped to spread the knowledge to the Western navigators and cartographers.

However, a closer examination of the right-side map in Fig. 44 shows that the 1418 Chinese World Map is crude by today's standard. It gives the gross outline of the Americas, and only a few of the internal geographic features are noted. The Hudson Bay is clearly shown to the north of Canada and Greenland is also visible. In the middle is the Isthmus of Panama. The large river emptying into a deep gulf is the Gulf of St. Lawrence. But, Florida, the Gulf of Mexico, and the Mississippi, Illinois and Missouri Rivers do not show up on the map.

There are three islands displayed in the Atlantic.

One of the northernmost islands is presumably Cape Breton Island, but it is shown too far south. The first European who visited the island was Venetian navigator and explorer John Cabot (1450–1500)[516] in 1497. However, European maps of the period are of too poor a quality for researchers to determine whether it was Newfoundland or Cape Breton Island which Cabot was the first to visit.

The fact that Cape Breton is shown on the 1418 Chinese World Map supports T.C. Bell's assertion that Chinese settlement existed on Cape Dauphin, Cape Breton Island, and that Cape Breton was the Chinese North Atlantic base during their earlier voyages as well as during Zheng He's last voyage.

One middle island group might be the Azores. The Azores archipelago began to appear on portolan charts[517] during the fourteenth century, well before its official discovery date. The first map to depict the Azores was the Medici Atlas of 1351.[518] We know from DNA that the Azores were inhabited by people with an East Asian admixture,[519] but here the island group is shown too close to the West Atlantic. This dislocation in longitude may be caused in part by a map projection which converted the Earth's spherical surface onto two overlapping two-dimensional flat surfaces.

The third island may be Bermuda.[520] The first European known to have reached Bermuda is the Spanish sea captain Juan de

Bermudez (1449–1570)[521] in 1505, after whom the islands are named.

Australia and New Zealand in Fig. 44 are too close to South America. This can be explained as due to the narrowing of the width of the Pacific Ocean, created when the map was projected from a three-dimensional curved surface on to two overlapping two-dimensional flat surfaces. The result is that the North and South American continents were drawn inside the same two-dimensional flat surface as that enclosing Australia and New Zealand.

As for major rivers, there are two river systems on the Atlantic coast of North America. The northernmost one is clearly the St. Lawrence River. The southernmost river system is the Roanoke River (Menzies and Hudson 184); this river is branched into three arms.

Finally, the last and one of the most important pieces of information revealed by the 1418 Chinese World Map is that the Mississippi River and its tributaries[522] are *absent* from the map. The Chinese did *not* know them yet. These rivers were also *absent* from Albertin de Virga's 1419 map and all other known European maps before 1419. The Europeans did *not* know them either. Only the Native Americans knew these rivers.

(4) Matteo Ricci's 1602 map, Kunyu Wanguo Quantu

In 1583, the Italian Catholic missionary Matteo Ricci (利玛窦; 1552–1610)[523] was among the first Jesuits to enter China from Macao. At the time, he had a small Italian wall map (made in 1570) in his possession. In 1584, he and his Chinese collaborators made the first Chinese world map, Yu Di Shan Hai Quan Tu 《輿地山海全图》[524] or Complete Terrestrial Map, which contains all the major continents of the world. For brevity, I shall call this map Ricci's 1584 map. There are straight lines indicating latitudes, and curved lines indicating meridians. It was China's first map with latitude and longitude. China is placed near the centre of the map.[525] The portrayal of Antarctica as vast and scattered indicates two important points; firstly, that the European missionaries at the time had no understanding of the Southern Hemisphere and secondly, that the Chinese who collaborated with Ricci were not aware of the

290

discoveries shown in the 1418 Chinese World Map, made by ancient Chinese.

Ricci's second world map, completed at Nanjing in 1600, was called Shan Hai Yu Di Quan Tu《山海輿地全图》or Complete Terrestrial Map (1600); it was based on a 1596 map that he made and which was called Shan Hai Yu Di Tu《山海輿地圖》or Terrestrial Map.[526] His second world map was engraved on a stele.

Another ancient Chinese map—also called Shan Hai Yu Di Quan Tu《山海輿地全图》[527] or Complete Terrestrial Map—is contained in the book, San Cai Tu Hui《三才图会》or *Encyclopedia of Assembled Illustrations of the Three Realms of Heaven, Earth and Man*, written by the Ming Dynasty Wang Qi (王圻) and his son Wang Siyi (王思义). The map was completed in 1607 and published in 1609. The 1609 map has often been confused with Ricci's Shan Hai Yu Di Quan Tu《山海輿地全图》or Complete Terrestrial Map (1600), which is no longer in existence.[528]

In 1601, Ricci was the first Jesuit to enter Beijing, the Ming capital, bringing atlases of Europe and the West, which were unknown to his hosts. The Chinese also had their own maps of the East, which were equally unfamiliar to Western scholars. In 1602, at the request of the Ming Wanli Emperor (明神宗; 1563–1620),[529] Matteo Ricci and his collaborators Zhong Wentao and Li Zhizao (李之藻; 1565?–1630)[530] printed his largest world map—Kunyu Wanguo Quantu《坤輿万国全图》or Complete Geographical Map of All the Kingdoms of the World.[531] It is the earliest known Chinese world map in the style of European maps with Chinese characters. It occupies a very important position in the history of China. Matteo Ricci was an important historical figure in China. Recently, however, Lee Siu-Leung has pointed out that Ricci's world map has a startling hidden secret: he used map data of the Chinese ancient navigators who had explored the Americas.

Lee analysed this map and writes that on the map near the region of Spain, there is this key Chinese text (李兆良,《坤輿萬國全圖解密》51):

此欧罗巴州有三十余国。。。去中国八万里，自古不通，今相通七十余载云。

My translation of the above passage is as follows:

This Europe has more than 30 countries. ...The distance from China is 80,000 *li*. Since ancient times, the place had no interaction with China. Now they have had diplomatic relations for some 70 years.

The last emperor Toghon Temür (元順帝; 1320–1370; he was the eleventh emperor and the last Khagan of the Mongol Empire) of the Yuan Dynasty, and Pope Innocent VI of the Holy See formally established diplomatic relations at the end of 1353 (李兆良,《坤輿萬國全圖解密》53).—Some 70 years (between 70 and 80 years) from 1353 means approximately the year between 1423 and 1433.—However, because An Nan (安南)[532] appeared on the map and the name of An Nan was changed from Jiao Zhi (交趾)[533] in 1428, the map must have been made between 1428 and 1433, a period after the sixth voyage, but overlapping the early part of Zheng He's seventh voyage. Given that, for the seventh voyage, the Ming Treasure Fleet embarked at Longwan near the Longjiang Shipyard on January 19, 1431, the map must have been completed by then to guide the new voyage. Hence, the contents of Ricci's 1602 map may be dated around 1428 to January 19, 1431, a narrower time range.

Matteo Ricci was in Beijing, the Ming capital, and had access to Chinese maps. He revised the European maps he had from the new sources of information obtained from these Chinese maps and made the Kunyu Wanguo Quantu. Lee Siu-Leung points out that the Kunyu Wanguo Quantu does not resemble European maps before 1602.

(5) Revelation by Ricci's 1602 map, Kunyu Wanguo Quantu

In Fig. 45, the two figures combined give the complete Kunyu Wanguo Quantu, which we may refer to, for brevity, as, "Ricci's 1602 map".

Fig. 46 shows a portion of the North and Central American continent in Ricci's 1602 map. This portion shows a North and Central America closer to its modern appearance than in the 1418 Chinese World Map, and gives a lot of detailed geographical information about the inland areas not displayed in the latter.

Portions of the Mississippi, Illinois and Ohio Rivers appear, although they are not named. These rivers are outlined in Fig 46. They were drawn at their correct locations, flowing into today's Gulf of Mexico. But only a relatively short upstream portion of the Mississippi River was drawn to the north of its confluence with the Illinois River.

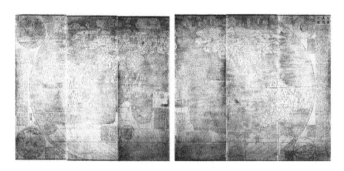

Fig. 45 Ricci's 1602 map

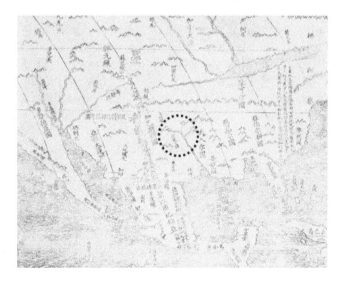

Fig. 46 Detail of North and Central America on
Ricci's 1602 map (Mississippi River and its tributaries, other than
the Missouri River, are outlined)

293

We can be sure that during the sixth voyage, the Ming mariners did not arrive at the Mississippi River from the Labrador coastal region as they did during the seventh voyage, because the Great Lakes do not appear in Fig. 46, which would be the only and important waterway for transportation from the Gulf of St. Lawrence and St. Lawrence River to the inland areas of the Mississippi. The Missouri River is not shown, indicating that it was not explored by the Ming mariners at the time.

As I have argued above,[534] the contents of Ricci's 1602 map may be dated around 1428 to January 19, 1431, a period which falls after Zheng He's sixth voyage, and right before the treasure fleet embarked for the seventh voyage. Hence, the rich information on the Americas revealed by the map could not be the fruits born out of the seventh voyage. The existing Chinese historical records show no evidence that the Ming Treasure Fleet had reached the Mississippi River in any of the first to fourth voyages (these voyages did not sail beyond the Indian Ocean). In relation to the fifth voyage, the only unsettled issue is the location of Mu-lan-pi. But, regardless of whether Mu-lan-pi was Namibia in West Africa, or the border area between the Patagonian Plateau and the Pampas in South America, it was far away from the Mississippi River in North America. Hence, it is not surprising that the river does not show up on the 1418 Chinese World Map shown in Fig. 44. The Mississippi, Illinois and Ohio Rivers outlined in Fig. 46 could have been explored by the Ming mariners only during their sixth voyage in the early 1420s. The Chinese cartographers were able to draw these rivers carefully in preparation for future voyage(s). Indeed, they explored the area again during their seventh voyage about ten years later!

Earlier I mentioned that Wang Ming's ex-wife Liu Shi was taken away during a raid by local American Indians on October 13 in the 21st year of the Yongle period (in late November 1423). This occurred during the sixth voyage of the Ming Treasure Fleet. The circumstantial evidence obtained from the above-mentioned map analysis clearly supports the idea that the Ming sailors *did* arrive at Fengdu/Cahokia Mounds State Historic Site in the central Mississippi Valley around 1423, once again supporting Luo Maodeng's narrative.

Disappointingly, among the European maps and other world maps before 1602, none was able to label the proper location with the correct name of the Mississippi River and its major tributaries

(李兆良,《坤輿萬國全圖解密》 98–109); hence, its identification has been confusing. This was despite the fact that the Mississippi River had already been reached in 1518 by the expedition sent out by the Spanish Basque conquistador Francisco de Garay (1475–1523), and drawn by an unidentified person on the Turin map.[535] Later, the Spanish explorer and conquistador Hernando de Soto was the first documented European to have crossed the Mississippi River in 1541. He led the first European expedition from 1539 to 1542 deep into modern American territory including the territory of modern-day Florida, Georgia, Alabama and most likely Arkansas. But the confusion found in European maps as to the name and location of the Mississippi river was not resolved.

Perhaps due to these complications, Ricci and his collaborators decided to use the information on the Chinese map, in which the Mississippi River and its tributaries had been drawn at the correct locations, but did not have names. Ricci and his collaborators transferred the unambiguous Mississippi River and its tributaries on the Ming map to their 1602 map, and the resulting map looks distinctly different from the European maps. This is clear evidence that Ricci's 1602 map could not have been a copy of the European maps before 1602.

Now we can have a good idea about where the Chinese mariners entered the Mississippi River during their sixth voyage. They most likely entered the Mississippi River from the Gulf of Mexico, which was named in Chinese Xin Yi Xi Ba Ni Hai 新以西把你海 (海 Hai; meaning Ocean) in Fig. 46.[536] They did not enter from the Labrador coastal area as they did during the seventh voyage, because the five Great Lakes do not show up. But Florida[537] and Cuba[538] appear on Ricci's 1602 map, giving new evidence that the Chinese sailors must have explored the Caribbean Sea as well during their sixth voyage.

There are many other geographical features on Ricci's 1602 map which deserve attention. Here are just a few examples relevant to the content of the present book:

1. As mentioned earlier, Australia already appears on the 1093 Chinese Wooden World Map and the 1418 Chinese World Map. On the latter, New Zealand is correctly shown as two main islands next to Australia. (See Fig. 44.) In this figure, both Australia and New

Zealand are closer to South America than to Asia. I have explained the cause in the earlier part of this chapter.

However, on Ricci's 1602 map the situation becomes very different. Australia is written as 鸚哥地, meaning Land of Parrots,[539] and labelled as a land mass below the southern end of Africa. (See Fig. 47.)

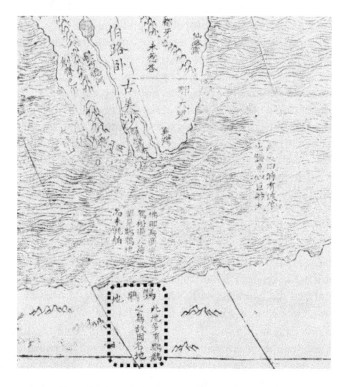

Fig. 47 Australia (framed) as a land mass
below the southern end of Africa on Ricci's 1602 map

Australia is too far west (an error of approximately 90° or ¼ of 360° in longitude) and too far south (an error of approximately 30° in latitude) from its actual position. The errors cannot be due to errors in measured latitude and longitude. We know that the Chinese mariners were able to measure latitude and longitude rather accurately; the earlier 1093 Chinese Wooden World Map and the 1418 Chinese World Map show reasonable accuracy for the positions of Australia and New Zealand. The errors also cannot simply be explained as due to the distortion generated when the map is projected from a three-dimensional round surface on to a two-dimensional flat surface. This leads me to think that Ricci and his Chinese collaborators still did not know the region of the Southern Hemisphere in 1602 and mistakenly placed Australia or 鸚哥地 at a "presumed" location (in their perception), as a huge land mass.

Dutch navigator Willem Janszoon was the first European to reach Australia (in 1606), four years after Ricci's 1602 map was completed. Another Dutch navigator Abel Tasman was the first European to reach New Zealand (in 1642), 40 years after Ricci's 1602 map was completed.

Moreover, the fact that New Zealand and the Antarctic region still do not appear on Ricci's 1602 map further supports the viewpoint that Ricci and his collaborators did not appear to have a good understanding of the Southern Hemisphere at the time. They simply covered that vast area with a huge blank area and filled it in with some text.

2. Ricci's 1602 map does not show Newfoundland as an island which is disconnected from the entire Canadian mainland and separated from continental Labrador by the narrow Strait of Belle Isle.

Historically, Newfoundland Island was long settled by indigenous peoples of the Dorset culture.[540] Later, it was visited by the Icelandic Viking Leif Eriksson (Leif Ericson or Leif Erikson; 970–1020)[541] in the eleventh century, who called the new land "Vinland". The next European visitors to Newfoundland were Portuguese, Basque, Spanish, French and English migratory fishermen. The island was visited by the Venetian navigator John Cabot on his expedition from Bristol in 1497. Later, in 1534, Breton navigator Jacques Cartier (1491–1557)[542] was the first European to enter the Gulf of St. Lawrence by the Strait of Belle Isle and then reached the inlet of the St. Lawrence River.

From the above brief summary, we know that between the eleventh and the mid-sixteenth century, Europeans explored eastern Canada. Several colonies were established and a few maps were drawn to record these explorations before 1602. So why did Ricci not draw Newfoundland as an island, a well-known fact since 1534?

Obviously, Ricci used information from a map earlier than 1534 and from a non-Europeam source to draw the east coast of today's Canada on his 1602 map. But what was the source of this map?

A close examination of the east coast of Canada on Ricci's 1602 map shows that it differs from any European map before 1602. Such an observation indicates that Matteo Ricci may have used the Chinese map drawn between 1428 and January 19, 1431, as the basis to draw his 1602 map. There are at least two reasons to support this conclusion: 1) he had kept Chinese geographical information including names and locations on his 1602 map which did not show on the European maps; and 2) he had added more Chinese names translated from the European maps or books, and placed them on his 1602 map at their "presumed" geographical locations. A few examples are shown in Fig. 48 as follows:

Fig. 48 East coast of Canada on the Japanese copy of Ricci's 1602 map. Cape Breton Island (framed) is shown as two separate islands

1. The Gulf of St. Lawrence in Fig. 48 has a wide opening to the Atlantic Ocean, since Newfoundland Island is not shown as an island. We now know that Newfoundland Island blocks a big part of the mouth of the St. Lawrence River as shown in Fig. 18, creating the Gulf of San Lawrence, the world's largest estuary. Mistakenly, Newfoundland is presented as a peninsula on Ricci's 1602 map and in two parts.

One part labelled in simplified Chinese characters as Ke Er De Le Ya Er De 可尔得勒亚尔地, translated from Portuguese "Terra Corterealis" (李兆良，《坤輿萬國全圖解密》122) is connected with Weng E Da or Wong Ak Dab 蓊厄答 ("Honguedo", perhaps translated directly from Native American pronunciation; 李兆良，《坤輿萬國全圖解密》123) or today's Quebec to its west side. In fact, Newfoundland Island does not connect with today's Quebec; rather Labrador is connected with Quebec.

The other part, labelled Ba Ge Lao De 巴革老地 (translated from the Portuguese "Terra de Baccalaos"; 李兆良，《坤輿萬國全圖解密》122), is located to the north of a big bay labelled Mo Luo Ta Hai 默罗它海 (it is the bay that separates Ba Ge Lao De 巴革老地 from Ke Er De Le Ya Er De 可尔得勒亚尔地; the map label is hard to read; this is the original Chinese name; later it was translated as "Mare Melotuo" or denoted as "G. de Merostro" in 1594 and 1606 European maps, respectively; 李兆良，《坤輿萬國全圖解密》123). This bay has a wide opening to the North Atlantic Ocean. This part of Newfoundland is connected with Yi Li Duo De Lan De 亦利多的兰地 (translated from Estotilant or Estotiland in European maps or books; 李兆良，《坤輿萬國全圖解密》122). This leaves De Er Luo Wu Luo Duo 得尔洛勿洛多 (translated from the Portuguese "Terra Labrador"; 李兆良，《坤輿萬國全圖解密》123) which is to the west of Ke Er De Le Ya Er De 可尔得勒亚尔地 or Newfoundland, having no direct access to the Gulf of St. Lawrence and the Atlantic Ocean. Lee Siu-Leung writes that De Er Luo Wu Luo Duo 得尔洛勿洛多 includes today's province of Newfoundland and Labrador (李兆良，《坤輿萬國全圖解密》123). If that is the case, then on Ricci's 1602 map, Labrador has no direct access to the Gulf of St. Lawrence and the Atlantic Ocean; only Newfoundland accesses both.

Under these conditions, what corresponds to the Mo Luo Ta Hai 默罗它海? It might be the combination of today's Groswater Bay, Happy Valley-Goose Bay and Lake Melville shown in Fig. 18. It was drawn as having a very wide opening to the Atlantic Ocean, further indicating that the source of this part of Ricci's 1602 map was an older map than the sixteenth century European map. If Mo Luo Ta Hai 默罗它海 is the combination of today's Groswater Bay, Happy Valley-Goose Bay and Lake Melville, then both Ba Ge Lao De 巴革老地 and Yi Li Duo De Lan De 亦利多的兰地 must be part of today's Labrador, shown in Fig. 18 for a comparison.

The above are examples showing that Matteo Ricci had added Chinese names which were translated European names. He placed these names on an ancient Chinese map at their "presumed" geographical locations (in Ricci's perception) to make his 1602 map. As a result, mistakes and confusions were created.

2. There are two islands labelled Gui Dao 鬼岛 or the Ghost Island (left island inside the outlined area of Fig. 48; 鬼 gui, meaning ghost; 岛 dao, meaning island; 鬼岛 Ghost Island, meaning notorious for its shipwrecks), and Jia Li Han Island 加里漢岛 (right island in the framed area of Fig. 48). They are near the entrance of the Gulf of St. Lawrence and off the mainland of today's Nova Scotia Province.

On Ricci's 1602 map, Gui Dao 鬼岛 or the Ghost Island, and the Jia Li Han Island 加里漢岛 combined together could be today's Cape Breton Island.[543] The Island was famous for its rocky coast, stormy Atlantic Ocean and stories of shipwrecks. In Fig. 48, Cape Breton Island is shown as two separate islands. Today we know that it is one large island separated from the mainland of Nova Scotia by the narrow Strait of Canso. (See Fig. 20 in Chapter 5.) The reason why Cape Breton Island was drawn as two separate islands on this ancient map may be explained by a finding by Paul Chiasson. He writes that an ancient canal existed across St. Peter's isthmus *long before* the sixteenth century (*Ruins*, 62–63). If this was true, the canal would have separated the Island into two separate islands. Chiasson writes further that the canal could have been built only by the Ming Chinese for navigation down through the centre of the Island from the Atlantic. The presence of Cape Breton Island labelled as 鬼岛 and 加里漢岛 in Fig. 48 *does* seem to support

300

Chiasson's theory, although the shapes and orientations of these two islands were not precisely surveyed during the sixth voyage of the Ming Treasure Fleet in the early fifteenth century.

In the 1418 Chinese World Map, Cape Breton Island is shown too far south. In Ricci's 1602 map, it is appropriately located. Since both maps show Cape Breton Island, they give strong support to our earlier finding in Section (2) of Chapter 5 that Cape Breton Island would appear to have been the Chinese North Atlantic base. Cape Breton is what Paul Chiasson identified as the Island of Seven Cities, due to its seven ports—Cape Dauphin, Chéticamp, Ingonish, Louisbourg, St. Peter's, St. Ann's and the area now known as Sydney. As I have mentioned in Chapter 5, the Seven Cities were the legendary cities of great wealth sought by earlier Spanish explorers. On Ricci's 1602 map, there is also an area called Zu Wa La 祖瓦蜡, translated from Ceuola or Cibola (李兆良,《坤輿萬國全圖解密》124–125), which is supposed to be where the Seven Cities were located. But Matteo Ricci mistakenly placed Zu Wa La 祖瓦蜡 in the mid-west of Canada.

In conclusion, a comparison of the 1418 Chinese World Map with Ricci's 1602 map indicates that the latter, with its lines of latitude and longitude, is a much-improved world map. It gives not only the locations and the general shapes of continents and oceans (with the exception of Australia, New Zealand and the Antarctic region), but also gives a richness of inland geographical information. Ricci's 1602 map also corrects the mistake in the 1418 Chinese World Map which shows California as an island. I suggest that all these achievements could be attributable to a circumnavigation made by the Ming Treasure Fleets during their sixth voyage. If these ideas are correct, they further validate the historical value of Luo Maodeng's account.

The Last Journey of the San Bao Eunuch

CONCLUSION

In the Preface to this book I mention that the extent of the epic voyages of the Ming Treasure Fleet, led by Chinese Admiral Zheng He, has sparked a continuous and lively worldwide debate. While some claim that the Fleet circumnavigated the globe, in the process exploring most of the world, others simply reject this claim entirely. And there are still many who are confused and caught in the middle, not knowing which side to take. As stated in Chapter 1, the debate in particular covers unsettled issues such as: did Zheng He and his mariners make the trans-Atlantic voyage to reach the Americas in the early fifteenth century? If they did, when and how did they do it? And why did Zheng He seemingly disappear from history in the middle of his seventh and last voyage? These issues can be resolved only if we know the detailed navigational routes and timelines, and explore all the evidence related to the visits of the Ming Treasure Fleet to the Americas. There can be no more than one truth, even if the process of seeking the truth may be tortuous.

In this book, a thorough analysis of Luo Maodeng's novel, San Bao Tai Jian Xi Yang Gi 《三宝太监西洋记》 or *An Account of the Western World Voyage of the San Bao Eunuch*, written in 1597, is made from a fresh angle, by eliminating its fanciful portions and then verifying Luo's hidden narrative about Zheng He's seventh voyage to the Western Ocean against other ancient and modern Chinese and western records.

I suggested that Luo's novel is an allegory, a concealed description of historical facts, which have to be extracted and interpreted to reveal the actual history hidden within the story. This way of writing was not uncommon in imperial China. As I mention in the Introduction, the famous novel, Hong Lou Meng 《红楼梦》 or *Dream of the Red Chamber*, one of China's Four Great Classical Novels, exposed the hypocrisy, decay and exploitation of the upper class in the feudal era. But, by portraying a fictional dynasty, hiding the truth and circumventing political issues, the author succeeded in avoiding persecution for his writings.

At the beginning of my book, such as in Chapter 1, I mention that soon after the seventh voyage, China decided to withdraw completely from the world stage. The Confucian scholars in the imperial court, who had opposed Eunuch Zheng He's costly voyages, finally won the political struggle against the powerful eunuchs who supported the voyages of Zheng He. The treasure ships were burned at anchor and the construction of new long-range ocean vessels was strictly forbidden. It then became dangerous to talk or write about Zheng He's voyages in the post-Zheng He era. Luo, knowing the history of some of these voyages and wishing to preserve a record of them, was conscious of the possible penalty; hence, chose to hide America's Cahokia under the veil of a fictitious Fengdu Ghost Country, to convey to readers what had really happened during the seventh voyage. For over 400 years, this has caused great difficulty in understanding Luo's novel.

However, despite all the challenges, my in-depth analysis of Luo's novel, as given in this book, has enabled me to extract, for the first time, the navigational routes and estimated timelines for the Ming Treasure Fleet during its seventh voyage, starting from Nanjing to North America, then back to China.

A closer examination shows that the squadrons in the treasure fleet did not stay together throughout this voyage. In the middle of the journey, when the entire fleet was at Ceylon (today's Sri Lanka), Zheng He divided the fleet and ordered Hong Bao to lead a squadron to Gu-li/Calicut in today's India (his next call), while he himself and Wang Jinghong together would lead the remaining fleet to other destinations.

Shortly after Hong Bao arrived at Calicut in December 1432, he commanded Ma Huan and six other senior officers to board a Calicut merchants' ship for *Tiangfang*/Mo-jia on pilgrimage and for trade. This Mo-jia is correctly mentioned in Luo's novel, and, in Chapter 2 of this book, is shown to be ancient Tunisia in North Africa during the Hafsid period. But the journey there was not recorded by Luo. Hong Bao himself had only a short stay at Calicut. After leaving Calicut, his squadron visited Dandi Bandar, farther north along the west coast of India, before crossing the Arabian Sea to arrive at Hormuz near the Persian Gulf. He stayed at Hormuz for over two months and returned to Calicut on March 31, 1433, where, shortly afterwards, his squadron regrouped with Wang Jinghong's squadron and from there they returned together to China in July 1433.

Next, my analysis in Chapter 3 enables me to deduce that after separating from Hong Bao at Sri Lanka, Zheng He and Wang Jinghong led the remaining fleet to visit Liushan in today's

Maldives and several kingdoms, which were located in today's India, on the east coast of Africa, on the Arabian Peninsula, and in the neighbourhood of Hormuz in today's Iran/Persia. Next, they visited Aden in today's Yemen. There Zheng He decided to visit *Tiangfang*/Yun Chong—Mecca, in today's Saudi Arabia—on pilgrimage. It was at Aden that envoys from Mecca came to greet Zheng He to show their respect and escort him and his crew to their country. It was most likely also at Aden, that Wang Jinghong separated from Zheng He and took the responsibility of escorting envoys from eleven countries (including Mecca) to visit China. Wang Jinghong's squadron re-joined Hong Bao's at Calicut in early April 1433 before they headed back to China. They arrived in Nanjing in July 1433.

According to Luo Maodeng, after Zheng He had completed his pilgrimage to Mecca, his fleet embarked on a long journey in a generally westward direction across a big ocean in search of a new land at the end of sky and sea (perhaps also for the purpose of recovering the lost Imperial Seal of China). Luo's novel gives a vivid and unique description of this trans-Atlantic voyage made by Zheng He's fleet to the North Atlantic coast. Such a description has never appeared in other historical records, Chinese or non-Chinese, and my detailed analysis of this navigation is presented in Chapter 4.

Luo's description of the length of time taken in the fleet's trans-Atlantic navigation, the climate and scenes near the Grand Banks, the steep cliff covered with yellow grass into which one of Zheng He's reconnaissance boats bumped, and the snow-covered North Atlantic inland around early-mid October to mid November 1433, are short but precise, and can stand the test of detailed scrutiny.

Luo did not give very detailed information as to how Zheng He's scout, Wang Ming, managed to travel from where the fleet landed initially to a strange city called Fengdu. Instead, Luo chose to project the image of Fengdu in North America under a veil, as a netherworld, perhaps in consideration of political sentiment in the post-Zheng He era in China, as I mentioned earlier. But Luo's novel did give enough hints to suggest that Zheng He's crew plausibly went to Cahokia—today's Cahokia Mounds State Historic Site in the central Mississippi Valley—a UNESCO World Heritage Centre, some 18 km/11 mi from the confluence of the Mississippi and Missouri Rivers. Cahokia was the largest pre-Columbian settlement north of Mexico. This inland journey is detailed in Chapter 5.

305

Then in Chapters 6 and 7, I list the multiple lines of evidence extracted from Luo's narrative after comparing them with what we know today about Cahokia's landscape, history, culture and archaeological findings to show that Luo's Fengdu was indeed Cahokia.

For example in Chapter 6, after I thoroughly explore the striking similarities between Luo's North American Fengdu and the Cahokia Mounds complex, I document the results in twelve categories. The vivid exchange between Zheng He's scout Wang Ming and his ex-wife Liu Shi in Cahokia in late November 1433 was not only an emotional event for them, but also an explicit line of evidence which shows that the Fengdu in Luo's novel was an entirely different place from the legendary Fengdu ghost town in China, and that Zheng He's mariners had explored Cahokia earlier, also, during their sixth voyage in 1423.

Then in Chapter 7, I offer evidence to show that both Fengdu and Cahokia shared the same moral standards and rewarded people who had good conduct and punished or reformed people who behaved badly. These methods convey without doubt a Native American flavour and Cahokia's Mississippian characteristics.

The comprehensive and detailed similarities presented in Chapters 6 and 7 can surely not be pure fantasy on the part of Luo Maodeng. Certainly, they cannot have been fed into Luo's writing by the French explorers who reached Cahokia in the late 1600s (about 100 years after the publication of Luo's work). The most reasonable explanation is that the city Luo names Fengdu in his novel was the real Cahokia, and that Luo read records or had access to information from Zheng He's mariners who had actually visited Cahokia in the early fifteenth century. Unfortunately, these records are no longer in existence today.

It took two years for Zheng He and his crew to make the trans-Atlantic navigation to Cahokia and then return to China, and I detail several possible home-bound navigational routes for these mariners in Chapter 8 of this book. Therefore, if Zheng He did return to China with them, the date would be in the summer or autumn of 1435, too late for him to be reappointed to serve as the defender of Nanjing in 1433. Also, if Zheng He did die in China, why does an official Chinese record in the Qing Dynasty state that there was a place in Niushou Mountain/Cattle Head Mountain, which was offered by the emperor as Zheng He's cenotaph? On the other hand, if he died at sea or Calicut in 1433 during his seventh and last voyage, who were the witnesses and where is the proof? Why didn't Ma Huan, Gong Zhen and Fei Xin, who joined Zheng He's seventh voyage, record his death in Calicut in 1433, in their books? Moreover, what is the connection between the Xuande Medallion, awarded to Zheng He and unearthed in North Carolina, and Zheng He's final whereabouts? Can we really rule out the possibility that Zheng He stayed in North America and died there?

Finally in Chapter 9, I present circumstantial evidence deduced from comparing two ancient Chinese maps to conclude further that Zheng He's mariners also explored the central Mississippi Valley in the 1420s during their sixth voyage. The 1418 Chinese World Map does not show the Mississippi River, but Matteo Ricci's 1602 map—which used Chinese map information obtained after Zheng He's sixth voyage but before the start of the seventh voyage—does show the Mississippi River and most of its tributaries, as well as the Gulf of Mexico. But neither map shows the Great Lakes. The finding implies that during the sixth voyage, Zheng He's mariners most likely entered the Mississippi River from the Gulf of Mexico and explored Cahokia. Although there exists no map which records the survey work performed by Zheng He's mariners during their seventh voyage, this book shows that the Chinese mariners had progressively advanced their geographical knowledge, and by the 1430s had explored the Great Lakes and found a new waterway to sail to the Mississippi River to explore the heartland of North America. It seems to me that Zheng He's crew must have sought help from the Native Americans.

Contrary to the generally-held viewpoint that the Ming Treasure Fleet never sailed beyond the East Coast of Africa, the complete navigational routes, timelines and multiple lines of evidence presented in the present book speak for themselves: the Ming sailors did explore the central Mississippi Valley during both their sixth and seventh voyages, in 1423 and 1433, respectively, almost sixty and seventy years before Columbus set foot in the Americas, and over one hundred years before Hernando de Soto led the first European expedition to cross the Mississippi River in 1541.

Taking a new perspective, the present in-depth analysis of an ancient Chinese novel, written in the late Ming Dynasty, has enabled me to extract realistic navigational routes, estimated timelines and multiple lines of evidence for the voyage of Zheng

He's fleet to North America. All these efforts seem to suggest a much larger and different story from most of those previously suggested in modern times, and it seems possible that this new story may become one of the first steps in bridging the gap in our understanding of ancient America-China history in the era before the Age of Discovery. The great contributions made by the Ming sailors should not be overlooked or forgotten, despite being largely erased from history. They deserve a proper place in the history books. More research and more archaeological excavations around the world are called for, in order to extend this work and to answer the question: did the early Chinese sailors explore most of the world?

APPENDIX
THE TEXT OF LUO MAODENG'S NOVEL

The original text of Luo Maodeng's 1597 novel San Bao Tai Jian Xi Yang Gi《三宝太监西洋记》or *An Account of the Western World Voyage of the San Bao Eunuch* in handwritten style is known in two published editions; first as published by Fu Chun Tang (富春堂；a Nanjing publishing house) in the 26th year of the Ming Wanli era (1598—but please note that Luo's Preface was written in 1597), and second as published by Bu Yue Lou (步月楼; a Suzhou publishing house) in the early Qing Dynasty. The latter edition is entitled Xin Ke Quan Xiang San Bao Tai Jian Xi Yang Ji Tong Su Yan Yi : Er Shi Juan《新刻全像三宝太监西洋记通俗演义：二十卷》or *New Edition of An Account of the Western World Voyage of the San Bao Eunuch: Twenty Volumes with Complete Figures*. Some researchers think that the content of these two editions is the same; Bu Yue Lou simply purchased the copyright and put their name on the book. The digitised form of the latter edition is available on several Chinese websites (for example, <https://list.shuge.org/书格文件/PDF/戏曲小说/新刻全像三宝太监西洋记通俗演义.二十卷.一百回/>), and also on the U.S. Library of Congress (LOC) website: <https://www.loc.gov/resource/lcnclscd.2012402020.1A002/?st=gallery/>.

Today, major libraries in the world have one or other edition of Luo Maodeng's novel in their collections and the book is considered an important document with regard to China-West maritime transportation. During the China Guardian 2017 Autumn Auctions (中国嘉德 2017 秋季拍卖会), the aforementioned Bu Yue Lou printed edition was priced at RMB 1,000,000-2,000,000!

Over the past four hundred or so years, many Chinese and foreign scholars have read this novel and offered their viewpoints. Mainly, there are two schools of thought.

One school of thought, represented by Lu Xun (鲁迅), a leading figure of modern Chinese literature, thinks that the author imitated some of the writing style from Xi You Gi《西游记》or *Journey to the West* and turned the historical facts of Zheng He's seven voyages in the Ming Dynasty into a fanciful novel. These scholars think that the novel hopes to inspire Ming Dynasty emperors to fight

309   317

against pirates at sea and reinvigorate the country. However, in section (2) of Chapter 8 of the present book, I quote conversations between Yama in Fengdu and Marshall Tang (one of Zheng He's generals) to show that Luo Maodeng actually condemned Zheng He and his soldiers for their military actions in several countries they explored.

The other school of thought, represented by the famous British biochemist, historian and sinologist, Joseph Needham, and the renowned Dutch Sinologist J.J.L. Duyvendak, was initiated in the early twentieth century by Western scholars who looked into the exploratory nature of Zheng He's voyages, and regarded Luo's novel as having historical value. Later, both American writer Louise Levathes and renowned Singaporean scholar Tan Ta Sen (陈达生) echoed their viewpoint, also considering Luo's novel as having historical reliability. This second school of thought is exemplified by Gavin Menzies' *1421: The Year China Discovered America* (2002), although Menzies did not, and could not read Luo's novel. (His knowledge of Chinese characters is very limited.)

My viewpoint is that it is certainly worthwhile to investigate Luo Maodeng's account as thoroughly as possible to see whether some valuable historical information can be extracted from his huge amount of work (100 chapters and over 750,000 characters).

Today, several modern editions of Luo's novel are available whether in printed book form or on the Internet. Those I have studied all show minor editing of Luo's original text as it is known from the digitized Bu Yue Lou version available on the LOC website. For convenience and efficiency, I have worked with an edition that I located on the Internet at the following URL: <http://mingqingxiaoshuo.com/guiguaishenmo/sanbaotaijianxiyangji/>.

In order to satisfy myself that each passage I cited from this particular Internet version is indeed an authentic representation of Luo's original work, I have done the following. I made a detailed comparison between, on the one hand, Luo's original passage as it appears in the Bu Yue Lou edition, as digitized and available on the LOC website (denoted in the table, 'Comparison of the Internet version used as the basis for the present study with the digitised version of the Bu Yue Lou edition of Luo's work available on the Library of Congress website' by "LOC digitised version of the Bu

Yue Lou edition of Luo's work") and, on the other hand, the passage (quoted in the present book) taken from the above-mentioned Internet version (denoted in the table by "Internet version used as the basis for the present study, as identified above"). I also list the page number where each of these passages is quoted in the present book.

In the same table, I use square brackets to show where differences between the two versions of each passage occur, and I also comment on the nature of these differences. In most cases, the meaning is essentially unchanged, and, generally speaking, the Internet version used as the basis for the present study may be considered as showing some improvement of Luo's original writing. It is clear that the differences between the two versions generally reflect a modern publisher's effort to correct a small number of what they may consider Luo's errors of style to make the text more suited to modern readers, without changing Luo's content. In one case only, as we see in Item 3, the modern Internet edition omits an amplification of a description of the weather. It seems that several Internet editions also show this omission. Could this be a printer's error?

I also compared Luo's descriptions of sailing (from Chapters 22 to 86 of his work), such as the length of time it took to sail from country to country and the countries Zheng He's fleet visited, as presented in these two versions, and found no difference in their contents.

On the basis of these comparisons, I feel comfortable that the edited Internet version that I used for my work is an authentic representation of Luo's original work.

Comparison of the Internet version used as the basis for the present study with the digitised version of the Bu Yue Lou edition of Luo's work as available on the Library of Congress website

#	Page no. in the present book	LOC digitised version of the Bu Yue Lou edition of Luo's work	Internet version used as the basis for the present study (as identified above)	Nature of difference
1	139	固[是]于此	固[尽]于此	"固是于此" means "all are here". "固尽于此" means "all ends here". In the context of the passage as a whole, "尽" better describes what the King of Aden was trying to convey than "是", because he then stopped his advice to Zheng He.
2	148	前[日]唐状元	前唐状元	"前日" means "the day before yesterday", or "previously", and "前" means "previously".
3	149 *Item 5 below also addresses this point in English.*	就像中朝冬月间的雾露天气，[朝不见日，暮不见月。不见星宿，不辨方隅，一丈之外，就不看见人。]	就像中朝冬月间的雾露天气。	The internet version omits 25 Chinese characters.
4	150	哪[个]敢转过身来？	哪敢转过身来？	The internet version gives a shorter and better description.
5	150	It was just like the winter weather in China when the air is filled with mist and dew. [There was no sun in the	It was just like the winter weather in China when the air is filled with mist	The omission of 25 Chinese characters in the internet version sacrifices details that make the situation more vivid.

			and dew.	
		morning, no star in the night, no way to estimate range, and one could not see people beyond a distance of one *zhang*.		
6	152	[水]深難辨路高低	[雪]深難辨路高低低	The snow, not the water, was too deep for Zheng He's crew to tell the height of the ground. If there had been no snow, there would have been no problem in estimating the height of the road. I am glad that the Internet version corrects Luo's misleading statement (Luo was describing the road seen by Zheng He's crew when they were ordered to stop sailing in front of a cliff. The height of the road was hard to estimate, not because of the depth of the sea water, but because of the snow covering the road).
7	167	上岸去[體]探	上岸去[打]探	"打探" is generally used in Chinese language for "inquiring" or "reconnaissance" work. "體探" means "physical exploration", and the meaning is limited.
8	167	一[張]戒手刀	一[口]戒手刀	The LOC version uses "一張戒手刀" to mean "a knife". This usage is very unusual, because "一張" is often used to describe "a bed" (一張床) or "a piece of paper" (一張紙), not a knife. The Internet version uses a more commonly used term for "a knife".
9	167	[也]盡稠密	[又]盡稠密	Both "又" and "也" mean "also".
10	183	[也]盡稠密	[又]盡稠密	Both "又" and "也" mean "also".
11	187	[都]凡人的	[大]凡人的	The LOC version "都凡人的" means, "In all cases, people are…". The internet version "大凡人的" means, "In all cases, people are…" without exception. The internet version "大

凡人的" means "Generally, people are…". The former strong statement has been given a more restricted meaning.

No.	Page			Explanation
12	187	连忙的[扒]将起来	连忙的[爬]将起来	"爬" means crawl or climb. "扒" can also mean "爬", but is less often used in describing the movement of "crawling up" or "climbing up".
13	188	为因机密军情，[?]然到此	为因机密军情，[才]然到此	The "?" mark denotes that the meaning of this character, used in the LOC version, cannot be identified. In the Internet version, the editor replaces "?" with "才" and combines it with "然", to make "才然". The two characters together mean "only then" or "only because". The whole passage then means "I came here only because I have to gather information", or simply, "I came here to gather information". The Internet passage conveys a clearer meaning.
14	188	两泪双[抛]	两泪双[流]	"抛" means "throw". Liu Shi did not "throw" her tears down. Her tears flowed (流) down. The Internet version is clearly better.
15	188	王明听见说道是他的刘氏妻[妾]	王明听见说道是他的刘氏妻[室]	Both passages are acceptable. In Chinese language, both "妻室" and "妾" mean "wife".
16	188	你既是我[刘]氏妻	你既是我[妻]刘氏	Both passages mean "my wife whose last name was Liu". While "刘氏妻" sounds smooth in speaking, "我妻刘氏" emphasises "my wife".
17	188	死了十[余]年	死了十[数]年	Both passages mean "over ten years", but less than twenty years". Each denotes a similar length of time.
18	188	怎么[人]在这里相逢我哩?	怎么[又] 在这里	"怎么人在这里相逢我哩？" means "How come there is

		相逢我哩?		a living person meeting me here again?" The Internet version "怎么又在这里相逢哩？" means "How come you are here meeting me here again?" Wang Ming thought his ex-wife had died ten years earlier, but this woman in front of him told him that she was his wife. Given this, it was natural for him to ask her directly, "How come you are meeting me here again?" "How come there is a living person meeting me here again?" connects less well with the emotional scene of this brief reunion.
19	191	[是]判官说[道]：	判官道：	Both passages have the same meaning. The Internet version is a shortened version of the original passage.
20	191	[我]方才	方才	"我方才" means "a moment ago, I"…, and "方才" simply means "a moment ago". But from reading the entire passage, it is obvious that this "方才" or "a moment ago" really means "a moment ago, I"… Both expressions are acceptable. The Internet version is trying to make the sentence shorter to avoid repetition.
21	194	[只]叫做鄥都鬼国	[这]叫做鄥都鬼国	The LOC version, "只叫做", means "It is only called", whereas the Internet version, "这叫做" means "This is called". Since Liu Shi was referring to the place where she was living, the editor of the Internet version clearly prefers to use "这", though it would be better to say, "This [place] is called".
22	198	忧心[悄悄]	忧心[悄悄]	The Internet version is an idiom in Chinese language meaning "worry seriously". "悄悄" means "quietly".

No.	Page	Version 1 (LOC)	Version 2 (Internet)	Commentary
23	199	见了天齐仁[圣]大帝	见了天齐仁圣大帝	"Worry quietly" is not a better expression for describing the mental state of the funeral mourners. Both "天齐仁圣大帝" and "天齐仁大帝" are correct titles for the god of Mount Tai.
24	204	王明[启]头一看	王明[抬]头一看	The Internet version is a commonly used Chinese expression. However, "启" means "open"; it is not meaningful to use "启头", which means "open the head". Perhaps Luo meant to use the character "起". "启" and "起" have the same pronunciation in modern Chinese. If Luo had used "起头", it would have had the same meaning as "抬头", "raising the head."
25	232	把头上的晋巾儿也打[吊]了	把头上的晋巾儿也打[掉]了	"掉" and "吊" have the same pronunciation in modern Chinese but different meanings: "fall" and "hang", respectively. Luo is describing how the five ghosts pulled the judge's scarf off his head. In this case, "掉" is the right word to use, not "吊".
26	236	只见远远的望见有一[路]倭倭的墙头儿	只见远远的望见有一[条]矮矮的墙头儿	The LOC's version, "路" means "road"; the Internet version's "条" means "an array-like structure". As referring to a wall, the Internet version seems more appropriate than the LOC version.
27	237	众[官][起]头一看	众[将][抬]头一看	There are two points here. First, the five people in front of Yama's residence were generals (将), not court officials (官). The Internet version is more accurate in the context of the whole. Second, both the LOC version's "起头" and the Internet version's "抬头" have the same meaning

28	237	一面[小]牌	一面牌	(raising the head). There seems no particular justification for this change. Evidently, the editor of the Internet version does not think the sign on the plaque of the gatehouse was (or could be) "small".
29	249	又生受野花行者。。。[为]送仙舟返帝京。。。又生受劳草行者。。。[遥]送仙舟返帝京。。。	又生受野花行者。。。[直]送仙舟返帝京。。。又生受劳草行者。。。[直]送仙舟返帝京。。。	Both passages say that the wild flowers and the green grass bade farewell to the ships for them to return to the capital.
30	251	[吊]下一个军士在海里去了	[掉]下一个军士在海里去了	"掉" and "吊" have the same pronunciation in modern Chinese, but different meanings: "fall" and "hang", respectively. From the context of the whole, we can see that the Internet version is a more correct description of what happened.
31	252	[吊]下去之时，得[他]乘住，虽然风大浪大，[他]浮沉有法	[掉]下去之时，得[它]乘住，虽然风大浪大，[它]浮沉有法	I have explained in Item 30 the difference between "掉" and "吊". "他" refers to "he" and "它" refers to a creature or an object. Since fish are creatures, "它" should be used. The Internet version is correct.
32	252	是[他]口里说道	是[它]口里说道	"他" refers to "he" and "它" refers to a creature or an object. Since fish are creatures, "它" should be used. The Internet version is correct.

The Last Journey of the San Bao Eunuch

NOTES

[1] This map is among the holdings of the United States Library of Congress Geography and Map Division.

[2] This map is among the holdings of the Library of the Tohoku University of Japan. I have used this Japanese copy of Ricci's 1602 map as a reference when it was difficult to read Ricci's 1602 map. The Japanese copy has differences, but these are not relevant to my analysis.

[3] As found in the electronic version on the internet at <http://mingqingxiaoshuo.com/guiguaishenmo/sanbaotaijianxiyangji/>).

[4] Zheng He's year and place of death remain unsolved.

[5] Menzies, Gavin. *1421: The Year China Discovered America*. New York, U.S.A.: HarperCollins Publishers, 2002.

[6] Zheng He, born Ma He, was made to serve as a palace eunuch and given the new surname "Zheng". He was promoted to Director of the Directorate of Palace Eunuchs. He was also known as Ma San Bao or Ma Sanbao. "San" means "three" and "Bao" means "jewels" or "treasures". "San Bao" or "Sanbao" literally means "Three Jewels" or "Three Treasures". Buddhists make a commitment to the Three Jewels or Triple Gem. The Three Jewels are: the *Buddha*, the fully enlightened one; the *Dharma*, the teachings expounded by the *Buddha*; and the *Sangha*, the monastic order of Buddhism that practices the Dharma. People often use "San Bao" as a symbol of Buddhism. Zheng He was originally a Muslim, but in the first year of the Yongle period (1403), he converted to Buddhism. People would honour him as "San Bao Eunuch", meaning the "Buddhist Eunuch" or Ma Sanbao.

[7] Low, C.C. & Associates. ed. and trans. "The Ending of the Xiyang Voyages." *Pictorial Series of Chinese Classics & History in English & Chinese: Zheng He's Voyages to Xiyang*, Singapore: Canfonian Pte Ltd, 2003, p. 249; b) Tan, Ta Sen. "Cheng Ho's Seven Grand Expeditions to Western Ocean." *Cheng Ho and Malaya*, Malacca, Malaysia: Cheng Ho Cultural Museum and Singapore: International Zheng He Society, 2014, pp. 37–40; c) Levathes, Louise. "The Treasure Fleet." *When China Ruled the Seas: The Treasure Fleet of the Dragon Throne, 1405–1433*, Oxford, U.K.: Oxford University Press, 1994, p. 180; d) Levathes, Louise. "The Auspicious Appearance of the Celestial Animals." *When China Ruled the Seas, op. cit.*, p.150; and d) Levathes, Louise. "The Sultan's Bride." *When China Ruled the Seas, op. cit.*, pp.183-193.

[8] "Dream of the Red Chamber." *Wikipedia: The Free Encyclopedia*, Wikimedia Foundation, Jan. 9, 2019, en.wikipedia.org/wiki/Dream_of_the_Red_Chamber.

[9] "曹雪芹", 自由的百科全书, 百度百科, 2019, baike.baidu.com/item/曹雪芹/14919

[10] The Mississippi Valley occupies the centre of the United States. It stretches 2,348 miles from Lake Itasca in northern Minnesota to the mouth of the Mississippi River in the Gulf of Mexico.

319

[11] The river either borders or passes through the states of Minnesota, Wisconsin, Iowa, Illinois, Missouri, Kentucky, Tennessee, Arkansas, Mississippi, and Louisiana; "Mississippi River." *Wikipedia*, Jan. 9, 2019, en.wikipedia.org/wiki/Mississippi_River

[12] Collections & Research Center. "Mississipian." www.museum.state.il.us, Illinois State Museum, 2000, www.museum.state.il.us/muslink/nat_amer/pre/htmls/miss.html

[13] "Fengdu Ghost City." *Wikipedia*, Jan. 9, 2019, en.wikipedia.org/wiki/Fengdu_Ghost_City

[14] Nickless, Mark, et al. (马克·尼克莱斯等.) Zheng He Fa Xian Mei Zhou Zhi Xin Je《郑和发现美洲之新解》or *New Evidence for Zheng He's Exploration of the Americas*. Beijing, China: World Knowledge Publishing House (世界知 识出版社), 2015.

[15] "Cahokia." *Wikipedia*, Nov. 16, 2018, en.wikipedia.org/wiki/Cahokia

[16] "File:Zhenghemap.jpg." *Wikimedia Commons: The Free Media Repository*, Wikimedia Foundation, Mar. 4, 2019, commons.wikimedia.org/wiki/File:Zhenghemap.jpg

[17] His book, Gu Di Tu Mi Ma : Zhong Guo Fa Xian Shi Jie De Mi Tuan Xuan Ji《古地图密码 : 中国发现世界的谜团玄机》or *Secret Code of Ancient Maps: The Mystery of China's Discovery of the World*, is an explanation of ancient maps.

[18] "Kunyu Wanguo Quantu." *Wikipedia*, Oct. 28, 2018, en.wikipedia.org/wiki/Kunyu_Wanguo_Quantu

[19] 李兆良,《坤輿萬國全圖解密: 明代測繪世界》, 聯經出版社, 2012 年。 He wrote the book, Kun Yu Wan Guo Quan Tu Jie Mi : Ming Dai Ce Hui Shi Jie《坤輿萬國全圖解密:明代測繪世界》or *Deciphering the Kunyu Wanguo Quantu, A Chinese World Map—Ming Chinese Mapped the World Before Columbus*. Taipei: Linking Publishing Company, 2012.

[20] "Christopher Columbus." *Wikipedia*, Feb. 12, 2019, en.wikipedia.org/wiki/Christopher_Columbus

[21] "Hernando de Soto." *Wikipedia*, Jan. 30, 2019, en.wikipedia.org/wiki/Hernando_de_Soto

[22] "Age of Discovery." *Wikipedia*, Dec. 29, 2018, en.wikipedia.org/wiki/Age_of_Discovery

[23] Needham, Joseph, et al. *Science and Civilisation in China, Vol. 4: Physics and Physical Technology, Part 3: Civil Engineering and Nautics*. Cambridge,U.K.: Cambridge University Press, 1971.

[24] Chen, Stephen. "Hunt for Ming dynasty admiral Zheng He's lost treasure ship heats up in Indian Ocean." www.scmp.com, South China Morning Post, 27 Nov., 2017. www.scmp.com/news/china/society/article/2118421/hunt-ming-dynasty-admiral-zheng-hes-lost-treasure-ship-heats

[25] Taicang is a city in Suzhou, Jiangsu province; the city is located in the south of the Yangtze River estuary; "Taicang." *Wikipedia*, June 11, 2018, en.wikipedia.org/wiki/Taicang

[26] Changle is a district located in eastern Fujian province; "Changle District." *Wikipedia*, Feb. 9, 2019, en.wikipedia.org/wiki/Changle_District

[27] It was an Indonesian city, now the capital of the South Sumatra province and southern Sumatra's largest port and trade centre.

[28] Xuande Emperor or Xuanzong 宣宗/Zhu Zhanji 朱瞻基; he took the throne in 1425 and passed away in 1435, aged 38; he decided to restart the magnificent feats of the treasure-fleet's voyages.

[29] "Ferdinand Magellan." *Wikipedia*, Nov. 30, 2018, en.wikipedia.org/wiki/Ferdinand_Magellan

[30] "Chinese treasure ship." *Wikipedia*, Jan. 8, 2019, en.wikipedia.org/wiki/Chinese_treasure_ship

[31] "*Santa María* (ship)." *Wikipedia*, Jan. 16, 2019, en.wikipedia.org/wiki/Santa_María_(ship)

[32] "Keel." *Wikipedia*, Jan. 7, 2019, Jan. 22, 2019, en.wikipedia.org/wiki/Keel

[33] Calicut or Kozhikode, the Chinese name being 古里 (Gu-li), was dubbed the "City of Spices" for its role as the major trading point of eastern spices during classical antiquity and the Middle Ages; it is a city in the state of Kerala in southern India on the Malabar Coast.

[34] 郑一钧, "郑和死於一四三三年"; see zhenghe.tust.edu.tw/doc/鄭一鈞鄭和死於一四三三年.pdf

[35] The Wanli Emperor (Zhu Yijun 朱翊鈞; 1563–1620) was the fourteenth emperor of the Ming Dynasty of China. "Wanli", the era name of his reign, literally means "ten thousand calendars"; see "Wanli_Emperor." *Wikipedia*, Jan. 7, 2019, en.wikipedia.org/wiki/Wanli_Emperor

[36] 林梅村, "鄭和忌日及身後事", www.cciv.cityu.edu.hk, 中國文化中心, 香港城市大學, 2004 年 12 月 1 日, www.cciv.cityu.edu.hk/publication/jiuzhou/txt/8-s-2.txt

[37] 陈平平, "明代相关史料对'郑和 1433 年死于古里国'说的否定", 《南通航运职业技术学院学报》, 南京晓庄学院生命科学系, 2014 年 第 13 卷第 13 期, http://www.cqvip.com/main/confirm.aspx?id=662646062

[38] The Kangxi Emperor ruled over China from 1661 to 1722.

[39] 張廷玉等, 万斯同等编修, 《明史》, 中华书局, 1974 年, 卷三百〇四, 列傳第一百九十二, 宦官一　鄭和。

[40] See note 35.

[41] "Category: Tomb of Zheng He." *Wikimedia Commons: The Free Media Repository*, Wikimedia Foundation, May 27, 2018, commons.wikimedia.org/wiki/Category:Tomb_of_Zheng_He; a "tomb" was built for Zheng He at the southern slope of Cattle Head Hill, Nanjing (南京牛首山). The original tomb was a horseshoe-shaped grave. It is a cenotaph

321

believed to contain Zheng He's clothes and headgear. In 1985, the tomb was rebuilt following a Muslim style.

[42] Levathes, Louise. *When China Ruled the Seas, op. cit.*

[43] It is not clear to me whether Gavin Menzies made a mistake, or it is just a typographical error.

[44] In Chapter 3 of this book, I shall point out that the fleet was actually in Beruwala in the west coast of Sri Lanka.

[45] "Hong Bao." *Wikipedia*, Feb. 11, 2018, en.wikipedia.org/wiki/Hong_Bao

[46] It is known that Zheng He's navigational knowledge and experience was shallow, and Wang Jinghong was responsible for managing the fleets and navigational routes.

[47] The Longjiang shipyards built ships classified in *liao*; a 2,000 *liao* ship is about 200 *chi* long, 37 *chi* wide and 13 *chi* draft (1 *chi* is 1/3 of a metre); it is about the scale of a medium-sized Zheng He ship. A 400 *liao* ship is about 160 displacement tons, tiny in comparison with Zheng He's treasure ships.

[48] 祝允明,《前聞記•下西洋》, 維基文庫, 自由的圖書館, 維基媒體基金會, 2018 年 5 月 1 日, zh.wikisource.org/zh-hant/前聞記#下西洋

[49] "Zhu Yunming." *Wikipedia*, July 27, 2018, en.wikipedia.org/wiki/Zhu_Yunming

[50] "Vasco da Gama." *Wikipedia*, Dec. 10, 2018, en.wikipedia.org/wiki/Vasco_da_Gama

[51] In Chapter 2 of this book, I shall show that this country is verified as ancient Tunisia in North Africa.

[52] This will be discussed in detail in Chapter 2 of this book again.

[53] 尤侗(編者),《明史外國傳》, 臺灣學生書局, 1977 年 6 月, www.cp1897.com.hk/product_info.php?BookId=2222003051188

[54] Hsu, Sheng-I and Yau-Zhih Chen. "Preliminary Study of Astronomical Navigation by Zheng He." *Zheng He and the Afro-Asian World,* edited by Chia Lin Sien and Sally K Church, Melaka Museums Corporation (PERZIM) and International Zheng He Society, 2012, pp. 86–98; 徐勝一和陳有志, "鄭和《過洋牽星圖》及丁得把昔與沙姑馬山地理定位之研究" or "Study on the Navigation Charts of Zheng-he's Expedition and Geographical Positioning of Dandi Baxi and Sha-Gu-Ma-San", 《地理学报》, 第 52 期, 2008 年, 第 93 至 114 页。

[55] *The Charts of Zheng He's Voyages* consists of twenty pages of nautical maps, 109 maps for terrestrial navigation, and four cross-ocean stellar maps for astronomical nagivation. The nautical map is 20.3 cm high and 560 cm long, containing 500 place names; see "郑和航海图", 维基百科, 自由的百科全书, 2018 年 3 月 10 日, zh.wikipedia.org/wiki/郑和航海图

[56] The method is called "astronomical nagivation". In the Northern Hemisphere, the observed angle (expressed by the unit of the "finger") with the Polaris star determined the coordinate (latitude) of the targeted destination. In the Southern Hemisphere, different stars were used. In this way, the ancient Chinese sailors

could correct their direction deviated from the north due to the effect of wind; also see "郑和航海天文导航技术及丁得巴昔古代军事基地的发现"一文, 于《郑和与亚非世界》, 作者张江齐, 编者廖建裕, 柯木林, 和许福吉, 国际郑和社团和马六甲博物馆（PERZIM）联合出版, 2012 年, 第 101 至 121 页。

[57] See note 54.

[58] Wang, Tai Peng. "Zheng He's delegation to the Papal Court of Florence." www.gavinmenzies.net, Gavin Menzies, Aug. 16, 2011, www.gavinmenzies.net/Evidence/3-tai-peng-wangs-research-1433-zheng-he%e2%80%99s-delegation-to-the-papal-court-of-florence

[59] Wang, Tai Peng. "Zheng He and His Envoys' Visits to Cairo in 1414 and 1433." www.gavinmenzies.net, Gavin Menzies, August 2008, www.gavinmenzies.net/wp-content/uploads/2011/08/wangtaipeng_zhenghevisittocairo.pdf

[60] Pope Eugene IV was Pope from March 3, 1431, to his death in 1447; he moved his palace to Florence after June 1434.

[61] Edward L. Dreyer has the date as January 17, 1433. The one-day difference is due to conversion from the Lunar calendar into the Gregorian calendar; Dreyer, Edward L. "Zheng He's Seventh and Final Voyage, 1431–1433." *Zheng He: China and the Oceans in the Early Ming Dynasty: 1405–1433,* London, U.K.: Pearson, 2006, pp. 150–163.

[62] 林贻典, "The Country of Tian Fang is in Tunisia",《郑和研究动态》, 第二期 (总第 24 期), 2014 年 7 月 30 日。

[63] 维基百科, 自由的百科全书, 维基媒体基金会, 2014 年 3 月 7 日, zh.wikipedia.org/wiki/西洋番国志

[64] 黄省曾,《西洋朝贡典录》, 维基百科, 2014 年 3 月 7 日, zh.wikipedia.org/wiki/西洋朝贡典录

[65] 景泰 or Jingtai was the title of the Chinese Ming Dynasty's seventh emperor Zhu Qi Yu 朱祁钰, who reigned from 1450 to 1456; the second year of Jingtai was 1451; 马欢 , "瀛涯胜览", 维基百科, 2017 年 10 月 30 日, zh.wikipedia.org/zh/瀛涯胜览

[66] "馬歡島", 维基百科, 2018 年 7 月 27 日, zh.wikipedia.org/wiki/馬歡島

[67] "Ma Huan." *Wikipedia,* Nov. 6, 2018, en.wikipedia.org/wiki/Ma_Huan

[68] 麒麟 Qilin or Kirin, a mythical Chinese animal or Chinese unicorn: it symbolises prosperity or serenity.

[69] Because they "bought" all kinds of unusual commodities and rare valuables, qilins, lions, ostriches and other things, instead of "receiving" them as tributes.

[70] Gong Zhen's dates of birth and death are not recorded.

[71] "Tuareg people." *Wikipedia,* Jan. 14, 2019, en.wikipedia.org/wiki/Tuareg_people

[72] "Tuareg man from Algeria." *Wikipedia,* Dec. 4, 2004, en.wikipedia.org/wiki/Tuareg_people#/media/File:Tuareg2.JPG

[73] "Tuareg woman with face veil." *Wikipedia*, Jan. 1, 2007, en.wikipedia.org/wiki/Tuareg_people#/media/File:Tuareg_woman_from_Mali,_2007.jpg

[74] "Tunisia." *Wikipedia*, Jan. 13, 2019, en.wikipedia.org/wiki/Tunisia

[75] "Hafsid dynasty." *Wikipedia*, Dec. 19, 2018, en.wikipedia.org/wiki/Hafsid_dynasty

[76] 费信,《星槎胜览》, 维基百科, 2016 年 10 月 18 日, zh.wikipedia.org/wiki/星槎胜览

[77] Later in Chapter 3 of this book, I shall mention that Ming Shi 《明史》or *The History of Ming* gives a different number—22 days—for the same journey.

[78] 1 knot (kn) is 1.852 km/hr or approximately 1.151 mi/hr.

[79] https://www.google.com/search?client=firefox-b-d&q=distance+from+Calicut+to+Aden

[80] Yack Yack. "The Straight Line Air Flying Distance from Jeddah Saudi Arabia to Aden Yemen." www.distantias.com, Yack Yack, Jan. 17, 2019, www.distantias.com/distance-from-jeddah-saudi_arabia-to-aden-yemen.htm

[81] Yack Yack. "The Straight Line Air Flying Distance from Jeddah Saudi Arabia to Mecca." *op. cit.*, www.distantias.com/distance-from-jeddah-saudi_arabia-to-mecca-saudi_arabia.htm

[82] "Flight Time from Cairo to Jeddah." www.prokerala.com, Ennexa Technologies Pvt. Ltd., 2019, www.prokerala.com/travel/flight-time/from-cairo/to-jeddah

[83] "Distance Between Mogadishu and Calicut." www.prokerala.com, Ennexa Technologies Pvt. Ltd., 2019, www.prokerala.com/travel/distance/from-calicut/to-mogadishu

[84] "Distance from Calicut to Elizabeth–South Africa." *Google: The Free Internet Search Engine*, Google LLC, 2019, google.com/search?q=distance+between+Calicut+and+Port+Elizabeth+in+South+Africa&ie=utf-8&oe=utf-8&client=firefox-b-ab

[85] "Djerba." *Wikipedia*, Jan. 1, 2019, en.wikipedia.org/wiki/Djerba

[86] https://www.distancesfrom.com/tn/distance-from-Gabes-to-Jerba-Tunisia/DistanccHistory/33245814.aspx

[87] "Distance from Kairouan to Gabes." www.DistanceCalculator.net, Distance Calculator, 2019, www.distancecalculator.net/from-kairouan-to-gabes

[88] "行宫", 维基百科, 2018 年 6 月 28 日, zh.wikipedia.org/wiki/行宫

[89] "Distance from Sousse to Chebba." www.distancefromto.net, DistanceFromTo, 2019, www.distancefromto.net/distance-from-sousse-tn-to-chebba-tn

[90] "Distance from Sousse to Kairouan." *Google: The Free Internet Search Engine*, Google LLC, 2019, google.com/search?q=distance+from+Sousse+to+Kairouan

[91] "Kairouan." *Wikipedia*, Jan. 1, 2019, en.wikipedia.org/wiki/Kairouan

[92] See note 78.

[93] "Agulhas Current." *Wikipedia*, Oct. 4, 2018, en.wikipedia.org/wiki/Agulhas_Current

[94] Joanna Gyory, Arthur J. Mariano, Edward H. Ryan. "The Benguela Current." Ocean Surface Currents. (). https://oceancurrents.rsmas.miami.edu/atlantic/benguela.html. (This special citation style is required by the four authors of this article.—Ed.)

[95] Statnikov, Eugene. "Speed of Ocean Currents." https://hypertextbook.com/, The Physics Factbook: An Encyclopedia of Scientific Essays, 2002, https://hypertextbook.com/facts/2002/EugeneStatnikov.shtml

[96] *Ibid.*

[97] Joanna Gyory, Arthur J. Mariano, Edward H. Ryan. "The Canary Current." Ocean Surface Currents. (). https://oceancurrents.rsmas.miami.edu/atlantic/canary.html. (This special citation style is required by the three authors.—Ed.)

[98] Sea-Distances.org, 2019, www.sea-distances.org

[99] Sfax is chosen because it is in the proximity of Chebba. In this crude calculation, this will minimize error in the estimated sailing time.

[100] "Distance from Sfax to Chebba." www.distancefromto.net, DistanceFromTo, 2019, www.distancefromto.net/distance-from-sfax-tn-to-chebba-tn

[101] "Distance between Cape Town and Cape Of Good Hope." alldistancebetween.com, AfiGIS(Pty)Ltd, Google, 2019, http://alldistancebetween.com/in/distance-between/cape-town-cape-of-good-hope-a2322344c47ed33d3ae98680ce20fd11/

[102] Menzies estimates that a ship sailing at an average speed of 4.8 kn would have taken 40 days to reach the Cape Verde Islands from the Cape of Good Hope.

[103] The distance from Calicut to the Cape of Good Hope would be 4,355 nm/5,012 mi/8,065 km (8,130 minus 65 = 8,065) and take 37 days and nineteen hours.

[104] "Agulhas Current." *Wikipedia*, Oct. 4, 2018, en.wikipedia.org/wiki/Agulhas_Current

[105] 427 *li* per day is for a ship sailing at an average speed of 4.8 kn.

[106] "Global Positioning System." *Wikipedia*, Jan. 16, 2019, en.wikipedia.org/wiki/Global_Positioning_System

[107] "South Atlantic Current." *Google: The Free Internet Search Engine*, Google LLC, 2019, sites.google.com/site/correntesoceanica/ocean-currents/surface-currents-of-the-atlantic/south-atlantic-currents

[108] The South Indian current band is an eastward current band in the Indian Ocean. This current, with the Antarctic Circumpolar Current, is known as the West Wind Drift (the current flows at a rate of about 111 cm/sec or 2.16 kn). As the South Indian Current reaches the coast of Australia, it becomes the West Australia Current; "Antarctic Circumpolar Current." *Wikipedia*, Feb. 3, 2019, en.wikipedia.org/wiki/Antarctic_Circumpolar_Current

[109] "Agarwood." *Wikipedia*, Jan. 16, 2019, en.wikipedia.org/wiki/Agarwood

[110] "Kaaba." *Wikipedia*, Jan. 11, 2019, en.wikipedia.org/wiki/Kaaba

[111] "Black Stone." *Wikipedia*, Dec. 24, 2018, en.wikipedia.org/wiki/Black_Stone

[112] "Kairouan." *Wikipedia*, Jan. 1, 2019, en.wikipedia.org/wiki/Kairouan

[113] "Great Mosque of Kairouan." *Wikipedia*, March 4, 2019, en.wikipedia.org/wiki/Great_Mosque_of_Kairouan

[114] "Minaret." *Wikipedia*, Dec. 23, 2018, en.wikipedia.org/wiki/Minaret

[115] "Great Mosque of Kairouan." *Wikipedia*, March 4, 2019, en.wikipedia.org/wiki/Great_Mosque_of_Kairouan

[116] 编辑, "欧格白清真寺", 自由的百科全书, 百度百科, 2019, baike.baidu.com/item/欧格白清真寺; "突尼西亞#15 世界四大清真寺之開羅安大清真寺 2014 Kairouan Great Mosque." *YouTube*, uploaded by Dd tai, Jul 14, 2014, youtube.com/watch?v=wda_7zb6aLM; also see "Great Mosque of Kairouan." *op. cit.*

[117] "Great Mosque of Kairouan." *op. cit.*

[118] *Ibid.*

[119] Anthony, John. "The Fourth Holy City." www. archive.aramcoworld.com, Aramco World, vol. 18, no. 1, Jan./Feb. 1967, https://archive.aramcoworld.com/issue/196701/the.fourth.holy.city.htm

[120] "Rose Water." *Wikipedia*, Jan. 14, 2019, en.wikipedia.org/wiki/Rose_water

[121] 黄省曾,《天方國第二十三》, https://ctext.org/zh, 中國哲學書電子化計劃, 2006, http://ctext.org/wiki.pl?if=gb&chapter=341111#天方國第二十三

[122] Stones, Rebecca J. ed. "Are lions mentioned in the Qur'an or any other Islamic source, and if so, are they positively mentioned?" www.islam.stackexchange.com, Islam Beta, July 9, 2017, http://islam.stackexchange.com/questions/5753/lions-in-the-quran

[123] Kjeilen, Tore. "Kairouan: Cemetery of Ouled Farhane." http://i-cias.com/e.o/, LookLex, 2019, http://i-cias.com/tunisia/kairouan07.htm; Jacobs, Daniel. *The Rough Guide to Tunisia*, London, U.K.: Rough Guides, 2009.

[124] DKQOEI8K, "欧格白清真寺 (Masjid 'Uqbah)" www.wenda.so.com, WEIBO 北京微梦创科网络技术有限公司, Dec. 15, 2013, http://wenda.haosou.com/q/1387293435060800, but the content of this article in no longer available.

[125] "Distance from Mecca to Medina." www.distancefromto.net, DistanceFromTo, 2019, www.distancefromto.net/distance-from-mecca-sa-to-medina-sa

[126] "File: Plan Kairouan 1916.jpg." *Wikimedia Commons: The Free Media Repository,* Wikimedia Foundation, Dec. 13, 2008, commons.wikimedia.org/wiki/File:Plan_Kairouan_1916.jpg

[127] 黄省曾, *op. cit.*

[128] "Kairouan." *op. cit.*

334

[129] "Entering Bir Barrouta Kairouan Tunisia April 2015." *YouTube*, uploaded by Jonny Blair, Apr. 3, 2015, youtube.com/watch?v=ch5Dktzqkwo

[130] The distance between Bir Baruta and Uqba Mosque is 1.0 km/0.62 mi via Avenue Habib Bourguiba/Rue Saussier and Rue De La Kasbah.

[131] This kind of precious gold band was worn around the head of the Mo-le (Mara in Sanskrit) Buddha; see "摩勒", 百度百科, 2019, baike.baidu.com/item/摩勒/639638. This kind of gold band is expected to have been produced in India.

[132] "History of early Islamic Tunisia." *Wikipedia*, Apr. 22, 2018, en.wikipedia.org/wiki/History_of_early_Islamic_Tunisia

[133] "Bartolomeu Dias." *Wikipedia*, Jan. 9, 2019, en.wikipedia.org/wiki/Bartolomeu_Dias

[134] 林贻典, "再论美洲由郑和船队发现的见解", 《海交史研究》第 2 期, 中国海外交通史研究会, 2003 年, http://iwaas.cssn.cn/webpic/web/cns/paper/uploadfiles/2/HJSY200302003.pdf

[135] Lam, Yee Din. "A Third Research on the Discovery of America by Zheng He's Fleet." www.gavinmenzies.net, Gavin Menzies, Aug. 16, 2011, www.gavinmenzies.net/Evidence/5-mr-lam-yee-din-a-third-research-on-the-discovery-of-america-by-zheng-he%E2%80%99s-fleet

[136] 刘钢, 《古地图密码: 中国发现世界的谜团玄机》, 广西师范大学出版社, 2009 年, 第 5 章.

[137] It was in what is today the central part of Vietnam; the place once had the largest and most widespread population of Asian rhinoceroses, including the Javan rhinoceros, also known as the Sunda rhinoceros or lesser one-horned rhinoceros; also see Ma, Huan. J.V.G. Mills, trans. *Ying-yai Sheng-lan: The Overall Survey of the Ocean's Shores (1433)*, London, U.K.: Hakluyt Society, 1970, p. 181.

[138] See Luo Maodeng, *op. cit.*, Chapters 22 to 32.

[139] It was in what is today's northern part of Shunhai Province (顺海省) and the southern part of Fuqing Province (富庆省) in southern Vietnam; "宾童龙", 百度百科, 2019, baike.baidu.com/item/宾童龙

[140] See Luo Maodeng, *op. cit.*, Chapters 32 and 33.

[141] Lopburi is the capital city of today's Lopburi Province in the central region of Thailand; "罗斛国", 维基百科, 2016 年 11 月 22 日, zh.wikipedia.org/wiki/罗斛

[142] See Luo Maodeng, *op. cit.*, Chapters 33 and 34.

[143] It was in today's Island of Java in Indonesia; "爪哇国", 百度百科, 2019, baike.baidu.com/item/爪哇国

[144] See Luo Maodeng, *op. cit.*, Chapters 34 to 45, inclusive.

[145] "郑和下西洋", 维基百科, 2019 年 1 月 16 日, zh.wikipedia.org/wiki/郑和下西洋

[146] It was a tiny village kingdom in what is today's Surabaya region, in East Java; "重迦罗", 维基百科, 2019 年 1 月 6 日, zh.wikipedia.org/wiki/重迦罗

[147] See Luo Maodeng, *op. cit.*, Chapter 45.

[148] Today's Palembang 旧港, in south Sumatra, Indonesia; "旧港", 百度百科, 2019, baike.baidu.com/item/旧港宣慰司

[149] See Luo Maodeng, *op. cit.*, Chapters 45 and 46.

[150] It is not clear where this place was. It might be in today's Sulawesi to the east of the Island of Java, Indonesia, where the Bugis people live. But this location is not on the route to Malacca, the fleet's next destination. Hence, it is more logical to place the Land of Many Perfumes at a location between Palembang and Malacca.

[151] See Luo Maodeng, *op. cit.*, Chapters 46 to 50.

[152] It was in the state of Malacca in Malaysia; "马六甲苏丹王朝", 维基百科, 2018 年 9 月 11 日, zh.wikipedia.org/wiki/马六甲苏丹王朝

[153] See Luo Maodeng, op. cit., Chapters 50 and 51.

[154] It was a very small kingdom in the northeast of today's Sumatra, near Deli River and Belawan; it was called Ya Lu 亞路 in *The Charts of Zheng He's Voyage* mentioned in note 55; "哑鲁", 维基百科, 2019 年 1 月 6 日, zh.wikipedia.org/wiki/哑鲁

[155] See Luo Maodeng, *op. cit.*, Chapter 51.

[156] It had almost the same Chinese name as Aru; it was a very small kingdom near the A-lu anchorage (Sungai Deli in today's north Sumatra, Indonesia); it was not far away from Aru according to Luo Maodeng's narrative; it should not be confused with the Aru Islands which are a group of about ninety-five low-lying islands in the Maluku province of eastern Indonesia.

[157] See Luo Maodeng, *op. cit.*, Chapter 51.

[158] Semudera was on the north coast of Sumatra; Lho Seumawe district; Ma, Huan. J.V.G. Mills, trans. *Ying-yai Sheng-lan: The Overall Survey of the Ocean's Shores (1433), op. cit.*, p. 218.

[159] See Luo Maodeng, *op. cit.*, Chapter 51.

[160] *Ibid.*

[161] In the Kollam District of Kerala State, India, there is Chirayil Kulam (a lake) and Temple Kulam. Kulam might be a small country in today's Kollam neighbourhood on the southwest coast of India; the country's people had black-coloured skin. Both *Ying Ya Sheng Lan* 《瀛涯胜览》 or *The Overall Survey of the Ocean's Shores* and Míng Shi • Wai Guo Zhuan 《明史•外国列传》 or *Foreign Countries in The History of Ming* interpret Kulam (故临国) as the Lesser Quilon/Xiao Gelan (小葛兰国), which Zheng He's main fleet actually visited in 1432 (the 26th country on the country list in Chapter 3). But the fact that Luo Maodeng listed Kulam (故临国) and Lesser Quilon/Xiao Gelan (小葛兰国) as two different countries may indicate that they were two small counties in the Kollam neighbourhood, in addition to the Greater Quilon/Da Gelan (大葛兰国；perhaps Kayankulam village). This deserves further investigation.

[162] It was ancient Tunisia during the Hafsid period, North Africa; the Hafsids were a Sunni Muslim Dynasty of Berber descent who ruled Ifriqiya (western Libya, Tunisia, and eastern Algeria) from 1229 to 1574; "Hafsid dynasty." *op. cit.*

[163] Battak (花面國) was in north Sumatra; "花面國", 白度百科, 2019, baike.baidu.com/item/花面國; Nakur/Nagur (那孤兒國) was in northwest Sumatra; "那孤儿", 百度百科, 2019, baike.baidu.com/item/那孤儿; people in these countries liked to tattoo their faces.

[164] It was in today's Egypt; "勿斯里国", 百度百科, 2019, baike.baidu.com/item/勿斯里国

[165] It was today's Mosul in northern Iraq; "Mosul." *Wikipedia*, Feb. 4, 2019, en.wikipedia.org/wiki/Mosul

[166] It was in today's eastern Afghanistan; "Ghazni." *Wikipedia*, Feb. 26, 2019, en.wikipedia.org/wiki/Ghazni

[167] Or Ma-li-pa, Ma-lo-pa (麻离拔国); it was a very small town on the south coast of Arabia, no longer in existence; Ma, Huan. J.V.G. Mills, trans. *Ying-yai Sheng-lan: The Overall Survey of the Ocean's Shores (1433), op. cit.*, p. 205.

[168] Li-fa/Li-de was in the Li-tai Meureudu district on the north coast of Sumatra; it was a very small country, no longer in existence; Ma, Huan. J.V.G. Mills, trans. *Ying-yai Sheng-lan: The Overall Survey of the Ocean's Shores (1433), op. cit.*, p. 202.

[169] It was today's Baghdad in Iraq; "白达国", CiDianWang.com, www.cidianwang.com/lishi/diming/4/23224gh.htm

[170] It was a small kingdom in the west of Sumatra; "南浡里国", 维基百科, 2017 年 9 月 13 日, zh.wikipedia.org/wiki/南浡里

[171] It was a small island country between Semudera in North Sumatra and Sri Lanka; people had black skin and blood-red hair.

[172] See Luo Maodeng, *op. cit.*, Chapters 52 to 59.

[173] It was today's Sri Lanka in the Indian Ocean; "斯里兰卡", 百度百科, 2019, baike.baidu.com/item/斯里兰卡/213964?fromtitle=锡兰&fromid=7670790

[174] See Luo Maodeng, *op. cit.*, Chapter 60.

[175] "Treasure voyages." *Wikipedia*, Jan. 5, 2019, en.wikipedia.org/wiki/Treasure_voyages

[176] The corresponding Lunar calendar date—November 18, 1432—would make it October 26 in the seventh year of the Xuande period, when the entire treasure fleet was still on its way to Ceylon/Sri Lanka.

[177] The Maldives and Laccadive Islands in the Indian Ocean are located about 500 km/311 mi southwest of Sri Lanka and India; "溜山国", 百度百科, 2019, baike.baidu.com/item/溜山国

[178] See Luo Maodeng, *op. cit.*, Chapter 60.

[179] "Distance between Galle and Beruwala." www.distancefromto.net, DistanceFromTo, 2019, www.distancefromto.net/distance-from-galle-lk-to-beruwala-lk

[180] It was a small country in today's Kollam (former name Quilon) region (perhaps Kayankulam village) in southwestern India; Kollam is about 318 km/198 mi south of Calicut; Ma, Huan. J.V.G. Mills, trans. *Ying-yai Sheng-lan: The Overall Survey of the Ocean's Shores (1433), op. cit.,*p. 219.

[181] See Luo Maodeng, *op. cit.*, Chapter 60.

[182] It was another small country in what is today's Kollam region in southwestern India; see discussion in note 161.

[183] See Luo Maodeng, *op. cit.*, Chapter 60.

[184] *Ibid.*

[185] It was a small country in today's Cochin region of southwestern India; about 213 km/132 mi south of Calicut; "柯枝国", 百度百科, 2019, baike.baidu.com/item/柯枝国

[186] See Luo Maodeng, *op. cit.*, Chapter 60.

[187] *Ibid.*

[188] It was in today's Kozhikode/Calicut region of southwestern India; "古里國", 百度百科, 2019, baike.baidu.com/item/古里国/5643127?fromtitle=古里佛&fromid=274188

[189] See Luo Maodeng, *op. cit.*, Chapter 61.

[190] See Luo Maodeng, *op. cit.*, Chapter 60.

[191] It was a small nation consisting of islands in the Bay of Bengal; the country no longer exists today; this island nation could be the Andaman Islands in the Bengal Bay, north of the Great Nicobar Islands.

[192] See Luo Maodeng, *op. cit.,* Chapters 61 to 68.

[193] See Luo Maodeng, *op. cit.,* Chapter 61.

[194] See Luo Maodeng, *op. cit.,* Chapter 62.

[195] Wolf Howl Organization. "Wolf Anatomy." www.runningwiththewolves.org, Running With The Wolves, Inc., 2019, www.runningwiththewolves.org/anatomy.htm

[196] It was located in the eastern part of the Indian subcontinent at the apex of the Bay of Bengal; "孟加拉(南亚地区)", 百度百科, 2019, baike.baidu.com/item/孟加拉/1257008

[197] See Luo Maodeng, *op. cit.,* Chapter 72.

[198] *Ibid.*

[199] *Ibid.*

[200] It was today's capital of Somalia in East Africa; "木骨都束国", 百度百科, 2019, baike.baidu.com/item/木骨都束国

[201] See Luo Maodeng, *op. cit.,* Chapters 72 to 77.

[202] The Earth Chronicles. "In Kenya, the remains of the Chinese of the era of sea voyages: Zheng He." www.earth-chronicles.com, Earth Chronicles News, July 30, 2017,

earth-chronicles.com/histori/in-kenya-the-remains-of-the-chinese-of-the-era-of-sea-voyages-zheng-he.html

[203] *Ibid.*

[204] Jubb or Jobo, a small country; Luo wrote that it was only about 50 *li* south of Mogadishu; it was in southwestern Somalia near the Juba/Zubba River region; "竹步国", 百度百科, 2019, baike.baidu.com/item/竹步国

[205] See Luo Maodeng, *op. cit.*, Chapters 72 to 77.

[206] It was a very small country; Luo wrote that it was only about 50 *li* north of Mogadishu; but actually the country was south of Mogadishu, and north of Zhubu/Juba; the three kingdoms were very close to each other; "卜剌哇国", 百度百科, 2019, baike.baidu.com/item/卜剌哇国

[207] See Luo Maodeng, *op. cit.*, Chapters 72 to 77.

[208] There have been debates about where this country was. Some scholars say that it was near Mogadishu, while others say that it was Zeila, a port city in the northwestern Awdal region of Somalia. But J.V.G. Mills analysed the Mao Kun map and found that Lasa appeared on the coast of the Arabian Peninsula, a few miles from Mukalla and could be reached from Calicut in twenty days sailing. Sailing data from Fei Xin and Ma Huan and analysis by J.J.L. Duyvendak support the location of Lasa near Mukalla, a seaport and today the capital city of Yemen's Hadhramaut governorate.

[209] See Luo Maodeng, *op. cit.,* Chapter 78.

[210] Sea-Distances.org, 2019, www.sea-distances.org

[211] Ma Huan in Ying Ya Sheng Lan 《瀛涯胜览》 or *The Overall Survey of the Ocean's Shores* gave a longer duration of 30 days. But this might be due to the different ships they used during the different voyages. Ma did not stay with Zheng He's main fleet during this part of the journey; hence, his data might be from earlier voyages.

[212] See note 208.

[213] Sea-Distances.org, 2019, www.sea-distances.org

[214] It was in today's Dhofar/Dhufar/Djofar region of southwestern Oman, on the eastern border with Yemen; "祖法儿国", 百度百科, 2019, baike.baidu.com/item/祖法儿国

[215] See Luo Maodeng, *op. cit.,* Chapter 78.

[216] It could be in today's Minab region of southeastern Iran; Minab is the capital of Minab County, Hormozgan Province, Iran. Minab is not far from Bandar Abbas. Both cities are close to the Strait of Hormuz. But recently, Zhang Leqi (章乐绮) has shown that Hormuz was Jerun (or Djeroun, Jaraun, Jiran) Island, instead of Qeshm Island proposed by J.V.G. Mills in his translated book *Ying-yai Sheng-lan: The Overall Survey of the Ocean's Shores (1433).* Since the Minab region, Jerun Island and Qeshm Island are all close to the Strait of Hormuz, Zheng He's mariners would have explored all of them for trade and for replenishment of supplies; "忽鲁谟斯国", 百度百科, 2019, baike.baidu.com/item/忽鲁谟斯; also see "郑和的舰队去到哪个忽鲁谟

斯?"一文, 于《郑和与亚非世界》, 作者章乐绮; 编者廖建裕, 柯木林, 和许福吉, 国际郑和社团和马六甲博物馆（PERZIM）联合出版, 2012 年, 第 205 至 212 页。

[217] See Luo Maodeng, *op. cit.*, Chapter 79.

[218] *Ibid.*

[219] There is no record of this small country.

[220] See Luo Maodeng, *op. cit.*, Chapters 80 to 84.

[221] The country was on the northwestern shore of the Gulf of Aden in today's Yemen; "阿丹国", 百度百科, 2019, baike.baidu.com/item/阿丹国

[222] See Luo Maodeng, *op. cit.*, Chapters 84 to 86.

[223] See Luo Maodeng, *op. cit.*, Chapter 84.

[224] The earliest date for him to arrive at Calicut would likely be April 6, 1433.

[225] Hong Bao's squadron arrived at Calicut on March 31, 1433.

[226] I will identify this later as Mecca in today's Saudi Arabia.

[227] See Luo Maodeng, *op. cit.*, Chapter 86.

[228] I will identify this later as today's Cahokia Mounds State Historic Site in the central Mississippi Valley.

[229] See Luo Maodeng, *op. cit.*, Chapters 87 to 93.

[230] "岭外代答", 百度百科, 2019, baike.baidu.com/item/岭外代答

[231] "宋会要", 百度百科, 2019, baike.baidu.com/item/宋会要

[232] "诸蕃志", 维基百科, 2018 年 4 月 24 日, zh.wikipedia.org/wiki/诸蕃志

[233] "汪大渊", 百度百科, 2019, baike.baidu.com/item/汪大渊

[234] 编辑, "'笃冲'在古代指的是哪个国家或地区？" www.zhihu.com, 知乎, 2015 年 10 月 15 日, www.zhihu.com/question/36534016

[235] "Tian (天)" means "sky" and "Shan (山)" means "mountain". The Tian Shan, also known as the Tengri Tagh, meaning the Mountain of Heaven, or the Heavenly Mountain, is a large system of mountain ranges located in Central Asia; "Tian Shan." *Wikipedia*, Jan. 15, 2019, en.wikipedia.org/wiki/Tian_Shan

[236] 拂菻: the Byzantine Empire.

[237] "西域", 维基百科, 2018 年 9 月 15 日, zh.wikipedia.org/wiki/西域

[238] "Climate of Mecca." *Wikipedia*, Jan. 16, 2019, en.wikipedia.org/wiki/Climate_of_Mecca

[239] Razwy, Sayyid Ali Ashgar. "Chapter 1: Makka in the Sixth Century." www.al-islam.org, Ahlul Bayt Digital Islamic Library Project, 2019, www.al-islam.org/khadijatul-kubra-sayyid-ali-asghar-razwy/chapter-1-makka-sixth-century

[240] "Quraysh." *Wikipedia*, Jan. 11, 2019, en.wikipedia.org/wiki/Quraysh

[241] "Allah as a lunar deity." *Wikipedia*, Jan. 6, 2019, en.wikipedia.org/wiki/Allah_as_ a_lunar_deity

[242] "Mecca." *Wikipedia*, Dec. 26, 2018, en.wikipedia.org/wiki/Mecca

[243] Beyhum, Toufic. "The Clothes of Mecca." www. vestoj.com, Vestoj, June 28, 2015, www.vestoj.com/the-clothes-of-mecca

[244] "Thawb." *Wikipedia*, Jan. 16, 2019, en.wikipedia.org/wiki/Thawb

[245] See Luo Maodeng, *op. cit.*, Chapter 86.

[246] I mentioned earlier in this chapter that an envoy from Mecca was escorted by Wang Jinghong to China at the end of the seventh voyage. Wang Jinghong and Zheng He arrived at Aden around March 15 to April 19, 1433. According to Ming Shi《明史》or *The History of Ming*, it would take 22 days to get to Calicut from Port Aden. If Wang Jinghong also went to the country of paradise/Yun Chong/Mecca with Zheng He, it would be too late for him to meet Hong Bao and lead the squadrons on April 9, 1433 from Calicut to China. However, if Wang Jinghong escorted the envoy from Mecca around March 14, 1433 (soon after he arrived at Aden, since Mecca's envoys were already waiting at Aden for the arrival of Zheng He's fleet), back to China, then he and his squadron could reach Calicut as early as April 6, 1433. Then, Wang Jinghong could rejoin Hong Bao and leave Calicut on April 9, 1433 heading for China. Hence, it is most likely that Wang Jinghong's squadron separated from Zheng He's main fleet in Aden soon after they arrived there.

[247] In ancient China, the Army of the Front was the large forces used for exploration; the Army of the Centre was the main strength of an army; the Army of the Back provided supplies to the large forces and served as their rearguard; in addition, there were the Army of the Left and the Army of the Right to protect the two flanks of the large forces and back up the actions of the large forces. Also, banners were usually installed on ships to send signals for various purposes including communication, training, commanding and seeking rescue. In the Ming Dynasty, banners could have five different colours representing the five elements metal (white), wood (blue), water (black), fire (red) and earth (yellow), which the ancient Chinese believed to be the elements composing the physical universe.

[248] "The Holly Mosque, Mecca." www.sacred-destinations.com, Sacred Destinations, 2019, www.sacred-destinations.com/saudi-arabia/mecca-haram-mosque

[249] Saad Judi. "Holy Mosque Twin Minarets." www.skyscrapercity.com, Bulletin Solutions Inc. and DragonByte Technologies Ltd., Aug. 7, 2014, www.skyscrapercity.com/showthread.php?t=1753731

[250] "Great Mosque of Mecca." *Wikipedia*, March 29, 2019, en.wikipedia.org/wiki/Great_Mosque_of_Mecca

[251] *Ibid.*

[252] "Mecca, ca. 1778." *Wikipedia*, circa 1778 date, en.wikipedia.org/wiki/Mecca#/media/File:Mecca-1850.jpg

[253] "Map of Makkah city." www.maps-makkah.com, Newebcreations, 2019, https://maps-makkah.com/map-of-makkah-city

[254] "Kaaba." *op. cit.*

[255] *Ibid.*

[256] *Ibid.*

[257] "Religion in pre-Islamic Arabia." *Wikipedia*, Jan. 17, 2019, en.wikipedia.org/wiki/Religion_in_pre-Islamic_Arabia

[258] 1 metre = 0.3 *zhang* (Chinese unit in length); 1 *zhang* = 3.33 m.

333   341

[259] 1 metre is equal to 3 *chi* (Chinese unit in length), or 3.28 ft.

[260] "Kaaba." *op. cit.*

[261] *Ibid.*

[262] "Distance from Mecca to Medina." www.distancefromto.net, Veeam Explorer for Exchange, 2019, www.distancefromto.net/distance-from-mecca-sa-to-medina-sa

[263] "Jannat al-Mu'alla." *Wikipedia*, Dec. 24, 2018, en.wikipedia.org/wiki/Jannat_al-Mu'alla

[264] 张华,《博物志》, www.sbkk88.com, 随便看看吧, 2019, www.sbkk8.cn/mingzhu/gudaicn/bowuzhi/273482.html

[265] 100,000 *li* = 50,000 km. It considerably exceeds our Earth's diameter of 12,742 km. This shows that before 300 AD, not all Chinese people knew that the Earth was round, or the correct diameter of the Earth.

[266] Zhang Heng (张衡; 78–139), the chief astronomer of the Eastern Han Dynasty, wrote about the round Earth in one of his books entitled, Ling Xian 《灵宪》or *The Spiritual Constitution of the Universe*, around 120 AD. He theorised that the universe was like an egg with the stars inside the shell and the Earth as the yolk; the moon was illuminated by the sun. He explained the solar and lunar eclipses, using something similar to the radiating influence theory, and compared the celestial circle to the diameter of Earth and obtained a raio of 736:232, thus π = 3.1724; "Liu Hui's π algorithm." *Wikipedia*, Dec. 14, 2018, en.wikipedia.org/wiki/Liu_Hui's_π_algorithm; 编辑,《灵宪》, 百度百科, 2019, baike.baidu.com/item/灵宪/3054310?fromtitle=《灵宪》&fromid=1776425

[267] Wang Jinghong in fact had separated from Zheng He in Aden and escorted the ambassadors of eleven countries, including Aden, Brava, Lasa and Mecca, to Calicut, before returning to China.

[268] The Suez Canal is a man-made sea-level waterway in Egypt, connecting the Mediterranean Sea to the Red Sea through the Isthmus of Suez. It extends from the northern terminus of Port Said to the southern terminus of Port Tewfik at Suez, a length of 193.30 km/120.11 mi, including its northern and southern access channels; "Suez Canal." *Wikipedia*, Jan. 11, 2019, en.wikipedia.org/wiki/Suez_Canal

[269] "Ocean current." *Wikipedia*, Jan. 17, 2019, en.wikipedia.org/wiki/Ocean_current

[270] "Gulf Stream." *Wikipedia*, Feb. 12, 2019, en.wikipedia.org/wiki/Gulf_Stream

[271] Cooper, John P. "Egypt's Nile-Red Sea canals chronology location seasonality and function." www.researchgate.net, ResearchGate, January 2009, www.researchgate.net/publication/41152508_Egypt's_Nile-Red_Sea_canals_chronology_location_seasonality_and_function

[272] Barbie Bischof, Arthur J. Mariano, Edward H. Ryan. "The North Atlantic Drift Current." Ocean Surface Currents. (2003).

https://oceancurrents.rsmas.miami.edu/atlantic/north-atlantic-drift.html. (This special citation style is required by the three authors. —Ed.)
[273] "Labrador Current." *Wikipedia*, Feb. 12, 2019, en.wikipedia.org/wiki/Labrador_Current
[274] "和氏璧", 百度百科, 2019, baike.baidu.com/item/和氏璧
[275] "Heirloom Seal of the Realm." *Wikipedia*, Sep. 28, 2018, en.wikipedia.org/wiki/Heirloom_Seal_of_the_Realm
[276] 秦王子婴; on the throne for only days.
[277] 西晋、前赵、后赵、冉魏、东晋、宋、南齐、梁、北齐、周、隋。
[278] 唐朝。
[279] 五代; 607–960。
[280] 十国; 902–979。
[281] Legend says that Mazu was a woman in Putian, Meizhou Island in China; her nickname is Niang Ma.
[282] "Trade winds." *Wikipedia*, Dec. 17, 2018, en.wikipedia.org/wiki/Trade_winds
[283] The Gulf Stream originates off the tip of Florida. It follows the eastern coastlines of the U.S. and Newfoundland before its northern extension, the North Atlantic Drift, moves towards Europe. It is a powerful and swift Atlantic Ocean current.
[284] 王恩双, 任建民, "中国第一艘远洋木帆船—'耆英号'", www.pep.com.cn, 人民教育出版社, 2008 年 9 月 23 日, http://old.pep.com.cn/czls/xs/lszs/201008/t20100827_807824.htm
[285] The ship was renamed after the Manchu official Keying; Keying (1787–1858) was also known by his Chinese name Qiying and his Manchu name Kiyeng.
[286] 王恩双, 任建民, "中国第一艘远洋木帆船—'耆英号'", www.pep.com.cn, *op. cit.*, http://old.pep.com.cn/czls/xs/lszs/201008/t20100827_807824.htm
[287] *Ibid.*
[288] Sea-Distances.org, 2019, www.sea-distances.org
[289] "Grank Bank." *Wikipedia*, Nov. 18, 2018, en.wikipedia.org/wiki/Grand_Bank
[290] "Polar climate." *Wikipedia*, Jan. 9, 2019, en.wikipedia.org/wiki/Polar_climate
[291] "Subarctic climate." *Wikipedia*, Jan. 11, 2019, en.wikipedia.org/wiki/Subarctic_climate
[292] Plazacic, Vesna. "5 unique islands to explore in Newfoundland and Labrador." www.Cottagelife.com, Blue Ant Media Canada, June 12, 2017, https://cottagelife.com/outdoors/5-unique-islands-to-visit-in-newfoundland-and-labrador/
[293] "Iceberg." *Wikipedia*, Dec. 30, 2018, en.wikipedia.org/wiki/Iceberg
[294] "Avalon Peninsula." *Wikipedia*, Dec. 26, 2018, en.wikipedia.org/wiki/Avalon_Peninsula

[295] Banfield, Colin. "Winter." www.heritage.nf.ca, Department of Geography, Memorial University of Newfoundland, 1998, www.heritage.nf.ca/articles/environment/seasonal-winter.php
[296] "Climate St. Anthony." *Wikipedia*, Jan. 8, 2019, en.wikipedia.org/wiki/St._Anthony,_Newfoundland_and_Labrador
[297] "Climate Happy-Valley Goose Bay." *Wikipedia*, Dec. 26, 2018, en.wikipedia.org/wiki/Happy_Valley-Goose_Bay
[298] "Climate Labrador City." *Wikipedia*, Dec. 27, 2018, en.wikipedia.org/wiki/Labrador_City
[299] Janzen, Olaf. "The Norse in the North Atlantic." www.heritage.nf.ca, Newfoundland and Labrador Heritage Web Site Project, 2004, www.heritage.nf.ca/articles/exploration/norse-north-atlantic.php
[300] "John Cabot." *Wikipedia*, Jan. 17, 2019, en.wikipedia.org/wiki/John_Cabot
[301] "The Island of Seven Cities (in three parts) Part 1: History and Geography." *YouTube*, uploaded by Paul Chiasson, Mar. 26, 2014, youtube.com/watch?v=KkxIP-gLLxU
"The Island of Seven Cities (in three parts) Part 2: The Site." *YouTube*, uploaded by Paul Chiasson, Mar. 26, 2014, youtube.com/watch?v=PWKeATzqXPQ;
"The Island of Seven Cities (in three parts) Part 3: The Indigenous People." *YouTube*, uploaded by Paul Chiasson, Mar. 26, 2014, youtube.com/watch?v=O4NDdiQZNvk;
"CBC The National's story on Island Of Seven Cities." *YouTube*, uploaded by CBC The National's, June 16, 2008, youtube.com/watch?v=HMrtibNAzAE
[302] "Paul Chiasson -The Island of the Seven Cities." *YouTube*, uploaded by Craig Rintoul, Feb. 21, 2007, youtube.com/watch?v=9JpRTN33hzw; "CBC The National's story on Island Of Seven Cities." *YouTube*, uploaded by joehistory2, Jun 16, 2008, youtube.com/watch?v=HMrtibNAzAE; Chiasson, Paul. *The Island of Seven Cities: Where the Chinese Settled When They Discovered America.* Toronto, Canada: Random House Canada, 2006.
[303] "Cape Dauphin." *Wikipedia*, June 24, 2018, en.wikipedia.org/wiki/Cape_Dauphin
[304] Caplan, Ronald. "The Early History of St. Ann's (Englishtown)." www.capebretonsmagazine.com, Cape Breton's Magazine, Jan. 1, 1986, http://capebretonsmagazine.com/modules/publisher/item.php?itemid=2039
[305] "St. Anns, Nova Scotia." *Wikipedia*, Nov. 10, 2018, en.wikipedia.org/wiki/St._Anns,_Nova_Scotia
[306] Author's private email communication with Paul Chiasson; courtesy of Paul Chiasson.
[307] "Chéticamp, Nova Scotia." *Wikipedia*, July 27, 2018, en.wikipedia.org/wiki/Chéticamp,_Nova_Scotia
[308] "Ingonish." *Wikipedia*, Aug. 15, 2018, en.wikipedia.org/wiki/Ingonish
[309] "Louisbourg." *Wikipedia*, Nov. 7, 2018, en.wikipedia.org/wiki/Louisbourg
[310] *Ibid.*

[311] "St. Peter's, Nova Scotia." *Wikipedia*, Jan. 8, 2019, en.wikipedia.org/wiki/St._Peter's,_Nova_Scotia

[312] Author's private email communication with Paul Chiasson; courtesy of Paul Chiasson.

[313] Canso is roughly southwest of St. Peter's; the Canso Straits, now partially blocked by a bridged causeway, separate Cape Breton Island from mainland Canada.

[314] Author's private email communication with T.C. Bell; courtesy of T.C. Bell.

[315] T.C. Bell also located the first complete Viking settlements in Cumbria, U.K.; courtesy of T.C. Bell.

[316] The main road to the Chinese site was built by the Chinese; it was there before the Viking Hogback grave markers were placed on it.

[317] Thompson, Gunnar. *Viking America*. Seattle, Washington, U.S.A.: Misty Isles, 2012.

[318] A unit of length equal to six ft.

[319] Author's private email communication with T.C. Bell; survey work was made by T.C. Bell; courtesy of T.C. Bell.

[320] As discussed earlier in this chapter, T.C. Bell's discovery has shown that the Chinese road in Cape Dauphin existed prior to the Viking arrival in North America in the tenth century. The tenth century covered the late period of the Tang Dynasty (618 to 907), the entire period of the Five Dynasties (a period of disunity from 907 to 960), and the early period of the Song Dynasty (960 to 1279).

[321] Author's private email communication with T.C. Bell; courtesy of T.C. Bell.

[322] Kahn, Joseph. "Storm over 1418 map: History or scam?" www.nytimes.com, *The New York Times*, Jan. 16, 2006, www.nytimes.com/2006/01/16/world/asia/storm-over-1418-map-history-or-scam.html

[323] "Kunyu Wanguo Quantu." *op. cit.*

[324] "Chicago Portage." *Wikipedia*, Nov. 5, 2018, en.wikipedia.org/wiki/Chicago_Portage

[325] Lake Chicago was a prehistoric proglacial lake that is the ancestor of what is now known as Lake Michigan.

[326] "Chicago Portage." *Wikipedia*, Nov. 5, 2018, en.wikipedia.org/wiki/Chicago_Portage

[327] "Chicago Portage National Historic Site." *Wikipedia*, Nov. 3, 2018, en.wikipedia.org/wiki/Chicago_Portage_National_Historic_Site

[328] The Illinois joins the Mississippi near Grafton, approximately 40 km/25 mi northwest of downtown St. Louis.

[329] Here are a few examples: 徐全, "發現美洲的是鄭和？", www.paper.wenweipo.com, 《文匯報》, 2015 年 9 月 14 日, http://paper.wenweipo.com/2015/09/14/FC1509140001.htm; 秋禾, "郑和发现美洲之新解", http://m.kdnet.net, 凯迪, 2017 年 3 月 6 日, http://m.kdnet.net/share-12149773.html; 神谷俗人, "盖棺定论—郑和船队确

337

曾抵达美洲", http://bbs.tianya.cn, 天涯社区, 2016 年 10 月 19 日,
http://bbs.tianya.cn/post-no05-437839-1.shtml

[330] Luo Maodeng's country of Fengdu was first suggested to be Cahokia in the unpublished book draft 'To the Gates of Feng-Tu: Discovering the Last Ming Expedition to North America, 1433', co-authored by Mark Nickless, Laurie Bonner-Nickless and Sheng-Wei Wang. The draft has been selectively translated into Chinese with Sheng-Wei Wang's additional input, and published as Nickless, Mark, et al. (马克·尼克莱斯等.) Zheng He Fa Xian Mei Zhou Zhi Xin Je《郑和发现美洲之新解》or *New Evidence for Zheng He's Exploration of the Americas*. Beijing, China: World Knowledge Publishing House (世界知识出版社), 2015.

[331] "Fengdu Ghost City." *Wikipedia*, Oct. 29, 2018, en.wikipedia.org/wiki/Fengdu_Ghost_City

[332] 氏 or Shi means "last name"; 刘氏 or Liu Shi means someone whose last name is Liu. Luo Maodeng did not introduce Wang Ming ex-wife's first name.

[333] Xi You Ji《西游记》or *Journey to the West* is a Chinese novel published in the sixteenth century during the Ming dynasty and attributed to Wu Chengen (吴承恩; 1506–1582). It is one of the Four Great Classical Novels of Chinese literature.

[334] "Lu Xun." *Wikipedia*, Jan. 16, 2019, en.wikipedia.org/wiki/Lu_Xun

[335] Jacobs, James Q. "Cahokia Mounds Photo Gallery: Earthworks of Eastern North America." www.jqjacobs.net, James Q. Jacobs, 2018, www.jqjacobs.net/archaeo/cahokia.html

[336] During the twelfth century Cahokia was a "melting-pot".

[337] "Trappists." *Wikipedia*, Nov. 6, 2018, en.wikipedia.org/wiki/Trappists

[338] Mound 55 is known as a platform mound in two books: 1) Iseminger, William R. *Cahokia Mounds: America's First City (Landmarks)*, Stroud, Gloucestershire, U.K.: The History Press, 2010, the Cover page; and 2) Dalan, Rinita A., et al. "Landscape Elements." *Envisioning Cahokia: A Landscape Perspective*, DeKalb, Illinois, U.S.A.: Northern Illinois University Press, 2003, pp. 151–166. But Mound 55 is considered a small conical mound by Fowler, Melvin L. "Descriptions of Mounds 39–88." *The Cahokia Atlas, Revised: A Historical Atlas of Cahokia Archaeology, No. 2 (Studies in Archaeology)*, Illinois, U.S.A.: Illinois Transportation Archaeological Research Program, 1997, p. 119.

[339] Teofilo. "Cahokia's Grand Plaza." www.gamblershouse.wordpress.com, Blog at WordPress.com, Feb. 19, 2012, https://gamblershouse.wordpress.com/2012/02/19/cahokias-grand-plaza/

[340] The reason for creating a terrace or terraces on top of the mound is to build structures on it.

[341] "Cahokia." *Wikipedia*, Nov. 16, 2018, en.wikipedia.org/wiki/Cahokia; Fowler, Melvin L. *The Cahokia Atlas, Revised: A Historical Atlas of Cahokia Archaeology, No. 2 (Studies in Archaeology). op. cit.*, 1997.

[342] Iseminger, William R. "Defending Cahokia: The Stockade/Palisade." *Cahokia Mounds: America's First City (Landmarks), op. cit.*, pp. 137–147.

[343] "Cahokia." *op. cit.*

[344] Britannica Group. "Cahokia Mounds." www.britannica.com, Encyclopædia Britannica, Inc., 2019, www.britannica.com/place/Cahokia-Mounds/images-videos

[345] Monks Mound is the largest pre-Columbian earthwork in the Americas and the largest pyramid north of Mesoamerica; "Monks Mound." *Wikipedia*, Jan. 13, 2019, en.wikipedia.org/wiki/Monks_Mound

[346] Seppa, Nathan. "Metropolitan Life on the Mississippi." http://www.washingtonpost.com, The Washington Post, Mar. 12, 1997, www.washingtonpost.com/wp-srv/national/daily/march/12/cahokia.htm?noredirect=on

[347] *Ibid*; Cahokia mound's archaeology is complicated, but evidence of human sacrifice can be made out, see Janus, Owen. "Cahokia: North America's First City." www.livescience.com, Live Science, Jan. 11, 2018, www.livescience.com/22737-cahokia.html

[348] 编辑, "酆都大帝", 百度百科, 2019, baike.baidu.com/item/酆都大帝

[349] "Distance from Fengdu to Cahokia Mounds State Historic Site." *Google: The Free Internet Search Engine*, Google LLC, 2019, google.com/search?q=distance+between+Fengdu+and+Cahokia&ie=utf-8&oe=utf-8&client=firefox-b-ab

[350] "The Cahokia Birdman Tablet." *YouTube*, uploaded by Chad Ryan Thomas, Aug. 9, 2012, youtube.com/watch?v=KHmmFl6Cnus

[351] 土地庙 or 土地公庙 means Land Deity Temple; 土地公 means "lord of the soil and the earth."

[352] 东岳庙 is the temple for the god of Mount Tai; the temple of the supreme lord in charge of birth, death, illness and old age in the netherworld; "东岳庙", 维基百科, 2018 年 11 月 14 日, zh.wikipedia.org/wiki/东岳庙

[353] For Monks Mound, see note 345, above.

[354] *Ibid.*

[355] "Mesoamerica." *Wikipedia*, Jan. 16, 2019, en.wikipedia.org/wiki/Mesoamerica

[356] "土星", 维基百科, 2019 年 1 月 14 日, zh.wikipedia.org/wiki/土星

[357] "木星", 维基百科, 2019 年 1 月 18 日, zh.wikipedia.org/wiki/木星

[358] Admin. "Mound 67." www.cahokiamounds.org, Cahokia Mounds State Historic Site (Museum Society), Oct. 23, 2015, https://cahokiamounds.org/mound/mound-67/

[359] Admin. "Mound 68." www.cahokiamounds.org, Cahokia Mounds State Historic Site (Museum Society), Oct. 23, 2015, https://cahokiamounds.org/mound/mound-68/

[360] A charnel house is a vault or building where human skeletal remains are stored; "Charnel_house." *Wikipedia*, Oct. 25, 2018, en.wikipedia.org/wiki/Charnel_house

[361] The name Yama originated from Buddhist scriptures in India. Originally ancient China had no conception of Yama. After Indian Buddhism was introduced into China in ancient times, the faith of Yama as the Lord of Hell became popular in China. It interacted with the Chinese indigenous religion of Daoism (Taoism), and evolved into the legend of the "ten Courts of Hell". In Chinese folklore, the general image of Yama is closer to that of a court judge, and Yama represents the Buddhist Dharma. According to Buddhism, the newly dead report to hell to face trial and accept Yama's judgement. Yama has a "book of life and death", which sets the length of life of each individual. The judgment of Yama depends on the acts of each individual in their lifetime. Meritorious people or people with good conduct will be allowed to live in Elysium to enjoy immortal bliss or be given a happy afterlife, whereas those who broke the law or committed evil will go to hell to receive all kinds of punishment or endure a bad afterlife; "Yama (Buddhism)." *Wikipedia*, Dec. 8, 2018, en.wikipedia.org/wiki/Yama_(Buddhism)

[362] The title of the eighth King of Mount Tai originated from China (it refers to the place where the Chinese thought hell was in the earliest days), whereas the remaining titles of the eight lords were given randomly by Chinese monks at that time.

[363] Admin. "Mound 59." www.cahokiamounds.org, Cahokia Mounds State Historic Site (Museum Society), Oct. 23, 2015, https://cahokiamounds.org/mound/mound-59/; about 1 *li*/500 m/1,640 ft directly south of Monks Mound are two of the more impressive mounds at the site. One of these—Mound 60—is a well-formed, flat-top platform mound. Directly to the west of Mound 60 is a conical mound of considerable elevation, Mound 59 (Moorehead's Mound 57), commonly known as Round Top Mound.

[364] Admin. "Mound 60." www.cahokiamounds.org, Cahokia Mounds State Historic Site (Museum Society), Oct. 23, 2015, https://cahokiamounds.org/mound/mound-60/

[365] Kane, Njord. "The Sacred Colors of the Maya." www.readicon.com, Spangenhelm Publishing, Dec. 4, 2016, http://readicon.com/the-sacred-colors-of-the-maya/

[366] This is because at the time of sunrise, the Sun is near the horizon. The light from the Sun should traverse a larger density of atmosphere than when the Sun is overhead. Blue and violet-coloured rays are scattered more than the red-coloured rays, hence, the setting/rising sun appears red; Varun. "Why does the setting/rising sun appear red?" www.quora.com, Quora, Mar. 7, 2015, www.quora.com/Why-does-the-setting-rising-sun-appear-red

[367] 彩 cai, means colourful; 幢 chuang, is an ancient flag, hanging like a vertical cylinder and decorated with feathers, see 编辑, "幢", 百度百科, 2019, baike.baidu.com/item/幢; it is a banner of victory and auspiciousness and is considered a Buddhist treasure; 绛 jiang, is a bright-red colour; 节 jie, means a banner used by emperors or gods.

[368] 羽 yu, means feather; 葆 bao, is a kind of ceremonial banner on a pole with bird feathers gathered as a cover like a crown; 花 hua, means colourful; 旌 jing, means feather-decorated flag.

[369] 云 yun, means cloud; 锦 jin, is a silk fabric.

[370] 透明の纯粹, "云锦的英文介绍", 自由的百科全书, 百度文库, May 1, 2011, wenku.baidu.com/view/d56226543c1ec5da50e2706f.html

[371] China's silk products entered different countries in Asia, Europe, and African countries in the first century BC or even earlier via the Silk Road trade.

[372] "Crusades." *Wikipedia*, Jan. 7, 2019, en.wikipedia.org/wiki/Crusades

[373] "History of silk." *Wikipedia*, Jan. 7, 2019, en.wikipedia.org/wiki/History_of_silk

[374] Carballo, David M. "Trade Routes in the Americas before Columbus." www.academia.edu, Academia, 2019, www.academia.edu/4998969/Trade_Routes_in_the_Americas_Before_Columbus

[375] "Maize." *Wikipedia*, Jan. 1, 2019, en.wikipedia.org/wiki/Maize

[376] *Zhong* was an ancient unit of capacity in China; 1 *zhong* was 64 *dou* (斗); one *dou* was ten litres.

[377] Shun lived between 2128 and 2025 BC; he was also known as Emperor Shun, a legendary leader of ancient China, and was regarded as one of the Three Sovereigns and Five Emperors (a group of mythological rulers or deities in ancient northern China).

[378] "刘殷", 百度百科, 2019, baike.baidu.com/item/刘殷

[379] "严震", 百度百科, 2019, baike.baidu.com/item/严震/2763083

[380] The old Ming Empire was decaying. Due to persistent drought and famine, two major popular uprisings gathered force. They were led by Zhang Xianzhong (张献忠) and Li Zicheng (李自成), both poor men from famine-hit Shaanxi (陕西) in northwestern China.

[381] "Chongzhen Emperor." *Wikipedia*, Jan. 11, 2019, en.wikipedia.org/wiki/Chongzhen_Emperor

[382] 普掠地狱 is translated as Pu Lue Hell. According to Buddhism, this is the name of one of the hells located in the centre of the netherworld.

[383] *Ren* was an ancient Chinese unit for measuring length, one *ren* equals seven or eight *chi*, one *chi* is about 30 cm or about one foot.

[384] "Palisade." *Wikipedia*, Jan. 10, 2019, en.wikipedia.org/wiki/Palisade

[385] 佛教术语, "夜叉 [印度神话中的妖怪]", www.baike.com, 互动百科, 2019 , www.baike.com/wiki/夜叉

[386] Bostrom, Peter A. "Birdman Tablet." www.lithiccastinglab.com, Lithic Casting Lab., Jan. 1, 2003, www.lithiccastinglab.com/gallery-pages/birdmantabletcahokialarge.htm; for a brief video exploring the meaning of the Cahokia Birdman, please view "The Cahokia Birdman Tablet." *YouTube*, uploaded by Chad Ryan Thomas on Aug. 9, 2012, youtube.com/watch?v=KHmmFl6Cnus

[387] Excavations of the copper workshops at Mound 34 – a small conical-shaped mound located on the Ramey Plaza (east of Monks Mound) outside downtown Cahokia – indicate that copper was worked there. Anvils were used for beating out the flattened sheets of copper; "Mississippian copper plates." *Wikipedia*, Nov. 20, 2018, en.wikipedia.org/wiki/Mississippian_copper_plates#Cahokia_and_the_Birdman

[388] "Sun dance." *Wikipedia*, Nov. 11, 2018, en.wikipedia.org/wiki/Sun_dance

[389] Young, Gloria A. Dianna Everett, ed. "Sun Dance Archived 2012-11-19 at the Wayback Machine." *Encyclopedia of Oklahoma History and Culture*, Oklahoma City: U.S.A.: The Oklahoma Historical Society, Accessed 28 December 2013.

[390] "四大天王", 维基百科, 2019 年 1 月 8 日, zh.wikipedia.org/wiki/四大天王

[391] "Metate." *Wikipedia*, June 1, 2018, en.wikipedia.org/wiki/Metate

[392] AgCultures. "Cahokia: The Great Native American City." www.agcultures.com, AgCultures, May 2017, https://agcultures.com/activity/cahokia

[393] Chen, Angus. "1,000 Years Ago, Corn Made This Society Big. Then, A Changing Climate Destroyed It." www.npr.org, National Public Radio, Inc. (US), Feb. 10, 2017, www.npr.org/sections/thesalt/2017/02/10/513963490/1-000-years-ago-corn-made-this-society-big-then-a-changing-climate-destroyed-the

[394] Golden carp: on each side of the abdomen of this fish there is a gold stripe.

[395] The other site is Trotier (11S861); Durst, Patrick, et al. *Excavations at the Trotier Site: French Cahokia, St. Clair County, Illinois (Research Reports, No. 122)*. Plastic Comb. Illinois, U.S.A.: Illinois State Archaeological Survey, 2009.

[396] "Snakes in central Mississippi Valley." *Google: The Free Internet Search Engine*, Google LLC, 2019, google.com/search?q=SNAKES+IN+central+mISSISSIPPI+rIVER+vALLEY&client=firefox-b-ab&tbm=isch&tbo=u&source=univ&sa=X&ved=2ahUKEwjZ38zdtujfAhXEZt4KHWEKAxsQ7Al6BAgDEA0&biw=1093&bih=451

[397] Admin. "Mound 66." www.cahokiamounds.org, Cahokia Mounds State Historic Site (Museum Society), Oct. 23, 2015, https://cahokiamounds.org/mound/mound-66/

[398] A mortar and pestle is a kitchen device used in many places in the world since ancient times to prepare ingredients or substances by crushing and grinding them into a fine paste or powder.

[399] Liu Shi said that Fengdu Ghost Mountain was a thousand *li* away to the west of Fengdu.

[400] "角带", www.zdic.net, 汉典, 2019, www.zdic.net/c/2/f0/249611.htm

[401] Tremain, Cara Grace. "Resource: Ancient Maya clothing." www.mexicolore.co.uk, Maya at Mexicolore, Nov. 23, 2014, www.mexicolore.co.uk/maya/teachers/what-did-the-ancient-maya-wear

[402] *Ibid.*

[403] "Maya maize god." *Wikipedia*, June 22, 2018, en.wikipedia.org/wiki/Maya_maize_god

[404] "The Cahokian Way of Living—Living in Paradise?" www.univie.ac.at, Universität Wien, 2001, www.univie.ac.at/Anglistik/webprojects/LiveMiss/Cahokia/LIFESTYLE.htm

[405] "Aztec Civilization." www.informationaboutaztec.weebly.com, Weebly, 2019, https://informationaboutaztec.weebly.com/priests-and-temples.html

[406] Admin. "Mound 51." www.cahokiamounds.org, Cahokia Mounds State Historic Site (Museum Society), Oct. 23, 2015, https://cahokiamounds.org/mound/mound-51/

[407] About 1 *li*/500 m/0.31 mi/1,640 ft directly south of Monks Mound are two of the more impressive mounds at the site. One of these, Mound 60, is a well-formed, flat-top platform mound. Directly to the west of Mound 60 is a conical mound of considerable elevation, Mound 59 (Moorehead's Mound 57), commonly known as Round Top Mound; Admin. "Mound 59." www.cahokiamounds.org, Cahokia Mounds State Historic Site (Museum Society), Oct. 23, 2015, https://cahokiamounds.org/mound/mound-59/

[408] Admin. "Mound 60." www.cahokiamounds.org, Cahokia Mounds State Historic Site (Museum Society), Oct. 23, 2015, https://cahokiamounds.org/mound/mound-60/

[409] Monks Mound is the largest pre-Columbian earthwork in the Americas and the largest pyramid north of Mexico; "Monks Mound." *Wikipedia*, Jan. 13, 2019, en.wikipedia.org/wiki/Monks_Mound

[410] Zhang Bo (张柏) or Zhang Langya (张狼牙; lang 狼 means wolf, and ya 牙 means tooth) always carried and used a weapon called *Langya Bang* (Bang 棒, meaning baton) which had many short, tooth-like blades around the edge of a club; these blades were as sharp as a wolf's teeth.

[411] "Illinois Adventure #1308 'Cahokia Mounds.'" *YouTube*, uploaded by WTVP, Mar. 8, 2014, youtube.com/watch?v=xt-u9FBBnhc

[412] Bostrom, Peter A. "Birdman Tablet." www.lithiccastinglab.com, Lithic Casting Lab., Jan. 1, 2003, www.lithiccastinglab.com/gallery-pages/birdmantabletcahokialarge.htm; for a brief video exploring the meaning of the Cahokia Birdman, please view "The Cahokia Birdman Tablet." *YouTube*, uploaded by Chad Ryan Thomas on Aug. 9, 2012, youtube.com/watch?v=KHmmFl6Cnus

[413] 晓愚, "如何超度亲人亡灵?" www.fo.ifeng.com, 凤凰新媒体, 2014 年 03 月 10 日, http://fo.ifeng.com/changshi/detail_2014_03/10/34588859_0.shtml

[414] In Buddhism, Nirvana is a transcendent state in which there is neither suffering, desire, nor sense of self; and the subject is released from the effects of karma and the cycle of death and rebirth. It represents the final goal of Buddhism.

[415] Traditionally, the period of 49 days after someone dies is seen as a time for that person's soul to perceive his karma. According to Buddhist teaching, the bodhisattva Ji Jang Bosal helps the deceased during these 49 days to perceive their karma, so that when they return, they are reborn to help this world, rather than continuing in the cycle of birth and death; see Lerch, Tim JDPSN. "49 Day Funeral Ceremony." www.providencezen.org, Providence Zen Center, Mar. 20, 2012, http://providencezen.org/49-day-funeral-ceremony

[416] Ma Fubo is considered one of the more famous generals in Chinese history, not only because of his military achievements, but also because he demonstrated perseverance and respect to his friends and subordinates.

[417] "Labrador Current." *Wikipedia*, Jan. 6, 2019, en.wikipedia.org/wiki/Labrador_Current; speeds for the Labrador Current are about 0.3–0.5 m/s or 0.58–0.97 kn along the shelf edge.

[418] It is a slow-moving body of water located about 50°–64°N and 10°–30°W.

[419] The northeast monsoon develops during late October and continues through early March, gradually becoming more intermittent. Later in April, more intermittent SSW winds associated with the Southwest Monsoon build up, though the Southwest Monsoon season really is in "full swing" during the period from mid/late May through early October; also see "Monsoon." *Wikipedia*, Jan. 7, 2019, en.wikipedia.org/wiki/Monsoon

[420] "Tropical cyclone." *Wikipedia*, April 12, 2019, https://en.wikipedia.org/wiki/Tropical_cyclone

[421] *Ibid.*

[422] "Vasco da Gama." *Wikipedia*, Dec. 10, 2018, en.wikipedia.org/wiki/Vasco_da_Gama

[423] "Strait of Gibraltar crossing." *Wikipedia*, Dec. 29, 2018, en.wikipedia.org/wiki/Strait_of_Gibraltar_crossing

[424] "Florence." *Wikipedia*, Jan. 18, 2019, en.wikipedia.org/wiki/Republic_of_Florence

[425] "Council of Florence." *Wikipedia*, Jan. 18, 2019, en.wikipedia.org/wiki/Council_of_Florence

[426] "Florence." *Wikipedia*, Jan. 14, 2019, en.wikipedia.org/wiki/Florence

[427] Menzies, Gavin. *1434: The Year a Magnificent Chinese Fleet Sailed to Italy and Ignited the Renaissance*. New York, U.S.A.: HarperCollins Publishers, 2008.

[428] A monsoon is a seasonal change in the direction of the prevailing, or strongest, winds of a region. Monsoons are large-scale sea breezes and always blow from cold to warm regions. During warmer months the land temperature rises more quickly than the ocean temperature, and the air above the land expands and develops low pressure, whereas the air above the ocean retains a higher pressure. This difference in pressure causes sea breezes to blow from the ocean to the land, bringing moist air inland. This moist air rises to a higher altitude over land and then it flows back toward the ocean. However, when the air rises, and while it is still over the land, the air cools. This decreases the air's

ability to hold water, and this causes precipitation over the land. This is why summer monsoons cause so much rain over land. In the colder months, the cycle is reversed. Then the land cools faster than the oceans and the air over the land has higher pressure than air over the ocean. This causes the air over the land to flow to the ocean.

[429] The Strait of Magellan was called the "Dragon's Tail", a navigable sea route in southern Chile, separating mainland South America to the north from Tierra del Fuego to the south. It is the most important natural passage of the three passages between the Atlantic and Pacific Oceans. Portuguese explorer and navigator Ferdinand Magellan (circa 1480–1521) became the first European to navigate the strait in 1520 during his voyage of global circumnavigation. At its narrowest point, the strait is approximately 570 km/350 mi long and about 2 km/1.2 mi wide. It is considered a difficult route to navigate due to the narrowness of the passage and unpredictable winds and currents. But it is shorter and more sheltered than the often-stormy Drake Passage, and less treacherous than the Beagle Channel; "Strait_of_Magellan." *Wikipedia*, Nov. 30, 2018, en.wikipedia.org/wiki/Strait_of_Magellan

[430] Author's private email communication with T.C. Bell; courtesy of T.C. Bell.

[431] *Weng Cheng* is an enclosure built on the outside (or inside; or both) of a city gate with defensive systems to protect towns and cities in China in pre-modern times; it is part of the walls of ancient Chinese cities; its shape is either semi-circular or square. The semi-circular one is called Weng Cheng 瓮城 or Weng City, or *Weng Cheng*; the square one is called Weng Cheng 方城 or Square City, Fang City or *Fang Cheng*.

[432] T.C. Bell does not want to reveal the location of the evidence to protect it from being destroyed; courtesy of T.C. Bell.

[433] Author's private email communication with T.C. Bell; courtesy of T.C. Bell; "Māori people." *Wikipedia*, Jan. 18, 2019, en.wikipedia.org/wiki/Māori_people

[434] Moeraki is a small fishing village on the east coast of the South Island of New Zealand; see "Moeraki." *Wikipedia*, June 19, 2018, en.wikipedia.org/wiki/Moeraki

[435] Author's private email communication with T.C. Bell.

[436] See T.C. Bell's unpublished booklet, 'A Chinese Boachuan (Treasure Ship): Ship Yard to Wreck'; courtesy of T.C. Bell.

[437] *Ibid.*

[438] Kitt, Jeffrey. "November earthquake uncovers 'dinosaur egg' boulders in Kaikoura." www.stuff.co.nz, Stuff Limited, Aug. 27, 2017, www.stuff.co.nz/national/96105986/november-earthquake-uncovers-dinosaur-egg-boulders-in-kaikoura

[439] Author's private email communication with T.C. Bell; courtesy of T.C. Bell.

[440] *Ibid.*

[441] T.C. Bell, 'A Chinese Boachuan (Treasure Ship): Ship Yard to Wreck', *op. cit.*

[442] "History of the anchor." *Wikipedia*, May 1, 2018,
en.wikipedia.org/wiki/History_of_the_anchor

[443] Author's private email communication with T.C. Bell; courtesy of T.C. Bell.

[444] Xiangyang is in the Hubei Province of China and was a place contested by all strategists in ancient times.

[445] 编辑, "襄阳炮", 百度百科, 2019, baike.baidu.com/item/襄阳炮

[446] "襄樊之战", 维基百科, 2018 年 12 月 10 日, zh.wikipedia.org/wiki/襄樊之战

[447] "Song dynasty." *Wikipedia*, Jan. 5, 2019,
en.wikipedia.org/wiki/Song_dynasty

[448] Polo, Marco and Ronald Latham. *The Travels of Marco Polo*. London, U.K.: Penguin Classics, 1958.

[449] "云梯", 维基百科, 2017 年 9 月 10 日, zh.wikipedia.org/wiki/云梯

[450] "Spring and Autumn period." *Wikipedia*, Dec. 16, 2018,
en.wikipedia.org/wiki/Spring_and_Autumn_period; it was from approximately 771 to 476 BC, or according to some authorities until 403 BC.

[451] The Eastern Zhou period is traditionally divided into two periods; the "Spring and Autumn" period which lasted from about 770 BC to 475 BC, and the "Warring States" period which lasted from about 475 BC to 221 BC.

[452] "重力抛石機", 维基百科, 2017 年 11 月 1 日, zh.wikipedia.org/wiki/重力抛石機

[453] 米爾軍事, "古代的超級武器：襄陽巨炮究竟多可怕", www. read01.com, 壹讀, June 10, 2015,
https://read01.com/QQgJLE.html#.XDrpvs1S_v9

[454] The above date of 1400 is only an estimate based on carbon-dating, which can be inaccurate.

[455] Bouscaren, Durrie. "New insights into the curious disappearance of the Cahokia Mounds builders."
www.news.stlpublicradio.org, St. Louis Pubic Radio, May 4, 2015,
http://news.stlpublicradio.org/post/new-insights-curious-disappearance-cahokia-mounds-builders#stream/0

[456] Iseminger, William. *Cahokia Mounds: America's First City (Landmarks)*. *op. cit.*, 2010.

[457] Dalan, Rinita A., et al. *Envisioning Cahokia: A Landscape Perspective*. *op. cit.*, 2003.

[458] Lee, Siu-Leung. "The Mystery of Zheng He and America."
www.ChianUSFriendship.com, Sheng-Wei Wang, Feb. 1, 2010,
www.chinausfriendship.com/article1.asp?mn=201; 李兆良, "郑和与美洲之謎–逸史尋跡", www.ChianUSFriendship.com, Sheng-Wei Wang, 2010 年 2 月 1 日, www.chinausfriendship.com/chinese/article1.asp?mn=167; 李兆良, 《宣德金牌啟示錄：明代開拓美洲》, 聯經出版社, 2013 年, 第 3 頁。

[459] Hamilton, Calvin and Rosanna Hamilton. "Cahokia Mounds." www. scienceviews.com, ScienceViews.com, 2011, http://scienceviews.com/indian/cahokia.html

[460] "Hernando de Soto." *Wikipedia*, Jan. 30, 2019, en.wikipedia.org/wiki/Hernando_de_Soto

[461] 徐波, "历史的投影与现实的折射—关于'中国人发现美洲'百年学术争议的国际政治思考", www.wap.sciencenet.cn, Feb. 29, 黄安年的科学网博客, 2016, http://blog.sciencenet.cn/blog-415-959364.html

[462] "Matteo Ricci." *Wikipedia*, Jan. 8, 2019, en.wikipedia.org/wiki/Matteo_Ricci

[463] Walter, Ted. "When did the Chinese first find out the Earth is round? How did the rulers and the people react to this? What changes did it make to Chinese society at the time?" www.quora.com, Quora, Dec 15, 2016, www.quora.com/When-did-the-Chinese-first-find-out-the-Earth-is-round-How-did-the-rulers-and-the-people-react-to-this-What-changes-did-it-make-to-Chinese-society-at-the-time

[464] "Zhang Heng." *Wikipedia*, Dec. 14, 2018, en.wikipedia.org/wiki/Zhang_Heng

[465] If you draw a circle with a diameter of 1; then the circumference is 3.14159265..., a number known as Pi, or the Greek symbol π.

[466] "Zhang Heng." *op. cit.*

[467] "Ptolemy." *Wikipedia*, Jan. 11, 2019, en.wikipedia.org/wiki/Ptolemy

[468] "History of the compass." *Wikipedia*, Jan. 13, 2019, en.wikipedia.org/wiki/History_of_the_compass

[469] 编辑, "郭守敬", 百度百科, 2019, baike.baidu.com/item/郭守敬

[470] This book specializes in recording unusual astronomical phenomena in different dynasties.

[471] "Book of Jin." *Wikipedia*, Nov. 15, 2018, en.wikipedia.org/wiki/Book_of_Jin; this is an official Chinese historical text covering the history of the Jin Dynasty from 265 to 420; compiled in 648 by a number of Tang Dynasty officials.

[472] 编辑, "浑天说", 百度百科, 2019, baike.baidu.com/item/浑天说

[473] 编辑, "盖天说", 百度百科, 2019, baike.baidu.com/item/盖天说

[474] 编辑, "宣夜说", 百度百科, 2019, baike.baidu.com/item/宣夜说

[475] Thompson, Gunnar. "Chinese Knowledge of the Spherical Earth Centered on the Sun." www. Gavinmenzies.net, Gavin Menzies, Aug. 18, 2011, www.gavinmenzies.net/Evidence/26-chinese-knowledge-of-the-spherical-earth-centered-on-the-sun-by-gunnar-thompson-ph-d

[476] In fact, the Earth is not perfectly round. Instead, it is an oblate spheroid—a sphere that is squashed at its poles and swollen at the equator. Another point is that the Earth's shape does change over time due to many other dynamic factors.

[477] "Angle gauge." *Wikipedia*, Feb. 6, 2018, en.wikipedia.org/wiki/Angle_gauge

347

[478] A "level" is a device for establishing a horizontal plane.

[479] "Crux." *Wikipedia*, Jan. 10, 2019, en.wikipedia.org/wiki/Crux; it is believed that Amerigo Vespucci was the first European explorer to see the "Four Stars", as he called them, while on his third voyage in 1501. See "Amerigo Vespucci." *Wikipedia*, Jan. 12, 2019, en.wikipedia.org/wiki/Amerigo_Vespucci

[480] Menzies, Gavin. "Zheng He's method of calculating latitude and longitude." www.gavinmenzies.net, Gavin Menzies, Aug. 11, 2011, www.gavinmenzies.net/Evidence/29-zheng-he%E2%80%99s-method-of-calculating-latitude-and-longitude

[481] "Dead reckoning." *Wikipedia*, Dec. 12, 2018, en.wikipedia.org/wiki/Dead_reckoning

[482] "Magnetic declination." *Wikipedia*, Nov. 5, 2018, en.wikipedia.org/wiki/Magnetic_declination

[483] "Arctic Ocean." *Wikipedia*, Jan. 7, 2019, en.wikipedia.org/wiki/Arctic_Ocean

[484] 刘钢，《古地图密码：中国发现世界的谜团玄机》，广西师范大学出版社，2009 年。

[485] USGS. "How much water is there on, in, and above the Earth?" www.water.usgs.gov, U.S. Geological Survey, Dec. 2, 2016, https://water.usgs.gov/edu/earthhowmuch.html

[486] 编辑，"大明混一图"，百度百科，2019, baike.baidu.com/item/大明混一图

[487] 编辑，"混一疆理历代国都之图"，百度百科，2019, baike.baidu.com/item/混一疆理历代国都之图

[488] Gavin Menzies succeeded in correcting the shape of Western Africa in the Kangnido Map by incorporating the effect of ocean currents, as I have mentioned in Section (4) of Chapter 6 of this book.

[489] 刘钢，《古地图密码：中国发现世界的谜团玄机》，广西师范大学出版社，2009 年。

[490] Temple, Robert and Joseph Needham. *3,000 Years of Science, Discovery, and Invention Revised Ed.* Rochester, Vermont, U.S.A.: Inner Traditions, 2007.

[491] "Charles Hapgood." *Wikipedia*, Jan 22, 2019, en.wikipedia.org/wiki/Charles_Hapgood

[492] "Portolan chart." *Wikipedia*, Dec. 25, 2018, en.wikipedia.org/wiki/Portolan_chart

[493] "華夷圖"，維基百科，2018 年 3 月 16 日, zh-yue.wikipedia.org/wiki/華夷圖

[494] "Caverio map." *Wikipedia*, May 22, 2018, en.wikipedia.org/wiki/Caverio_map

[495] "Pietro Vesconte." *Wikipedia*, April 10, 2017, en.wikipedia.org/wiki/Pietro_Vesconte

[496] 刘钢，《古地图密码：中国发现世界的谜团玄机》，广西师范大学出版社，2009 年，彩图 19 和 20。

[497] Admin, "第三节 与《张匡正世界地图》相似的《天下全图》", www.wakbook.com, 我爱看书, 2019, www.wakbook.com/Article/1x0000000002/174040x13547/STANZA_44.html

[498] 编辑, "天下全舆总图", 百度百科, 2019, baike.baidu.com/item/天下全舆总图

[499] 刘钢, "《天下诸番识贡图》收藏者：此图无声胜有声", www.tech.sina.com.cn, Sina Corporation, Mar. 23, 2006, tech.sina.com.cn/d/2006-03-23/1727875871.shtml

[500] Thompson, Gunnar. "Chinese Knowledge of the Spherical Earth Centered on the Sun." www.gavinmenzies.net, Gavin Menzies, Aug. 18, 2011, www.gavinmenzies.net/Evidence/26-chinese-knowledge-of-the-spherical-earth-centered-on-the-sun-by-gunnar-thompson-ph-d

[501] 刘钢, "《天下诸番识贡图》收藏者：此图无声胜有声", www.tech.sina.com.cn, Sina Corporation, Mar. 23, 2006, http://tech.sina.com.cn/d/2006-03-23/1727875871.shtml

[502] "De Virga world map." *Wikipedia*, May 22, 2018, en.wikipedia.org/wiki/De_Virga_world_map

[503] Menzies, Gavin. "Albertin di Virga's map and Zheng He's 1418 map." www.gavinmenzies.net, Gavin Menzies, Aug. 11, 2011, www.gavinmenzies.net/Evidence/18-albertin-di-virgas-map-and-zheng-hes-1418-map

[504] *Ibid.*

[505] 刘钢,《古地图密码：中国发现世界的谜团玄机》, 广西师范大学出版社, 2009 年。

[506] Thompson, Gunnar. "Dr. Gunnar Thompson's opinion of the 1418 map." www.gavinmenzies.net, Gavin Menzies, Aug. 18, 2011, www.gavinmenzies.net/Evidence/12-dr-gunnar-thompsons-opinion-of-the-1418-map

[507] He reigned from 1402 to 1424.

[508] "Treasure voyages." *Wikipedia*, Jan. 5, 2019, en.wikipedia.org/wiki/Treasure_voyages

[509] Beijing served as the Imperial capital of the Ming Dynasty from New Year's Day 1421.

[510] 林贻典, "再论美洲由郑和船队发现的见解",《海交史研究》第 2 期, 中国海外交通史研究会, 2003 年, http://iwaas.cssn.cn/webpic/web/cns/paper/uploadfiles/2/HJSY200302003.pdf; Lam, Yee Din. "A Third Research on the Discovery of America by Zheng He's Fleet." www.gavienmenzies.net, Gavin Menzies, Aug. 16, 2011, www.gavinmenzies.net/Evidence/5-mr-lam-yee-din-a-third-research-on-the-discovery-of-america-by-zheng-he%E2%80%99s-fleet

[511] "Kunyu Wanguo Quantu." *op. cit.*

[512] 刘钢,《古地图密码：中国发现世界的谜团玄机》, 广西师范大学出版社, 2009 年, 第 5 章。

[513] The Pampas are large treeless plains in South America.

[514] "Andes." *Wikipedia*, Jan. 15, 2019, en.wikipedia.org/wiki/Andes

[515] "Pampas." *Wikipedia*, Jan. 11, 2019, en.wikipedia.org/wiki/Pampas

[516] "John Cabot." *op. cit.*

[517] Portolan charts are ancient nautical charts known for their high cartographic accuracy; "Portolan chart." *Wikipedia*, Jan. 22, 2019, https://en.wikipedia.org/wiki/Portolan_chart

[518] "Medici-Laurentian Atlas." *Wikipedia*, May 22, 2018, en.wikipedia.org/wiki/Medici-Laurentian_Atlas

[519] Author's private email communication with T.C. Bell; courtesy of T.C. Bell.

[520] "Bermuda." *Wikipedia*, Jan. 15, 2019, en.wikipedia.org/wiki/Bermuda

[521] "Juan de Bermúdez." *Wikipedia*, Feb. 13, 2019, en.wikipedia.org/wiki/Juan_de_Bermúdez

[522] "Mississippi River." *Wikipedia*, Jan. 9, 2019, en.wikipedia.org/wiki/Mississippi_River; the word *Mississippi* itself comes from *Messipi*, the French rendering of the Anishinaabe (Ojibwe or Algonquin) name for the river, *Misi-ziibi* (Great River). The Mississippi River's confluence with the Missouri River is north of St. Louis, Missouri, and the Mississippi River's confluence with the Ohio River is near Cairo, Illinois.

[523] "Matteo Ricci." *Wikipedia*, Jan. 8, 2019, en.wikipedia.org/wiki/Matteo_Ricci

[524] 中央研究院档案馆, "中國西元 1500 年後的地圖", www.sinica.edu.tw, 中央研究院, 2019, http://www.pro-classic.com/ethnicgv/cmaps/中國西元 1500 年後的地圖.htm

[525] 杰杰, "中國第一張有經緯線的地圖", www.tw.answers.yahoo.com, Yahoo, 2006, https://tw.answers.yahoo.com/question/index?qid=20051029000014KK10012

[526] Days, John D. "The Search for the Origins of the Chinese Manuscript of Matteo Ricci's Maps." *Imago Mundi,* vol. 47, 1995, pp. 94–117. Matteo Ricci prepared four editions of Chinese world maps before 1603 during his mission in China: 1) a 1584 early woodblock print called Yu Di Shan Hai Quan Tu 《輿地山海全图》; 2) a 1596 map carved on a stele, called Shan Hai Yu Di Tu 《山海輿地圖》; 3) a 1600 revised version of the 1596 map, usually named Shan Hai Yu Di Quan Tu 《山海輿地全图》; and 4) a larger and much refined 1602 edition of the 1584 map, in six panels, printed in Beijing, called Kunyu Wanguo Quantu 《坤輿万国全图》; www.myoldmaps.com/renaissance-maps-1490-1800/441-ricci.pdf

[527] "《山海輿地全图》", フリー百科事典, 2017 年 2 月 8 日, ja.wikipedia.org/wiki/山海輿地全图

[528] Most of Matteo Ricci's maps are now lost. Later copies of the 1602 edition of the Kunyu Wanguo Quantu may be found in China, Korea, London, Vienna, and the U.S. Library of Congress; one copy of the map was recently discovered

in the storerooms of the Shenyang Museum (沉阳博物馆) in China; www.myoldmaps.com/renaissance-maps-1490-1800/441-ricci.pdf

[529] "Wanli" is the era name of his reign; it literally means "ten thousand calendars."

[530] "李之藻", 维基百科, 2018 年 8 月 28 日, zh.wikipedia.org/zh-tw/李之藻

[531] See "Kunyu Wanguo Quantu." *Wikipedia*, Oct. 28, 2018, en.wikipedia.org/wiki/Kunyu_Wanguo_Quantu

[532] "安南", 维基百科, 2018 年 9 月 29 日, zh.wikipedia.org/wiki/安南

[533] It is today's Red River Delta basin in Northern Vietnam.

[534] See p. 292.

[535] Cartographer unknown. "Turin Map." www.scholar.library.miami.edu, University of Miami Libraries, 1969, http://scholar.library.miami.edu/floridamaps/view_image.php?image_name=dlp00020000520001001&group=spanish

[536] The large river in Fig. 46 flowing from west to east is the St. Lawrence River.

[537] Ninety years later, in 1513, Juan Ponce de Leon reached Florida, and in 1518 Alvar Nunez Cabeza de Vaca began exploring the regions that later became the states of Texas, New Mexico, and Arizona. By 1540, Francisco Coronado had travelled up the Colorado River, and Hernando de Soto had explored the Mississippi River in 1541.

[538] The first European to reach Cuba was Christopher Columbus on October 28, 1492.

[539] Parer, David and Elizabeth Parer-Cook. "Australia Land of Parrots." www.docuwiki.net, DocuWiki, Feb. 8, 2018, docuwiki.net/index.php?title=Australia_Land_of_Parrots

[540] "Dorset culture." *Wikipedia*, Jan. 16, 2019, en.wikipedia.org/wiki/Dorset_culture

[541] Leif Erikson was a Norse explorer from Iceland. He is the first known European to have reached continental North America (excluding Greenland), before Christopher Columbus; "Leif Erikson." *Wikipedia*, Dec. 22, 2018, en.wikipedia.org/wiki/Leif_Erikson

[542] "Jacques Cartier." *Wikipedia*, Jan. 9, 2019, en.wikipedia.org/wiki/Jacques_Cartier

[543] The Mi'kmaq had lived in Nova Scotia for centuries; the French arrived there in 1604.

The Last Journey of the San Bao Eunuch

GLOSSARY

Introduction

1418 Chinese World Map

The first world map on a scroll, produced by Chinese people; owner of the map is Liu Gang (刘钢), a Beijing lawyer, map collector and analyst, and author of the Chinese book entitled Gu Di Tu Mi Ma: Zhong Guo Fa Xian Shi Jie De Mi Tuan Xuan Ji《古地图密码: 中国发现世界的谜团玄机》or *Secret Code of Ancient Maps: The Mystery of China's Discovery of the World.*

Age of Discovery

A period from the early fifteenth century to the early seventeenth century, during which European ships travelled around the world to search for new trading routes.

Cahokia Mounds State Park

Similar names are Cahokia Mounds City, Cahokia Mounds complex, or simply Cahokia; located in the central Mississippi Valley; the largest urban centre north of Mexico—now a UNESCO World Heritage Centre in the central Mississippi Valley.

Christopher Columbus

1451–1506; an Italian explorer, navigator, and colonist who completed four voyages across the Atlantic Ocean. He set foot in the Americas for the first time on October 12, 1492; his landing place was an island in the Bahamas, but the exact location is uncertain.

Fengdu (酆都)

In Luo Maodeng's novel, Fengdu was in North America, today's Cahokia Mounds State Park in Collinsville, Illinois, U.S.A.; the city of Fengdu in Chongqing, China is a large complex of shrines, temples and monasteries dedicated to the afterlife.

Hernando de Soto

1496/1497–1542; a Spanish explorer and conquistador who led the first European expedition to cross the Mississippi River on May 8, 1541.

Mississippi River

The second-longest river (Missouri River is the longest river in the continent) and chief river of the second-largest drainage system on the North American continent, second only to the Hudson Bay drainage system.

Mississippi Valley

Occupies the centre of the United States and stretches 2,348 miles from Lake Itasca in northern Minnesota to the mouth of the Mississippi River in the Gulf of Mexico.

New Zealand

A country in the southwestern Pacific Ocean; it consists of two main islands—the North Island and the South Island.

353

Qing Dynasty

The last imperial dynasty ruled China proper from 1644 to 1912.

San Bao Eunuch

"San Bao" literally means "Three Jewels", a symbol of Buddhism. Buddhists make a commitment to the Three Jewels or Triple Gem: the *Buddha*; the *Dharma*; and the *Sangha*. Zheng He was originally a Muslim, but later converted to Buddhism. He was a eunuch, and people honoured Zheng He as "San Bao Eunuch", meaning the "Buddhist Eunuch".

Tianfang (天方)

In ancient China, Mecca and the Arab region were called *Tianfang*— "the heavens". However, according to the interpretation of some scholars, the "country of *Tianfang*" can refer to a very distant country or any country far beyond the horizon.

Zheng He (郑和)

1371–?; Zheng He's year and place of death remain unsolved. Originally born as Ma He in a Muslim family, he later adopted the surname Zheng conferred by Emperor Yongle. Zheng He was a Chinese mariner, explorer, diplomat, fleet admiral, and court eunuch during China's early Ming Dynasty. He was sent by Ming emperors to lead treasure voyages to the Western Ocean seven times in the fifteenth century starting from 1405. Many believe that Zheng He's fleet circumnavigated the whole world including the New World before Christopher Columbus did. Zheng He's epic voyages successfully promoted trade and diplomacy to the many countries his fleet visited.

《三宝太监西洋记》

An Account of the Western World Voyage of the San Bao Eunuch was written in 1597 by Luo Maodeng (罗懋登) in the Chinese Ming Dynasty. The novel is believed by some scholars to provide an abundant amount of information on Zheng He's overseas voyages and to have historical value. But extracting reliable historical information from Luo's novel has been challenging for both Chinese and non-Chinese researchers, since Luo's narrative is written in classical Chinese, rather than modern Chinese, and since the more than 750,000-character text is full of fanciful stories mingled with an overwhelmingly large number of ancient Chinese legends and historical events.

《红楼梦》

Dream of the Red Chamber is one of China's Four Great Classical Novels, written by Cao Xueqin (曹雪芹; 1715–1763). The novel is believed to be semi-autobiographical, mirroring the rise and decline of the author's own family and, by extension, of the Qing Dynasty. The novel exposed the hypocrisy, decay and exploitation of the upper class in the feudal era. However, by using a fictional dynasty, hiding the truth and not touching on political issues, the author succeeded in

354

avoiding political persecution for his writing. There is controversy over the novel's completion date.

《坤輿万国全图》

The Complete Geographical Map of All the Kingdoms of the World (abbreviated as "Ricci's 1602 map") was made in 1602 by Italian Jesuit priest Matteo Ricci (利马窦; 1552–1610) and his Chinese collaborators in the Ming Dynasty. They used information contained in ancient Chinese maps. It is the earliest known Chinese world map in the style of European maps with Chinese characters. Ricci became the first European to enter the Forbidden City of Beijing in 1601 when invited by the Wanli Emperor, who sought his services in matters such as court astronomy and calendrical science. Matteo Ricci occupies an important position in Chinese history.

Chapter 1

Astronomical navigation

Ancient Chinese mariners verified the observed angles of the stars with stellar maps they had on hand for specific destinations, to confirm their arrival at those destinations. These maps helped them to confirm the latitudes of their destinations by reducing the errors due to winds.

Ceylon (锡兰国)

Today's Sri Lanka in the Indian Ocean.

Changle (长乐)

A district located in eastern Fujian province.

Confucian scholars

Officials in the Ming imperial court; some opposed Zheng He's costly voyages, and finally won the political struggle against the powerful eunuchs who supported Zheng He's voyages.

Dandi Bandar

A small city, near latitude 16.2°N and longitude 73.4°E, in the middle of the west coast of India.

Fei Xin (费信)

1388–?; Zheng He's scribe; his year of death is unknown. He joined the 1409, 1412, 1415 and 1430 voyages and wrote a book in 1436, entitled Xing Cha Sheng Lan 《星槎胜览》 or *The Overall Survey of the Star Raft*.

Ferdinand Magellan

Circa 1480–1521; a Portuguese explorer who organised the Spanish expedition to the East Indies from 1519 to 1522. After Magellan's death in the Philippines, Juan Sebastián Elcano, a Spanish explorer, took command of the ship and completed a circumnavigation of the Earth.

Florence

A city in Italy, and a centre of medieval European trade and finance; one of the wealthiest cities of that era.

Gu-li/Calicut (古俚/古里)
> In today's Kozhikode/Calicut region of southwestern India.

Haijin
> A series of related isolationist Chinese policies restricting private maritime trading and coastal settlement; imposed during most of the Ming Dynasty and part of the Qing Dynasty; *Haijin* or Sea Ban was partially lifted starting from 1567.

Hong Bao (洪保)
> A Chinese eunuch sent on overseas diplomatic missions during the reigns of the Ming Yongle Emperor and the Xuande Emperor; one of the five Assistant Envoys sent by the Xuande Emperor to explore the countries of the Western Ocean during Zheng He's seventh voyage.

Hulumumosi/Hormuz (忽鲁谟斯国)
> It could be in today's Minab region of south-eastern Iran. However, Zhang Leqi (章乐绮) has shown that Hormuz was Jerun Island, instead of Qeshm Island proposed by J.V.G. Mills earlier. Since the Minab region, Jerun Island and Qeshm Island are all close to the Strait of Hormuz, Zheng He's mariners could have explored all of them.

Jabal Khamis Mountain
> Near 22.4°N and 59.5°E, in today's northeast of Oman.

Kangxi (康熙)
> 1654–1722; the Kangxi Emperor was the fourth and the longest-reigning emperor (1661–1722) of the Qing Dynasty (also in Chinese history); one of the longest-reigning rulers in the world.

Keel
> A long piece of wood or steel structure along the base of a ship to support the framework of the whole; it may extend downwards as a ridge to increase stability.

Liu Daxia (刘大夏)
> 1436–1516; a senior Chinese official at the Ministry of War in the post-Zheng He era, who opposed Zheng He's voyages and may have ordered the destruction of the logs and records of Zheng He's expeditions.

Long Gu (Dragon Bone 龙骨)
> Timber used to minimize the damage caused by grounding. *Dragon Bone* is like a keel.

Ma Huan (马欢)
> Circa 1380s–circa 1460; participated in the fourth, sixth, and seventh voyages of the treasure fleet, and set to work on a book entitled Ying Ya Sheng Lan《瀛涯胜览》or *The Overall Survey of the Ocean's Shores,* starting from 1416. The book describes his personal experiences and what he had learned during his voyages. The book was completed in 1451. He knew several classical Chinese and Buddhist texts, and learned Arabic well enough to translate into Chinese.

Mamluk Sultanate

A medieval realm ruled by the Mamluks, spanning Egypt, the Levant, and Hejaz from 1260 to 1517.

Mediterranean Sea

A sea that is connected to the Atlantic Ocean, surrounded by the Mediterranean Basin; it is almost completely enclosed by land.

Ming Treasure Fleet

Many of the ships in Admiral Zheng He's fleet were treasure ships—a type of large wooden ship—the fleet is referred to as the Ming Treasure Fleet.

Niushou Mountain/Cattle Head Mountain (牛首山)

Zheng He's cenotaph was located on the western side of this mountain.

Pope Eugene IV

1383–1447; he was Pope from March 3, 1431, to his death in 1447; he moved his palace to Florence after June 1434.

Red-Sea-Nile-Canals/Red Sea Canals

Man-made east-west waterways linking the Red Sea to the Nile.

Renaissance

A period in European history, covering the span between the fourteenth and seventeenth centuries; marking Europe's transition from the Middle Ages to the Modern Era.

Santa María de la Inmaculada Concepción

The largest of the three ships used by Columbus in his first voyage to America.

Semudera (苏门答剌)

Country on the north coast of Sumatra, in the Lho Seumawe district.

Taicang (太仓)

A city in Suzhou, Jiangsu province, China; it is located south of the Yangtze River estuary.

Terrestrial navigation

Zheng He's fleet used detailed maps for terrestrial navigation. Each map includes the mountains, rivers, islands, buildings, and the depth of water along the sea route, etc. to set the direction of travel. They also used compasses to set their direction and measure the sailing distances towards their targeted destinations.

Tianfang (天方国)/Mo-jia

The country was ancient Tunisia, North Africa.

Treasure ship

A type of large wooden ship in the fleet of Admiral Zheng He in the early fifteenth-century Ming Dynasty.

Vasco da Gama

Circa 1460s–1524; a Portuguese explorer; the first European to reach India by sea, and to land in Calicut (May 20, 1498).

357

Wang Jinghong (王景弘)

A Chinese eunuch, mariner, explorer, diplomat and fleet admiral; sent on overseas diplomatic missions during the reigns of the Yongle Emperor and the Xuande Emperor in the Ming Dynasty. He became one of the two Principal Envoys (the other one was Zheng He) during the seventh voyage. It is known that Zheng He's navigational knowledge and experience was shallow, and Wang Jinghong was responsible for managing the fleets and navigational routes.

Xuande (宣德) period

1425–1435; the era of the Ming Xuande Emperor Zhu Zhanji (朱瞻基); "Xuande" means "Proclamation of Virtue".

Yongle (永乐) period

1403–1424; the era of the Ming Yongle Emperor Zhu Di (朱棣).

Zhu Yunming (祝允明)

1461–1527; a famous Chinese calligrapher, poet, writer, and scholar-official of the Ming Dynasty; he wrote the book, Qian Wen Ji • Xia Xi Yang《前闻記•下西洋》or *A Record of History Once Heard: Down to the Western Ocean*, which records the history of the early period of the Ming Dynasty.

《大明都知监太监洪公寿藏铭》

"The Inscription on the Tombstone of Eunuch Hong Bao of the Great Ming Dynasty" was on the tombstone of Hong Bao in the Ming Dynasty. It was prepared before his death and was dated in the ninth year of the Xuande period (1434). It was discovered on Zutang Hill (祖堂山) in Nanjing.

《天妃灵应之记》

"A Record of *Tianfei* Showing Her Presence and Power" was the inscription on the memorial stele in the Nanshan Temple in Changle, Fujian Province. The stele was erected in 1431, right before Zheng He embarked on his seventh voyage.

《太宗实录》

Taizong's Veritable Records of Ming records the history of two Ming emperors (1398–1424): Huizong (惠宗)/Zhu Yunyu (朱允炆) and Chengzu (成祖)/Zhu Di (朱棣).

《江宁县志》

Jiangning County Records; a new version was written by Zhou Shi (周诗) in 1985 based on the engraved county records in 1598 /the 26 year of the Wanli era, Ming Dynasty.

《西洋番国志》

The Annals of the Foreign Countries in the Western Ocean was written in 1434 by Gong Zhen (巩珍; fl. 1400s–1434). Gong Zhen participated in Zheng He's seventh voyage.

《明史》

The History of Ming was written in 1739 by Zhang Tingyu *et al.* (張廷玉等) in the Qing Dynasty. It records the history of the Ming Dynasty from 1368 to 1644.

《明史・外国传・天方》

Tianfang Section of the Chapter of Foreign Countries in The History of Ming records that Zheng He ordered one of his deputy commanders to lead a squadron to Calicut. This deputy commander must have been Hong Bao; as confirmed by Gong Zhen in Xi Yang Fan Guo Zhi 《西洋番国志》 or *The Annals of the Foreign Countries in the Western Ocean.*

《明实录》

The Veritable Records of Ming contains the imperial annals of the Ming emperors (1368–1644). It is the single largest historical source for the dynasty. It covers historical events which span thirteen dynasties and contains sixteen million words.

《非幻庵香火聖像記》

"Record of Holy Images at the Incense- and Candle-burning Feihuan Nunnery" was written in 1457 by an anonymous author. The note was originally the inscription on a monument (which no longer exists) that stood in the Nanjing Bifeng Temple (碧峰寺). The anonymous author thought that a few last words spoken by Zheng He to a Buddhist Master in the Bifeng Temple prior to Zheng He's seventh voyage were Zheng He's will.

《娄东刘家港天妃宫石刻通番事迹碑》

"Inscription on the Stele in the Temple of the Heavenly Princess at Liujiagang in Eastern Lou, Recording the History of Contacts with the Barbarians" was the inscription on the memorial stele in the Temple of the Heavenly Princess in Taicang, Jiangsu Province. The stele was erected in 1431, right before Zheng He embarked on his seventh voyage.

《郑和航海图》

The Charts of Zheng He's Voyages consists of twenty pages of nautical maps, 109 maps for terrestrial navigation (each map contains detailed sketches of mountains, rivers, islands, buildings, and depth of water along the sea route, etc.; see note 55) and four cross-ocean stellar maps for astronomical navigation (and to confirm the arrival at a destination). The nautical map is 20.3 cm high and 560 cm long.

《星槎胜览》

The Overall Survey of the Star Raft was written by Fei Xin (费信; 1388–?) in 1436. He was Zheng He's scribe, who joined the 1409, 1412, 1415 and 1430 voyages.

359   367

《瀛涯胜览》

Ma Huan (马欢) participated in the fourth, sixth, and seventh voyages of the Ming Treasure Fleet. *The Overall Survey of the Ocean's Shores* describes Ma Huan's personal experiences and what he had learned during his voyages. After 35 years of modifications, the book was completed in 1451 by Ma Huan.

Chapter 2

A-bi San-san

This water spring is in Mo-di-na, the old town centre of Kairouan, behind the tomb of the descendants of the Prophet Muhammad.

Agarwood

Agarwood or aloeswood is a fragrant dark resinous wood used in incense, perfume, and small carvings.

Agulhas Current

A western coastal current of the southwest Indian Ocean; it flows down the east coast of Africa; a swift and strong current, with mean peak speed 136 cm/sec (second). This means 4.89 km/hr or 2.64 knot (kn), but the current can reach 245 cm/sec (this means about 4.76 kn). (The average walking speed for adult humans is about 2.7 kn (5 km/3.1 mi/hr).)

Al-Masjid al-Harām

The Sacred Mosque, the Holy Shrine, the Great Mosque, or the Grand Mosque in Mecca of Saudi Arabia.

Bartolomeu Dias

Portuguese explorer (1451–1500); the first documented European mariner to sail around the southernmost tip of Africa in 1488, and to reach the Indian Ocean from the Atlantic.

Benguela Current

A cold-water current; travels along the west coast of Africa from south to north; the mean speed is about 0.33 kn.

Bir Barrouta

A small town not far from the centre of Kairouan, Tunisia; has tombs of descendants of Prophet Muhammad.

Black Stone

A stone altar venerated at the *Kaaba* of the *al-Masjid al-Harām* mosque in Mecca; it has been broken into a few fragments after being touched by millions of Islamic prayers.

Calicut

A coastal city in south Indian; was an important spice trade centre.

Caliphate

A state under the leadership of an Islamic steward with the title of caliph.

Canary Current
A very slow wind-driven surface current (0.054–0.136 kn); part of the North Atlantic Gyre. It joins the Atlantic North Equatorial Current near Senegal.

Cape of Good Hope
About 150 km/90 mi west-northwest of Cape Agulhas (the geographic southern tip of the African continent).

Cape Town
About 65 km/40 mi north of the Cape of Good Hope.

Cape Verde Islands
An archipelago in the Atlantic Ocean; approximately 570 km/350 mi west off the Cape Verde Peninsula off the coast of Northwest Africa.

Chebba (Sheba)
Harbour where the Ma Huan delegation arrived at in early 1433 for trade; in *Tianfang*/Mo-jia or ancient Tunisia.

Gabes
The nearest city to the west of Jerba in Tunisia.

Hafsid
A Sunni Muslim Dynasty of Berber descent; ruled Ifriqiya from 1229 to 1574.

Hajj
An annual Islamic pilgrimage for Muslims to the holiest city Mecca in Saudi Arabia.

Heavenly Hall mosque/ Mosque of Uqba
In Kairouan, Tunisia; spreads over a huge surface area of 9,000 m²; one of the oldest places of worship in the Islamic world.

Hemp silk
A fabric made by combining the smooth texture of silk with the natural strength of hemp (a variety of the Cannabis sativa plant species).

Huang Shengzeng (黄省曾)
1490–1540; author of the 1520 book entitled Xi Yang Chao Gong Dian Lu 《西洋朝贡典录》 or *Records of Tributes from the Western Ocean Countries* in the Ming Dynasty.

Ishmael (Si-ma-yi)
A holy man and the son of Ibrahim; built the Sacred Mosque in Mecca around 2130 BC with his father. But some scholars regard Si-ma-yi as Ismaili, a branch of Islam, and Si-ma-yi can be interpreted as Ismaili believers (namely the Shia faction of Islam).

Jerba (Djerba)
An island near 33.81°N, 10.85°E, off the coast of today's Tunisia.

Kaaba
A cuboid stone building at the centre of Islam's holy mosque in Mecca, Saudi Arabia; the House of God.

K'ai-a-pai
K'ai-a-pai in Arabic is "The Cube", or "a cube-shaped building".

361

Kairouan

The fifth largest city in today's Tunisia; an inland desert city near 35.68°N, 10.09°E, and today's capital of the Kairouan Governorate in Tunisia; now a UNESCO World Heritage town. "Kairouan" means "caravan", indicating the city's origin as a settlement where desert trade caravans stopped.

Knot (kn)

A unit of speed (for water, current, ship, etc.); 1 knot = 1 nautical mile/hr = 1.852 km/hr or about 1.15078 mi/hr (mph).

Ma Huan Island (马欢岛)/Nanshan Island (南尚岛)

To the north of the Spratly Islands; it is named after Ma Huan (马欢), who participated in four of Zheng He's voyages and was author of the famous and important Chinese book entitled Ying Ya Sheng Lan《瀛涯胜览》or *The Overall Survey of the Ocean's Shores*. The book records his travel experiences.

Medina or Mo-di-na (蓦底纳)

Old town of Kairouan; not to be confused with Medina in Saudi Arabia, which is 338 km/210 mi from Mecca. The Prophet Muhammad, after his death, was buried at his original residence in the Mosque of the Prophet in Medina, Saudi Arabia.

Mihrab

An ornamental indentation in the wall of a mosque; marks the direction (of Mecca) to which Muslims turn in prayer.

Ming Dynasty

Ruled China from 1368 to 1644 following the collapse of the Mongol-led Yuan Dynasty.

Mosque of Uqba

In Kairouan, Tunisia; the oldest and largest Islamic mosque in North Africa; Muslims regard it as the Mecca of North Africa.

Mu-lan-pi (木兰皮国)

Near today's Namibia in West Africa, or a border area between the Patagonia Plateau and the Pampas in South America. The location of his country is still under debate.

Ostriches

Large flightless birds native to Africa.

Paolo del Pozzo Toscanelli

1397–1482; an Italian astrologer, mathematician, and cosmographer.

Persian Gulf

Off today's southern Iran.

Persian rosewater

Scented water made by immersing rose petals in water; Persian rosewater is made from the gorgeous Persian Rose.

Qilins

Giraffes; a precious gift to the emperor in the Ming Dynasty; their homeland was today's Kenya in Africa.

Sfax

A city in Tunisia; about 270 km/170 mi southeast of Tunis.

Sousse

Tunisia's third largest city; near 35.82°N, 10.63°E; located to the northwest of Chebba. The king of ancient Tunisia had a palace here.

South Equatorial Current

A broad, slow-flowing, westward current; it can be divided into three branches. The current travels at a speed of 0.058–0.116 kn.

Tianfang (天方国)/Yun Chong

Mecca in today's Saudi Arabia; Luo Maodeng regarded it as *Tianfang*, the Heaven.

Tuareg people

Semi-nomadic Muslim people; believed to be the descendants of the Berber natives of North Africa; called the "blue people" because of the indigo-dyed clothes they traditionally wore and which stained their skin.

Well of Zamzam

Located 20 m/66 feet east of the *Kaaba* inside the Sacred Mosque in Mecca.

Western Ocean

It is *not* limited to the Indian Ocean, but extends as far as the Atlantic Ocean.

申位

Compass direction representing "southwest" ("shen").

《西洋朝贡典录》

Records of Tributes from the Western Ocean Countries; written by Huang Shengzhen in 1520. Huang recorded the geographies, customs, products, languages, and cultures of the 23 countries which Zheng He visited, corrects some text errors in Ying Ya Sheng Lan 《赢涯胜览》 or *The Overall Survey of the Ocean's Shore*, and Xing Cha Sheng Lan 《星槎胜览》 or *The Overall Survey of the Star Raft*, and adds information about the local products and tributes not available in these two books.

兑位

Compass direction represented by "due west" or "dui" point.

Chapter 3

Aden (阿丹国)

In today's Yemen.

Alu (阿鲁国)

Almost the same Chinese name as Aru; a very small kingdom near the A-lu anchorage (Sungai Deli in today's North Sumatra, Indonesia); not far away from Aru.

Aru (哑鲁国/亞路国)

A very small kingdom in the northeast of today's Sumatra; was called Ya Lu 亞路 in Zheng He Hang Hai Tu《郑和航海图》or *The Charts of Zheng He's Voyages*.

Baghdad (白达国)

Today's Baghdad in Iraq.

Beruwala (别罗里)

A town in Kalutara District, Western Province, Sri Lanka; it is only 55 km/34 mi (shortest distance) from Galle.

Bintonglong (宾童龙国)

In today's northern part of Shunhai Province (顺海省) and the southern part of Fuqing Province (富庆省) in southern Vietnam.

Brava/Barawa (卜剌哇)

A small kingdom; south of Mogadishu in today's Somalia and north of Zhubu/Juba; the three kingdoms, Mogadishu, Brava/Barawa and Zhubu/Juba, were very close to each other.

Champa (金莲宝象国/占城)

City of the Chams; in the central part of today's Vietnam.

Cochin (柯枝)

A small country in today's Cochin region of southwestern India; about 213 km/132 mi south of Calicut.

Fengdu (酆都)

Today's Cahokia Mounds State Historic Site in the central Mississippi Valley: Now a UNESCO World Heritage Centre and the largest pre-Columbian settlement north of Mexico; some 18 km/11 mi northeast of St. Louis, Missouri.

Five Tiger Passage (五虎门)

The passage exiting the Min River (闽江) estuary in Fujian, China.

Galle

A major harbour city on the southwest coast of Sri Lanka.

Ghazni (吉慈尼/加兹尼)

In today's eastern Afghanistan.

Greater Quilon/Da Gelan (大葛兰)

A small country in today's Kollam (former name Quilon) region (perhaps Kayankulam village) of southwestern India; Kollam is about 318 km/198 mi south of Calicut.

Hatīm

In today's Sacred Mosque in Mecca; *Hatīm* is a semi-circular low wall. According to western scholars, the graves of Ishmael and his mother Hagar were located in the space between the *Hatīm* and the *Kaaba*.

Hong Luo Mountain (红罗山)

Near the border of Xi-ge-la/Bengal. There is no English name for it.

Janggala (重迦罗)

A tiny village kingdom in today's Surabaya region, in the east of the Island of Java, Indonesia.

Kulam (故临)

A small country in the Kollam area on the southwest coast of India; the country's people had black-coloured skin.

Lasa (剌撒)

J.V.G. Mills analysed the Mao Kun map and found that Lasa appeared on the coast of the Arabian Peninsula, a few miles from Mukalla and could be reached by sailing from Calicut in twenty days. Sailing data from Fei Xin and Ma Huan and analysis by J.J.L. Duyvendak support the location of Lasa as being near Mukalla, a seaport and today the capital city of Yemen's Hadhramaut governorate.

Java (爪哇)

A region in today's Island of Java of Indonesia.

Jeddah

An important harbour city in the Tihamah region of the Hejaz on the coast of the Red Sea; the shortest distance from Jeddah to the Holy City Mecca is 64 km/40 mi.

Juffair/Dhufar (祖法儿)

In today's Dhofar/Dhufar/Djofar region of southwestern Oman, on the eastern border with Yemen.

Lambri/Lamuri (南浡里)

Was a small kingdom in west Sumatra.

Lesser Quilon/Xiao Gelan (小葛兰)

A small country in today's Kollam region of southwestern India. Both Ying Ya Sheng Lan 《瀛涯胜览》 or *The Overall Survey of the Ocean's Shores* and Míng Shi • Wai Guo Lie Zhuan 《明史•外国列传》 or *Foreign Countries in The History of Ming* interpret Kulam (故临) as the Lesser Quilon/Xiao Gelan. But Luo Maodeng lists Kulam and Lesser Quilon/Xiao Gelan as two different countries, in addition to the Greater Quilon/Da Gelan (大葛兰; perhaps Kayankulam village). This deserves further investigation.

Li-fa/Li-de (黎伐/黎代)

In the Li-tai Meureudu district on the north coast of Sumatra; a very small country, no longer in existence.

Liujiagang (刘家港)

It is now called Liuhe (浏河, meaning Liu Creek). It is a town in Jiangsu province, China, on the lower reaches of the Yangtze River.

Liushan/Maldives (溜山/马尔代夫)

The Maldives and Laccadive Islands in the Indian Ocean are located about 500 km/311 mi south-west of Sri Lanka and India.

Longwan (龙湾)

Dragon Bay at Nanjing, China, near the Longjiang Shipyard.

Lopburi (罗斛)

The capital city of today's Lopburi Province in Thailand (in the northern part of today's Gulf of Thailand).

Malacca (满剌伽)

A city in the state of Malacca in Malaysia.

Ma-li-ban (麻离板)

Also Ma-li-pa/Ma-lo-pa (麻离拔); a very small town on the south coast of Arabia; no longer in existence.

Misr (勿斯里)

In today's Egypt.

Mogadishu (木骨都束)

Today's capital of Somalia in East Africa.

Mosul (勿斯离)

Today's Mosul in northern Iraq.

Nagur/Nakur (那孤兒) **or Battak** (花面)

Countries of the Tattooed Faces, in the northwest and north, respectively, of today's Sumatra.

Palembang (浡淋邦／浡淋国)

The Country of Old Haven; today's Palembang (旧港) in Sumatra, Indonesia.

Sa Fa (撒发)

A small island country between Semudera in North Sumatra and Sri Lanka; people had black skin and blood-red hair. This island country could be the Great Nicobar Islands.

Siyu

A strange village of more than 1,000 residents on a small island, Pate Island, which is only 8 km/5 mi away from the continent to the east of Kenya (it borders Somalia). The villagers claim that they are the offspring of Zheng He's sailors.

"Country with people with silver-coloured eyes" (银眼国)

There is no record of this small country; it was on the route from Hulumumosi/Hormuz to Aden after Zheng He's fleet sailed for a few days.

"Country with people with yellowish-coloured or golden-coloured eyes" (金眼国)

A small nation consisting of islands (which could be the Andaman Islands) in the Bay of Bengal; the country no longer exists today.

Land of Many Perfumes (女儿国)

It is not clear where this place was. It might be in today's Sulawesi to the east of the Island of Java, Indonesia, where the Bugis people live. But this location is not on the route to Malacca, the fleet's next destination after leaving Palembang. Hence, it is more logical to place the Land of Many Perfumes at a location between Palembang and Malacca.

Quraysh tribe

Mecca was ruled by the Quraysh tribe with a tribal chief, and the Islamic religion kept the society in good order. The Quraysh were a powerful merchant tribe that controlled Western Arabia including Mecca and its *Kaaba*. According to pre-Islamic and Islamic tradition, they were descended from Ishmael.

Western Regions (西域)

The name refers mostly to the many countries and regions to the far west of China in the Han Dynasty (202 BC–220 AD).

Xi-ge-la/Bengal (吸葛剌/榜葛剌)

A region in South Asia, specifically in the eastern part of the Indian subcontinent at the apex of the Bay of Bengal.

Zhubu/Juba (竹步)

Jubb or Jobo; a small country near the Juba/Zubba River region; close to Mogadishu, Somalia.

Zu-la-fa

Giraffe.

《宋会要》

Decrees and Laws Collected in the Song Dynasty; they are the records collected in the Song Dynasty by the official historians in the imperial court after they had arranged the original imperial edicts and memorials to the throne into different classifications.

《岭外代答》

Answers to the Questions Concerning Foreign Countries is a book written by Zhou Qufei (周去非; 1134–1189) in 1178 of the Southern Song Dynasty.

《诸蕃志》

Records of Many Foreign Countries is a masterpiece written by Zhao Rugua (趙汝适 1170–1231) in 1225 during the Southern Song Dynasty. This book records maritime trade and transportation between China and foreign countries from Japan in north-eastern Asia to Europe, and to Morocco in North Africa.

《岛夷志略》

Descriptions of Barbarians and the Islands is a significant book written in 1349 by Wang Dayuan (汪大渊; 1311–1350), a traveller and prominent navigator from Quanzhou, China, during the Mongol Yuan Dynasty in the fourteenth century.

Chapter 4

Brazil Current

The Brazil Current is a weak and warm ocean current that flows southward along the Brazilian south coast to the mouth of the Río de la Plata. The current flows at less than half of the speed of the Agulhas Current.

367   375

Equatorial Counter Current

An eastward flowing current in the Atlantic, Indian, and Pacific Oceans; the current is located between the North and South equatorial currents and flows in the opposite direction to them, that is, from west to east.

Grand Banks

The "Grand Banks", where the cold southbound Labrador Current mingles with the warm eastbound Gulf Stream, is the foggiest place in the world. It is a vast and shallow continental shelf to the east of Newfoundland and an ideal fishing ground. Zheng He's fleet passed this area during its seventh voyage.

Great Bitter Lake

A saltwater lake (a salt flat, which rarely accumulated enough water to become a true lake before the Suez Canal was built) in Egypt; connects to the Mediterranean Sea and the Red Sea via the Suez Canal.

Gulf of St. Lawrence

In eastern Canada; the outlet of the North American Great Lakes via the St. Lawrence River into the Atlantic Ocean.

Gulf Stream

Together with its northern extension the North Atlantic Drift, this is a warm and swift Atlantic Ocean current that originates in the Gulf of Mexico and stretches to the tip of Florida, then follows the eastern coastlines of the United States and Newfoundland before crossing the Atlantic Ocean. The current velocity is fastest near the surface, with the maximum speed typically about 2.5 m/sec (4.85 kn/5.6 mph).

Imperial Seal of China/Heirloom Seal of the Realm

A Chinese jade seal carved out of the He Shi Bi (和氏璧), a historically famous piece of jade.

Jin Bifeng (金碧峰)

The monk accompanying Zheng He on his voyages; Jin's job was to resolve doubts, to dispel suspicion, and practice virtue to pray for blessings.

Junk Keying

A Foochow (福州) Chinese trading junk in the 26th year of the Daoguang Emperor (道光二十六年; 1846) of the Qing Dynasty; in 1846–1847 set the distance record for Chinese sailboats in the post-Zheng He era. It proved the excellence of construction technology and performance of ancient Chinese wooden boats.

Labrador Current

A slow and cold current in the North Atlantic Ocean; flows from the Arctic Ocean south along the coast of Labrador and Newfoundland, continuing south along the east coast of Nova Scotia; speeds vary from 30–50 cm/sec (0.58–0.97 kn).

Mazu (媽祖)

A Sea God belonging to the faith of people living on the southeast coast of the mainland of China and other maritime areas in East Asia.

Newfoundland

A large Canadian island off the east coast of the North American mainland; Newfoundland and Labrador form the most easterly province of Canada.

North Atlantic Drift

A slow-moving body of warm water located between about 50°–64°N and 10°–30°W, leading to the British Isles. It reaches speeds of about 2 knots (103 cm/sec) near the North American coast.

North Equatorial Current

A significant current in the Pacific and Atlantic Oceans; flowing east-to-west between about 10°N–20°N; it travels at an approximately similar speed as the Canary current. Despite its name, the current has no connection with the equator.

Prince of Yan (燕王)

Emperor Yongle, Zhu Di (朱棣). When Hongwu (洪武皇帝; 明太祖朱元璋), the founding emperor of the Ming Dynasty died, he did not pass the throne to his son but to his grandson Zhu Yunwen (朱允炆), who became Emperor Jianwen (建文帝). Zhu Di, the Prince of Yan (燕王), the fourth son of Emperor Hongwu, was not satisfied. He successfully invaded the capital Nanjing and changed the era name to Yongle. After that, Emperor Jianwen disappeared.

Qin Shi Huang (秦始皇)

He was born Ying Zheng (嬴政) or Zhao Zheng (趙政), a prince of the state of Qin. He became Zheng, the King of Qin (秦王政) when he was thirteen. In 221 BC at the age of 39, he unified China by defeating six other countries and established a powerful country, the Qin Dynasty.

River Nile

The River Nile is about 6,670 km/4,160 mi in length and is the longest river in Africa. The man-made Red-Sea-Nile-Canals in Egypt linked the Red Sea to the Nile.

Small Bitter Lake

Adjoined to the Great Bitter Lake.

South Equatorial Current

Flows east-to-west between the equator and about 20°S; in the Pacific and Atlantic Oceans, it extends across the equator to about five degrees north; this current travels at an approximately similar speed as the Canary Current.

St. Helena Island

Junk Keying which set the distance record for Chinese sailboats in the post-Zheng He era, reaching this island in the South Atlantic Ocean on April 17, 1847, during its global sailing.

Suez Canal
> A sea-level waterway in Egypt, connecting the Mediterranean Sea to the Red Sea through the Isthmus of Suez. The canal was officially opened on 17 November 1869.

Tang Zhuangyuan (唐状元)
> Tang Ying (唐英); one of the military chiefs under Zheng He's command during the western expeditions.

Yun Gu (云谷)
> A Buddhist disciple on board Zheng He's treasure ship during the seventh voyage.

《灵宪》
> *The Spiritual Constitution of the Universe* was written around 120 AD by Zhang Heng (张衡; 78–139 AD), the chief astronomer of the Eastern Han Dynasty (25–220 AD). In this book, he argued that the Earth was round.

《博物志》
> *Natural History*; written by Zhang Hua (张华; 232–300 AD) in the Western Jin Dynasty (西晋时期; 266–316 AD).

Chapter 5

Avalon Peninsula
> The southeast portion of the island of Newfoundland in Canada.

Bras d'Or Lake
> An inland sea in the centre of Cape Breton Island, Nova Scotia, Canada.

Cahokia
> Cahokia Mounds State Historic Site; a pre-Columbian Native American city directly across the Mississippi River from modern St. Louis, Missouri, U.S.A. This historic park lies in southern Illinois between East St. Louis and Collinsville.

Cape Breton Island
> An island on the Atlantic coast of North America and part of Nova Scotia, Canada.

Cape Dauphin
> One of the peninsulas of Cape Breton Island in Nova Scotia, Canada; 300 m/984 ft high, heavily forested, with steep cliffs on three sides.

Chéticamp River
> A river on Cape Breton Island, Nova Scotia, Canada; located at the western entrance to Cape Breton Highlands National Park.

Chicago Portage
> A land route which allows the carrying of water craft and cargo between the watersheds and the navigable waterways of the Mississippi River and the Great Lakes.

The Last Journey of the San Bao Eunuch

Chicago River
> A system of rivers and canals with a combined length of 156 miles which runs through the city of Chicago.

Chippewa
> The town of Chippewa lies by the Niagara River in Canada, about 2 km/1.2 mi upstream from the Niagara Falls.

Des Plaines River
> A river that flows southward for 133 miles through southern Wisconsin and northern Illinois in the United States Midwest, eventually meeting the Kankakee River west of Channahon to form the Illinois River.

Forbidden City in Beijing
> A palace complex in central Beijing, China; served as the home of emperors and their households; was the ceremonial and political centre of Chinese government for almost 500 years from the Ming Dynasty to the end of the Qing Dynasty.

Happy Valley-Goose Bay
> A town in the province of Newfoundland and Labrador, Canada; located in the central part of Labrador on the coast of Lake Melville and the Grand River.

Grand River
> A large river in Southwestern Ontario, Canada.

Great Lakes
> Five interconnected freshwater lakes: Lakes Superior, Michigan, Huron, Erie, and Ontario; primarily in the upper mid-east region of North America, on the Canada-United States border; they connect to the Atlantic Ocean through the St. Lawrence River.

Iceberg
> A large piece of freshwater ice that has broken off a glacier or an ice shelf and is floating freely in open water.

Illinois River
> A principal tributary of the Mississippi River, approximately 273 mi/439 km long; important among Native Americans and early French traders as the principal water route connecting the Great Lakes with the Mississippi. Zheng He's mariners may have taken this water route to arrive at the North American Fengdu—*Cahokia*—in the central Mississippi Valley during their seventh voyage to the Western Ocean in the 1430s.

Island of Seven Cities
> Cape Dauphin, Chéticamp, Ingonish (also known as Portuguese Bay), Louisbourg (also known as English Harbour), St. Ann's (also known as Englishtown), St. Peter's (also known as St. Peters), and the area now known as Sydney (also known as Spanish Bay) are the seven cities on Cape Breton Island, Canada.

Labrador Sea
> An arm of the North Atlantic Ocean between the Labrador Peninsula and Greenland.

371   379

Lake Chicago
A prehistoric proglacial lake; the ancestor of today's Lake Michigan.
Lake Melville
This is on the Labrador coast in the Canadian province of Newfoundland and Labrador.
Mi'kmaq
A First Nations people indigenous to Canada's Atlantic Provinces and the Gaspé Peninsula of Quebec as well as the north-eastern region of Maine. They had oriental features, used strange hieroglyphs, and wore clothing with golden oriental patterns and Chinese-style earrings.
Missouri River
The longest river in North America; rising in the Rocky Mountains of western Montana, the Missouri flows east and south for 2,341 miles before entering the Mississippi River north of St. Louis, Missouri.
Nain
The northernmost permanent settlement in the Canadian province of Newfoundland and Labrador.
New Brunswick
One of four Atlantic Provinces on the east coast of Canada (New Brunswick, Nova Scotia, Prince Edward Island, and the easternmost province of Newfoundland and Labrador).
Newfoundland and Labrador Province
The most easterly province in Canada. The Strait of Belle Isle separates the province into Labrador—a large area of mainland Canada—and Newfoundland, an island in the Atlantic Ocean.
Niagara Falls
The collective name for three waterfalls which straddle the international border between Ontario in Canada and the state of New York in the United States.
Niagara River
Flows north from Lake Erie to Lake Ontario; forms part of the border between Ontario and the state of New York.
Norse settlers
Settlers who came from Scandinavia and travelled by boat as far as North America in the west and Central Asia in the east from about 700 to 1100 AD.
Nova Scotia
One of Canada's four Maritime Provinces.
Polar tundra climate
Cool summers and very cold winters; a polar climate results in treeless tundra, glaciers, or a permanent or semi-permanent layer of ice.
Prince Edward Island
One of eastern Canada's Maritime Provinces in the Gulf of St. Lawrence, off New Brunswick and Nova Scotia.

Queenston

This town lies by the Niagara River in Canada, about 5 km/3.1 mi downstream from the Niagara Falls.

St. Anthony

A town on the northern reaches of the Great Northern Peninsula of the Province of Newfoundland and Labrador.

St. Lawrence River

A large river in the middle latitudes of North America; flows in a roughly north-easterly direction, connecting the Great Lakes with the Atlantic Ocean and forming the primary drainage outflow of the Great Lakes Basin.

St. Louis

A major U.S. port in the state of Missouri, built along the western bank of the Mississippi River, which marks Missouri's border with Illinois.

Strait of Belle Isle

145 km/90 mi long and 20 km/12 mi wide; the narrowest passage separating Newfoundland from the mainland of Canada.

Subarctic climate

A climate characterized by long, usually very cold winters, and short, cool to mild summers.

Grand Bank, Newfoundland

A small rural town located on the southern tip of the Burin Peninsula, 360 km from Newfoundland's capital of St. John's.

Viking

Norse seafarers, mainly speaking the Old Norse language, who, during the late eighth to late eleventh centuries, raided and traded from their Northern European homelands across wide areas of Europe, and explored westwards to Iceland, Greenland, and Vinland (now called Newfoundland Island).

Viking Hogbacks

Stone-carved Anglo-Scandinavian sculptures from tenth- to twelfth-century England and Scotland; grave-markers.

Wang Ming (王明)

In Luo Maodeng's novel, Wang Ming was Zheng He's scout, who discovered North American Fengdu—Cahokia.

Witless Bay

A small town on the Avalon Peninsula in the Canadian province of Newfoundland and Labrador; located 35 km south of the provincial capital, St. John's.

Chapter 6

Aztec civilisation

A Mesoamerican culture, which flourished in central Mexico from 1300 to 1521.

Cahokia civilisation

The Cahokians built more than 100 earth mounds near today's St. Louis, Missouri, U.S.A., representing the largest prehistoric earthen construction site north of Mesoamerica. They were advanced people who did not appear to be related to any major known Native American tribes.

Cahokia Creek

Outside downtown Cahokia; it is a stream in Madison County, Illinois, U.S.A.

Conical mound

A cone- or oval-shaped mound.

Cui Jue (崔珏)

In the famous Chinese classical mythical novel, Xi You Ji《西游记》or *Journey to the West*, Cui Jue is a judge, whose official rank is lower only than that of Yama, King of Hell. In the court of Yama, Cui Jue was responsible for handling the trials of the ghosts who came to register in the netherworld. In Luo Maodeng's 1597 novel entitled San Bao Tai Jian Xi Yang Gi《三宝太监西洋记》or *An Account of the Western World Voyage of the San Bao Eunuch,* Cui Jue had the same title and the same job; he was also responsible for handling trials of the ghosts who came to register themselves in Fengdu Ghost Country. This Fengdu Ghost Country in Luo's novel was actually Cahokia, and these ghosts were Cahokians or captured outsiders. Cui Jue was Liu Shi's new husband.

Downtown Cahokia

Archaeologists have identified more than 100 mounds in the Cahokia Mounds City near today's St. Louis, Missouri, U.S.A., and these mounds are all numbered. Eighteen of them are inside the fenced downtown Cahokia (named as "Forbidden City" in Luo Maodeng's novel).

Fengdu Ghost Country

North American Fengdu/Cahokia; Wang Ming's ex-wife Liu Shi lived there with her new native-American husband Cui Jue.

Fengdu Mountain

The mountain where the ghosts and the Fengdu Emperor (Yama) resided; it was in the legendary ghost city, Fengdu, in China.

Gate tower (八字门楼)

A gate with a roof, shaped like the Chinese character, "八".

God of Mount Tai

Mount Tai is in eastern China, and the supreme god living there is the Eastern Great Emperor (东皇太; 东 means "east", 皇太 means "supreme god"), or Tianqi Emperor (天齐帝), or the Master of the East.

Gou Si Gui (勾死鬼)

The ghost whose task is to take away the human soul and bring it to the netherworld. In Cahokia, they were the local court guards.

Grand Plaza
> A ceremonial plaza in the central area of downtown Cahokia; it served as the central focus of the community.

Great Sun Chief
> Cahokia's Great Sun Chief ruled the earth and spoke to the sky; his counsellors were members of the élite class composed of priests and chieftains.

Land Deity Temple
> Temple of the "lord of the soil and the earth".

Ling Yao (灵曜)
> The Chinese meaning of Ling Yao (灵曜) is the "sun".

Ling Yao Palace
> The place where Yama works and lives in Luo Maodeng's novel.

Liu Shi (刘氏)
> Ex-wife of Wang Ming (王明), Zheng He's scout.

Lu Xun (鲁迅)
> Lived, 1881–1936; a leading figure of modern Chinese literature.

Maya civilisation
> A Mesoamerican civilisation developed by the Mayan peoples. The Maya civilisation had the most sophisticated and highly-developed writing system in the pre-Columbian Americas, and was well-known for its art, architecture, mathematics, calendar, and astronomical system.

Monks Mound
> Mound 38 in Cahokia; the largest pre-Columbian earthwork in the Americas and the largest pyramid north of Mexico. It is where the Sun Chief of Cahokia lived and worked.

Palisade
> A low wall made of wood and then plastered over with clay. Downtown Cahokia was surrounded by a low wall (palisade) with several gates to facilitate entry for the populace.

Platform mound
> Any earthwork or mound intended to support a structure or activity; these mounds are usually four-sided truncated pyramids, steeply-sided, with steps built of wooden logs ascending one side.

Ridgetop mound
> The base of the mound is like that of a platform mound, but the top forms an extended ridge.

Ten Courts of Hell
> The phrase "ten Courts of Hell" started from the Tang Dynasty (618–907) when Buddhism blossomed in China. Yama divided hell into ten courts, each with the name of their Lord or King; each court, with a different kind of hell.

Yama
> A god of death, who rules the netherworld.

《西游记》
  Journey to the West is one of the Four Great Classical Novels of Chinese literature; written by Wu Chengen (吴承恩; 1506–1582) in the mid-sixteenth century in Ming Dynasty.

Chapter 7

Baffle gates
  Gates which permit passage in one direction only.

Birdman tablet
  Discovered in 1971, during excavations at the base of the eastern side of Monks Mound in Cahokia. Archaeologists theorise that the bird on the front of the tablet symbolizes the Upper World, the human figure represents the Middle World, and the snake-skin pattern on the back of the tablet represents the Lower World.

Cahokia Mounds State Historic Site
  A UNESCO World Heritage Centre and the largest pre-Columbian settlement north of Mexico; some 18 km/11 mi northeast of St Louis, Missouri.

Emperor Shun (舜)
  Circa 2128–2025 BC; a legendary leader of ancient China; regarded by some sources as one of the Three Sovereigns and Five Emperors.

Gulf Coast
  The coastline along the Southern United States where they meet the Gulf of Mexico. The Gulf States—Alabama, Florida, Louisiana, Mississippi, and Texas—have a shoreline on the Gulf of Mexico.

Li Zicheng (李自成)
  Lived, 1606–1645; a former minor Ming official who became the leader of a peasant revolt. He overthrew the Ming Dynasty in 1644 and ruled over northern China as emperor of the short-lived Shun Dynasty before his death a year later.

Liu Yin (刘殷)
  Lived, ?–312; a high-ranking official in the imperial court, and dutiful son in the Jin Dynasty (晋朝; 265–420).

Emperor Chongzhen (崇祯)
  Lived, 1611–1644; the seventeenth and last emperor of the Ming Dynasty.

Mississippian culture
  A mound-building Native American civilisation dated from about 800 AD to 1600 AD, varying regionally.

Mound 72
  In Cahokia, archaeologists have found over 20,000 marine shell beads in Mound 72, a small ridge-topped mound with a height of 3.05 m/10 ft, located less than 0.8 km/0.5 mi south of the Monks Mound.

384

Pu Lue Hell (普掠地狱)

In Buddhism, this is the name of one of the hells located in the centre of the netherworld.

Rattlesnake Mound

Mound 66 (a long, ridge-topped mound) is one of the largest mounds at the Cahokia site and is referred to by the U.S. Geological Survey as the Rattlesnake Mound. What was locally referred to as Rattlesnake Mound (Mound 64) was partially destroyed by the construction of railroad tracks. Nests of rattlesnakes were found at these mounds.

Shun Dynasty (大顺)

In power, 1644–1645; a short-lived dynasty in the transition from Ming to Qing rule. It was created by Li Zicheng (李自成), the leader of the peasant revolt.

Yan Zhen (严震)

Lived, 724–799; a famous minister and a dutiful son in the Tang Dynasty (唐朝; 618–907).

Chapter 8

Arabian Peninsula

Located in western Asia, and situated northeast of Africa; includes today's Jordan, Iraq, Kuwait, Bahrain, Qatar, the United Arab Emirates, Oman, Yemen and Saudi Arabia.

Australia

It consists of the mainland of the Australian continent, the island of Tasmania and numerous smaller islands.

Chao Du (超度)

In Buddhism, "chao du" is chanting to relieve ghosts from misery. The deeper meaning is to pass through life and death and to reach the other side of Nirvana.

Emperor Yinzhong (明英宗)

Emperor Zhengtong (正統帝 ; 1427–1464) of the Ming Dynasty; ascended the throne in 1435, at age seven.

Fang Cheng (方城)

A square enclosure built on the outside of the city gate, the hallmark of a Chinese development.

Forbidden City in North American Fengdu

Downtown Cahokia.

Gate of Hell (鬼门关)

Entrance to the underworld in Chinese legend.

Ling Yao Government Offices

Temple-palaces inside the Forbidden City of Fengdu or inside downtown Cahokia.

Liu Guxian (刘谷贤)

Zheng He's sergeant. He fell into the sea but was saved by a big fish as he was about to drown. The sea was in the Grand Banks region near the Gulf of St. Lawrence, and the "fish" was most likely the narwhal, a regional whale.

Ma Fubo/Ma Yuan (馬伏波 /马援)

A great military strategist in the Eastern Han Dynasty (25–220 AD).

Malindi

A town at the mouth of the Galana River; lies on the Indian Ocean coast of Kenya.

Maya maize deity

The Maya believed in many gods who represented aspects of nature, society and the professions. The maize god was one of the most important.

Moeraki balls

Stone spheres (balls) found at Moeraki harbour site in New Zealand.

Mombasa

A seaport city on the coast of Kenya, along the Indian Ocean.

Mozambique

A southern African nation.

Spring and Autumn Period

A period in Chinese history from approximately 770–476 BC, or according to some authorities until 403 BC.

South Atlantic Current

An eastward ocean current, fed by the Brazil Current; it travels at a speed of 37–148 cm/sec (0.72–2.88 kn).

South Indian Current

An eastward current band in the Indian Ocean. This current, with the Antarctic Circumpolar Current, is known as the West Wind Drift (the current flows at a rate of about 111 cm/sec or 2.16 kn). As the South Indian Current reaches the coast of Australia, it becomes the West Australian Current.

Strait of Gibraltar

A strait (about 14 km/9 mi wide at its narrowest point) connecting the Atlantic Ocean to the Mediterranean Sea.

Weng Cheng (瓮城)

A semi-circular enclosure built on the outside of the city gate, the hallmark of a Chinese development.

Xiangyang Dapao/Xiangyang Cannon (襄阳大炮)

Also known as the huge stone catapult, named after its use in the famous Battle of Xiangyang, a war between the Southern Song Dynasty (1127–1279) and the Mongols.

Xuande Medallion
Early in the 21st century, a plain copper medallion of seven centimetres in diameter with the inscription, "Authorised and awarded by Xuande of Great Ming", was unearthed four inches under the surface in North Carolina. This old copper piece is considered to be the medallion awarded to Zheng He by Ming Emperor Xuanzong (Xuande Emperor) before Zheng He embarked on the seventh voyage.

Zhang Bo (张柏) or Zhang Langya (张狼牙)
Zheng He's Deputy Chief Commander responsible for reconnaissance and alert missions during the Western Expedition.

《元史·阿里海牙傳》
The Biography of Ali Hai Ya in the History of the Yuan Dynasty.

《马可·波罗游记》
The Travels of Marco Polo is a thirteenth-century travelogue written by Rustichello da Pisa from stories told by Italian explorer Marco Polo (1254–1324), an Italian merchant, explorer and writer; it describes Marco Polo's travels in Asia (1271–1295), and his experiences at the court of Kublai Khan.

Chapter 9

Albertin de Virga
Famous Portuguese cartographer, who made the Albertin de Virga Map. He obtained a copy of Zheng He's Integrated Map of the World, 1418, which he copied.

Australia on Ricci's 1602 map
Australia is written as 鸚哥地, meaning Land of Parrots, and labelled as a land mass below the southern end of Africa. It is too far west (an error of approximately 90° or ¼ of 360° in longitude) and too far south (an error of approximately 30° in latitude) from its actual position. But the earlier 1418 Chinese World Map places Australia near its correct position.

Azores
An archipelago in the mid-Atlantic Ocean.

Bermuda
An island in the North Atlantic Ocean.

Caverio Map
A world map drawn by the Genoese cartographer Nicolay de Caveri, circa 1506.

Dead reckoning
In navigation, dead reckoning is the method of calculating a ship's current position by using its previously determined position, and advancing that position based upon known or estimated speeds over elapsed time and direction.

379   387

Greenland

A massive island between the North Atlantic and Arctic Oceans.

Gui Dao (鬼岛)

Ghost Island, meaning that it was notorious for its shipwrecks; it is drawn on Ricci's 1602 map. The Island was famous for its rocky coast, stormy Atlantic Ocean and stories of shipwrecks. The Ghost Island and the adjacent Jia Li Han Island (加里漢岛), combined, could be today's Cape Breton Island.

Guo Shoujing (郭守敬)

Lived, 1231–1316; an astronomer, mathematician and hydrologist in the Yuan Dynasty (1271–1368). He predicted that the Earth was round.

Hudson Bay

A large body of saltwater in north-eastern Canada.

Isthmus of Panama

The narrow strip of land that lies between the Caribbean Sea and the Pacific Ocean, linking North and South America; contains the country of Panama and the Panama Canal.

Jacques Cartier

Lived, 1491–1557; in 1534, he was the first European to enter the Gulf of St. Lawrence, by the Strait of Belle Isle; he then reached the inlet of the St. Lawrence River.

Jia Li Han Island (加里漢岛)

It is separated from the Ghost Island and off the mainland of today's Nova Scotia Province.

John Cabot

Lived, circa 1450 to circa 1500; in 1497, this Venetian navigator and explorer was the first European to visit Cape Breton Island. However, European maps of the period are of too poor a quality to be sure whether it was Newfoundland or Cape Breton Island which Cabot visited.

Latitude

A geographic coordinate that specifies the north-south position of a point on the Earth's surface; an angle which ranges from 0° at the Equator to 90° at the poles; there are 180° of latitude (90°N ↔ 90°S). Each degree can be broken into 60 minutes (') and each minute can be broken into 60 seconds ("). 16.29°N means 16°17'24". Lines of constant latitude run east-west as circles parallel to the equator.

Longitude

A geographic coordinate that specifies the east-west position of a point on the Earth's surface; an angular measurement expressed in degrees (°); there are 360° of longitude (180°E ↔ 180°W). Each degree can be broken into 60 minutes (') and each minute can be broken into 60 seconds ("); 73.46°E means 73°27'36"E. Lines of constant longitude form north-south-oriented circles (meridians) passing through both poles.

Magnetic declination

The angle on the horizontal plane between magnetic north and true (geographic) north; it varies depending on the geographical location of the traveller on the Earth's surface and this angle also changes over time due to the rotation of the internal parts of the Earth.

Matteo Ricci (利玛窦)

Lived, 1552–1610; in 1583, the Italian Catholic missionary Matteo Ricci was among the first Jesuits to enter China, from Macao. In 1584, he and his Chinese collaborators made the first Chinese world map, called Yu Di Shan Hai Quan Tu《舆地山海全图》or Complete Terrestrial Map (1584), which contains all the major continents of the world. Matteo Ricci is an important historical figure in Chinese history.

Medici Atlas

An anonymous set of maps, explicitly dated 1351.

Ming Wanli Emperor (明神宗)

Lived, 1563–1620; Zhu Yijun (朱翊鈞) was the fourteenth emperor of the Ming Dynasty. "Wanli", the era name of his reign, literally means "ten thousand calendars".

Monk Yi Xing (僧一行)

Lived, 683–727; Zhang Sui (张遂). He became a monk in his youth. Yi Xing was his Dharma name (a new name acquired during a Buddhist initiation ritual in Mahayana Buddhism and the ordination of a monk in Theravada Buddhism). He was an astronomer in the Tang Dynasty and measured the length of the meridian of one degree.

Niccolò de' Conti

Circa 1395–1469; an Italian merchant and explorer; travelled to Asia during the early fifteenth century to participate in the Chinese voyages; helped to spread Chinese knowledge to Western navigators and cartographers.

Plane trigonometry

Deals with the relationships between the angles and sides of triangles that have three vertices located on a plane surface.

Polaris

Polaris/the North Star is very close to the north celestial pole. It is the brightest star in the constellation of Ursa Minor. It makes a small circle (seven-tenths of a degree away from the Earth's rotational axis) around the actual pole as the Earth rotates. Hence, Polaris stands almost motionless in the sky and all the stars of the northern sky appear to rotate around it. Polaris is used to measure latitude. If you measure the angle of Polaris above the horizon, that angle will be the same as your latitude. Hence, the North Pole is at latitude of 90° north, and the equator is at 0° north.

Roanoke River

A river in southern Virginia and north-eastern North Carolina in the United States; branched into three arms.

Southern Cross constellation

One of the best-known asterisms (groups of stars) in the night sky, and the most familiar star pattern in the Southern Hemisphere; contains two bright stars, Acrux and Gacrux, which point the way to the Southern Celestial Pole.

Spherical trigonometry

Deals with the relationships between the trigonometric functions of the sides and angles of spherical polygons defined by intersecting "great circles" (also known as orthodromes) on the sphere.

St. Peter's isthmus

Paul Chiasson writes that an ancient canal existed across St. Peter's isthmus long before the sixteenth century. If this is true, the canal would have separated Cape Breton Island into two separate islands. Chiasson writes further that the canal could only have been built by Ming Chinese, for navigation down through the centre of the Island from the Atlantic Ocean.

Strait of Canso

This narrow strait separates Cape Breton Island from the mainland of Nova Scotia.

Sun or star transit time

The time at which the sun or star passes over the observer's meridian line and is thus highest in the sky over the horizon.

Three ancient Chinese theories of the universe

They were 1) "浑天说" or the "Theory of Sphere-Heavens" or the "Geocentric Theory in Ancient Chinese Astronomy"; 2) "盖天说" or the "Theory of Canopy Heavens"; and 3) "宣夜说" or the "Theory of Unlimited Universe with Celestial Bodies Floating in the Void". Until the early fifteenth century, the "Theory of Sphere-Heavens" dominated ancient Chinese views on the universe.

Zhang Heng (张衡)

Lived, 78–139 AD; the chief astronomer of the Eastern Han Dynasty (25–220 AD). He theorised that the universe was like an egg with the stars on the shell and the Earth as the yolk in the centre. Modern scholars have compared his work in astronomy to that of the Greco-Roman Claudius Ptolemy (86–161 AD).

《大明混一图》

Amalgamated Map of the Great Ming Empire; drawn by Chinese cartographers. It is the oldest map of the African continent, dating back to 1389 in early Ming Dynasty. The author is unknown. This map shows that the Chinese in the fourteenth century already knew the ocean, today's Atlantic Ocean, lying to the west and to the south of Africa.

《天下全图》

1722 Complete World Map; this shows a close resemblance to the 1093 Chinese Wooden World Map, and to better representations of Europe, Africa and the Americas, indicating that the 1722 Complete World Map might be an updated version of the 1093 map.

《天下全舆总图》

Overall Map of the Geography of All Under Heaven; the map was a rendition made by Mo Yi-tong (莫易仝) in 1763 in the Qing Dynasty, based on the 1418 Ming map of Tian Xia Zhu Fan Shi Gong Tu 《天下诸番识贡图》or Map of the Barbarians from All under Heaven Who Offer Tribute to the Court, known as the 1418 Chinese World Map; Gavin Menzies calls this map, Zheng He's Integrated Map of the World, 1418.

《天下诸番识贡图》

Map of the Barbarians from All Under Heaven Who Offer Tribute to the Court was the source of the 1418 Chinese World Map, but no version is extant.

《旧唐书》

History of the Early Tang Dynasty was written by Liu Xu (刘昫) during the Tang Dynasty (618 to 907). Jiu Tang Shu • Tian Wen 《旧唐书•天文》or the *History of the Early Tang Dynasty on Astronomy* is one of the volumes related to astronomy.

《华夷图》

Map of China and Barbaric Countries; this 1137 Ancient Chinese Map was carved in stone. The map existed before 1137. The source of the map was Hai Nei Hua Yi Tu 《海内华夷图》or Map of China and Barbaric Countries within the Seas, which was drawn by Jia Danyu (贾耽于) in 801, Tang Dynasty.

《周髀算经》

Classic of Arithmetic from the Gnomon of the Zhou Sundial is China's first astronomical book on calendar calculations and a collection of Chinese mathematics; completed around the first century BC.

《张匡正世界地图》

Zhang Kuangzheng World Map or 1093 Chinese Wooden World Map was discovered in 1971 in an ancient Daoist tomb in Beijing; it drew the world inside a circle.

《晋书》

Book of Jin was written by Fang Xuanling (房玄龄) in the early Tang Dynasty. Tian Wen Zhi 《天文志》or *Astronomical Records* is one of the volumes in the *Book of Jin*, in which an explicit account is given of the shape of the Earth.

383

《混一疆理历代国都之图》

The Kangnido Map or Map of Integrated Lands and Regions of Historical Countries and Capitals was made by Koreans in 1402 based on two ancient Chinese maps and supplemented with maps of Korea and Japan. There is a big ocean to the south and to the west of Africa.

384

BIBLIOGRAPHY

English

Andro, Anatole. *The 1421 Heresy: An Investigation into The Ming Chinese Maritime Survey of the World.* Bloomington, Indiana, U.S.A.: AuthorHouse, 2005.

Appleton, Le Roy H. *American Indian Design & Decoration.* Mineola, New York, U.S.A.: Dover Publications. 1971.

Baires, Sarah E. *Land of Water, City of the Dead: Religion and Cahokia's Emergence.* Tuscaloosa, Alabama, U.S.A.: The University of Alabama Press, 2017.

Bonner-Nickless, Laurie L. *To the Gates of Fengtu: The first full modern translation of the final fifteen chapters of Luo Mao Deng's Epic Account of Chinese Exploration of North America.* Amazon Digital Services LLC, 2017.

Brockman, Norbert C. *Encyclopedia of Sacred Places.* Oxford, U.K.: Oxford University Press, 1999.

Burckhardt, Johann Ludwig. *Travels in Arabia, Comprehending an Account of Those Territories in Hedjaz which the Mohammedans Regard as Sacred, Volume 1.* Kindle edition. Los Angeles, California, U.S.A.: HardPress, 2018.

---. *Travels in Arabia, Comprehending An Account Of Those Territories In Hedjaz Which The Mohammedans Regard As Sacred, Volume 2.* Charleston, South Carolina, U.S.A.: Nabu Press, 2011.

Chiasson, Paul. *The Island of Seven Cities: Where the Chinese Settled When They Discovered America.* Toronto, Canada: Random House Canada, 2006.

---. *Written in the Ruins: Cape Breton Island's Second Pre-Columbian Chinese Settlement.* Dundurn, Saskatchewan, Canada: Dundurn, 2016.

Cook, Arthur Bernard. *Zeus: A Study in Ancient Religion.* Cambridge, U.K.: Cambridge University Press, 2010.

Dalan, Rinita A., *et al. Envisioning Cahokia: A Landscape Perspective.* DeKalb, Illinois, U.S.A.: Northern Illinois University Press, 2003.

Dreyer, Edward L. *Zheng He: China and the Oceans in the Early Ming Dynasty: 1405–1433.* London, U.K.: Pearson, 2006.

Durst, Patrick, *et al. Excavations at the Trotier Site: French Cahokia, St. Clair County, Illinois (Research Reports, No. 122).* Plastic Comb. Illinois, U.S.A.: Illinois State Archaeological Survey, 2009.

Everett, Dianna., ed. *Encyclopedia of Oklahoma History and Culture-Two Volumes.* Oklahoma City, U.S.A.: The Oklahoma Historical Society, 2009.

Federal Highway Administration. "Mississippi River Crossing Relocated I-70 and I-64 Connector, St. Louis County, Missouri: Environmental Impact Statement." Evanston, Illinois, U.S.A.: Northwestern University, Report/Paper Numbers: EPA 010126, FHWA-MO-010126, Accession Number: 01073796, Sep 12, 2007, 11:20 PM.

Fowler, Melvin L. *The Cahokia Atlas, Revised: A Historical Atlas of Cahokia Archaeology, No. 2 (Studies in Archaeology)*. Illinois, U.S.A.: Illinois Transportation Archaeological Research Program, 1997.

Fyle, C. Magbaily. *Introduction to the History of African Civilization: Precolonial Africa*. Lanham, Maryland, U.S.A.: University Press of America, 1999.

Goodrich, Anne Swann. *Chinese Hells: The Peking Temple of Eighteen Hells and Chinese Conceptions of Hell*. Abingdon-on-Thames, U.K.: Routledge, 1981.

Hapgood, Charles H. *Maps of the Ancient Sea Kings: Evidence of Advanced Civilization in the Ice Age*. Kempton, Illinois, U.S.A.: Adventures Unlimited Press, 1997.

---. *The Earth's Shifting Crust: A Key To Some Basic Problems Of Earth Science*. Scotts Valley, California, U.S.A.: CreateSpace Independent Publishing Platform, 2015.

Hastings, Robert W. *The Lakes of Pontchartrain: Their History and Environments*. Jackson, Mississippi, U.S.A.: University Press of Mississippi, 2014.

Iseminger, William. *Cahokia Mounds: America's First City (Landmarks)*. Stroud, Gloucestershire, U.K.: The History Press, 2010.

Jacobs, Daniel. *The Rough Guide to Tunisia*. London, U.K.: Rough Guides, 2009.

Kavasch, E. Barrie. *The Mound Builders of Ancient North America: 4000 Years of American Indian Art, Science, Engineering, & Spirituality Reflected in Majestic Earthworks & Artifacts*. Bloomington, Indiana, U.S.A.: iUniverse, 2003.

Krus, Anthony Michal. "Fortifying Cahokia: More Efficient Palisade Construction through Redesigned Bastions." Bloomington, Indiana, U.S.A.: Glenn A. Black Laboratory of Archaeology, Department of Anthropology, Indiana University Bloomington, 2011.

Levathes, Louise. *When China Ruled the Seas: The Treasure Fleet of the Dragon Throne, 1405-1433*. Oxford, U.K.: Oxford University Press, 1994.

Little, Stephen, *et al. Taoism and the Arts of China*. Oakland, California, U.S.A.: University of California Press, 2000.

Lorenz, Albert Lorenz and Joy Schleh. *Hero, Hawk and Open Hand: A Story About Cahokia*. New York, U.S.A.: Harry N. Abrams, 2005.

Low, C.C. & Associates. ed. and trans. *Pictorial Series of Chinese Classics & History in English & Chinese: Zheng He's Voyages to Xiyang*. Singapore: Canfonian Pte Ltd, 2005.

Ma, Huan. J.V.G. Mills, trans. *Ying-yai Sheng-lan: The Overall Survey of the Ocean's Shores (1433)*. London, U.K.: Hakluyt Society, 1970.

McLaughlin, Raoul. *Rome and the Distant East: Trade Routes to the ancient lands of Arabia, India and China*. London, U.K.: Continuum, 2010.

---. *The Roman Empire and the Indian Ocean: The Ancient World Economy and the Kingdoms of Africa, Arabia and India*. Barnsley, U.K.: Pen and Sword Military, 2018.

Menzies, Gavin. *1421: The Year China Discovered America*. New York, U.S.A.: HaperCollins Publishers, 2002.

---. *1434: The Year a Magnificent Chinese Fleet Sailed to Italy and Ignited the Renaissance*. New York, U.S.A.: HarperCollins Publishers, 2008.

---. and Ian Hudson. *Who Discovered America? The Untold History of the Peopling of the Americas*. New York, U.S.A.: HarperCollins Publishers, 2013.

Midlarsky, Manus I. *Handbook of War Studies II*. Ann Arbor, Michigan, U.S.A.: University of Michigan Press, 2000.

Morgan, M. J. *Land of Big Rivers: French and Indian Illinois, 1699–1778*. Carbondale, Illinois, U.S.A.: Southern Illinois University Press, 2010.

Needham, Joseph, *et al*. *Science and Civilisation in China, Vol. 4: Physics and Physical Technology, Part 3: Civil Engineering and Nautics*. Cambridge, U.K.: Cambridge University Press, 1971.

Nickless, Mark E. and Laurie L. Bonner-Nickless. *Chasing Dragons: The True History of the Piasa*. Scotts Valley, California, U.S.A.: CreateSpace Independent Publishing Platform, 2012.

Polo, Marco and Ronald Latham. *The Travels of Marco Polo*. London, U.K.: Penguin Classics, 1958.

Sien, Chia Lin and Sally K. Church, ed. *Zheng He and the Afro-Asian World*. Malacca, Malaysia: Melaka Museums Corporation (PERZIM) and Singapore: International Zheng He Society, 2012.

Swanton, John. *Source Material for the Social and Ceremonial Life of the Choctaw Indians (Contemporary American Indian Studies)*. Kindle Edition. Tuscaloosa, Alabama, U.S.A.: University of Alabama Press, 2009.

Tan, Ta Sen. *Cheng Ho and Malaya*. Malacca, Malaysia: Cheng Ho Cultural Museum and Singapore: International Zheng He Society, 2014.

Temple, Robert and Joseph Needham. *3,000 Years of Science, Discovery, and Invention*. Rochester, Vermont, U.S.A.: Inner Traditions, 2007.

Thompson, Gunnar. *Viking America*. Seattle, Washington, U.S.A.: Misty Isles, 2012.

Thompson, John Eric Sidney *Maya History and Religion (The Civilization of the American Indian Series)*. Norman, Oklahoma, U.S.A.: University of Oklahoma Press, 1990.

Winter, Joseph C. *Tobacco Use by Native North Americans: Sacred Smoke and Silent Killer (The Civilization of the American Indian Series)*. Norman, Oklahoma, U.S.A.: University of Oklahoma Press, 2001.

Chinese

Anonymous author. Wen Renjun (闻人军) and Cheng Zhenyi (程贞一), ed. Zhou Bi Suan Jing Yi Zhu 《周髀算译注》 or *Classic of Arithmetic from the Gnomon of the Zhou Sundial: Interpretations and Comments*. Shanghai, China: Shanghai Ancient Books Publishing House (上海古籍出版社), 2012.

387

Cao Xueqin 曹雪芹 (1715–1763). Hong Lou Meng《红楼梦》or *Dream of the Red Chamber*. Beijing, China: People's Literature Publishing House (人民文学出版社), 2008.

Fang Xuan ling 房玄龄 (579–648). Jin Shu《晋书》or the *Book of Jin*. Beijing, China: Zhonghua Book Company (中华书局), 1974.

Fei Xin 费信 (1388–?). Xing Cha Sheng Lan《星槎胜览》or *The Overall Survey of the Star Raft*. Beijing, China: Sino-Culture Press (华文出版社), 2019.

Gong Zhen 巩珍 (fl. 1400s–1434). Xi Yang Fan Guo Zhi《西洋番国志》or *The Annals of the Foreign Countries in the Western Ocean*, *Appendix 6:* Qian Wen Ji • Xia Xi Yang《前闻記•下西洋》or *A Record of History Once Heard: Down to the Western Ocean*. Beijing, China: Zhonghua Book Company (中华书局), 2000.

Huang Shengzeng 黄省曾 (1490–1540). Xi Yang Chao Gong Dian Lu《西洋朝贡典录》or *Records of Tributes from the Western Ocean Countries*. Beijing, China: Zhonghua Book Company (中华书局), 2000.

Institute of History and Philosophy, Academia Sinica (中研院历史语言研究所) and Huang Zhangjian (黄彰健). Ming Shi Lu《明实录》or *The Veritable Records of Ming*. Beijing, China: Zhonghua Book Company (中华书局), 2016.

Lee Siu-Leung (李兆良). Kun Yu Wan Guo Quan Tu Jie Mi：Ming Dai Ce Hui Shi Jie《坤輿萬國全圖解密:明代測繪世界》or *Deciphering the Kunyu Wanguo Quantu, A Chinese World Map—Ming Chinese Mapped the World Before Columbus*. Taipei, Taiwan: Linking Publishing Company (聯經出版社), 2012.

---. Xuan De Jin Pai Qi Shi Lu：Míng Dai Kai Tuo Mei Zhou 《宣德金牌啟示錄：明代開拓美洲》or *The Mystery of Zheng He and America*. Taipei, Taiwan: Linking Publishing Company (聯經出版社), 2013.

Liao Jianyu 廖建裕, *et al.*, ed. Zheng He Yu Ya Fei Shi Jie 《郑和与亚非世界》 or *Zheng He and the Asian and African World*. Singapore: International Zheng He Society and Malacca, Malaysia: Melaka Museum Corporation (PERZIM), 2012.

Liu Gang 刘钢. Gu Di Tu Mi Ma：Zhong Guo Fa Xian Shi Jie De Mi Tuan Xuan Ji《古地图密码:中国发现世界的谜团玄机》or *Secret Code of Ancient Maps: The Mystery of China's Discovery of the World*. Guangxi, China: Guangxi Normal University Press Group (广西师范大学出版社集团), 2009.

Liu Xu 刘昫 (887–946). Jiu Tang Shu 《旧唐书》or the *History of the Early Tang Dynasty*. Beijing, China: Zhonghua Book Company (中华书局), 1975.

Nickless, Mark, *et al.* (马克·尼克莱斯等.) Zheng He Fa Xian Mei Zhou Zhi Xin Je《郑和发现美洲之新解》or *New Evidence for Zheng He's*

388

Exploration of the Americas. Beijing, China: World Knowledge Publishing House (世界知识出版社), 2015.

Shanghai Bookstore Publishing House. Ming Shi Lu 《明实录》 or *The Veritable Records of Ming.* Shanghai, China: Shanghai Bookstore Publishing House (上海书店出版社), 2015.

Wang Dayuan 汪大渊 (1311–1350). Dao Yi Zhi Lue 《岛夷志略》or *Descriptions of Barbarians and the Islands.* Kindle edition. Beijing, China: ChineseAll Digital Publishing Group Co. Ltd. (中文在线), 2012.

Wu Chengen 吴承恩 (1506–1582). Xi You Ji《西游记》or *Journey to the West.* Beijing, China: Foreign Language Teaching and Researching Press (外语教学与研究出版社), 2015.

Xi Longfei 席龙飞, *et al.,* ed. Zhong Guo Ke Xue Ji Shu Shi: Jiao Tong Juan 《中国科学技术史:交通卷》or *History of Science and Technology in China: Transportation.* Beijing, China: Science Press (科学出版社), 2004.

Zhang Hua 张华 (232–300). Bo Wu Zhi 《博物志》or *Natural History.* Shanghai, China: Shanghai Ancient Books Publishing House (上海古籍出版社), 2012.

Zhang Tingyu 张廷玉 (1672–1755), *et al.* Ming Shi《明史》or *The History of Ming.* Zhonghua Book Company (中华书局), 1974.

Zhao Rugua 赵汝适 (1170–1231). Yang Bowen 杨博文, ed. Zhu Fan Zhi《诸蕃志》or *Records of Many Foreign Countries.* Beijing, China: Zhonghua Book Company (中华书局), 2000.

Zhou Qufei 周去非 (1134–1189). Ling Wai Dai Da《岭外代答》or *Answers to the Questions Concerning Foreign Countries.* Beijing, China: Chinese Bookstore Publishing House (中国书店出版社), 1999.

FROM PROVERSE HONG KONG
SELECTED TITLES
set mainly in China, Hong Kong,
Hong Kong China, as well as Macau

Biography, Historical Source Materials, Memoirs,
Social Science, Translations From Chinese,
Travel Journals

Jean Berlie	The Chinese of Macau a Decade after the Handover.
Gillian Bickley, Ed.	The Complete Court Cases of Magistrate Frederick Stewart.
---	The Development of Education in Hong Kong, 1841-1898.
---	A Magistrate's Court in Nineteenth Century Hong Kong, 1st ed. 2005, 2nd ed. 2009.
---	Through American Eyes: The Journals (18 May 1859 - 1 September 1860) Of George Washington (Farley) Heard (1837-1875).
---	Journeys with a Mission: Travel Journals of The Right Revd George Smith (1815-1871) first Bishop of Victoria (Hong Kong) (1849-1865).
Rupert Chan	Chocolate's Brown Study in the Bag.
Richard Collingwood-Selby and Gillian Bickley, Eds	In Time of War (Diary entries and letters by Lt. Cmdr. Henry C.S. Collingwood-Selby, R.N. (1898-1992)).
Jun Fang and Lifang He	The Romance Of A Literatus And His Concubine In Seventeenth-Century China. Annotated translation into English of "Reminiscences Of The Plum-shaded Convent" (Yingmeian Yiyu影梅庵憶語) by Mao Xiang (1611-1693) with the original Chinese text.

Brian Finch	A Faithful Record Of The *Lisbon Maru* Incident. (Translation from Chinese with additional material).
Emily Ho	Memoirs of an Ice-Cream Lady.
Sophronia Liu	A Shimmering Sea: Hong Kong Stories.
James McCarthy	The Diplomat of Kashgar: A Very Special Agent. The Life of Sir George Macartney, 18 January 1867 to 19 May 1945.

Novels And Other Fiction

Andrew Carter	Bright Lights and White Nights.
Feng Chi-shun	Three Wishes in Bardo.
Peter Gregoire	Article 109.
---	The Devil You Know.
Lawrence Gray	Cop Show Heaven.
Dragos Ilca	HK Hollow.
Caleb Kavon	Revenge from Beyond.
---	The Monkey in Me: Confusion, Love and Hope under a Chinese Sky.
---	The Reluctant Terrorist: In Search of The Jizo.
James Tam	Man's Last Song.
Jan Pearson	Black Tortoise Winter.
---	Red Bird Summer.
---	Tiger Autumn.
Jason S Polley	cemetery miss you.
James Tam	Man's Last Song.
Paul Ting	Bao Bao's Odyssey: From Mao's Shanghai to Capitalist Hong Kong.

FIND OUT MORE ABOUT PROVERSE AUTHORS, BOOKS, INTERNATIONAL PRIZES, AND EVENTS

Visit our website:
http://www.proversepublishing.com
Visit our distributor's website: www.cup.cuhk.edu.hk

Follow us on Twitter
Follow news and conversation: <twitter.com/Proversebooks>
OR
Copy and paste the following to your browser window and follow the instructions:
https://twitter.com/#!/ProverseBooks

"Like" us on www.facebook.com/ProversePress
Request our free E-Newsletter
Send your request to info@proversepublishing.com.

Availability
Most books are available in Hong Kong and world-wide
from our Hong Kong based Distributor,
The Chinese University Press of Hong Kong,
The Chinese University of Hong Kong, Shatin, NT,
Hong Kong SAR, China.
Website: Web: www.cup.cuhk.edu.hk

All titles are available from Proverse Hong Kong
http://www.proversepublishing.com
and the Proverse Hong Kong UK-based Distributor.
We have stock-holding retailers in Hong Kong,
Canada (Elizabeth Campbell Books),
Andorra (Llibreria La Puça, La Llibreria).
Orders can be made from bookshops
in the UK and elsewhere.

Ebooks
Most Proverse titles are available also as Ebooks.

392

CPSIA information can be obtained
at www.ICGtesting.com
Printed in the USA
LVHW080456261219
641711LV00009B/402/P